MURDER ON WA

By the same author

WHITE LIES

MURDER ON WARD FOUR

The Story of Bev Allitt, and the Most Terrifying Crime
since the Moors Murders

Nick Davies

Chatto & Windus
LONDON

First published 1993

1 3 5 7 9 10 8 6 4 2

© Nick Davies 1993

Nick Davies has asserted his right under
the Copyright, Designs and Patents Act, 1988
to be identified as the author of this work

First published in the United Kingdom in 1993 by
Chatto & Windus Ltd
Random House, 20 Vauxhall Bridge Road, London SW1V 2SA

Random House Australia (Pty) Limited
20 Alfred Street, Milsons Point, Sydney,
New South Wales 2061, Australia

Random House New Zealand Limited
18 Poland Road, Glenfield,
Auckland 10, New Zealand

Random House South Africa (Pty) Limited
PO Box 337, Bergvlei, South Africa

Random House UK Limited Reg. No. 954009

A CIP catalogue record for this book
is available from the British Library

ISBN 0 7011 4813 6

Phottypeset by Intype, London
Printed in Great Britain by
Mackays of Chatham

CONTENTS

PROLOGUE

In the old days, before the newspapers were taken over by accountants, when journalists were still honest, they used to say that 'News is what someone somewhere doesn't want you to know'. The story of what happened on Ward Four at Grantham Hospital in Lincolnshire in the spring of 1991 was, for a long time, ringed with secrecy. Almost everyone who was involved had a reason to hide what they knew. For some of them, this was simply a matter of emotion. There were nurses, for example, who were so full of anxiety and shame that they couldn't bear to look back and admit what had happened, even though there was often no good reason for them to feel anxious or ashamed about anything. Some were scared of causing trouble for themselves or for their colleagues. Some had been told that their careers would suffer if they were caught talking. There were union officials who were afraid that if the truth came out, it might cost their members' jobs. There were health service officials who were willing to use thousands of pounds of public money to barricade themselves away from prying public eyes. This book is evidence of their failure.

Those who tried to hide the truth failed, because all kinds of people refused to play the game of secrecy. Nurses pocketed their shame, hospital staff defied their heavy-handed employers, union leaders saw the light, and a number of individuals who might still suffer if they were ever identified took real risks with their careers to make sure that—however painful or awkward—the truth was shared and not stashed away as if it were the private property of bureaucrats and lawyers and public relations consultants. One particular group of people were especially striking in their willingness to set aside self-interest and to piece together all the tiny fragments of evidence: the parents of the children from Ward

Four. They had the best of reasons to refuse to help me. They were sad and confused and full of distrust. They had been plucked without warning out of obscurity and tormented, painfully and publicly. They could have been forgiven for wanting nothing more than to forget everything. Instead of which, they agreed to recall it all in excruciating detail and then to recall it all again and again when I needed to know more and to help me, too, with ideas they had had or rumours they had heard. Some of them stuck with me all the way through the production of this book and became unofficial co-authors as well as good friends.

It seems inadequate simply to say that I am grateful to all these people. I don't think they helped me in order to earn my gratitude. I think they did it because they knew that it mattered, that the events on Ward Four added up to more than merely a sad and extraordinary story, that there were all kinds of lessons to be learned—about doctors and their fallibility, about hospitals and their relentless commercialization, about secrecy and power, and about even more fundamental things that float to the surface of life only when they are stirred up by some terrible crisis, things like luck and fate, or evil and the limits of human cruelty, or families and how much they matter to you. Still, the best I can do is to thank them all, to be glad that they stood up to the people who didn't want us to know, and to hope that this book does justice to their efforts.

PART ONE

ENDLESS NIGHT

Every night and every morn,
Some to misery are born.
Every morn and every night,
Some are born to sweet delight.
Some are born to sweet delight.
Some are born to endless night.

(William Blake, *Auguries of Innocence*)

I

Chris and Joanne Taylor had nothing to worry about. They were young, healthy, happy, making their way in the world. They lived in a brand new semi-detached house with clean carpets and a fitted kitchen and a blue Ford Sierra on the forecourt outside. Their neighbours were solid, successful people—teachers and accountants and policemen. They had no debts, no feuds, no fears.

Chris had done well. He was only 24, but he already ran his own business, installing suspended ceilings, and although he had to work long hours, he was earning the kind of money that his father had only ever dreamed of. Joanne was the same age and, like Chris, she handled the world with an easy-going, almost cheeky style. She was always good for a laugh. She had plenty of friends, some of them from the hairdressers where she worked part-time, but mostly from her childhood because, even though she had settled down now with Chris and she had two small boys and a house to look after, she still went out for a drink with the people she had known since school.

The street where Chris and Joanne Taylor lived was on a new estate on the north west edge of Grantham, a small, quiet town—so quiet, in fact, that some outsiders call it dull. At first glance, they seem to be right, for Grantham is an utterly ordinary place. It is lost somewhere in the shallow valleys of south Lincolnshire, an hour or so north of London on the newly electrified railway line, an hour or so away from the clatter and cash of Skegness on the gaudy coastline to the east, nowhere very special at all. It is too big to appeal to the rural middle classes who prefer the honey-stoned cottages of Waltham on the Wolds for their weekend retreats. It is too small for the Japanese motor manufacturers or Whitehall agencies who are seduced instead by the pools of cheap labour in the cities that circle it, Nottingham and Leicester and Peterborough.

Grantham is ordinary in a very English way. You could be kidnapped on the other side of the planet, drugged, disorientated and thrown out of a train speeding past the edge of the town and as soon as you caught the first flying glimpse of your surroundings—the slate grey skies, the damp tufts of grass, the little red houses and the church spire in the distance—you would know immediately that this was England. In the old days, perhaps, the town had something of its own character. It was too poor to change, and for centuries it grew peacefully, selling sheep, making shoes, making arms in the war, making ends meet in its own quiet way. The last remains of this old town still provoke the occasional passing American into exercising his camera: the twelfth century church, the thick brown river, an old coaching inn which Charles Dickens once mentioned. But in their lifetime, Chris and Joanne Taylor had seen these old peculiarities invaded and overwhelmed by the same tide of commerce that had swept through scores of other little English towns. The Great North Road which used to run through Grantham and the surrounding villages like a dying river, clogged with queues of cars, grew wider and burst past the bottle necks with new bypasses; the new electric trains leaped up from London; all through the 1980s, 'retail enterprises' arrived like weeds in a country garden, filling every naked patch, webbing their roots beneath the surface, slowly choking the frail life of the old town.

Grantham's most famous son, Isaac Newton, is now remembered not so much by his severe statue outside the Guildhall, nor even by his initials in the window sill of the Kings School where he carved them one dull afternoon three centuries ago, as by the brand-new, purpose-built, all-weather Isaac Newton Shopping Centre in the high street. Here, in the covered mall, beside the artificial indoor bushes, old men sit with their hands clasped over their walking sticks, while piped muzak fills the air and children tug on cigarettes beneath the sign that bans the consumption of food and drink in this area. Old women in old clothes shuffle by the window full of portable CD systems ('Unbeatable deal—save £10') with shopping bags weighted to the end of each arm. The thick brown River Wytham now wears an oily veil, broken only by drowning cider bottles and crumpled carrier bags. The occasional American tourist now snaps the same sights and symbols that he has left behind at home, the McDonalds and the video stores on St Peter's Hill, the rows of burger joints and cheap motels along the Great North Road.

In the late 1980s the new work that had arrived so suddenly in Grantham, started to wither, just as it did in the rest of the country, and so, at Newton's bronze feet, on most days now, you can see baggy-eyed men sitting with broken bits of cigarette between their fingers and runaway newspapers blowing round their heels, and beside them, on the taxi rank, the cabbies sit for hours on end waiting for someone who can afford a ride.

Yet there is something about a town like Grantham which might escape an outsider's eye. It is the reason why its people defend its dullness, why they may even snap their teeth at the outsider's sneer: it is safe. There are no nasty surprises in Grantham, no earthquakes or epidemics, no riots or demonstrations, no ghettos, no tramps or junkies on the pavement. If someone is attacked in the street in Grantham, it makes the front page of the *Grantham Journal*. Fate and ill fortune have always ignored it. Grantham may not be rich and it may be drenched in its own ordinariness, but it is secure.

As Chris Taylor left home on this particular morning, Thursday 21 February 1991, things seemed better than ever. Everyone was feeling happier now that the fighting in the Gulf was over; they were even talking about the first troops coming home. The building trade was in a bad way, but he had managed to keep his orders coming in. Things were fine. Even the weather was better. Last week there had been snow as deep as a gumboot, and Grantham had been cut off for 48 hours with nothing but sledges for transport, but now the thaw had arrived, all the streets were dribbling and there was a blue sky and a tang of spring in the air.

If anyone had stopped Chris Taylor as he walked past the shiny blue Sierra and climbed into his battered old builder's van that Thursday morning and dared him to imagine some event which might have the power to shunt his whole life off the rails, he would have been lost for an answer. If someone had really pushed him, he might have grasped at the chance of his van crashing in the melting snow or maybe of the house catching fire from an electrical fault—something remote and unpredictable like that—but the truth is that he would have waved away the whole idea. He could scan the horizon for as far as he could see and find no hint of a threat out there.

If he felt at all bad, it was only because he and Joanne had been up half the night with their baby boy, Liam. He had a heavy cold and since he was only seven weeks old, he dealt with it the way that babies seemed to deal with most of their problems. He cried.

All through the night, they had tried everything they could think of—feeding him, burping him, putting him down, picking him up, pacing up and down with him, bouncing him in his rocker chair, even filling the kitchen with steam to try and clear his tubes. Liam had just cried. In the end, they had put him in his cot round on Chris's side of the bed and Chris had lain half asleep with his arm through the bars, stroking him and patting him, as he tripped in and out of sleep.

Liam was tough, but he seemed to have been ill on and off for most of the month. He had caught this cold in the first week in February and they'd had the doctor out several times and got some penicillin drops, and, at first, that had seemed to do the trick. Liam had got much better, and for a week he had been all cheerful again and kicking his legs and flashing his little pink gums at anyone who caught his eye. Then, for some reason, the cold had come back again, and this time it really seemed to have got a grip on him.

In the last two nights, they had had the doctor out twice. Joanne had called him first on Tuesday night, although she had felt bad about doing it. It had been snowing and the roads were terrible, but Liam was so unsettled and Chris had said 'Go ahead, that's what the doctor's there for'. So the doctor had struggled out to see them and he'd taken a look at Liam and given him a poke and a prod and said it was just sniffles and nothing to worry about. But he had got no better and by yesterday morning, Liam was so blocked up that he couldn't feed properly and then he was so hungry that he couldn't sleep, and all he would do was cry.

Finally, last night, Joanne had got so fed up that she had plucked up her courage and called the doctor out again. He had looked in Liam's ears and tugged up his vest and listened to his lungs and said 'He's all right, it's not gone to his chest, though I'm afraid you're in for a rough night'. He had been right about that.

Still, there was nothing unusual about any of this. Kids got colds, then they got better. They had been through it all before with Liam's elder brother, Jamie, who was two now. Liam would be all right. And as Chris Taylor climbed into his van that bright Thursday morning and coasted off down the hill into the middle of Grantham, he was secure in the knowledge that all was well in his world. There was nothing to worry about.

It was not yet 7.00 when Chris drove off to work, but inside the trim, red-brick house, Joanne Taylor was already awake. Liam was crying again. She really couldn't call the doctor out any more—he would only come and say Liam was all right again—so she did her best on her own, and after a while it began to seem that she had done the right thing. Liam finally stopped crying.

It was quiet in the house. Jamie was still asleep upstairs. Joanne made herself a cup of tea and looked down at Liam in his cot and felt a tiny worm of fear in her heart. He was quiet, but he was not right. He wasn't asleep, his eyes were open and they were dull, and he seemed all limp and listless. Joanne could see he was full of mucous and it suddenly seemed to her that he was not breathing properly; it was too shallow to do him any good. Or maybe she was wrong. Maybe he had just exhausted himself. She couldn't call the doctor. But she couldn't do nothing. Finally, she called out her health visitor and told her all about it, and she took one look at Liam in his cot, panting and wheezing, said 'Nonsense' and phoned the doctor herself.

When he came in the late morning, the doctor looked long and hard at Liam. Joanne stood watching. Jamie played in the kitchen. The doctor frowned as he snapped his stethoscope together. 'Well, I know what this little chap needs,' he said.

'What's that?'

'Hospital.'

'Oh, no,' said Joanne.

Joanne had never liked hospitals. It was odd really. Her mum, Shirley, worked at Grantham Hospital as a tea lady, and Chris's dad, Derek, had been head porter there for years until he retired, but she couldn't stand the place herself. Hospitals just made her feel squeamish. But there was no arguing: Liam had to go to hospital. For a while, Joanne was racing: get Chris's sister to come round, take Jamie next door to wait for her, leave loads of messages for Chris, grab spare nappies, pack Liam's clothes, call her mum, get in the car, drive to the hospital, don't panic. It made her tearful, the thought of her tiny baby being so ill that he needed to go to hospital, but it was a relief, too. For all that she hated the place, at least she could stop worrying about him—not knowing what was wrong with him or what to do for the best—and she could stop ringing up the doctor, too.

Her mother was waiting to meet her at the main door, and together they carried Liam and his little bundles of things down the long, wide central corridor, round the dog-leg corner, and through the double doors on the left with the brightly coloured banner over them that said 'Welcome to Ward Four'.

Joanne was so glad she'd brought him. It was 1.00 when they arrived, and by 1.30 Liam had been seen by a doctor and he was settled down in a cot in a little cubicle at the side of the ward. The nurses were all great. They said he had bronchiolitis. Joanne thought that sounded pretty bad, but there was a nice nurse called Clare who reassured her. It was just a bad cold that had gone to his chest, she said. 'Don't you worry. He'll be all right. He'll be home again in a couple of days. And don't you spoil him!'

They put an oxygen mask on him and although it made him look like some kind of alien creature, it helped him to breathe better, and before long he perked up and he started grinning at Joanne through the mask. 'Oh, bless him,' she thought.

Her mother went, Chris turned up, everything calmed down. Liam kept knocking the oxygen mask off with his chubby little fist—he was strong for a seven-week-old baby, the nurses said—and so they moved him into an incubator. Chris and Joanne sat and watched their son, with the colour back in his cheeks now, and every time they caught his eye, they grinned and waved at him and he gurgled back at them, and Joanne thought 'Thank God that's over'.

It struck them then that this was not the first time that this little hospital had come to Liam's rescue. It had been just about the same on the night of his birth. Of course, Chris had known that

Joanne's date had arrived and they had been joking about whether her waters would break suddenly when they were round at their friend Diane's house, but when it started to happen, it had still been a shock. It happened so fast. They say second babies are like that; they just can't wait to get out in the world. One moment they were sitting there talking to their friends and then—it was just after 8.oo in the evening—Joanne said she thought something was happening and, before Chris had time to protest, she was calling the hospital and calling home to warn the friend who was baby-sitting Jamie, and then they were out of the house and they were off, the two of them in the front of the blue Sierra, Chris driving too fast and wanting to laugh, Joanne with her hands pawing her volcano-belly, both of them jabbering with nervous excitement, and their teeth chattering in the cold as they whooshed through the night-time streets.

It was not far to the hospital—down into the middle of Grantham, out along Manthorpe Road and in less than ten minutes they were pushing through the heavy door at Casualty and they were inside, in the cosy yellow light, in the warmth, and the sister said Joanne looked too well to be in labour and the nurses came and said everything was fine and what a good job it was they'd come so quick because this little chap is in a hurry, and before they knew it Joanne was wanting to push, and the nurses were telling her to go for it, push now, good girl, and there was Liam— all nine pounds and three ounces of him, shaking his bloodied fists and yelling his little war cry. One very big, very healthy boy. It made Chris want to cry.

Eventually, when Liam was settled with Joanne on the maternity ward, Chris had gone back home and slept for a while until he heard Jamie downstairs having breakfast with the babysitter and he had got up to tell him the news. He had been so funny about it. When Chris had crouched down by the breakfast table and told him 'Hey, you've got a baby brother', Jamie had looked at him with a knowing smile, as if to say he was sorry that his dad had left his brain on a bus but there was really not too much he could do about it, and he had gone back to his bowl of cereal. But Chris could see him thinking about it, working it all out, and when he took him down to the hospital to see Joanne, Jamie had taken one look at his mother holding the baby, clambered up on the bed and given his new brother a big, messy hug. Chris had stood there grinning from wall to wall. Two boys—two mates. They'd be able to run around and play together, they'd go to school together, they would grow up and go drinking together. Of course, they might fight once in a while—all kids do—but they'd always be there for each other, always be mates.

It had been a hectic day. Chris had called his dad and Joanne's parents, and they must have made a few calls of their own and pretty soon there was a small traffic jam of relatives round the bed, all trying to welcome the new baby, with Joanne's dad wielding his video camera and all the aunts and uncles having a laugh, and Jamie hopping up to defend Liam from the crowd and even planting a kiss on his brother's forehead to stake his claim. That was 30 December.

By the next day, New Year's Eve, the hospital had let Joanne and Liam come home. They had spent the holiday doing a grand tour of their relatives: up to Chris's dad; then round to Chris's sister; tea with Joanne's mum; and then a big dinner with Joanne's dad and her stepmother, with everyone including Jamie sitting round the table and Liam on the floor in his rocker chair, looking very pleased with himself, as if to say 'Well, if this is what life's like, it's all fine with me'. And everyone agreed that it was a great way to start a new year.

He was a good baby. He fed well, he put on weight, he had no jaundice, pretty soon he had started sleeping through the night. Little Jamie never left him alone for a minute. He was always chattering in Liam's ear—'See this, Liam, look here, Liam, play with this, Liam.' One day, Joanne had been in the kitchen and she had heard Jamie in the sitting room babbling away at the baby, going 'Look at this, Liam, look at this, look at this' and she had gone in to see what he was getting so excited about and she had found him banging Liam over the head with a rattle to get his attention. Liam was just sitting there blinking. He was tough all right.

All through January, Liam had gone from strength to strength and life was calm and mostly happy. It was still tiring, of course, but Chris had felt they were on top of things and somehow it was easier than it had been with Jamie. He and Joanne knew what they were doing this time around and they hardly fought at all.

Chris knew that if Joanne was bathing and changing Liam, then he had to get on and bathe and change Jamie. It all worked well. They both agreed that it was an ideal size for a family, just what they had dreamed of. Chris had never wanted more than two children. This was just right.

At the end of January, when he was four and a half weeks old, Liam had delivered his first smile. And here he was now, three weeks later, still smiling, even in his incubator.

At about 4.30, a couple of nurses came into the room. One of them seemed to be a staff nurse—she was certainly in charge—with curly grey hair and glasses, and the other was much younger, a stocky girl with a pudgy face and short brown hair and the look of a tomboy about her. The staff nurse told them it was time that Liam had something to eat. She was very kind and she explained exactly what was happening: 'You can't really feed him yourself, he's too bunged up, so we'll feed him with a little tube in his throat. It doesn't hurt and that way we're sure he gets it. All right? You can pop home if you like. Fetch his little brother up here. We'll look after him. This is Bev. She's going to feed him. All right? See you in a little while.'

The staff nurse left. They picked up their coats and as they headed out of the cubicle door, Chris turned and saw Liam grinning and waggling his legs, while the young tomboy nurse called Bev fussed gently with his cot. They went home, got changed, picked up Jamie and their friend Diane, had something to eat, drove back to the hospital and as soon as they walked back on to Ward Four, they knew there was something wrong.

Someone said 'We were about to call you. He's taken a turn for the worse.'

In his little room, Liam was lying on the cot with his eyes shut. He was naked apart from his nappy. He was completely white. He was completely still. He might not have been breathing. Joanne cupped her hand over her mouth and stared for a moment, then turned to Bev.

'What's wrong wi' him?' said Chris.

Bev was standing by the door with her arms folded. 'He just went off on me. I was feeding him and he suddenly threw up. It went right across the room.' She swept one arm through the air to demonstrate, and then the other. 'Everywhere. He messed out the other end, too. It was all bright yellow, same colour as them curtains. It went all over me. I had to go and change my uniform.'

Chris and Joanne almost felt like apologizing for the mess, but they were too shocked to say anything sensible, and Bev went on.

'I think he might have stopped breathing. He was choking on his vomit. If he'd been at home, you'd probably've lost him.'

Now Joanne was crying. A consultant came. His name was Nanayakkara, and he was tall and trim in a tweed jacket with a breast pocket full of pens. Chris was telling Jamie it would be all right. A second doctor came, more junior. Two nursing auxiliaries came, one called Nadine, one called Wendy. Liam was still not moving. Joanne wanted to know what was going on: 'Is he going to be all right?'

The babble of talk stopped. The posse of nurses pushed Liam's cot out of his little room, on to the main ward and then into a side room full of drug cabinets and complicated electronic equipment. The sign on the door said 'Treatment Room'. Liam lay limp in the incubator. Dr Nanayakkara leaned over him. Chris and Joanne stood outside with Jamie and their neighbour Diane, and then the door was shut.

Jamie stared around him as if he had just landed on a new planet. Chris and Joanne waited. Was Liam going to die? The thought was too terrible to confess. Liam would be OK. Of course he would. All he had was a bad cold. Everything would be all right. The hospital would make sure of that. That's what hospitals are there for. They asked Diane to take Jamie home with her. Someone got them a cup of tea. Someone said 'Don't worry now. The doctor will look after him.'

When the door of the Treatment Room opened again half an hour later, Dr Nanayakkara's face was heavy with worry. Chris and Joanne were allowed to go and stand by the little bed, where Liam lay now in a web of tubes and wires. They felt as small as him, like you do when you're called in to see the head teacher, like you do when you're full of fear.

'Your baby has deteriorated very rapidly,' the consultant told them. 'The next 24 hours will be critical. He has some pneumonia on his lung. He is a very poorly baby, and he may need breathing support. The next 24 hours will be critical. Do you understand what I am telling you?'

They thought they understood. They thought he was telling them that they were right to be frightened, that they were about to lose Liam. But he was not quite saying that, and none of it made any sense anyway. It was only last night that another doctor had come to their house and told them that Liam would be fine. Understanding did not help. Even if they understood, what could they do about it? They weren't doctors. They couldn't do anything to help. All they could do was hope, and so they sat down in the Treatment Room, perched at the side of the bed, and together they waited to see whether their family would survive.

Chris could hardly believe that all this was happening. One minute, everything was just grand. Then, suddenly, it was all in pieces. A kid had a cold. It happens all the time, then they get better. How could this be happening? Only this morning, everything had seemed so good. But maybe that was the problem. Maybe life had been a bit too good to him. Everyone in Chris's family had always said the same thing about him: he was lucky. He could fall up to his neck in muck and come up smelling sweeter than rich tea. With him, it had always been money to money, luck to luck. Maybe God or someone had looked down on him and seen him walking along with a spring in his step and thought 'that little bugger's not getting his fair share of the hard things in life' and this was supposed to make up for it.

It wasn't right. It wasn't as if he had never had any bad times. There was his mother, for one thing. She'd died when he was just a kid—on his eleventh birthday. She had been ill for a long time, and the doctors couldn't work out what was wrong with her. She had kept getting these dizzy spells and she went through times when she would slur her speech and she couldn't walk properly. Then she had died and they had done a post-mortem and found out she had multiple sclerosis. But it was too late to do anything about it then. Chris just hoped the doctors did better with Liam.

In a way, Chris had been fighting all his life to bury his childhood. It was not his dad's fault. He had worked from hell to breakfast, portering in this very hospital, but he had been on his own with Chris and his three brothers and sisters, cooking and mending and minding the house, and, try as he might, he simply never could afford to do more than keep them just barely afloat. They had no fancy Christmas presents—no computers or remote control cars like some of his mates at school had—and they couldn't go shooting off on day trips like some of them. If Chris wanted a treat, he used to go down the Ford motor car showroom in the middle of Grantham; the salesman used to let him sit in the driver's seat and whizz the electric windows up and down and imagine that he was a rich person who could afford a flash car like this.

Sitting silently now, staring into the wires that ringed his son, Chris couldn't help feeling a little anger rising inside him. Surely, he deserved his luck as much as anyone else. It wasn't as though he had just woken up one morning and found the good life lying on the door mat, like a free gift that had been posted through the letter-box. He and Joanne had really fought to put their lives together.

They had been married more than four years now. They had had to pay for most of the wedding themselves, but they didn't mind. It was a laugh and they knew what they were doing. They were always careful with money. They never bought furniture on HP; they waited until they could afford to pay cash. They had wanted their own place, so they had chosen somewhere they could afford; it had only cost £14,000. Chris's wages had got better, and they had bought their first car, a second-hand Escort. Then, after Jamie was born, and Chris's new business was doing well, they had decided to buy a bigger house and when they sold the first one—only a year after they bought it—they made a profit of £16,000. Just luck, really. They had bought the new house, and Chris's wages had got better still and so they had sold the old Escort and one fine day they had gone down to the Ford motor car showroom in the middle of Grantham and bought themselves their own Sierra. That was a moment to cherish.

But life wasn't about money. It was about family. That was why he worked so hard. Chris was going to give his kids all the things that he'd wanted as a kid but couldn't have. He'd have the time to go to parents' evenings at the school and he'd be able to afford to take them on proper holidays, too. At Christmas, when he'd given Jamie his big red toy tractor, it had filled his heart with pride. His own family. It was the most important thing in his life. Second to none.

And now there was this. His youngest son was lying here, pale and breathless, hooked up to all kinds of medicines and monitors that were supposed to help him, and maybe they would and maybe they wouldn't, and all that Chris had was his hope, and his lucky streak.

It took only a few hours for the luck to start doing its work. Chris and Joanne hardly dared to believe it, but all that Thursday night, as they watched sleeplessly over him, they saw Liam's breathing grow stronger. All Friday morning, he did well, his colour came back and then, finally, one bright moment early on Friday afternoon, he opened his eyes and smiled at Chris. Chris beamed back and asked him if he was all right now.

The nurses moved Liam out of the Treatment Room, into a quiet cubicle. On the door, there was a picture of a cartoon man with a big yellow head and a crazy smile and 'Mr Happy' written underneath. Liam started kicking and cooing and sucking on a bottle. By Friday evening, they were talking about sending him home in a few days. Nobody seemed to know what had happened to him to make him so ill. The doctors took blood and X-rays and Dr Nanayakkara said he had some pneumonia and possibly septicaemia and it seemed perhaps he had been too bunged up with mucous. Anyway, he seemed to be as right as rain now.

Chris was full of thanks for Dr Nanayakkara—he really rated him—and for the nurses, particularly Bev. She had been sitting with Liam for hours, 'specialing' him, they called it. It turned out that she had only just qualified the week before, but she seemed really interested in him and she was always willing to talk to Chris and Joanne about what was going on. Some of the other nurses seemed a bit shy. They would say Liam was doing well, but they wouldn't give out any detail. But Bev told them exactly what was happening: they were giving him a drug called salbutamol through a face mask to open up his airways and they had set up a drip to feed him antibiotics to tackle his chest infection. She showed them the little pouch on the drip by Liam's wrist where they could inject the antibiotics without him feeling anything, and then she explained all the monitors to them, so that they could look at this machine called a pulseoximeter and see how much oxygen Liam had in his blood (98 per cent was about normal, she said), and they could make sense of the scratchy graph which was scribbling out the rhythm of Liam's heartbeat. She told them about the apnoea monitor which she said was really for preventing cot deaths. If Liam had trouble breathing, a little red light would come on and the apnoea monitor would scream out so loud that she said they'd hear it all over the ward. It was all really reassuring, because they could see for themselves that Liam truly was better.

Chris had been wondering whether they should try and transfer Liam down the road to Nottingham, to the Queen's Medical Centre, where they had a new intensive care unit specially for children, but Bev said they shouldn't worry.

'You're better off leaving him here. We can special him. They wouldn't have enough staff to do that at Queen's Med. They're always too busy there.'

Chris thought that made sense and, on Friday morning, when he heard Bev talking to a staff nurse about taking some time off, he made a point of asking her to come back that night, so that she could carry on specialing Liam. He felt she knew him so well now that she was the best person to keep an eye on him. He was really relieved when she agreed.

'I'll go and do some shopping and get a bit of sleep this afternoon, and I'll be back about 7.30.'

Chris thanked her.

Late that Friday night, after the last family visitors had left, Chris finally decided to catch up on his sleep in the little parents' room on the side of the ward. Joanne was already in there, dead to the world. She had more or less gone to sleep in the canteen a couple of hours earlier and dragged herself down to the bedroom. Chris went and had a bath and on his way to bed, he popped his head round Mr Happy's door, saw that Liam had 99 per cent oxygen in his blood and said goodnight to Bev and a male charge nurse who was with her. Just as he was about to go, one of the monitors started to wail and, for a second, Chris's heart fell through his chest, but the charge nurse rolled Liam onto his side, tapped him on the back and told Chris it was all right, Liam had just got a little mucous caught in his throat. They would get the physiotherapist to come and have a look, but he was sure there was nothing to worry about. Chris was happy that Liam was in good hands. He stumbled off to sleep. It was just after midnight.

When the night sister woke him, shaking his shoulder, Chris hardly knew where he was for a moment, and then he heard her voice telling him that Liam had had a relapse. What's a relapse?

'He has stopped breathing for a few minutes. Dr Nanayakkara is with him now and he'll talk to you as soon as he is finished.'

'What happened? What time is it?'

'It's nearly 5.00. Saturday morning. I don't know what happened. All I know is that he stopped breathing for a while.'

Chris did not believe her. Liam had had 99 per cent oxygen a few hours ago.

'The doctor will tell you. Would you like me to call the hospital chaplain?'

Chris shrugged off the question. Why would Liam have stopped breathing? They must have got the wrong baby or something.

He pulled on his clothes and padded barefoot down the corridor. There was Mr Happy, grinning in the night lights. And there, through the door, were Dr Nanayakkara and Bev and half a dozen other people all standing round Liam's cot, peering down, working away, all hands and elbows and wires and lights. That was his Liam. There was no mistake. And this time, when Dr Nanayakkara finally emerged with his verdict, he provided no shelter from the truth, no room to misunderstand what he was saying.

'Liam has suffered cardiac arrest and he has stopped breathing for a period of time. I estimate it may have been as long as one hour and 15 minutes. He is now breathing again but he is having some convulsions, which does indicate brain damage. It is my professional opinion that this damage is likely to be severe.'

On top of the bright white mattress, Liam's body was twitching and twisting like an angry snake.

Chris Taylor sat alone in the room. In his arms, he held a bundle of blankets which were wrapped around his baby son.

It was not a pretty room. The walls were bare, painted in a watery brown the colour of old mushrooms. The curtains were yellow with a cream check and a soiled look. There was a sink with a sign that said 'Not suitable for drinking' and a waste bin with a green plastic bag in it. There were no flowers, no toys, no games, no books. The only splash of life was Mr Happy outside on the door. Inside the room, it was as grey as rain. Chris had been sitting there for hours.

He was tired, stiff with fatigue. He had not slept since the night sister woke him, but he did not mind. If his back ached, it was because it needed to ache to stay in this shabby old armchair, hour after hour. If his arms were numb, that was fine, that was Liam lying on them. If his eyes were red, it was only natural. None of it mattered. Nothing else mattered. He would sit here for as long as it took, for as long as he had to. Joanne had gone upstairs to sit with relatives. In the whole world, there were only him and Liam and this room.

It was a small room. There was just enough space on the beige vinyl floor for Chris's heavy armchair with its bruised brown cushions, a couple of white plastic chairs, the little sink over in the corner to Chris's left and, immediately in front of him, a cot— not the kind of cot that children have at home, full of round-eyed bears and blinking dolls, but a steel-framed box on wheels called a Resuscitaire, more like a trolley, with a flat white plastic cover on the top, a bank of dials on the right-hand side, and a waterfall of wires pouring out of its insides and streaming across the room to the bundle of blankets in Chris's arms. Monitors. There was the cardiograph, slowly pumping out a strip of paper like a till-roll, with a jagged pencil line scribbling out the rhythm of Liam's heart. There was a sleek black computer screen flipping up a sequence of green figures, counting and recounting every fragile reflex of Liam's lungs. But the one that Chris watched was the little metal-grey box which lay in his lap, the apnoea monitor. It was the size of a television remote control, with two little lights on its face. From time to time, nurses slipped into the room to check that the thin grey wire was still running from it down through the blankets to the electrode-pad on Liam's warm abdomen. All the time that Chris sat there, the left-hand light was flashing green, constantly and regularly blipping away like a miniature lighthouse. The other light was still. As long as the little green light flashed, Liam was alive and there was hope. But if the light moved across and started to shine red, if the apnoea monitor started to scream, then Liam was losing.

Chris looked down at his son, at his soft yellow-pink face, at the frown around his eyes, and he could almost imagine that he was still fine.

He was breathing well. He seemed so calm, and everything on his little eight-week-old body was still so perfect, the fingers curled into a pudgy fist, the soft flake of nail waiting to be cut at the top of his thumb, his long eyelashes curving together, the blond fluff down the side of his cheeks. He still had that milk-sweet scent of new baby. But there was no pretending. If Chris had managed, just for a moment, to fool himself, to let his imagination run away with him and show him pictures of Liam waking up and smiling, and him and Joanne taking him home and everyone heaving a sigh of relief, of Liam growing up and running and talking and being his son, even then he could not have escaped. Liam's body would not let him. All the while he sat there, Chris could feel the steady pat-pat-pat of his baby son's left leg as it twitched uselessly against his thigh, like a blind man prodding with a cane. Then every so often, all the monitors would panic, and Liam's whole body would suddenly stiffen and his back would arch upwards and his fists would screw tight and his tiny arms would shoot up and beat the air like a clockwork toy soldier, as if some bony claw had grabbed his heart and squeezed it till it tried to burst with pain. There was no pretending. Liam was damaged.

Soon after dawn, the nurses had pushed a stainless steel trolley into the cubicle and laid out a white linen cloth, a small silver bowl full of water and a crucifix, and then the hospital chaplain had come and muttered a blessing and scooped a palmful of the water into his right hand. The nurses and the doctors had stood quietly. The chaplain had leaned over Liam. 'In the name of the Father and the Son and the Holy Spirit', he had passed the shape of a cross over the little boy's forehead and given him his name, Liam James Taylor.

Outside the door a trolley rolled by. Chris heard the nurses' voices drop and fade away. He had a fair idea what they were saying, because earlier he had seen it for himself in their faces: they thought he and Joanne were playing God. They were thinking like nurses—thinking about all the weird and wonderful medical ways they had of keeping Liam going against his will, thinking of sticking him full of needles and drips, and pumping his lungs and wiring up his heart. But Liam was hurt. Something inside this little boy had collapsed and all the most delicate, vital parts of his life had been broken and scattered about, and God alone knew what kind of state they were in. No one seemed to know why it had happened, but they all agreed he was damaged.

He and Joanne were thinking like parents. They didn't want their son messed around with any more. They wanted him to have some peace, one way or the other. So, whatever the nurses might think, they had asked for him to be taken off the ventilator and all the mysterious drugs that were forcing him to stay alive.

If the damage was so bad that he died, then that was the way it had to be and at least he would be free of all these needles and wires; if Liam was strong enough to survive, then that meant he might still have a life worth living. None of these doctors and nurses seemed to understand.

Their family doctor had driven to the hospital that morning and taken them aside with a low voice and a worried look. 'What are you going to do if Liam comes round?' he had asked.

'We'll feed him, of course,' Chris had told him. 'We're not going to starve him to death. We're just saying we don't want him hurt any more, we don't want him messed around with any more. It's up to Liam. And no one else. It's his decision.'

Just then, the door opened, and Chris was plucked out of his day dream. It was a nurse called Lynn, a chunky middle-aged woman with a worn face. 'The doctor wants to see you,' she said. 'Here, I'll look after him while you're gone.'

Chris sucked in a deep breath and handed Liam over. He felt a bit dizzy walking back up the corridor, round past the beds full of smiling children who were getting better in the main part of Ward Four to the consulting room, where he found Dr Nanayak-kara sitting with Joanne and her father, Harry. Joanne had her hands clasped between her knees, her face was grey. Chris sat next to her. The conversation started to whirl past them like a fair-ground ride.

Nanayakkara was trying to say that Liam was doing well. They were asking how well. He was saying he didn't know. He was saying he thought maybe they should put him back on his medi-cine. They were asking if Liam would survive then. He was saying he couldn't tell. They were asking if Liam's brain was still damaged. He was saying he didn't know. No—he was saying that the brain was definitely damaged. Severely damaged. He just didn't know how severely. So what was he saying? He was saying that Liam was doing well—not very well, but better than he had expected. So, maybe they should put him back on the drugs. Chris and Joanne looked at each other. It had been hard enough to take Liam off the medicine in the first place, to take their baby's damaged life and hand it over to fate. Now they had to go all through that decision again.

They dragged themselves out of Dr Nanayakkara's office, through the long hospital corridors and up to the door of the canteen. It was full of their relatives, waiting for news, so they slipped into a side office to talk privately. But what could they say?

Their son was damaged. Joanne couldn't shake off the feeling that Liam had had enough. 'I just feel like he wants to go,' she said. 'He wants them to leave him alone.'

For Chris, it stirred up something deep inside him. Most of the time he was easy-going and happy and he was not one to sit around feeling gloomy and wondering about death. But, buried down inside, he had this fear. He didn't talk about it, or even think about it very often, but he had this idea that maybe when you die and when you're buried, your mind still might be alive and working. It was only doctors and people like that who said that they knew that your mind died too. But what did they know? They didn't know about his mother having multiple sclerosis. They didn't even seem to know what had happened to Liam, unless they were hiding it from them. So maybe they didn't really know about dying either.

He remembered how this thought had come to him, one day, when he was 14, and he was walking back from St Wulfram's Comprehensive, and his route took him past the end of Grantham Cemetery. And as he walked along, he noticed a dead bird lying on the pavement and he stopped and looked and he was puzzled to see that it seemed still to be breathing. Its damp-feathered flanks were heaving in and out, and he didn't know why, it was just a reflex, but he poked it with his shoe and, to his horror, the little bird's body just collapsed—fell apart—and there was a terrible stench and all these fat white maggots came tumbling out. And that stuck with him. When he thought about death, he thought about that bird's horrible corpse and how it had seemed to be breathing—and he thought about all those maggots shifting around inside you while your mind was still alive, still conscious. It filled him with dread.

And now, sitting here with Joanne, he felt that same dread for Liam. Nanayakkara was saying he would be damaged, maybe a total wreck of a body, unable to move or do anything for himself, or perhaps just handicapped, maybe unable to speak properly or to have any will of his own. But if somewhere inside that wreck Liam's mind was alive and alert and suffering, if Liam was more or less buried alive inside his own body . . . It was too much to think of. They couldn't do that to him. They both agreed that he looked more peaceful now that he was off the drugs. Liam wanted to be left alone. He would decide whether to survive or not.

They went back downstairs and, for the second time that day, they told Dr Nanayakkara that Liam had had enough medicine. Then, together, they went back into the little room with Mr Happy on the door. Lynn the nurse left. Chris took Liam in his arms. Joanne sat beside him. And they waited for Liam's decision.

In front of them, beyond the window, the sun had found its way down through the clouds, cars swished through the melting snow on the road into Grantham, buses puffed and wheezed along behind them, small boys shouted on the playing fields. Behind them, on the other side of the door, they could hear from time to time the mumble of voices, the clacking of heels on the polished floor, laughter. Inside the room it was quiet. Only their thoughts disturbed them.

Joanne was watching her little boy's face. She was afraid that he was running out of time. It was after 2.00 in the afternoon now, more than nine hours since the night sister had woken them. Nanayakkara had already told them that Liam had done better than he had expected, just to last this long. She felt he was going, slowly going away.

It was not fair. It didn't make sense. But somehow she felt this was the way it was supposed to be. Looking back now, it was strange: the way he had caught that cold that just wouldn't let go; the way he'd got better and then got worse again straightaway.

Almost as if he was meant to go, as if he had just been lent to them for a while.

Joanne only had to look at him to see it. When they had first woken her in the night and told her what had happened, she had been too upset to go near him. But it was all right now, he was so relaxed now, so peaceful. His eyes had never opened again, not since the night sister woke them. He just lay quietly in Chris's arms, as if he was snoozing, with the little green light on the apnoea monitor flashing away.

Chris was still hoping. He had never really believed in fate. We are all free, he used to say, free to do good or do bad. Things turn out the way you make them. Liam had been ill on Thursday evening. Dr Nanayakkara had warned them then to expect the worst. But he'd got better. And he'd get better again now. They'd be lucky.

Chris stiffened. The green light on the apnoea had started to flicker, green to red, back to green, green to red.

'Is he going?' asked Joanne.

For a moment, she wondered whether she should throw open the door and call in the nurses, but she waited. They would only come and fuss with him and hurt his body, trying to force him to be alive a little longer. There was nothing they could do. Liam was here, in the quiet, where he was safe, with the people who loved him.

Chris shook his head. The two lights were flickering faster now. But Liam would be OK. He was tough. He was fighting. Kids got colds, then they got better. This wouldn't happen. They still had their luck. And the doctors—they would help. That's what they were there for. There was nothing to worry about. Liam would open his eyes and smile at them and want his bottle, and they'd pack up their things and go home in the blue Sierra and it would be fine, all fine again. Liam opened his mouth and took a tiny gasp. Suddenly, the apnoea was shrieking with a wail like a burning witch. The light was red.

Joanne looked at Chris: 'He's gone.'

2

Ward Four was a calm place. It always had been. Life ran through it like an old steam engine chugs through a children's book, puffing gently along the same old route at the same old speed.

Every morning, at 7.30, the day nurses arrived and drew back the big heavy curtains and turned out the dim yellow night lights and woke up the children for breakfast. At 8.00, Sister Barker would come and take the report from the night staff and go to her office to look after her paperwork. Soon after that, one of the consultants would start his round with a junior doctor, and Sister Barker would trip along behind them scribbling notes in an old diary as they wandered in and out of the six cubicles at the far end of the ward, round the corner to the four beds behind the nurses' station and then finally to the six beds next to the playroom. Every day they followed the same route. At noon the nurse in charge would walk through the ward with the drugs trolley, making sure she finished the round in time for the children's lunch at 1.00 so that they were ready for an afternoon of visitors and playing. Around 3.00, the afternoon shift arrived, took their report from the day staff, had a cup of tea, prepared for the final drugs round at 5.00, supper at 6.00, and by the time that the night staff arrived at 9.00, the children were tucked up safe and asleep in their beds again.

The steady rhythm ran unchanged from day to day. The children on the ward were not usually very ill. Maybe once or twice a year, a child might be in a really bad way and Ward Four would simply arrange a transfer to the Queen's Medical Centre, 20 miles down the road to the west in Nottingham, where they had a sparkling new paediatric intensive care unit staffed by a small army of nurses and paediatricians. But most children who came to Ward Four had broken legs or the complications of colds, or they needed minor operations to take grommets out of their ears or Lego out of their nostrils. Nothing nasty. There were more of them nowadays, since Grantham had merged with the little hospital down the road in Newark, and there were a few regular patients, children with cerebral palsy, for example, who came in every couple of months for observation or treatment. But mostly, there was a steady turnover of children who turned up crying and then left smiling.

Ward Four was popular with most of the nurses. There were a few who steered clear, because, as they all knew, sick babies could be very difficult. They couldn't tell you where they were hurting or what was wrong at all, and, if they were seriously ill, they had a habit of deteriorating terribly quickly, 'going off' as the nurses called it. But, for most of them, it was a favourite place.

Some of them had worked there for so long that their work had become almost a habit. Sister Barker, who was in charge of the ward, had been there for 16 years and she was often not seen for hours on end. She stayed in her little office and dealt with her paperwork, or popped off for a cigarette in the Ladies. You were not really supposed to smoke in there because it made the linen room next door smell, but everybody knew she did and nobody really cared. She always turned out for the doctor's morning rounds or if there was any crisis, and the rest of the time she could afford to leave things to the staff nurses. They ran the ward perfectly well. Sister Barker knew there was nothing to worry about.

Her number two, Margaret Geeson, who was the senior staff nurse on the ward, had been there ten years and she held the reins from day to day. She spent much more time on the ward than Sister Barker, she even drew up the rotas. She relied on half a dozen other staff nurses—senior nurses who had gone through a full three-year training course—although some of them, like Clare Winser, worked part time because they had their own children at home. A rank below them were the State Enrolled Nurses, who had trained for only two years. Some of them, like Bev Allitt, had only just qualified, but others, like Betty Asher and Lynn Vowles, had been there for so long that even though they were only SENs, Margaret and the other staff nurses treated them as equals. They had a steady turnover of student nurses and a back-up of auxiliaries with no medical training, to help them out. Everyone got on pretty well with each other, at least among the nurses.

The children seemed to like it, too. They were often frightened when they first arrived but the nurses had done their best to make the ward look cheerful, although the strange layout did not help them. The architects who designed it in the 1960s were very proud of it. 'A racecourse model', they called it, because there was a block of service rooms—baths, loos, offices, the Treatment Room—grouped in the middle, with a corridor running round the edge of them like a four-sided race-track. Then, on the far side of the race-track, there were offices and kitchens and all the children's beds fanned out like grandstands. The nurses thought it would have been fine, if only they could have seen round corners, and they doubted whether the architects had ever considered how to make such a place feel cosy and homely.

They had done what they could to disguise the ward. As soon as new children arrived, through the double doors from the main hospital corridor, they found the central block of service rooms on their right decorated with posters of Garfield the cat and Postman Pat, and an aquarium with a goldfish and a toy treasure chest. If they followed this first stretch of race-track corridor past the doctors' offices and a little kitchen on their left, they could turn right and walk down the next section of race-track passing most of the ward on their left, all brightly lit by floor-to-ceiling windows on the far side. There was the play area with toys and tables where some children ate their meals, then the six-bed area for the children who needed least attention and where there was sometimes a television with children's programmes, and finally the four-bed area which was right next to the nurses' station for children who needed to be watched. The nurses' station had a desk with a phone and a computer terminal, the special secure cupboard where they kept dangerous drugs under a double lock, a fridge and a panel of lights which lit up if any of the children pushed the call button by their bed. On their right, as they walked down this corridor, children passed Sister Barker's office and then the Treatment Room, where they kept less dangerous drugs and all the hi-tech monitoring equipment on the mobile Resuscitaire on which very sick children could lie to be revived. Although this piece of the race-track ran through the busiest part of the ward, the nurses had done their best to pretend it was a nursery, with a confetti of cartoon characters on the wall—Dumbo and Thomas the Tank Engine, Granny Dryden and Reverend Timms—and a board of Ward Four jokes ('Doctor, doctor, I feel like a pound coin'. 'Go shopping, the change will do you good').

Past the nurses' station, the children could turn right again down a third track of corridor between the six little isolation cubicles on their left, each named after one of the Mister Men who sat grinning on the doors, and the bathrooms and loos on the right. Most of the children went no further than this. Straight ahead, through swing doors at the end of the corridor, were the four little bedrooms and a sitting room set aside for parents staying in the hospital. Off to the right was the fourth track of corridor, leading past the Day Room for out-patients on the left, back to the double doors and the main corridor.

Despite the nurses' efforts, there was no concealing the fact that it was a hospital ward—it had that special smell of antiseptic and canteen cooking—but Ward Four was a warm, inviting place, reassuring, trustworthy, content to be calm.

From time to time, there might be some minor incident to disturb the surface peace. Some money had gone missing from the little store opposite the Day Room where the nurses left their coats and handbags when they came on duty. No one seemed to know who had taken it or how to stop them, but several of the nurses had decided to carry their purses around with them on the ward. And back in mid February, the key to the fridge by the nurses' station had got lost. It didn't matter too much—the fridge was only used to store eye-drops and insulin for diabetic children, nothing that was particularly dangerous—and no one even bothered to send an Untoward Incident Report to the management. The nurses just borrowed a key from the maternity ward (all the fridges had the same lock and the same key) until the Works Department came round and gave them a new one. But these little incidents soon passed and calm returned to its natural place on the ward, like a cat in a basket.

Even the death of Liam Taylor soon sank into the daily tranquillity. Some of the younger nurses had been a bit upset, like Wendy Sorrell, who was only 19 and was filling in as an auxiliary until she started her teacher training. She had been the first into Liam's room when they had heard his apnoea monitor screeching that Saturday afternoon and she had had to comfort the parents and, not being used to it, she had just burst into tears herself. She couldn't help it. It was a terrible thing to see a child die. There were nurses who had worked on the ward for years and never had to deal with a death themselves, so no one blamed her. It had been even worse for poor Bev Allitt who had only just finished her training. She had seen Liam go off on the Thursday afternoon when he had first arrived on the ward and then again in the early hours of the Saturday morning, and she had had to stay there when the Crash Team were working on him. All that could be pretty tough, but she had taken it in her stride without appearing to be upset by it at all.

Dr Nanayakkara had dealt swiftly with the crisis. He had examined the body, asked the parents if he could take some blood, sent that off to Leeds for tests, and concluded that the child must have died from some kind of blood poisoning. He signed a death certificate and, being an honest and scrupulous man, he acknowledged some doubts about his own diagnosis by giving the cause of death as 'probable septicaemia'. As far as Dr Nanayakkara was concerned, that was accurate and adequate, and he sent Liam's body, now placed in a Moses basket with flowers and a white shawl, to the mortuary so that funeral arrangements could be made.

It certainly was a strange case. The night charge nurse David Wiles who had been on duty when Liam's heart stopped had told Dr Nanayakkara that the suddenness of the baby's collapse was just extraordinary. Nanayakkara himself could not understand why it had been so difficult to revive the baby; that was not normal. But soon the waves of calmness lapped back over Ward Four, gently erasing the grief and fear that briefly had lain there, returning the ward to its regular rhythm, quiet, predictable, secure, just like any children's ward in any hospital in a small town in England.

And yet it was not quite so tranquil. Out of sight of the nurses and their patients, unremarked by the parents or the GPs who had sent them there, a distant squall was forming. It began when

Dr Nanayakkara's death certificate was rejected by the Grantham coroner, T. J. Pert.

Pert had been coroner in the town for as long as anyone could remember (for 41 years, in fact). He was a first-edition Dickensian character, rather like the old English actor Alastair Sim to look at, with curly grey feathers of hair, a cockerel's beak supporting his half-moon glasses, and an air of uncontrollable impatience which had him constantly strutting and scratching and pecking and prodding at everyone and everything around him. T. J. Pert was not at all happy with Dr Nanayakkara's death certificate. He wanted to know what had happened to this baby. Either this child had died of septicaemia, or he hadn't. He wasn't interested in what 'probably' had happened. 'Probable' was not a word that belonged on death certificates. At least, not in Grantham, not as long as T. J. Pert was coroner. So he rejected Dr Nanayakkara's death certificate and told the pathologist at Grantham Hospital to conduct a post-mortem. Nanayakkara protested and pleaded that if they had to have a post-mortem, at least it should be conducted by a paediatric pathologist, who specialized in understanding the deaths of children, but his protests were ignored.

In the mortuary at Grantham Hospital, at 11.30 on the morning of Tuesday 25 February, Dr Terry Marshall, the consultant pathologist, set to work with his assistant, Darren Whitton. They found that Liam Taylor's body was normally nourished and they recorded no unusual external features. The brain appeared normal. Examining the alimentary system, the urogenital system, the reticulo-endothelial system, and the endocrine system they found no sign of abnormality. They looked at the lungs and found no areas of pneumonia (although Dr Nanayakkara had said the baby was pneumonic). But when they looked at Liam Taylor's eight-week-old heart, they found that the left ventricle, which is responsible for pumping fresh blood out to the rest of the body, was terribly damaged. The tissue had been almost completely destroyed.

This was not, in itself, an unusual sight for a pathologist, and Dr Marshall recognized it as the classic symptom of myocardial infarction: a heart attack. In adults, it was a relatively common experience, but in a small baby, Marshall knew, it was extremely rare. He looked for a cause. He examined the rest of the heart, the coronary arteries and the aorta, but he found nothing. All the blood vessels seemed entirely normal. There was no structural fault, no sign of infection. There was, in short, no reason for the heart to have died. It was a medical mystery.

Dr Marshall found it all rather disturbing and most unsatisfactory from a medical point of view and he had a photograph taken of the damaged heart. But what could he do about it? The coroner wanted a death certificate and Dr Marshall decided that he had better provide him with one and so he explained his doubts in his official report and then went ahead and recorded that Liam Taylor had died of a myocardial infarction, a natural death.

T. J. Pert was happy. Dr Nanayakkara was not. It was not simply that the pathologist had overturned his own view about septicaemia, nor even that he had challenged his view that Liam had been suffering from pneumonia, but that the conclusion of the post-mortem made no sense to him. If this child really had suffered a myocardial infarction, there had to be a cause. Since no such cause could be identified, Nanayakkara strongly suspected that the pathologist had come up with the wrong conclusion and, being a forceful character (and, if the truth be told, no stranger to arrogance), he contacted Dr Marshall and told him so. He went further. He said that in his opinion, there should be a second post-mortem, and it should be conducted by a paediatric pathologist, who would be capable of establishing the real cause of death in this case—which might well turn out to be septicaemia, as he continued to suspect. But Dr Nanayakkara was too late. The coroner had his death certificate. He was not prepared to order a second post-mortem. Liam Taylor's body was removed for cremation.

Nanayakkara wrote to the Queen's Medical Centre, to the eminent paediatrician in charge there, Professor David Hull, urging that all children's deaths be handled by specialists, and he telephoned the Queen's Med paediatric pathologist, Dr David Fagan, who agreed that even if there was no second post-mortem, they might at least examine the histology samples—the various specimens of organic tissue from Liam Taylor's body. Nanayakkara relayed this suggestion to Dr Marshall in his office next to the Grantham mortuary, and he agreed to send the samples for further examination.

In their neat, new home on the edge of Grantham, Chris and

Joanne Taylor saw nothing of this squall. They had done their best to return to their old lives in the normal world. Chris had gone back to work, rising early, nodding hallo to his neighbours and heading off down the hill in his old van for a day of sweat and builders' dust. Joanne had picked up on her old routines in the house and gone back to her part-time job in the hairdressers. They had tried to explain to Jamie that Liam would not be coming back. But the truth was that their normal life was still shredded.

They had followed all the rituals of mourning—flowers and cards and a funeral at Grantham Cemetery. They bought a head-stone with a teddy bear on it, and they planted a special tree to grow over the spot where Liam's ashes lay. Chris stood and stared at the hard ground and thought about how cold it was up here in the ordinary world and how much colder it must be down there, and he was glad that Liam was only ashes now and couldn't feel a thing, couldn't feel any pain any more. They took their best picture of him, sitting safe on Chris's lap, and framed it and put it on the wall in their front room, with his full name written underneath, so that everyone knew that they were not forgetting him, that they still missed him. But there was something else which was caught in their thoughts, though it took them a while before they realized what it was.

One day, about a week after Liam's death, the coroner's officer came to call. His name was Maurice Stonebridge-Foster. He sat in the sitting room, on the new green settee, and he looked uncomfortable, feeding the rim of his hat through his hands. He looked at the carpet and glanced up at them and told them that the pathologist had done his work and he had to inform them that young Liam had died of a heart attack, and he was sorry. Chris and Joanne nodded.

'But why?' asked Chris.

The coroner's officer looked blank, he was obviously ready to leave, but Chris persisted.

'You're telling me Liam died of a heart attack. But I don't understand why. I mean, why did he have a heart attack?'

'Well, I don't know why. The pathologist didn't say. All I know is that it was a heart attack, myocardial infarction they call it.'

'But all he had was a bad cold. Apart from that, he was a healthy baby. Far as we know. I mean, why would he suddenly have a heart attack?'

'I don't know,' said the coroner's officer.

'Well, there must have been some reason.'

'It's just one of those things. I'm sorry.'

Now they knew what it was they needed. If they couldn't have Liam, if they couldn't go back and have their old life, at least now they should have the truth. If they could understand it, if they could explain why this thing had happened to them of all people, maybe then they could start to forget. Until then, they could not be happy.

In his consulting room on Ward Four, Dr Nanayakkara was not happy either, but it appeared to him that there was nothing more that he could do. He would wait to see the full report from the pathologist. He was sure there was something wrong here but, for now, he pocketed his doubts and went on about his business. The squall passed.

It was a Tuesday morning, 5 March, just over two weeks after the death of Liam Taylor. In a quiet street on the edge of Newark, 12 miles north west of Grantham, in a brightly-coloured classroom in Appleton Gate Special School, Tim Hardwick was sitting, as he often did, strapped into his wheelchair, his head rolling on to his chest, while the clatter of the day swept around him.

Tim Hardwick was 11 years old, but he had never learned to speak. His brain and body had been ruined at birth by cerebral palsy, which had nearly killed him. His arms and legs were thin and brittle and almost beyond his control. He weighed only two and a half stone. He was epileptic. He was almost blind. He was utterly dependent on other people to fulfil his every need. But he was alive. Inside his broken body his heart was still beating and his lungs were still breathing, and, deep below the surface, in a wordless, almost lightless cave, he was still there, still hearing the sounds and following the blurred outlines of the world outside, still awash with feelings, and still trying to send signals to the world outside, mostly with laughter.

He had a bright, clear little face, like a pixie, and he squealed with delight when he heard his favourite sounds: a dog barking or loud music or, best of all, the sound of someone clicking their finger-nails by his ear. Something about that sound made him squirm with joy. It was the same with food. He liked baked beans and Weetabix and he encouraged the social workers who looked after him to feed him more of them by grinning and giggling. But if he had to, he could fill his throat with a grunt of disgust to register his disapproval, particularly if someone tried to make him eat banana custard.

Tim had been home that weekend, to be with his mother and father and his elder sister, Elaine. He knew their voices and their little terraced house in Beeston near Nottingham, its smells and sounds, and he was relaxed and happy there, lying on the sofa. His mother, Helen, always made a tremendous fuss of him, tickling him and teasing him and showing him off to anyone who would watch. Giving him up into council care had been the greatest pain of her life. She had done it when he was only three months old, when it was obvious that he was damaged and that she could not cope. She was disabled herself. A stroke had withered her left arm and reduced her left leg to a broken reed, now caged in a metal caliper; she suffered severe epileptic attacks—the excitement of a dream was enough to provoke one—and when she was pregnant with Tim she had had a particularly long fit which seemed to have damaged him. For Tim's sake, she had had to put him into the care of Nottinghamshire County Council, but she had refused to let him go. She kept photographs of him and wrote poems about him and accepted that in some way she could not understand it was God's will that Tim should be like this. The council had looked after him well. They had made him a brace to stop him rolling into a ball and they had managed to find drugs to control his epileptic fits. Some of the social workers obviously really cared for him, they took him riding and swimming and played him music in bed and spoiled him with his favourite things, but still Helen Hardwick liked to see him, to have him home again, back with his family.

It was about 10.30 that Tuesday morning when the first fit seized Tim. A teacher saw it, ran to him, tried not to frighten the other children, hooked his tongue out of his mouth and wrestled him out of his chair, hanging on to his crazy limbs to stop him breaking his own bones as he beat his useless body against the ground. The teachers at Appleton Gate were used to dealing with epileptic fits, and calmly they carried Tim to another room and gave him rectal valium, which was usually enough to cure the problem. But something in Tim's body chemistry had changed and the epilepsy which had been contained in a medicinal cage for all these years now broke loose and started to rampage through him. Tim had no sooner recovered from his first fit than another, even more powerful attack overwhelmed him. By 1.30 he had been consumed by a sequence of five epileptic fits, he was drenched with sweat and urine, his face was flecked with spittle, and his whole frame was rigid with the effort. The head teacher phoned Caudwell House, the residential home where he lived, and told the social workers there that they were taking him to hospital.

Those who cared for Tim knew that in his remote and secret way, he would realize that there was something wrong and he would be terribly scared, and so they were determined that he should not be alone. When he arrived at Newark Hospital at 2.00, a teacher from the school was with him, holding his hand. The doctors quickly dosed him with five milligrams of rectal valium, fitted a pink plastic cannula to the back of his left hand, hooked it up to an intravenous drip and slowly fed another 2.5 milligrams of valium into his bloodstream. Tim's jaw started to loosen, his limbs to bend and his body to sag as the epilepsy crawled away, defeated. His breathing steadied, and the nurses tucked him into bed and left him gurgling quietly, as he often did. Tim slept. Two social workers from Caudwell House came and sat with him.

Now that the crisis was over, the doctors at Newark looked down at his sleeping form and agreed that he was out of danger. But there was always a chance that he might produce another fit and, since they could not keep him overnight in Newark, they decided to have him transferred to another hospital for observation. One of his social workers, Sue Young, said she would go with him.

Tim was still asleep as nurses lifted him from his bed, wrapped him into a stretcher, slid him into the back of an ambulance and drove him southwards, across the border of Nottinghamshire, into Lincolnshire, to the outskirts of Grantham, down Manthorpe Road, out on the stretcher, past the reception desk, through the Casualty department, down the white corridor where the old people slept in their dressing gowns, through the double doors, and into Ward Four. It was 3.15 in the afternoon.

The ward was not busy that day and Tim was the only patient in the four-bed area. Sue Young, the social worker, sat beside him, talking softly to him as he slept. He was still asleep an hour later when Dr Nanayakkara came to look at him and established that he showed no sign of further fits and told one of the junior doctors to take Tim's blood for tests and to give him more valium through the cannula which still pierced the skin on the back of the boy's hand. Soon after that, Tim woke.

From somewhere deep in his dark, private world, he smiled his recognition when Sue Young held his hand and told him he would be all right. He grunted in discomfort as Sue leaned him up in his bed to show Bev Allitt and a student nurse called Heather Skayman how to fit him into his brace, and then he lay back, apparently contented, as Sue calmed him and told him she was going now but she would be back to see him tomorrow and not to worry.

Alone now, he lay motionless in his bed, a helpless bundle, surrounded for once by strangers who, like most people, could make no sense of his secret life. His almost useless eyes still blinked, sweeping the ward like a lighthouse in the mist, recognizing nothing, knowing no one. Perhaps it was his eyes which warned him. Perhaps they caught a shape, some unfamiliar blur that signalled danger. Perhaps he simply sensed that something was not right. Whatever it was, he started to make a whirring sound in his throat. Bev Allitt who was nearby called out to the staff nurse in charge, Mary Reet, a hearty fresh-faced country girl with a bush of brown hair swept back off her face. She was just starting the 5.00 drugs round.

'Mary, he's coughing. Can you come and look at him?'

Mary came and looked and called the doctor, who listened to his urgent grunt and said he had a dry cough, and not to worry. The hands of strangers turned Tim Hardwick on his side, and went away and left him on his own again.

Perhaps this time it was a sound. A strange sound. Or a movement. Unfamiliar, unexplained. Or a pain. Something wrong. Something piercing. A warning reaching right inside him. Alarm. Danger. Another child, whose brain was ripe with health, could have burst into tears, or cried out for a parent, or even pushed

aside the blankets and stumbled out of bed to safety. But Tim
could do none of this. He was strapped inside his useless brain.
He could only make that sound again, that frantic hum deep in
his throat, a choked and muffled whirring sound—not a dry cough
at all but a scream for help in a language no one understood.

It was 5.45 when Bev Allitt raised the alarm. She called Mary
Reet to him again and this time, when Mary looked, she saw that
Tim's face was as white as chalk. The skin around his mouth was
blue. He was just barely breathing. She felt his pulse. Nothing.
Nothing at all. Tim's heart had stopped.

'222, Bev! And get the resus trolley!'

Mary turned the young boy on his back, pinched his nostrils
and started breathing into his mouth.

Bev dialled 222 on the phone at the nurses' station and went
straight through to the switchboard.

'Switchboard,' said the operator.

'Cardiac arrest,' said Bev, following the procedure she had
learned in training. 'Ward Four.'

The operator repeated her words. She pressed the Crash Team
button on the switchboard. In different parts of the hospital,
bleepers started to pulse: a junior doctor who specialized in heart
attacks broke into a run; the most senior nurse in the hospital
started out of her office; a junior doctor attached to Ward Four
raced down the long central corridor; an anaesthetist and a physician followed them; a porter hurried over to Ward One, grabbed
the defibrillator which was always waiting there fully charged,
looped his way up through Casualty to pick up the child-sized
paddles and headed for Ward Four.

On Ward Four, Bev had fetched the resus trolley from the
Treatment Room. By the side of Tim's bed, Mary Reet had pushed
a clear plastic airway into the top of Tim's throat, clipped an
Ambubag to the open end of it, and now she was squeezing it,
forcing air into the lifeless limp body. Within minutes, the whole
Crash Team had arrived with Dr Nanayakkara in their wake. They
removed the airway, fed a long tube down his throat and into his
lungs, hooked it up to the anaesthetist's oxygen supply, injected
him with atropine and adrenalin to stimulate his heart, stuck
electrodes like little white coins on to his naked chest to search
for a heartbeat, held the fat red paddles of the white enamel

defibrillator to his bony rib cage, one over his heart and one at his side, and fired him with 15-second bursts of electricity, trying to shock his heart out of its quivering spasm. But they were too late.

His heart had failed. Death had finally completed its unfinished business with Timothy William Hardwick, aged 11 years and two months. On his notes, the doctors wrote 'cardiac arrest, cause not clear'. It was just after 6.15 in the evening of Tuesday, 5 March.

Chris Taylor wanted the truth.

At first, after they had lost Liam, he had thought it must have been something to do with his cold, that somehow it had got him so bunged up inside that his heart had stopped. But now he wondered. Maybe it was something else. It could have been some strange infection and for all he knew it was going to attack other children on the ward as well, so someone ought to find out about it. Or it might have been some inherited weakness of the heart, which he and Joanne should know about in case it affected Jamie. Or maybe it truly was just a side-effect of the bronchiolitis. But whatever it was, he wanted to know the whole story.

When the coroner's officer had failed to answer his questions, Chris had called the pathologist at the hospital, Terry Marshall, and asked if he could come and see him. The pathologist had offered to meet him in his lab, but instantly Chris had seen a mental picture of Marshall's work in there and suggested instead that they meet in the hospital canteen.

It was lunch-time. The canteen was loud with the clatter of knives and forks and most of the tables were crowded with hospital staff and patients' relatives, but Chris managed to find an empty table in a corner, where he sat and drummed his fingers while Dr Marshall went and bought him a cup of coffee. Chris was not sure whether he was going to understand what Marshall had to say to him, but he was sure he was going to try. This man had looked inside Liam, he had seen his heart and his other vital organs with his own two eyes and he would have known what he was looking for. If he didn't have the whole answer, he would at least have clues.

Marshall came back with the coffee. He was a small, slightly chubby man who was beginning to lose his hair. Chris started the questions he had rehearsed, but he soon discovered that he was not going to get the answers he had hoped for. Marshall could not tell him why Liam's heart had stopped. He had found no cause for it at all, no blocked valve, no structural defect, no sign of infection. All he would say was that death was caused by heart failure, and that this had been accepted by the coroner. But he said one thing which left Chris with a whole new battery of questions.

'Your son's heart was in a very poor condition, really very poor.'

'How's that then?'

The pathologist told him, between sips of coffee, that Liam's heart had been ruined, reduced to the sort of condition he had previously seen only in middle-aged or elderly men who had spent a lifetime smoking and drinking.

'What? But Liam was a baby. What do you mean? He was a baby.'

Marshall shrugged. 'I can't explain it, I'm afraid.'

The pathologist said that it was most unusual, but he thought he knew of another similar case. He would try and dig out the details and send them on to Chris, but that was really all he could do. Chris wanted to say that this was not enough, that he wanted a second opinion, somebody else to do the job if Marshall couldn't come up with the right answers, that it didn't make sense, that doctors were supposed to understand these things, but he could see he was getting nowhere, so he finished his coffee and thanked Dr Marshall and went home with a fire burning in the back of his mind.

That evening Chris Taylor slumped in front of the television, gazing at the screen, wondering about Liam, gazing back again, and, by sheer chance, he found himself watching a programme about heart disease. It was late and Joanne was already asleep upstairs. He started to watch intently, looking for some sort of clue, but they were talking about diet and exercise and nothing that really affected Liam. Then, at the end, they flashed up the phone number of an advice line, and right there and then, Chris decided to call it.

He was quiet about it. He didn't want to wake Joanne or upset her with all this, so he went into the kitchen and shut the door.

He dialled and quickly a voice answered, and Chris explained as clearly as he could about his baby son's heart attack and the big question—why? The voice at the other end paused.

'I'm not sure that I can help you very much,' it said.

'How do you mean?'

'Well, so far as I know, it is very rare for a baby to have a heart attack.'

'Is it?'

'In fact, if you ask me honestly, I would have to say that I've never come across it. Babies don't have heart attacks.'

Chris thanked the voice and hung up. He was no doctor and he didn't claim to have anything more than common sense and a love of Liam on his side, but it was as clear as day to him that there was something wrong here.

Chris Taylor did not know it, but Liam's was not the only post-mortem that had thrown up a mystery. Dr Marshall also had been asked to have a look at Tim Hardwick, not because the coroner had any problem this time, but because the law said you had to conduct a post-mortem on anyone who died in hospital after a stay of less than 48 hours.

The pathologist had done the usual job, worked his way through the various systems and organs, and found nothing really to explain why Tim Hardwick's heart had stopped, although there were some tiny bleeds in the lungs, usually a sign of asphyxia. The Crash Team couldn't make sense of it either; it was a mystery. However, Dr Marshall had read the boy's medical notes and seen that he had a history of epilepsy, he understood that he had had a number of fits earlier on the day of his death, and that could explain the damage to the lungs. So he had settled for that. 'Status epilepticus', he had written on the death certificate—continuous epilepsy. Which was perfectly plain. The only mystery was that, according to the doctor on Ward Four who had referred the case to him, the boy had not actually been having a fit at the time of death. In fact, it seemed he hadn't had a fit for some four or five hours before he died. That was mysterious. If that was right, the boy couldn't, in fact, have died in 'status epilepticus' at all. Still, in the absence of any other clue, the pathologist had plumped for epilepsy even if the facts didn't fit. He had to come up with some explanation and it looked like the only runner. The coroner had accepted it. A natural death.

The result of the post-mortem was taken to the little house in Beeston, where Helen Hardwick was still reeling from the news of Tim's death. On the day after he died, she had been taken from her home and driven to the hospital. They had sat her in her wheelchair and pushed her through the strange, empty corridors to the chapel of rest where she had looked and seen Tim's frail, familiar face. She had always known that he would not live for long. The doctors had told her that in the beginning, but even so it was a shock to see him there. He had seemed to be doing so well. She had thought she would have him for a few more years. She did not try to understand it, she trusted the doctors to do that for her. She was used to suffering and she coped with this new hardship as she always did, with quiet despair and profound faith. Perhaps in some way, she thought, this was the will of God.

Some lives never seem to get started. There are people who are born poor and stay that way, or who fall sick and never get better, or who for one reason or another never even have dreams let alone fulfil them. Kayley Desmond's life had been like that.

She was only 15 months old but already she had been in and out of hospital more times than her parents could count. She was so weak when she was born that it was five months before the hospital would let her go home for the first time. She had a cleft palate so she had trouble feeding and she didn't grow properly, and she would scream in a high-pitched haunting way that no one could understand. Specialists had started probing into her genetic history to find out whether she had inherited her problems from her parents or whether perhaps she had been damaged at birth. They feared that she was suffering from some kind of brain damage. They didn't know.

If Kayley's life was bad when she was in hospital, it was little better at home. She lived with her parents and her four-year-old sister, Zara, in a council house in Princess Drive in Grantham. The family's life was wretched. They had none of the luxuries that other homes took for granted: no car, no phone, no television (not one that worked, only a dead black and white one with a twisted coat-hanger for an aerial), they never ate in restaurants or went to the cinema, they had never been on holiday, not even for a day at the seaside, the house was dirty and untidy. The one and only possession which brought a little colour to their lives was a second-hand music centre which Kayley's father, Finbar, had bought in a sale, and half a dozen tapes: Elvis Presley, Jim Reeves, Roy Orbison. That was his music.

It made Finn's heart ache to hear it. It reminded him of his days in the army — 12 years with the Second Royal Anglians — when he had played rhythm guitar in a band called the Power Game and he had dreamed of being a rock star. That was his ambition. It had never happened. He had left the army ten years ago and begun an uneven struggle with life which he had never come close to winning. He hadn't worked more than a couple of weeks since he left the army and from time to time he succumbed to bouts of terrible depression, when he would go off and get 'canned up' and end up slumped on some bench in a dog-turd public park with a belly full of cider and sherry. He knew he shouldn't do it, but life got on top of him. Often, he talked about killing himself, about stringing himself up, or laying down on the railway line. All he had left now of his dreams of stardom was a second-hand acoustic guitar which he had picked up for a pound. The strings were broken.

Finn's marriage to Maggie was the unstable centre of Kayley's home life. They had been married for 15 years, but they were still an odd couple: Finn, a stooping giant with tattooed arms, hands like axe heads, a rugged face and stumbling speech; and Maggie, tall and heavily built like an over-sized girl. She walked with a slow, lumbering gait, as if all her joints were worn to the nerve, she wore ankle socks on her thick, bare legs, her big full-moon face was lined with care, her black hair lay lank on her scalp. As a child she had had learning difficulties. As an adult, she coped as best she could, but she remained slow, dependent on Finn for support, on social security for money, and on doctors for help with her children's flickering health.

There were times when life in Princess Drive became so bad that the neighbours called the police to investigate the screaming and then the social workers closed in, buzzing angrily around the door, demanding assurances, while Finn swatted them away and swore that everything was fine. Once, when Kayley was nine

months old, Maggie left and took both the girls with her to stay
at her parents. Finn boiled with anger and collapsed in sadness
which he swamped with sherry until he made up his mind to fight
back. He snatched Zara from her bed early one morning and
brought her home to Princess Drive, where he looked after her
and was happy with her for three weeks, until he got drunk and
forgot to pick her up from the day nursery. Then the social
workers came buzzing round again and put both girls on the
Child Protection Register, with the category of grave concern, and
Maggie came back and they stumbled on together.

But Kayley survived. Finn believed that everyone had a guardian
angel who looked after them and, recently, it looked as though
Kayley's angel had been paying her more attention. She was feeding properly and putting on weight at last. When they called out
the doctor at the beginning of March, it was only because she had
a red rash on her trunk. It was probably measles, or just a reaction
to an anti-measles injection which she had had a week earlier, no
great cause for concern, yet the doctor was worried. He discovered
that Kayley had not been to her day nursery for three months,
and, even though Finn and Maggie insisted that she was eating
better, he could see that she was thin, she was coughing, she had
a temperature, and she looked dehydrated as if she was not getting
enough liquid. The doctor called again the next day and saw she
was no better and, knowing that her life was not easy, decided
that she should go into hospital once more, if only to give everyone
a rest.

On Ward Four, Kayley did little better. It was not that she was
dangerously ill, but apart from her rash, she obviously had some
kind of chest infection which made her cough and she kept on
throwing up her food. The nurses put her in one of the cubicles
with Maggie sleeping in there with her. Kayley was often disrup-
tive and unrewarding. She had an unattractive, pinched little face
and she was always complaining with that high-pitched whine of
hers. They tried to clear up her chest infection by putting her on
a drip of erythromycin antibiotic, and they had to put her in a
cubicle where she wouldn't disturb the other children. They chose
the one with Mr Happy on the door.

It was a Saturday, 9 March, late evening. Kayley was asleep in
her cot in her cubicle. Finn had gone home with Zara, and Maggie

was ponderously working her way through her routine before settling down for the night. The ward was full of shadows, broken only by the dull yellow pools of the night lights. Maggie closed the cubicle door, she turned off the light, she climbed into bed. The room was shut and sealed like a safe, and soon mother and daughter were both asleep, side by side, breathing gently in their peaceful little place with the darkness wrapped around them like a leather glove. Time passed. The ward fell quiet. Darkness everywhere. Midnight. 1.00. Peace—until something moved and the door was opened. A slice of yellow light fell across the floor, then vanished as the door was shut again.

A minute passed, maybe two. The door opened again, and closed. Outside on the ward, a nurse was coming.

'Lynn!' she called. It was Bev Allitt, working a night shift. 'Lynn, can you give me a hand here?'

At the nurses' station, Lynn Vowles, like Bev an SEN, but older and more experienced, put down her book and started walking. Bev wanted to change the counter on Kayley's drip, the little monitor that logged the antibiotics feeding into her vein, and she couldn't remember how to do it. Together, the two nurses walked into Kayley's cubicle and quietly, so as not to wake the child or its mother, they started to work. But then Bev stopped, as Maggie started to stir, and Bev pointed down at Kayley.

'Look at her colour,' she said. Maggie started to wake. Lynn shoved down the side of Kayley's cot.

'She's not breathing,' said Lynn. 'Call 222!'

Lynn straightened the little girl out on her back and ducked down towards her, her fingers on her nose, her mouth over the child's, breathing down, bobbing up for air, breathing down, while Bev ran out of the door and Maggie sat up in bed and said 'What's happening?'

Bev was on the phone. Lynn was pumping Kayley's chest. Maggie was starting to panic, her face blanked by confusion.

'What's happening? What's wrong with Kayley?'

Then Lynn felt the little girl's chest heave. She was starting to breathe but her face was twitching strangely and Lynn guessed it was something to do with not having enough oxygen.

'It's all right,' she told Maggie, not quite truthfully. 'Kayley's all right.'

By the time that the Crash Team arrived with their coats flapping, Kayley was definitely breathing though she still seemed very weak, and Maggie was disintegrating before their eyes. Bev told the night sister that she had heard Kayley crying and gone into her cubicle to investigate and found her collapsed.

Maggie was lost, like a cat in a storm, pelted with terrifying thoughts. Kayley was dying, what did it mean? It was her fault, what would Finn say? What were they doing to Kayley? Some of these thoughts came out in words. Others simply scared her, leaving her rooted, trembling to the spot. A nurse helped her out of her bed and told her to go to the kitchen and get herself a cup of tea. Maggie did as she was told, but when she got to the kitchen she couldn't remember how to make the tea.

She started pacing the corridor, weeping with fear, up and down past Mr Happy's grinning face. Then the cubicle door opened and they carried Kayley out, wrapped in tin foil. They said it must have been the chest infection which did it, and it was lucky that Bev and Lynn had spotted her colour when they did or she might have gone right under in her sleep. She was breathing now, they said, but they wanted her in the Treatment Room.

Maggie paced some more in the half-light, clasping and unclasping her hands beneath her chin. In the rest of the ward, she could see the shapes of sleeping children. On the other side of the door, she could hear the doctors working on Kayley. She didn't know what they were doing. She thought Kayley was probably dead. Whatever could she do? Whatever would she tell Finn?

Inside the Treatment Room, Kayley was breathing regularly again and screaming her usual high-pitched scream, but they were still groping to find out what the problem had been. They had hooked her up to the cardiograph and were picking up a steady heartbeat. She seemed free of mucous. They wondered whether she had vomited in her sleep and inhaled it, but there was no sign of any vomit in her cot. Perhaps her lung infection had got much worse. They X-rayed her chest. Whatever it was, she seemed to be stable now.

A nurse went to tell Maggie that Kayley was all right again. The night sister borrowed an extra nurse from another ward and left her and Bev in the Treatment Room with clear instructions not to take their eyes off Kayley and to hit the call button if she went off again. The doctors left the ward, Maggie was sent up to the canteen on the first floor, Lynn Vowles went back to the nurses' station, and in the Treatment Room Kayley lay sleeping, sealed into the darkness under the watchful eyes of two nurses. Time passed. Kayley was as safe as a baby at its mother's breast. Nothing could harm her now. Nothing could get close.

No one saw it happen.

All anyone knew was that her lungs had given up again, just slumped like busted balloons, and this time her heart was fading too, her pulse was flickering like a butterfly's wings, she was losing her grip, fading from them. When Dr Nanayakkara and the Crash Team arrived at her side, for the second time that night, just after 4.00 in the morning, they found her flaccid and unresponsive. Her heart had ground to a halt. They shot her a dose of aminophyline to bump-start her breathing and massaged her heart. Her breathing fluttered but failed again. Her pulse was distant and weak. They kept working, her lungs coughed back, her pulse came stronger, her breathing was regular, and Dr Nanayakkara said they would transfer this little girl to Queen's Med while they had the chance.

They tucked Kayley into a stretcher, packed Maggie's bags, shut both of them in an ambulance and sent them down the road to Nottingham, to the Queen's Medical Centre. Bev Allitt volunteered to go with one of the doctors to make sure Kayley was OK.

As the sun rose, at about 6.00 that morning, Sunday 10 March 1992, two police officers took their patrol car to Princess Drive and woke Finn Desmond to tell him the news. At first, Finn felt as though the bottom had fallen out of his heart but then he thanked God and Kayley's guardian angel for saving her life. She could have died, he thought, if those nurses had not gone in to change her drip. She was lucky to be alive.

By that time, Kayley and Maggie were settled in the paediatric intensive care unit in Nottingham, both calmer and stronger. Kayley was recovering so fast that the doctors there found it hard to believe that she had stopped breathing at all.

And in a brown manila file, tucked in amongst the nursing notes and fluid charts that traced the history of Kayley's stay on Ward Four, there lay an X-ray.

It had been taken at 1.45 that morning, when Kayley was being examined in the Treatment Room, just after her first attack, and it showed all the detail of the inside of her upper torso: her lungs with their dark clouds, her ribs like devil horns, a foggy swirl of heart and vein.

The doctors had looked at it then in the rush of the moment and they had seen the shadows on the lung, where the infection lay, and they had made their diagnosis as well as they could. But they were tired and they were busy and they were only ordinary doctors.

They never saw the streak of darkness, tucked away in the soft tissue and vessel of Kayley's underarm, up near the pit of her right arm, in the area known to doctors as the right axilla. It was an air bubble—in Kayley's flesh. It should not have been there. It was a clue. But no one saw it.

No one expected ordinary doctors to understand all the mysteries of X-rays. They weren't specialists. They were bound to miss things. And for that reason, there was a safety net: every X-ray for every patient had to be sent to the radiology department, where the specialists could search them with an expert eye and spot every tiny detail. But somewhere between Grantham and Nottingham, somewhere between the children's ward and the radiology department, Kayley's brown manila file lost its way. The X-ray was never sent to the experts. The clue was never seen.

On Ward Four, life chugged on as usual.

3

On Ward Four, some of the nurses were rattled.

Wendy Sorrell came into work on the day after Kayley Desmond had been transferred and she couldn't believe that the Crash Team had been on the ward again. It had been bad enough when Liam Taylor had died and she had had to go straight into his cubicle and try to comfort his parents. Then Tim Hardwick had died and she'd said 'Hold your horses, what's going on here?' but the other nurses had said it was all right. Now, Kayley.

Wendy knew she was only an auxiliary, she didn't claim to know very much about medicine—and she'd heard that Kayley was safe and doing well now at Queen's Med in Nottingham—but it seemed obvious to her that there must be something wrong. Hospitals made mistakes just like anyone else; her own mother was suing this very hospital for leaving surgical equipment inside her after an operation. But no one on Ward Four seemed to want to admit that they had a problem.

Still, Wendy could see that some of the others were jittery. A little girl called Natalie was brought on to the ward. She'd had an asthma attack and when Wendy started her shift, and she was having her report and being told what was happening, the staff nurse said to her 'Keep an eye on Natalie. She should be all right, but with what's been going on, we'd better be careful.' Wendy watched that little girl like a bird watches her eggs.

On some shifts, if the ward was quiet, Wendy was allowed to take her break with one of the nurses. There was one night when she went up to the canteen with Bev Allitt, who was only a couple of years older than her, and Wendy asked her if she thought there was something funny going on in the ward, and Bev said she didn't know what was happening, but she wished it would stop. She'd been specialing that little baby Liam when he'd gone off, she said, and then she told Wendy all the gory details and by the time their break was over, Wendy felt worse than ever.

Other nurses talked about it, too, quietly so as not to upset the patients or the parents, wondering what on earth was happening to this place. One of the nurses said there might be some sort of new virus that was attacking the children's hearts and there was talk of testing Mr Happy's cubicle, because that was where Liam and Kayley had been. But Tim had been in the four-bed area, nowhere near any of the cubicles. Even the experienced nurses admitted that they were baffled.

One of the night sisters, Pam Measures, said she had worked at Grantham Hospital for 26 years and in all that time she had known only two children to suffer arrests. Lynn Vowles who had been an SEN on Ward Four for seven years had only ever seen one arrest and that had been a child with whooping cough. She had been left quite speechless on the Saturday morning when she had come to work, expecting to find Liam Taylor as bright and cheerful as he had been the night before, and she had met his grandmother in the car park and heard that he had had a heart attack and that they were waiting for him to die. Mary Reet could not understand what had happened to Tim Hardwick. She had heard that he was supposed to have died of epilepsy, but she had been near the boy all the time he was on the ward and there was no way that that child was fitting. And Kayley? She had always been sickly, but why should she suddenly have two arrests in one night?

The nurses knew very well that sick children did die from time to time, but normally you would get only one or two deaths in a whole year on the ward and even then you were talking about children who were dying slowly, from leukaemia or a brain tumour or some kind of lingering illness, not sudden deaths, like Liam and Tim. The nurses all agreed that sudden deaths were really very rare and none of them could remember the ward ever having two in only ten days. And even stranger, Liam, Tim and Kayley all had suffered cardiac arrests. Children did occasionally suffer respiratory arrests but a cardiac arrest in a child was almost unheard of. And yet the older nurses insisted that there was nothing to worry about. They had seen so many odd things in hospitals, and they said that medicine was just like that. Every so often, you came across something that you couldn't explain, and you learned to accept it and get on with the job. There were unexpected clusters of deaths from time to time in any hospital. Like a couple of years ago, on the maternity unit, there were suddenly five still-births in one month—far more than usual—and then the next month, it was back to normal. There was no explaining it. It was just the way the cards fell, just a matter of luck.

Patients might think that doctors always knew what was wrong with them; the truth was that doctors often had no idea. Often, they just guessed—even the best of them guessed. They always looked grave and knowledgeable and they took great care to be reassuring, but often, inside, they were fumbling for an answer. The nurses knew that some of the doctors had a special diagnosis which they liked to use when they had tried everything they could think of and they still couldn't work out what was wrong with a patient. They said it was GKW. It sounded impressive. It stood for God Knows What. And that was really all you could say about Liam and Tim and Kayley. No one could say why it had happened, they'd probably never know and now it would be years before the ward saw another sudden death or unexplained arrest. That was medicine, full of mysteries.

There was another reason why some of the older nurses did not worry. There was no point to it. They could hardly complain even if they did think there was something wrong. Nurses were trained to obey, to defer to the doctors. It had always been like that. Nurses couldn't complain. Nurses never did. They had learned that it didn't pay. It was bad enough if you got a colleague into trouble, but the chances were that you would get yourself into hot water, too. You daren't even admit your own mistakes, for fear of being disciplined. There was a staff nurse in the papers just the other day who had been disciplined for writing a letter to *Nursing Times* daring to criticize her hospital. And look at Graham Pink, the charge nurse in Manchester who had lost his job after complaining about staff shortages. The doctors wouldn't want to hear their opinion anyway. Doctors looked down on nurses. There were doctors sitting on the nurses' new ruling body, the UK Central Council for Nursing. You could bet there were no nurses running the doctors' business at the BMA.

Sometimes, when they were chatting privately together, the

nurses shook their heads in wonder at their junior doctors. They were not really doctors at all. They were students, most of them fresh out of university, trying to complete their training, and suddenly thrown into the deep end and forced to make decisions which were way beyond their experience. They had no special training at all for dealing with children. They were supposed to go to Queen's Med for a fortnight to learn the ropes there, but the personnel department had started saying that they couldn't afford to hire replacements while they were away, so now even that was stopping. They wouldn't let an engine driver loose on British Rail until he had passed all his tests, but the National Health Service let learners loose on their patients. It was particularly worrying in a place like Ward Four which was too small to justify hiring a registrar to supervise them. There was no one between the junior doctors, struggling to learn as they worked, and the consultants who were far too busy to spend all day on the ward keeping an eye on them. The nurses knew that Grantham was not even likely to get the best of the junior doctors. Most of them chose to go to the big teaching hospitals in London or to one of the big provincial centres like St Jimmie's in Leeds or the Radcliffe in Oxford. A little district general hospital with no teaching facilities and no special interests was hardly going to attract the pick of the crop. None of these junior doctors seemed to stay more than a couple of months anyway; you no sooner got to know a face, than it vanished.

Take this Harshad Tailor who was working on the ward now. He had started at the beginning of January but he was only there as part of his training to be a GP, and by June he'd be gone again. When Liam Taylor had had his first arrest on the Thursday that he arrived on the ward, Margaret Geeson had bleeped Dr Tailor and he hadn't arrived. Of course, he must have had a very good reason but she'd had to bleep him again and, by the time he did come, she was very agitated, though she made sure the parents didn't notice. Then there had been that dreadful business in the early hours of Saturday morning, when Liam had had the arrest which killed him. Dr Tailor had been bleeped and this time he had got there quickly, before the Crash Team, and he had started work on Liam by pushing a tube down his throat into his lungs and pumping oxygen down it. At least, that was what he thought he had done. When the Crash Team turned up, Dr Tailor had asked the anaesthetist to check the tube and it turned out he had forced it down the baby's food pipe by mistake and he was blowing all this oxygen into the baby's stomach. You couldn't blame Dr Tailor. It was notoriously difficult to intubate a small child and he simply never had been trained to do it. Yet the hospital expected him to. The anaesthetist had been so worried about it that he had called the ward later to warn them, in case it had done the baby any extra damage. So the nurses knew all about it.

If the nurses saw little point in talking to the junior doctors, they saw even less chance of catching the attention of the two consultants on Ward Four. Dr Nanayakkara was fine with the children and, despite the pathologist finding that he was wrong about the cause of Liam Taylor's illness and death, everyone still said he was very good at his job, very precise and clear. The trouble was that he was such an overbearing man, inclined to shriek down telephones and shout across rooms, and he was particularly bad at dealing with women. He had reduced nurses to tears before now. Some of the nurses said it was his Sri Lankan upbringing. Others reckoned he was just an arrogant grouch who couldn't bear to have his opinion questioned. He always had to be right about everything. They had heard that he was trying to blame them for Kayley Desmond's arrests, trying to make out that they had failed to keep a close enough eye on her. Typical consultant! Only the other day, he had turned to a staff nurse, Kate Lock, and told her to fetch him something, but he should have known that she was a bank nurse who hadn't been on the ward long enough to discover where everything was kept. And when she told him that she couldn't find what he wanted, he yelled out at the whole room: 'Will someone get me a nurse who knows what she's bloody well doing?' That frightened the children as well as the staff.

The other consultant, Nelson Porter, would never roar at anyone. The nurses liked him. He was rather gentle and sincere, like Father Christmas with a stethoscope, but the trouble was that he was so nervous that, in his own way, he was just as difficult to talk to as Dr Nanayakkara. Dr Porter looked like the kind of empty-headed professor you see in children's books. He had a

bushy beard, thick glasses, scruffy clothes and a funny flat-footed
walk that made him look like a penguin. He seemed very
approachable, but even the simplest question seemed to torment
him with doubt and he would wander off on a ramble of half-
completed sentences, searching anxiously for the precise and perfect answer, and the nurses would wish they had never troubled
him in the first place.

It was not just that the nurses could not speak to the two
consultants. The two men didn't seem to enjoy speaking to each
other very much either. Nurses in hospitals often joked about the
secret School for Eccentrics where doctors went just before they
qualified as consultants, where they learned to wear dickie bows
with matching silk handkerchiefs and half-moon glasses and to
throw instruments around and generally behave like madmen and,
most of all, to treat each other like an infectious disease. Consultants seemed to take a pride in their professional rivalry, though
in the case of Ward Four, the two men were also completely
different characters. Nanayakkara was decisive and strong, while
Porter had the manner of a humble bumbler. The two men sometimes seemed to drive each other mad. There were good days
when the two men settled down and got along fine but then some
little irritant would set them off again. Nanayakkara was a great
one for drawing up guidelines and procedures and he would
proudly present his latest work to Dr Porter who might then
reject it and refuse to sign it. Then there'd be a rumpus. If they
were both on the ward at the same time, the nurses could feel the
friction and, sometimes, they heard them arguing in their rooms.
If there was only one of them on the ward, he might start tutting
and sighing about the other's work. They even changed each
other's prescriptions.

The nurses simply watched the lightning crackle around the two
men and did their best to conceal it from the patients and their
parents. It was childish, but they put up with it. It had always
been like that, they couldn't change it and, anyway, it had never
really mattered.

Kate Lock was determined not to be worried. She was a staff
nurse of 14 years' standing and she had done a lot of work with
sick children and she was sure that there was a simple explanation

for all this. It was probably just because they were getting extra patients from Newark. She had not worked on the ward long—she was a bank nurse who had been called in for a couple of months to fill a gap in the rota—but it was obvious that the merger with Newark must have doubled the workload so it was bound to have doubled the number of arrests. Whatever it was, she was pretty sure she had seen it before.

Until she moved up to Lincolnshire five years earlier, she had worked as a staff nurse in some of the big hospitals in London, Queen Elizabeth's in Hackney and the children's hospital in Great Ormond Street, and wherever she went now as a bank nurse, whether it was to old people's homes or different wards in Grantham Hospital, she took everything in her stride and she liked to think that she had a calming influence. She was not trying to say that she knew everything—she was no show-off and she was happy to take orders from a good SEN like Betty Asher who was really her junior—but it was a mood thing, really. Some nurses seemed to make things happen, to have little crises wherever they went. Nurses like Kate Lock calmed them down.

She was a large, motherly woman and she liked to follow a steady routine whenever she started a shift. She would go for her report and find out who was new on the ward and who was causing any little worries, then she'd have a walk round on her own, to say hallo and to see for herself that everything was all right, and then, all being well, she'd have a cup of tea and a chat before getting down to work. Despite the little ripples of panic after Kayley Desmond's illness, she made sure that, for her part, she worked each shift in her usual calm way, and by the time she came into work on Saturday afternoon, 23 March, almost exactly two weeks after Kayley's troubles, she was happy to see that the ward had relaxed again.

It was after 4.30 by the time she finished her walkabout and her cup of tea, and she knew that Betty Asher would want to start the drug round at 5.00, so that it was all done and out of the way in time for tea at 6.00. She had noticed on her walkabout that a baby boy called Paul Crampton had been sound asleep in one of the cubicles and she decided she would go and wake him up and feed him so that he was ready for his medicine. She had been told about him at report: 'Five months old, a happy wheezer, over the worst of it, going home tomorrow, mum resident.'

Kate Lock couldn't see the mother or father, she guessed they were spending Saturday afternoon with their other children at home, so she asked Bev Allitt to help her feed him. She had known Bev for some time. They lived in neighbouring villages about ten miles south of Grantham, and Bev had done some baby-sitting for her three or four years ago. In fact, Kate remembered telling her then about the work she did as a nurse, but she had never realized that Bev had gone off and qualified until she saw her on Ward Four and she wondered whether she had been the one to put the idea of nursing into Bev's head.

The two of them went over to Paul's cubicle, Mr Tickle, chatting about this and that as they walked, and they found he was still asleep. Bev started to wake him up while Kate popped back through the busy part of the ward to the kitchen to make up his bottle. She mixed up the SMA formula in the bottle, boiled the kettle, poured hot water into a jug, stood the bottle of milk in the hot water and took it back to the cubicle. By the time she got back, a minute or two later, Paul was awake in his cot, naked apart from his nappy, and blinking at Bev. He was a nice-looking little boy with blond hair and blue eyes and a big round face with a healthy flush in his cheeks. Kate took him on her lap and started to feed him. Bev stood by her chatting.

After a while, Kate noticed that Paul was feeding a bit slowly and thought probably he had not yet woken up properly. 'Come on now,' she coaxed him.

Just then, Betty Asher, the most experienced SEN, a stout little woman with curly white hair and a cheeky grin, came into the cubicle with one of the student nurses. They had the drugs trolley, and Betty explained that Paul was starting new drugs today. During the week, Dr Porter had been treating him for bronchiolitis but now that the weekend had arrived and Dr Porter was off duty Dr Nanayakkara had taken over the patient. He had changed the diagnosis to asthma, cancelled all Dr Porter's prescriptions and substituted his own regime. Betty moved on with the trolley, Bev was still chatting about how she was moonlighting on her days off in an old people's home so that she could afford to pay for her car, but Kate was distracted by Paul's behaviour. He was still very dozy and, unless she was mistaken, he was beginning to look rather grey.

'Come on now, Paul,' she clucked, and turned to Bev. 'He's had a good long sleep but he's not waking up properly.'

Kate smoothed his hair back from his forehead. She thought he felt sticky. 'He doesn't seem very well at all for a child that's supposed to be going home tomorrow.'

Bev leaned over them. Kate could see him getting worse. He was definitely grey now and he was clammy, too, and he was obviously having trouble keeping his eyes open. Kate couldn't understand it.

Then Bev spoke. 'He's having a hypo.'

As soon as she said it, Kate saw what she meant. Paul looked exactly as if he were having a hypoglycaemic attack, as if his blood sugar was falling. She hadn't thought of it herself, because there was no reason to. Paul had no history of diabetes, which was the most common reason for trouble with blood sugar, and he was being fed, which should have made his blood sugar rise.

But Bev seemed sure. 'We'd better do a BM stick.'

'Well, I don't know,' said Kate, still puzzled. 'It probably won't show anything but I suppose it won't hurt to have a go.'

Bev slipped out to the Treatment Room and returned with a grey box the size of a pack of cigarettes, a three-inch tube, a lancet and a medi-swab. She swabbed the end of one of Paul's limp fingers, pricked it with the lancet and then shook a white plastic stick out of the tube and smeared a little bulb of Paul's blood on to the end of it. They waited half a minute while the blood soaked into the yellow and blue strips of chemical at the end of the stick. Paul grizzled on Kate's lap. Bev took a tissue, wiped the surplus blood from the end of the stick and then slipped it into a slot in the grey box and waited again while the machine absorbed the information. Sixty seconds later, the machine bleeped and the electronic panel at the top of the box lit up and flipped up two green numbers — 3.7

'Three point seven?' said Kate. 'Well, that is rather low. But not what you'd call a hypo. I don't know what the trouble can be.'

Kate Lock was determined to stay calm. She sent Bev off to get some Calpol, fed a spoonful to Paul, sent Bev off again to warn

Betty Asher, looked up and was surpised to see an attractive woman with red hair and blue eyes walking into the cubicle. It was Paul's mother. Kate saw her face drop.

'I've given him some Calpol. But he doesn't seem right.'

'I think we'd better call the doctor.'

Now, for all Kate's calmness, there was no disguising the fact that this was a crisis. Paul was getting limper and drowsier, his face was cloudy grey, and he was now wet with sweat. His mother tried to give him a bottle of water. Paul was too weak to take it. Then Paul's father arrived, a compact, muscular man, with a tightly clipped black beard and a certain tension in his manner.

'What's going on?' he asked.

'I don't know,' said Kate. 'We've sent for the doctor.'

'When's he coming?'

Dr Tailor arrived, swept Paul into the Treatment Room, gave him oxygen, put him on a nebulizer of Atrovent, and took X-rays. The parents waited outside. Bev used another BM stick. This time his blood sugar was only 1.7—dangerously low. Now there was no doubt. Paul was having a hypoglycaemic attack. Bev had been right all along. This was serious. Without sugar, Paul's nervous system had no fuel. He would sink into a coma and, if the process was not reversed, he could even die. Dr Tailor clearly had not stopped the decline. He had treated him for bronchiolitis, not for hypoglycaemia. Dr Nanayakkara arrived, summoned from his home. Paul was now nearly unconscious. Nanayakkara saw what was happening and instantly ordered dextrose. That would restore his blood sugar. He told Dr Tailor to insert a drip in the boy's forehead. Dr Tailor tried, fumbled, drew blood but failed to get the drip in place. Nanayakkara took over and did it for him, hooked the drip up to a 10 per cent dextrose solution and then ordered more oxygen. The dextrose did its work. Paul's sweating stopped, the grey faded from his cheeks. Twenty minutes later, the crisis had passed. Nanayakkara went out to face the parents.

He told them that he thought perhaps the problem was simply that Paul had not been eating properly. David Crampton asked one or two questions but was obviously more interested in seeing whether his son was still grey and apparently slipping into a coma. He went into the Treatment Room to find Paul sitting up, leaning against Betty Asher's hand, happily reaching for his feet and trying to pull off his toes. At the sight of his child, a wave of relief punched through David Crampton's tension with such force that his eyes filled with tears.

'There, Paul, you naughty boy,' said Betty Asher. 'Look what you've done to your daddy. You've frightened him half to death.'

Kate Lock went on to finish her shift, staying busy, spreading calm, and at 9.00 that evening, she walked through the ward one last time to be sure that all was well and, just as she turned the corner to leave, she happened to look back and she caught sight of David Crampton talking to Dr Nanayakkara outside the Treatment Room. She paused a moment. She could see Nanayakkara explaining as best he could what had happened. She could see David Crampton, nodding and taking it in. He had a determined look about him. She pushed through the double doors and walked off to fetch her coat and handbag and as she left Ward Four that night, she said to herself: 'Somebody is going to have to answer that man's questions.'

She knew she couldn't.

David Crampton was not the sort of man who liked unanswered questions. He was a straight-in-the-eye, straight-to-the-point high achiever. He worked long hours as a construction company manager in Grantham pounding from office to building site with a hard hat and a car phone, juggling figures, knocking heads and shooting trouble. He was sharp and he was fit and he was fuelled by large quantities of barely controlled aggression. He would get home to Leadenham, a little village 15 miles north west of Grantham where he lived with Kath and their three children, and no matter how long the day had been or how rough the weather, he would go straight out jogging. Once a week he went aerobic training with the local football team. In David Crampton's world, targets were there to be met, problems were there to be solved. He did not like foul-ups.

The morning after Paul's hypoglycaemic attack, Sunday 24 March, David Crampton was up early. He had been calling the hospital every hour until he went to bed, and then he had slept badly. Kath had stayed the night at the hospital and now he had to get the two oldest children, Louise and Simon, out of bed, give them breakfast, reassure them about Paul, call Kath at the hospital, call her mother, call his mother, drive to the hospital with Louise and Simon, visit Kath and Paul on Ward Four, drive the two older children 16 miles over to his mother for lunch, drive on to a sports meeting, call Kath to check on Paul, call Kath's niece to get her to pick up Kath and drive her over to her mother's for a decent meal, and then drive back to Grantham Hospital and be sitting with Paul before 2.00. By 1.15 he had organized everything, made one last call on his car phone to make sure Paul was OK, and he was sitting tight in his blue Vauxhall Cavalier heading for Grantham Hospital.

As he drove, he had time to reflect that yesterday they had been very lucky indeed. If Paul had had this hypoglycaemic attack at home, they would have had no idea what to do and it could have got very serious. On Wednesday, five days ago, when the GP had said Paul should go into hospital, it was only for observation in case his bronchiolitis got worse, 'just to be on the safe side' as the doctor had put it. Paul had not been that ill. They had had no idea that he was suffering from this hypoglycaemia. It had hardly seemed worth letting him go to hospital at all.

As a matter of fact, they had heard a few rumours about the hospital. Kath, who was famous for getting on with everyone, went to a weekly pottery class a couple of miles down the road, where she made friends with a woman called Diane who told her how her best friends had had a little baby called Liam who had died on Ward Four, and Diane had explained that the parents couldn't get an explanation out of anyone about why it had happened. Diane had some theory that it must be something to do with the contraceptive pill. Kath also had heard a few odd things about the ward from a friend who worked for the health authority. She mentioned that she had heard that they were worried about some kind of infection on Ward Four. They seemed to think they might have legionnaires' disease or a heart virus or some such thing.

But these were only rumours, they probably didn't mean a thing. All three of the Crampton children had been born in the hospital and it went without saying that they trusted the place. And thank God they had. David shuddered to think of what might have happened if they had kept Paul at home.

And now it seemed that he was over it all. According to Kath on the phone, the doctors were saying it was a one-off incident probably because he had not fed properly or he had been sick and choked a bit. The tomboy nurse, Bev, was on duty and she had written in Paul's notes: 'Still a little drowsy, but condition much improved.' They had taken the drip out of his forehead and they were saying he could come home in a day or two. As he slowed the Cavalier down Manthorpe Road and swung into the hospital car park, David Crampton felt like a lucky man. The problem was solved.

Paul was alone in his cubicle, Kath had gone off to her mother's an hour ago, and the little boy was sleeping soundly. David sat down and was surprised within minutes to see Paul stir and start to wake up. He picked him up and held him on his knee and a mystery began to unfold before his eyes as his baby son curled his lips and started to grizzle, rolled his head, cried a little, turned pale, hesitated, slumped a little, rubbed his eyes, twisted and turned and refused to sit calm, turned paler still then grey, became cold and clammy and greyer still and, whimpering now, began to sweat with terrible force and finally to flop backwards like a rag doll. David tried to comfort him, tried to hold him up to show him his reflection in the little mirror by the sink, tried to joggle him in his arms, tried for a moment to control the wave of sheer terror which was breaking over him. Then he headed out of the door, to the nurses' station, and told the blur of faces there that it was happening again.

It seemed worse than last time. Paul was now slumped limp in David's arms, his skin icy cold and his eyes rolling stupidly in their sockets, not even crying any more. There was a rush of people around him. Dimly, David was aware of a BM stick. He knew Dr Tailor was there. Someone mentioned Nanayakkara. Someone said the BM stick was very low. 'Less than one', he thought they said. Then some hands took Paul away and a voice told him to wait in the cubicle, and so he did.

David Crampton was not used to feeling like this. He was used to acting and reacting, to making plans and giving orders, to getting up and going and taking control, but here, he was utterly powerless. He thrived on information, but he had none. He liked to intervene, but he couldn't, not without jeopardizing his son's safety. There was nothing he could do. He had no control. Yet his whole personality demanded that he had to do something and so, although it ran against the grain of several deeply-held beliefs, he sat alone in the abandoned cubicle and he said a prayer.

The next thing he saw was Kath's face, as she returned from her family lunch. He knew he must have seen a lot of other things as he had sat crumpled in the cubicle with his forehead resting on his hand, but Kath's face was the first thing that broke through. He had never seen her look so frightened. The words 'abject horror' came into his mind. He tried to reassure her but there was precious little he could say. They simply had to trust the hospital.

Eventually the doctors and the nurses emerged again from the Treatment Room. Paul was still alive. The evil-looking drip was back in his forehead. Dr Nanayakkara talked about the causes of the attack, about diet and aspiration and the effect of glucose on blood sugar and, for a while, David stood and took it, but as he listened, his own blood began to flow again and the numbness that seemed to have paralysed his brain began to wear off and, for the first time, he felt himself starting to ask the right questions. What exactly was hypoglycaemia? It was a lowering of blood sugar. And what could cause it? A number of things: starvation; an abnormality in the pancreas; insulin, which was used by diabetics whose blood was overdosed with sugar. And how were they treating it? Through the drip to Paul's forehead which was now attached to two different fluids, glucose to raise his blood sugar, and hydrocortisone steroids to help his breathing. Steroids? David made it clear that he didn't like the sound of that. When Dr Nanayakkara told him that they would be taking more X-rays, David insisted on going with him, and, kitted out with a lead apron, he watched every move, asked every question that came into his head and complained that they seemed to be taking too many. Couldn't that be dangerous? Nanayakkara assured him that Paul was in good hands.

All that afternoon Paul was ill. He would improve for half an hour and then fall back. He seemed to be having trouble breathing. Several times, the nurses called for Dr Tailor. As nurses came and went, David Crampton hovered, making sure he was not in the way but gathering information so that he could understand.

It was not just that he was asking questions. Something else was happening to David and Kath Crampton. They did not see it themselves until later that night when they went to the little bedroom at the side of the ward to attempt to sleep and, alone now, Kath sat on the bed and wept and said that Paul was going to die and what was more, it was the hospital's fault, because they must have given him the wrong drugs. Paul had been getting better. They'd said he could go home. The hospital must have done something that had made him ill like this, probably mixed up drugs that weren't supposed to be mixed up—a cocktail—or they'd just given him the wrong drug. They had changed his drugs just yesterday because they had decided he'd got asthma. She was sure it was their fault. Somehow, the hospital had caused this. And now that she said it, so was David. For the first time, neither of them trusted the hospital.

Chris and Joanne Taylor had almost abandoned any hope of ever understanding what had happened to Liam. They had waited for the pathologist, Dr Marshall, to contact them with details of the similar case which he had said he would send them, but he didn't. They had thought they might hear something from the hospital manager or from the consultants, but they didn't. They tried their GP, but he seemed to know nothing.

All the time they waited, their confusion grew deeper. There was one little thing they had remembered. It probably meant nothing, but Chris and Joanne had suddenly realized that they had never heard any alarms go off when Liam had had his final attack. Bev and the other nurses had shown them all these monitors—the apnoea and the pulseoximeter and the others—and they were loud, easily loud enough to have reached the little room at the end of the corridor, where the two of them had been asleep. So when Liam's heart stopped just after 4.00 that Saturday morning, all the alarms should have rung. But Chris and Joanne had heard nothing. Maybe they were just too deep asleep or maybe a nurse had been right there and turned them off before they'd rung for too long, or maybe they were broken or maybe something else was wrong. They didn't know and no one could tell them.

They began to accept that they would never know the truth. All they could do was to put it down to experience, treat it as one of life's bitter flukes, and try to get over it.

For the first time since it happened, Joanne agreed to go out for a drink with some of her mates. It was an important step in putting Liam's death behind her. But it seemed to follow her. They walked into one pub and bumped straight into the doctor who had come out to the house and told them that Liam just had the sniffles and there was nothing to worry about. And in the next pub, there was a whole group of nurses in there including Bev Allitt, who had spent so much time with Liam.

As soon as Joanne saw her, she wanted to go across and sit down with her and ask her questions: Did you hear about the post-mortem result? Can you believe it? What do you think it was that made his heart stop? But she was not sure whether she should.

She told one of her friends, who said 'Go on, go and talk to her.'

'No,' said Joanne. 'I can't. She's out with her mates for a drink, she doesn't want me goin' on at her.'

She could see that Bev had seen her and was sort of watching her out of the corner of her eye. Joanne went to the Ladies and on her way back, she put her hand on her shoulder and said 'Hallo, I've just come to say thanks for looking after me.'

Bev looked a bit shy. 'Oh, well,' she said.

'I've been wanting to talk to you, but you're with all your friends, so thanks, anyway. All right?'

Joanne smiled at Bev and walked away. She felt a little better.

The tranquil face of Ward Four was drawn and tired. It still wore its cheerful smile and insisted on normality, pursuing its daily rituals like a tired housewife pushing her broom, smiling for her children while her life decays inside her. But life no longer chugged so cheerfully through the ward.

It wasn't just the children falling ill, nor even this silly business of the petty thieving on the ward—there were children's clothes going missing now. There was something else which dragged the nurses down, nothing so upsetting as the sudden illnesses, but something just as bewildering and even more demoralizing. The fact was that Ward Four was not the place it used to be. At times, it felt more like a sweat shop to the nurses. The work got harder, the pay got worse, the thanks got rarer. They were not alone. It was happening all over the National Health Service. It was all changing.

The NHS had always been a big, ugly mountain of a place, its sides littered with hundreds of little clinics and hospitals, its summit ringed by councils and committees, half of them lost in the clouds of bureaucracy, none of them sure what all of the others was doing, but at least it was solid, one of the great, unmovable objects of British life. Now, suddenly it had exploded, hurling new guidelines and reports and instructions into the air, belching out an unstoppable flow of change which filled every naked patch with circulars and memos and codes of conduct, invading and overwhelming all the hospitals and clinics, slowly choking the frail life from them. Slowly but certainly, the nurses feared, their hospitals were being changed into new 'retail enterprises'.

The hospital was no longer an institution, it was a 'provider unit in an internal market'. Every department, every ward had a budget. Every treatment, every operation was costed and billed. Sister Barker, officially, was now no longer a sister, but a ward manager. The hospital was no longer run by nurses and doctors and managers together, but by a manager alone, who might be well-meaning and humane but who had never worked on a ward or studied medicine for one day of his life.

For the nurses on Ward Four, the worst effect of all this was simply that there were not enough of them. Their workload had increased as they took more patients from shrinking hospitals like Newark; but their ward budget had been cut and then frozen. On day shifts now, there were often only two trained nurses on the ward—just enough to administer controlled drugs without breaking the law. By night, there was usually only one, who had to keep running to the night sister for help. If anything went wrong—if a nurse was ill, if there was a rush of sick children, if a nurse was called down to Casualty to help with a child—there was a crisis. Margaret Geeson often sat for two hours at a time at the nurses' station ringing round bank nurses trying to find someone who could fill a hole in the rota. Sometimes, there was no alternative but to ask someone to come in on their day off. Just this week, Sister Barker had had to cancel a holiday she had booked for the end of the month. It was bad enough when nurses volunteered to give up their free time, but lately they had been told in no uncertain terms that if they didn't volunteer, there was a risk that the ward would close and they would all lose their jobs.

The ward was stretched so thin that holes were beginning to appear. Even though it was a children's ward, there were only two staff who were qualified as Registered Sick Children's Nurses. Others wanted to qualify, but the budget wouldn't allow it. Mary Reet had had to ask for five years before they would give her RSCN training and then they had paid her only £45 towards the costs; others tried and got nothing except permission to go for training at their own expense and in their own time. On some shifts, there were no staff nurses of any kind at all and so an SEN had to take charge, even though they were not really supposed to. Only two years ago, there had been a part-time teacher for the children and a play-leader on Ward Four, but not any more — they had left and their salaries had been grabbed and stuffed into some crack in the budget. The outpatient clinic had lost its staff so that Sister Barker had to run it as well as the ward. The ward had been relying on student nurses to keep them going, but now it looked as though they were going to lose them too: the Nursing School had just carried out an 'educational audit' of Ward Four and found that the senior nurses were too busy to teach.

The ward had been howling for help for months. The nurses had gone to their unions, the unions had gone to the management, Margaret Geeson had gone to Sister Barker, Sister Barker had written letters. In reply they had been told they could use more bank nurses under certain circumstances. It was not enough, but it did not surprise them. The line of management that ran from Ward Four to the regional health authority was about as effective as a ladder with no rungs.

Sister Barker was supposed to report to her nursing manager, Moira Onions. Mrs Onions had been a nurse in the days of regulation hair nets and starched pinafores; she was tall, thin and rather correct. And she had never wanted to manage Ward Four. She was a midwife by training and she had been perfectly happy managing the maternity ward and the Special Care Baby Unit until fifteen months ago when the hospital manager had suddenly told her to take on Ward Four as well. He hadn't consulted her about it. He hadn't even offered her any more money for it. He had simply passed her this unruly child and told her to look after it. She and Sister Barker had got off on the wrong foot.

Mrs Onions felt that the sister resented her, that she was distinctly cool, if not downright unfriendly. She could see that this ward had settled into a lot of stuffy old routines and when she tried to jog it out of its rut, it seemed to her that the sister treated her as an intruder. Sister Barker, for her part, wondered why she was working for a manager with no paediatric training and began to complain that Mrs Onions was doing things behind her back. One day, she walked on to the ward and found all the shelves had been taken down from the nurses' station and the books and files had been piled into her office. Then she found that shifts were being changed without her consent. And job descriptions for new nurses were drafted without her approval. The two women never actually fell out, although they came close to it in a dispute about whether the ward should have new camp beds or reclining chairs for parents to sleep on. Sister Barker used to say that if this management had got a plan for Ward Four, she was afraid she didn't know what it was. Mrs Onions used to say that she could walk on to a ward and smell trouble—just know what was happening by instinct—but not with Ward Four. There, all she knew was that she didn't know.

The next link on the ladder was no stronger. Moira Onions was supposed to report to an assistant manager, Hannah Newton. Miss Newton was often, and inevitably, compared to a mouse. She was small and frail and nervous, a deeply religious spinster. If Moira Onions needed more funds or new equipment, she relied on Miss Newton to win them for her. She needed Miss Newton to roll up her sleeves and stride down the corridors of power, kicking down doors, banging on tables, holding her own in bare-knuckle bargaining sessions. Mrs Onions was afraid that it was asking too much.

It was not simply the weak links between Sister Barker, Moira Onions and Hannah Newton that made the nurses on Ward Four feel neglected. Two years earlier, the whole ward had been given away like an unwanted orphan. Grantham Hospital had passed its management to Pilgrim Hospital, 30 miles away in Boston. That was where Hannah Newton was based and she was responsible to people who Sister Barker and Moira Onions barely knew. The nurses sometimes felt that Ward Four was not really managed at all; it just dangled by a thread.

On the day before Paul Crampton suffered his first hypoglycae-mic attack, Moira Onions had written the managerial equivalent of a begging letter to Hannah Newton, pleading with her for more staff for Ward Four. She said it was urgent. She knew it would make no difference.

The older nurses muttered about some of the things that were happening. They were routinely having to borrow equipment from other wards—incubators and monitors. They felt it was all wrong bringing that young Bev Allitt back to work on Friday night when Liam Taylor had his fatal arrest. She had already been at work in the morning and they had sent her home and told her to come back again for the late shift. Margaret Geeson had asked the management to pay for a bank nurse to come in instead, but they'd said they couldn't afford it. But nurses needed sleep. Their work was bound to suffer and it was hard to stick to the letter of every rule when you were running from dawn to dusk. Sometimes, for example, they just had to unlock the drug cupboard in the Treat-ment Room and leave it open.

The doctors didn't make life any easier. Even before Paul Crampton started having these hypos, the doctors couldn't agree about what was wrong with him. Dr Porter said he had a severe chest infection. Dr Nanayakkara said he thought there was no infection at all. Paul was Dr Porter's patient, and Dr Porter was quite clear that the boy was suffering from bronchiolitis—just as his GP had diagnosed—and he said he needed a nebulizer of Atrovent and a syringe of salbutamol squirted into his mouth. But as soon as Dr Nanayakkara took over on Saturday morning, he had started quarrelling with Dr Porter's diagnosis. He had asked Kath Crampton if there was any asthma in the family, she had said there was, and with that he had just changed everything. He said the boy had mild asthma, he cancelled all Dr Porter's drugs and put him instead on a drug called terbutaline. The oddest thing about it was that there was precious little difference between the two diagnoses, and the terbutaline which Nanayakkara had prescribed was effectively the same as the salbutamol which he had stopped—the only real difference between them was the name—but now the nurses were watching to see how Dr Porter would react when he returned from his weekend at home to find that his instructions had been overturned.

The nurses would not have minded all this tension so much if the ward still felt like a caring place. But money was all that counted now, in the brave new world of the NHS. Not patients. They still counted for all the individual nurses and doctors, but not to the NHS. It had lost its heart.

Now there was all this worry about the children to deal with as well, and there wasn't enough time. In the old days, the nurses would have held a meeting after each incident to put their heads together and see what had happened, but now they rushed from one end of the shift to the other and everyone was too busy and too bothered to be able just to stop, and take a long, cool look at the problem. Sometimes, they did not even have the time to write up their notes, let alone to sit down and wonder if they contained some hidden clue. It was all they could do to get enough equipment on the ward to deal with these arrests.

When Liam Taylor had his first arrest, they had to send both auxiliaries running off to different ends of the hospital to fetch kit. Wendy Sorrell had to go all the way up to the Special Care Baby Unit to fetch an oxygen tent. It was three floors up and she was in a terrible state about whether to run up all those stairs or wait for the lift and hope that that was quicker. In the end, she went for the lift and it wasn't too slow, but she still felt it was such a waste of precious time. Just before he had his second arrest, on the Friday night, the one that killed him, Bev Allitt had to send an auxiliary called Allison Clegg up to the Special Care Baby Unit to get some baby U-bags to catch his urine, and when she got there, she found they'd run out. There was no defibrillator on the ward—they had never needed one before. That was kept down the corridor on Ward One, but the special little child-sized paddles were over in Casualty. The nurses were worried about how they would cope if there were any more of these arrests on the ward, and the more senior ones asked for their own defibrillator and paddles on the ward. That didn't mean they were going to get them.

Joan Cottam was worried about something more specific. She was one of the few nurses on the ward who had been specially trained to work with children. She was officially a Registered Sick

Children's Nurse and, like Kate Lock, she had worked in some of the big children's hospitals in London. She had seen children suffering hypoglycaemic attacks before and she knew, in her bones, from her own long experience, that there was something very odd about Paul Crampton's hypos. Whenever she had seen them before, they had always developed slowly, whereas Paul's had hit him like a truck. And there had always been a reason for them. There had to be. But, in Paul's case, there was none. The doctors had not told the parents, but they had been wondering whether he might have a tumour in his pancreas, yet they knew he had none of the other symptoms that would have signalled that. So they had been trying to say that Paul must have been short of food, but she knew that was wrong, too. She'd seen him eat a rusk on the day he had his first hypo. And even if he had been hungry, it was hard to see how that could have made his blood sugar dive the way it did. It couldn't be that. Joan Cottam didn't know what it was. All she knew was that there was something very odd here. So she went to see Moira Onions.

David Crampton was not going to let this go. He took Monday off work and spent the whole day in the hospital. He monitored the BM sticks which were being tested on Paul every two hours. He realized that the nurses did not welcome his attentions. During the night, as they lay awake in the parents' room, they had heard Paul crying repeatedly but when Kath had gone to help him, the nurses had turned her away because they had no time to answer her questions. Still, he persisted. He pressed to have the dose of steroids reduced. He checked and rechecked Paul's condition and was disturbed to find his body heat soaring as he lay on the Resuscitaire. He queried it. The nurses looked at the temperature gauge on the Resuscitaire. No, they said, the heat lamp was at the right level. But Paul was getting hotter. David insisted that they check again. They discovered then that the temperature gauge was broken.

David shook his head and told Kath. 'They've been cooking him half the night,' he said.

He cornered Nelson Porter who had come back on duty after the weekend and insisted on an explanation for Paul's hypoglycaemia. Could it have been a reaction to some cocktail of drugs he had been given? Dr Porter, diffident as ever, suggested that it might have been the sudden withdrawal of the salbutamol which had caused the trouble. But then again, he said, it might not have been. In any event, he said, now that he had returned from his weekend off, he had restored the salbutamol. He had also restored his own diagnosis of bronchiolitis. Equally, he said, the problem might have been some side effect of the terbutaline which Paul had been prescribed on Saturday. But perhaps not. In any case, he had now stopped the terbutaline. There again, it might have been caused by Paul's chest infection (he was sure he did have a chest infection, not asthma) or, alternatively, they might be dealing with an insulinoma residia blastosis or, in fact, Reye's syndrome although, of course, the absence of jaundice and vomiting suggested that that was perhaps unlikely.

David Crampton strained to see through the fog. He wanted to know what specific steps were going to be taken to establish the cause of his son's illness. Dr Porter hesitated, squinting into the middle distance. He would speak to Queen's Med and take advice, he said. Yes, said David, but what would he do with Paul? If it happened again, the consultant told him, he would take blood and send it for tests, a wide range of tests. Indeed, he would take blood now and send that for urgent tests, specifically to see if he had too much insulin in his blood. That was really all he could do, in the circumstances. And yes, certainly, he would make sure that Mr Crampton was given the results of the tests.

Dr Porter then retired to his office where he took a step about which he said nothing to David Crampton. He had a word with the hospital pharmacist and then filed an official report with the Committee on Safety of Medicines in London, recording the change of medication which Dr Nanayakkara had ordered in his absence over the weekend and noting that the patient had suffered a suspected adverse reaction to his colleague's prescription. It was a rare move—either an extraordinarily thorough piece of thinking or the consultant's equivalent of a swift knee to his colleague's groin.

On Monday afternoon, as Kath sat with Paul in his cubicle, she saw a woman talking to the nurses at the nurses' station. Something in her manner suggested she had some authority and, when she asked, Kath was told that this was Moira Onions the nursing manager. Kath Crampton was a calm person—David sometimes complained that she was too relaxed—but when she saw Moira Onions wandering towards her with her clipboard and her efficient smile, something rose inside her.

Pointing down towards her sickly son on the Resuscitaire, she demanded: 'I want to know what they've done to him.'

Moira Onions stopped and stared at her.

'Look at him,' said Kath. 'We only came in here with a chest infection and now look what's happened.'

Moira Onions stammered, but Kath had not finished. 'He was supposed to be going home. What are we doing here now? I don't know what it is but I know they've done something to him.'

Moira Onions did her best to be polite and then faded away.

The Cramptons' confidence in the hospital was getting no stronger. No one seemed to understand what was wrong with Paul. No one seemed really to be sure how to treat him. They remembered too, how, when Louise was born in this same hospital, and she had had jaundice, one of the doctors had told Kath that Louise might have brain damage. It turned out that he had misread some instrument and that Louise's jaundice was very mild. David had wanted to wring the doctor's neck. Now, he and Kath talked about trying to move to another hospital, perhaps even down to Great Ormond Street in London if that was the only place where they could get to the bottom of this. In the meantime, he was determined to control his anger and gather information without doing anything which might affect the way that Paul was being treated.

David realized that if he visited the ward in the middle of the morning, he would catch at least one consultant doing the morning round. So, each morning that week, he took Louise to school, dropped Simon at the neighbour's, went to the office for an hour and then to the ward. He would question the doctors, return to his office, come back to the ward at lunch time, again during the afternoon and again in the evening with Louise and Simon, constantly pushing for answers, and getting none.

He pressed the doctors to reduce Paul's glucose intake, to get him back to normal health. On Tuesday, he discovered that Paul had not been receiving most of the glucose drip anyway: it had come loose from its site and was dribbling uselessly into the cot.

He brought in the Ventolin which Paul had been taking at home in case that was the cause of the problem. On Ward Four, the doctors told him that they could not test it and advised him to throw it away. He wondered if there was any result to the urgent blood test for insulin which Dr Porter had ordered on Monday morning. There was none. The path lab had done a preliminary test and decided not to proceed with the test for insulin. But no one mentioned that to David Crampton. That evening, they took Paul off the Resuscitaire, not because he no longer needed it, but because the Special Care Baby Unit wanted to borrow it.

Still, Paul certainly was getting better. There were even times when David and Kath relaxed and talked to the other parents on the ward. There was a man called Peter Phillips, a small, wiry figure with a permanent twinkle in his eye as if he was just about to tell you a raunchy joke or slip you some second-hand gear. His whole family seemed to be in the hospital: two little twin girls with feeding trouble, a three-year-old boy with constipation, and a teenage daughter down the corridor with a gynaecological problem. When Peter Phillips spoke to the Cramptons, he was full of praise for the hospital.

David had a regular routine with a 12-year-old boy called Paul Lilley who used to sit in his bed staring glumly at his feet, while his father sat beside him, arms crossed, staring just as glumly at the floor. They seemed to sit like that for hours on end—as if they were in the back seat of a car on a never-ending journey—and David got into the habit of breaking the silence every time he walked past by asking the boy how he was.

'Ah got blude in mah wee,' he'd say, nothing more, and then stare back at his feet.

It became a sort of catch phrase in the ward.

That Tuesday night, one of the nurses sat with Kath in her cubicle and chatted quietly with her. They were short of staff, the nurse admitted, and of equipment, too. It was not easy. Kath asked her about the rumours she had heard of a heart virus on the ward, and the nurse said it was true that they had had a lot of very sick children recently, but she reassured Kath that there was no heart virus here. She was sure of that. She paused.

'It's up to you and your husband,' she went on, 'but if I were you, I'd move Paul from here.'

Kath was quite startled and showed it.

'I mean it. He'd be better off in another hospital.'

'Why ever?'

Kath was trying to work out whether the nurse meant there was something wrong on Ward Four, or just that Paul needed a specialist hospital and not a little general hospital like Grantham. But the nurse would be drawn no further. 'I just think he'd be better off if you moved him.'

The next morning, Kath told David and they talked about it, but the problem was that they didn't know where to take him and they decided that since Paul obviously was getting better — he was off the steroids now and the antibiotics, his glucose drip was being reduced, and his BM sticks were all fine — the best thing would be to leave him on Ward Four, where at least they now knew the ropes, and they would hope to get him home in a day or two. The next day, Paul Crampton had another attack.

It happened at lunch-time. The whole morning had become confused when David took a message on his car phone out at the site of a new sports complex he was building, to say that Louise had been taken ill at school, so he had to make a flurry of calls to arrange that he would go and sit with Paul in the hospital, while Kath took the car to fetch Louise and go shopping. He arrived about 12.30, sent Kath off in the car and sat with Paul who was sound asleep and apparently better than ever. Ever vigilant, David spotted a little air bubble in Paul's glucose drip and called Betty Asher, who sorted it out. After ten or fifteen minutes, he felt hungry and told a nurse he was going to the canteen, where he bought himself a pasty which appeared to be made of cardboard. He was sitting there, stirring a cup of unattractive tea when he noticed that it was 1.15 and automatically felt he should go back to the ward, simply because his lunch break at work always ended at 1.15 and his disciplined nature insisted that he stick to his normal schedule. As soon as he walked back into Paul's cubicle, he was plunged into an action replay of the previous Sunday: Paul waking, grizzling and quite unbelievably descending into this cold, clammy, grey-faced nightmare.

As the nurses answered his call for help, swarming around him, he caught Sister Barker's eye.

'Just tell me,' he pleaded. 'This is real? I'm not imagining it?'

'No, you're not imagining it. There is a problem.'

And the look on her face told him he was in real trouble, and there was nothing that his logical, well-informed mind could grasp to explain it. He heard the sister telling someone to get him a cup of tea.

A few minutes later, Nelson Porter arrived with Dr Tailor in his wake. Dr Porter noticed that Paul's drip was loose and leaking fluid. He couldn't imagine why. He and Dr Tailor started pumping glucose into Paul and then, while Bev Allitt and Betty Asher looked on and David grimaced, Dr Porter stooped over Paul, reached down to his groin with a syringe, slipped a needle into the little blue veins and drew off a substantial quantity of blood. After Paul's earlier attacks, the doctors had taken only pin-pricks of blood, 'capillary samples' as they called them. Now Dr Porter explained that they were taking extra blood and he was going to ask for a full range of tests: potassium, blood glucose, insulin, cortisol, growth hormone, blood gases, bicarbonate, urea. They would trawl through all the possibilities. He sealed the blood into a little perspex bottle. Through his terror, David felt some glimmer of relief that at last someone looked like getting hold of some reliable information. But would Paul survive to benefit from the results?

Dr Porter arranged to transfer Paul to Queen's Med in Nottingham. Kath came back to the hospital, David went off to pick up the children, Paul seemed to be stable, the glucose lifting his blood sugar (though it was hard to be sure because the electronic gadget which measured the BM sticks had broken). Nurses wrapped Paul in a space blanket, laid him out on a stretcher with his drips and tubes and wires, and offered Kath a kidney bowl in case she was sick in the ambulance. They told her that Dr Tailor and Bev Allitt would come with her to look after Paul on the journey. As they waited on the ward, Paul started to decline, his breathing became shallow, and his colour faded. Dr Tailor and Bev headed him straight out to the ambulance, Kath threw his clothes into a bin bag, and was about to run after Paul when David called on the ward phone.

'He's much worse,' Kath cried to him. 'We're going straight away. You'd better be quick.'

Kath left the ward in a blur, vaguely aware of the frightened faces of the other parents as she left, Peter Phillips, his cheeky face now creased with anxiety, Paul Lilley staring more glumly than ever at his feet. As she broke through the double doors, Peter Phillips turned to his wife, Sue, and said: 'I wouldn't put much money on that lad's chances.' They thanked their lucky stars they weren't in Kath Crampton's shoes.

It was only when Paul's ambulance hit the traffic outside the hospital that Kath realized it was Good Friday the next day, and the road to Nottingham was clogged with cars setting off for a long weekend. For a while the ambulance waded through the traffic, then Dr Tailor tested Paul's blood with a BM stick, the ambulance man glanced down at his wax-mask face and said this was a full emergency. Kath could hardly breathe. The siren started to scream, they burst straight through a red light and the holiday traffic parted before them.

At home in Leadenham, David was pacing the floor, waiting for his mother to arrive to look after the older children, checking his watch, calling the hospital, pacing the floor some more. Finally, he called in a neighbour to look after Louise and Simon, hurtled out of the house and launched the blue Cavalier on to the road. He was normally a careful driver, but not now, not when his son was dying. He stood on the accelerator. He had some half-formed idea that he'd see a police car and flag it down and get them to drive him the rest of the way, but there wasn't one. His normal poise and self-control had shattered, he was cannoning round corners, jumping lights, sweeping past everything in front of him, anything, just as long as he could get there before it was too late.

As he sped towards Nottingham, he sobbed with pain.

On Ward Four, a sort of peace descended. In the kitchen, Kate Lock and some of the other nurses talked. They admitted they were bewildered. All they could think was that it was something to do with the different drugs that Paul had been given over the weekend. He must have had some sort of reaction to them. Kate agreed that that must be it. With any luck, the blood tests would show it up. Still, Kate Lock knew that she would probably never find out. They no longer needed her on Ward Four, and this was her last shift.

And, privately, Kate knew it was nothing to do with the drugs that he had had. She guessed the other nurses knew that, too. That little boy had been better again, ready to go home. The drugs he had been on today were quite different to the ones that Nanayakkara had given him over the weekend. No, it was something else. She didn't know what. And if Paul Crampton hadn't been on a glucose drip when this latest hypo hit him, he would not have survived. As she worked out her last shift on Ward Four, she was no longer full of calm. She was deeply worried.

Wendy Sorrell had had enough. She had only ever gone to work on Ward Four by accident. She wanted to be a teacher, not a nurse. Six months earlier, she had gone to see Moira Onions about a sponsored event she was trying to run at a playgroup and, to her surprise, she had been offered work as an auxiliary.

She had agreed because she liked working with children, but she had never expected it would be like this: all these deaths and terrible arrests, and the Crash Team always in and out of the ward. It was heart-breaking, and it was just not the way it was supposed to be, and no one seemed to be able to do anything about it. So Wendy Sorrell handed in her notice and left.

Moira Onions talked to the two consultants. She told them she was most anxious about the number of very sick children on the ward, and she suggested that it might be a good policy to start screening children as they arrived on the ward. They could take a sample of each child's blood, test it for a range of infections and then, if—Heaven forbid—any of these children then suffered an arrest, they could test their blood again and try to see if anything had changed. She thought this was important because despite all the talk about a heart virus or legionnaires' disease, they had not actually conducted any special tests at all. Not one. The path lab had found nothing of note in any routine blood tests and had not, therefore, triggered the system by asking the Control of Infection officer to visit the ward. And the ward itself had not called in anyone. But if now they adopted this screening policy, they might discover something, some clue. At least they would be doing something instead of just talking about it.

The two consultants said no. They made it clear to Moira Onions that this was a pointless idea. If there was no specific indication of infection, there was no reason to start testing. She suggested an alternative, that at the very least they should screen the doctors to make sure that they were not bringing any infection on to the ward themselves. She was thinking of Dr Tailor, who had a terrible chest infection. The two consultants said no, and Moira Onions thought to herself that doctors always said no because they liked to think they were above the law. By the time the two consultants had finished squashing her plans, she felt like a junior nurse again.

Dr Porter and Dr Nanayakkara went their separate ways as usual. As far as they were concerned, there was no special problem here. They had not even sat down and talked to each other about it all. They had barely mentioned it at their weekly doctors' meetings. Dr Nanayakkara had complained about the pathologist who dealt with Liam Taylor and by coincidence, at their meeting on Thursday morning, Nanayakkara had been talking about Paul Crampton just before he had suffered his final hypo. Nanayakkara thought Dr Porter had made a mistake. He thought this baby should have been transferred to Queen's Med as soon as he was well enough on Monday morning. And he said so. He thought this baby had nearly died at the weekend. Probably he had a tumour in the pancreas, he said. Dr Porter stammered a defence of his decision. Nanayakkara went on. There was another possibility, he said—Munchausen Syndrome. The junior doctors at the meeting had never heard of it. Dr Nanayakkara told them that it was a rare personality disorder, an obsession with hospitals which sometimes made adults attack children so that they could enjoy the thrill of the medical alert that followed. Dr Nanayakkara said they should keep an eye on the boy's parents. You could never be sure. But he had little time to develop his theme. A nurse interrupted the meeting to say that Paul was having another attack. Dr Porter rushed off to deal with it, with Dr Tailor in his wake. The meeting ended.

Everyone agreed that they were dealing with mysteries. Moira Onions, the two consultants, Sister Barker, they all agreed that there had been some bizarre and unexpected events. They all shook their heads and they worried and they wondered, but none of them did anything to solve the mystery of Ward Four.

Paul Crampton had gone from Grantham Hospital, but in a small, plastic bottle with a white lid and a white label, he had left his blood behind him, the blood which Dr Porter had taken from his groin that afternoon. Dr Porter had scribbled out some details on the request form that was fastened around the bottle's neck—doctor's name, patient's name, illness 'unexplained hypoglycaemia'—and he had passed it to an auxiliary nurse called Nadine Shelbourn. That was soon after 1.30.

Nadine had taken the little bottle and set off down the long corridor to the front of the hospital, round to the left by the main door and into the path lab, where she had handed it to the receptionist, Jo Cockcroft. The journey had taken her less than three minutes.

Jo Cockcroft had noticed that Dr Porter had not completed all the details on the label, and so Nadine had done her best to fill in the gaps. Then Jo Cockcroft had recorded the details on her central register, given the bottle a path lab number, 30-10-90-AA, and placed it in the specimen area. The work had taken her less than five minutes.

A lab technician had come and collected the sample and spun the little bottle in a Beckman TJ6 centrifuge to separate the straw-coloured plasma from the blood cells, divided the plasma samples into three little bottles—different bottles for different tests in different places. Then he had taken them back out to reception. It was routine work. It took less than 15 minutes.

This blood mattered. It could end the confusion and the doubt. It contained the clue—the hard, unassailable chemical clue which could unravel the mystery and stop the pain. Dr Porter was sure he had told Nadine that this was an emergency. Nadine was sure that she had taken it straight to the path lab without delay and told them there that it was urgent. Jo Cockcroft, a policeman's wife, was sure that she had handled it with all due speed. The technician was sure that he had followed procedures as fast as possible. But someone had dawdled.

The blood had been taken at 1.30. Its processing should have taken less than half an hour. But at 3.45 that afternoon, two and a quarter hours after the blood was taken, when the porter came round to the path lab to collect the outgoing mail, it was still not ready. The blood that was so urgent missed the post.

That night, as Paul's almost lifeless body arrived at Queen's

Med in Nottingham, his blood still lay in a freezer in the path lab at Grantham Hospital, untouched and untested.

On Ward Four, nothing changed. Wendy Sorrell's fears, Kate Lock's worries, Chris and Joanne Taylor's questions, Joan Cottam's attempt to raise the alarm, David Crampton's ceaseless effort to find the truth—all were lost like a whistle on the wind. Paul Crampton had gone, whisked down the road to a safer place. Behind him, in Ward Four, the source of the threat was safer, too. Clues to the truth lay unheeded like a baby crying in the dark.

4

Judith Gibson couldn't sleep. It was nearly midnight and she was still lying on the settee in the sitting room, stubbing out cigarettes and keeping the dog awake. She just hated the thought of Brad lying all alone in a hospital bed. She wished she had stayed with him, but they'd said she couldn't sleep right next to him, so she couldn't see the point. She was not too keen on hospitals anyway, not since she'd been cooped up in one for six weeks with pneumonia when she was 16, and today she'd spent hours on Ward Four without anyone offering her so much as a cup of tea or telling her anything about Brad, and so she'd come home. Now she was full of guilt and worry. Brad had never been away from home before and he'd never been ill before either, not since he was born, when he had managed to get the cord wrapped round his neck. There had been one time, three months ago, when he'd had his routine health check at school and the school doctor had reckoned he had heard a murmur in his heart, but she had taken him along to Grantham Hospital and Dr Porter there had made him run up and down the corridor to get his heart beating faster and said there was nothing wrong at all and he couldn't understand what the school doctor had heard. This time, however, he was certainly ill.

Brad had woken up that morning, coughing and choking and wheezing terribly, and when she had tried to get some antibiotics down him, he had just retched and thrown the sticky yellow stuff all over his chest. The GP had said the only solution was to get him into hospital and put him on an antibiotic drip. Brad had been upset because it was Good Friday, the first day of the Easter holidays, and they had planned for him to go off for the weekend with his grandparents in their caravan to Boston in east Lincolnshire but he'd been very good about it. Considering he was only five, he was very grown up in his ways. He'd looked at Judith and said: 'I think I'd better not go.'

On the ward, they said he had pneumonia, though he seemed happy enough. One of the nurses had told him he looked like Thomas the Tank Engine when they put him on a nebulizer of salbutamol and steam had come pouring out of his face mask. There were two other little boys near him; one of them had come in because he had fallen out of bed at home and given himself concussion.

Judith was not quite so happy. Apart from being cut off from all food and drink, it had taken her most of the day to persuade the nurses to stop trying to feed Brad medicine on a spoon and to put him on a drip, which was the whole point of his being there anyway. As soon as they had taken her word for it and tried him on a drip, Brad had started to look much better. A little Chinese boy had been running round the ward and he had stopped at the foot of Brad's bed and stood with his legs astride and his hands clasped behind his back and given them a rather serious look, and Judith had said 'Look, here's Prince Philip come to see you' and Brad had chuckled away. By the time Steve had come to pick her up, he had been sleeping peacefully and just as they were leaving the ward, Steve had turned and seen him open his eyes and Brad had given him a little smile and waved at them.

But now all Judith could think of was the senior staff nurse, Margaret Geeson. Steve had asked her, as they were leaving, if Brad could come home the next day, since he was doing so well, and she'd snapped 'No, he's a very poorly boy' and Steve had felt quite small.

Finally, just after midnight, Judith could stand it no longer and she telephoned the hospital and asked to be put through to Ward Four. The nurse who answered assured her that Brad was fine, he was just as they had left him, fast asleep and breathing well: 'There's nothing to worry about. You get some sleep.'

Judith sighed, stubbed out a last cigarette and fell asleep on the settee, which is where she was at 3.10 in the morning when the phone rang, and someone from the hospital told her that Brad's condition was causing concern. 'Can you and your husband come to the hospital straightaway, please?'

Judith was too alarmed to ask questions. She went straight

upstairs, woke Steve, told him the news, saw the look on his face, popped her head in on her teenage twins, Richard and Russell, both fast asleep and old enough to be left alone, hurried Steve into his clothes and went out to the car. Judith drove. She stared at the street. Steve was still half-asleep, he kept asking what the hospital had said. She couldn't tell him. They'd said nothing. All Steve could think of was his mate David, whose dad had gone into hospital a month or so ago and, in the middle of the night, they'd called him and told him to come in and by the time he'd got there, his dad had died.

'I've heard all this before,' he said quietly.

Judith was driving as fast as she could, skipping the red lights on the deserted streets, but the tired old Austin was no racer. It was all Steve could afford on his labourer's pay. Still, it was only a few miles to the hospital and soon Judith was turning in to the car park. The whole building seemed to be in darkness. Which door were they supposed to go to? The main door was locked and bolted. They hurried down the side. There was a door there, they knew, next to maternity. It was locked. There was no sign of anyone. They found an intercom and pushed the button. A voice said it was coming. An age passed. Steve had never liked this hospital. He'd been in here himself once when his first marriage was breaking up and he'd been in a terrible state and he'd fallen down stairs and cracked his head and come round on one of the wards. He'd taken one look and decided to leave and, even though he was still concussed, he had managed to find his clothes, wander off down the corridor and get out on to the road without anyone noticing.

Finally, a porter came and let them in, down the side of the maternity unit, across the main corridor, through the double doors, into Ward Four, where a nurse met them. She was the night sister, Jean Savill. She seemed very efficient, with grey hair and glasses, and she led them to a side room. It was brightly lit, there was a coffee table and some old magazines and a sign that said 'No Smoking'. But where was Brad?

Sister Savill told them the news. Brad had stopped breathing. His heart had stopped.

She said that the Crash Team were working on him now and it was too soon to go in and see him but she would come back to them as soon as there was any more news, and perhaps they would like the hospital chaplain to come and sit with them.

'Why?'

'Well, some people find it a comfort. In this sort of situation.'

But a chaplain meant only one thing. Judith and Steve didn't want a chaplain.

'We're not really religious,' Steve said. Then, glancing up at the No Smoking sign, he added: 'I'd like a cigarette, though.'

Sister Savill said that would be fine and just ignore that notice, and she said the chaplain was waiting on the ward anyway and he might as well come and talk to them, just so there was someone there, not to spout religion. Then they were alone in the little room and both of them started crying.

Steve lit a cigarette and saw his fingers were fluttering. He slumped forward with his forearms on his knees, sighing hard and counting the minutes and watching the door. He didn't want to be sitting in this little room, he wanted to be with Brad. 'Any second now,' he thought, 'someone's going to walk through that door and look at me and say "We're sorry, Mr Gibson, we've lost him." '

The door opened. Steve reared back. It was the chaplain, a small man in his mid 30s with a tight-clipped beard and a dark jacket. All Steve and Judith wanted was to sit quietly and nurse their fears, but he wanted to talk to them, to comfort them. Steve took one look at him and knew he was there for the last rites. The sight of him filled him with despair. Judith could tell the chaplain was finding it hard to think of anything to say, he seemed almost as upset as they were. They asked if he would go to their home and wake their two older boys, Richard and Russell, to tell them what was happening. They were alone again.

'How many minutes have we been here?' asked Steve.

'I don't know. About 15.'

'What do you think they're doing?'

'I don't know. How should I know?'

Steve went back to watching the door. Another cigarette. Just yesterday, Brad had been with him on the site of the new Swallow Hotel where Steve was labouring, wearing his black Batman sweatshirt, mucking about in a heap of sand while Steve worked on a water pump. He'd been so happy. He always was happy, grinning under his blond hair, in his go-kart, messing about with his trains. Oh, this was like being in a film here, that scene where they're in the waiting room and the doctor comes in with a long face and a soft voice and says 'I'm sorry, we've lost him'. The door opened again. It was Sister Savill with two cups of coffee in blue china cups.

'What's happening?' asked Judith.

'I'm afraid,' the sister said, 'that they're still working on him.'

Steve and Judith were frozen, watching her face.

'But the longer he can keep going the better,' she added, 'the better his chances. They're trying to stabilize him.'

She left them with the coffee. The cups were too hot. They stared at the walls, full of meaningless posters.

'How many minutes do you think it's been?' asked Steve.

'Twenty. I don't know.'

Steve hated tension. He didn't like fights or people shouting or any of that nastiness. He liked to leave the worries of life to Judith. It was not that he couldn't cope; beneath his slow, soft-spoken exterior, he always surprised people with his shrewdness. But Judith was quicker off the mark, tougher, much more confident in dealing with people. She had brought up Richard and Russell on her own for eight years after splitting up with their father, and even though she had been with Steve now for nine years, she still ran her own life and Steve's too. Steve liked familiar things: working on the building sites, gardening, doing tug-of-war at the village fetes. And Brad. He and Judith loved that little boy.

'How many minutes has it been now?'

'I don't know,' said Judith. 'Half an hour or something.'

They lit more cigarettes. Judith's mind was trying to rescue her. She realized she was sitting staring at the floor, playing through all the details of how she would have to arrange a funeral. Since she'd only ever been to one funeral she had no idea how it was done and she wondered who she should talk to and whether she had to tell the police that Brad had died and whereabouts in the cemetery they would bury him. Then she snapped out of it. Brad was not dead. But all of this was just too much to bear, and so her mind had jumped forward to the next stage, hoping somehow all this would go away.

The chaplain came back with Richard but without Russell who

had been so fast asleep that they couldn't wake him. They sat and sighed and smoked and, finally, the door opened and a stocky man with a beard and thick glasses came in and said he was Dr Porter and that Brad seemed to be holding his own now, he seemed to be stable.

Judith asked: 'Why did it happen?'

'We don't know.'

Judith thought Dr Porter seemed terribly timid. 'Can we see him now?'

Dr Porter said they could but he felt he ought to warn them that Brad might look rather terrible to them, then he led them out of the little room into the dim lights of the corridor, past the posters of Garfield the cat and Postman Pat, past the slumbering shapes of children whose hearts had not stopped, dozing in the safety of their little cubicles, past the nurses' station to a wild place.

This is where they had last seen Brad, in the four-bed area, where he had been lying under the dim lights in his own bed, blankets tucked around him, smiling goodbye from his clean white pillow, and waving one hand as he drifted off with his bear called Ted beside him. Now the room was white with light. The other beds were pushed away. Only one bed remained, stripped to the boards. The mattress gone. The blankets all pulled off. On it lay a naked boy. Machines had gathered round him, dipping their feelers into his veins, sucking on him. The boy was all white. Arms and legs stretched straight and limp. Eyeballs rolling backwards under half-opened lids.

Judith and Steve walked closer. Now they could see his chest, where the pale, thin skin was drawn tight across the breastbone, shrunk around the ribs, and they could see that it was scarred. There were seven or eight red rings on the skin, burn marks, they realized, where his dead heart had been shocked back into life.

They began to see more people in the room, eight or nine of them, hovering around Brad's bed, men and women with white coats. One of them was sitting by Brad's head, squeezing an air bladder into a pipe which forced itself down Brad's throat so that his chest fluttered in and out with every squeeze. Somehow, Steve felt better when he saw that, and he wanted to share his morsel of relief—anything to break the silent tension—so he caught the anaesthetist's eye and smiled at him.

'Have you been doing that long? You'll get cramp.'

Dr Porter led them away, showed them some X-rays, talked about infection and inhalation and cardiac rhythm and other things they could not get a grip on, and the night sister came and asked if they would agree to their transferring Brad to Queen's Med, and they said yes, they would agree to anything, anything the doctors said, they were so full of thanks for them saving Brad's life.

Judith asked if she could go with him in the ambulance.

'No,' said Sister Savill. 'There's not enough room. The anaesthetist is going with him, on escort, and we'll send a nurse as well.'

Bev Allitt volunteered to go, but the sister said that it was better if she stayed with her patients, and she borrowed a nurse from another ward.

'Is he going to be all right?' asked Judith.

'We've done all we can,' said the sister and left them in the darkness.

Forty-eight hours passed, night fell, it was the evening of Easter Sunday, 31 March, about 9.00.

On Ward Four, in the Treatment Room, Margaret Geeson was talking to one of the staff nurses, Catherine Morris, a Chinese woman in her early 40s who was still recovering from the shock of witnessing Brad Gibson's heart attack. Catherine was saying that there was something wrong with the Ambubag, which was used to squirt air into a child's mouth if it stopped breathing.

Around the corner in a cubicle with a picture of Mr Happy grinning on the door, was a two-year-old boy, Yik Hung Chan, known as Henry Chan. He'd been brought in three days earlier, on Thursday morning, after launching himself out of his first-floor bedroom window at home and landing on a paved patio below. His skull was fractured in two places but he had recovered well and he had been in effervescent form, running all round the ward grinning at everyone. He would have gone home yesterday but he had been sick after drinking some Ribena, so they were keeping him in for observation and giving him his liquids through a drip. He would be home tomorrow, all being well.

Now Catherine was telling Margaret Geeson about Brad's collapse. She had been on the night shift with Bev Allitt when it
happened. She could still hardly believe it. The boy had been
restless all night. He had wet the bed and she and Jean Savill had
had to change his sheets, then he had kept complaining that his
arm hurt where the drip went into his wrist and then he had been
wheezing so they had given him some salbutamol in a nebulizer.
But all the same, his collapse had taken her completely by surprise.
Bev had gone over to see him because he had been complaining
about his arm again, Catherine had been sitting at the nurses'
station—she'd just got back from her break—and Bev had suddenly shouted 'Catherine, come quick' and she had turned round
just in time to see Brad slump forwards on the bed. Then it had
been pandemonium. She had run over to the boy's bed and found
he had no pulse. She had started giving him mouth to mouth, and
he had choked and brought some fluid up into her mouth.

Around the corner, Henry Chan still slept.

Catherine was telling Margaret that by the time the Crash Team
had arrived a few minutes later, Brad had no vital signs. No pulse,
no spontaneous breathing. They had put him on an ECG monitor
but the trace was flat. It had taken them 32 minutes to get him
going again. Even then, it was only because they had started giving
him adult doses of electric shock from the defibrillator. They had
started him on 50 joules, then they had given him two lots of 100
joules, then they had tried 200 joules and when he had still failed
to respond they had gone all the way up to 300 joules and given
him a series of five shocks. It was a desperate tactic. Then his
heart had started, racing along at 170 beats a minute, and his lungs
had got going again and they knew they had him back.

Bev Allitt poked her head in the door. There was something
wrong with Henry Chan, she said. He was crying and she thought
Catherine might be able to shut him up, since she spoke the same
language.

Catherine and Margaret held open the Treatment Room door
and listened. There was no sound of crying at all. Catherine had
her doubts about Bev Allitt. She had been with her when Liam
Taylor and Brad Gibson had had their arrests and it seemed to
her that Bev did not work very well in a crisis. She seemed to
flap and start dropping things. She and Margaret finished their

conversation. They still couldn't understand why Brad's heart had stopped. Dr Porter who had been called out of his bed had thought at first that it must have been brought on by his pneumonia, but they had X-rayed his lungs and found there was nothing like enough infection to explain it. The potassium in his blood tests had been high, but that didn't seem to mean anything. The doctors had started saying that he must have asthma instead of pneumonia, but they didn't seem at all certain about anything.

Margaret Geeson said she must go. She'd been running the ward all day with no qualified staff—nothing but two student nurses. It was time she was home. She and Catherine turned right out of the Treatment Room and walked up past the row of cubicles on their left. As they went, they paused to peep at Henry, just to be sure that he was not crying any more, and that was how they came to see his face. It was blue, a deep, dark blue, like the belts around their waists.

Once more, the Crash Team headed out for Ward Four. By now, they did not even stop to ask where the arrest was taking place. They simply ran when their bleepers started screaming and headed straight for the dying children.

Henry came coughing back to life, whining in a tearful muddle of English and Chinese. Catherine Morris and Bev Allitt fed him oxygen. Henry's mother, Jenny Chan, arrived innocently on the ward to kiss him goodnight and found herself swallowed up in the chaos. Catherine Morris came out and put her arm around her, led her away and explained that Henry had had a fit, but the worst was over, Henry was fine again now. More doctors pushed their way into Henry's cubicle.

Jenny Chan went out into the corridor to phone her husband, Eddie, at his restaurant in Stamford, half an hour's drive south of Grantham. He said he would come quickly. After she had spoken to him, she felt calmer and she drifted cautiously back to Henry's door, from where she could see a nurse holding a mask to his face, giving him oxygen. The other nurses and doctors had gone away now, his colour was better, he was lying normally on the bed, his eyes were open. But as she watched, the nurse with the oxygen snapped into life. Henry's face was going blue again and his eyes were rolling. Now his face was black-blue, like a thunder-cloud, his lips were puffed, his eyes were rolled up into their sockets, his back was arched stiff, clear off the bed, he was quivering. All this, Jenny Chan saw in a moment.

She started to cry and to shout in Chinese, she didn't even know what she was saying, but she couldn't stop herself, she was wailing very loud, jabbering through her fingers, sobbing for help, and some nurses came and led her away, into one of the parents' rooms, while doctors hurtled back through the ward to work once more on her small son's body.

When she came back to her ten minutes later, Catherine Morris said that Henry was all right. The doctors thought the fits were caused by the fractures in his skull. They were normal with that sort of injury, they said, and really nothing to worry about, but they had decided to transfer him to Queen's Med in Nottingham, and a nurse would travel with him in the ambulance. Her name was Bev.

Catherine Morris went back to the ward, puzzling over Henry's fit. Dr Titley, the junior doctor who was looking after Henry, said that they had been febrile convulsions—fits brought on by high temperature—but she had seen a dozen febrile convulsions in children and none of them had been like Henry's. He had not been twitching and his temperature was not high enough. She had told Dr Titley that he was wrong, and Margaret Geeson and Bev Allitt had backed her up, but the doctor had stood his ground. And maybe he was right. There was no telling with medicine.

Jenny Chan watched with Eddie as their son was strapped into a stretcher. Bev climbed into the back of the ambulance and Henry was bundled in after her, in amongst the shadows.

Thirty-six hours passed. It was Tuesday morning, 2 April. In the pathology lab at Grantham Hospital, a clerk named Sue Barker had come in to work and was now pursuing her normal daily routine. She was a little busier than usual, because she had been away for four days for the Easter holiday and now there was a backlog of work waiting for her.

She cleared her desk and then she checked the freezer where she found a cluster of sample bottles waiting for her to wrap and dispatch to their various destinations. Following her normal routine, she took each one from the freezer, sealed it in parafilm to stop it leaking, wrapped it in cellulose, slipped it into a biohazard bag, then into a Jiffy bag and left it in the mail tray to be collected by the porters on their round. She noticed as she did so that three of them were blood samples, marked up by the lab technicians. One was for Lincoln County where it was to be tested for cortisol; one was for Pilgrim Hospital down the road in Boston where it was to be tested for growth hormone; and the third had to go all the way to the University Hospital of Wales in Cardiff where they had specialist equipment to test for insulin. And all three were samples for the same patient—Paul Crampton from Ward Four.

Five days had passed now since Dr Porter urgently drew the crucial sample of blood from Paul Crampton's groin. In that time, Brad Gibson and Henry Chan had been hurled into the darkness. And Paul Crampton's blood sample with all its clues had still not been tested. One hundred and twenty hours later, it had not yet even found its way to the hospital post room.

David Crampton was feeling better now. Ever since he had hurtled into Queen's Med five days earlier, on that Thursday evening—abandoning the Cavalier in the car park, chasing into the hospital, arriving breathless and hopeless at the side of Paul's bed—he had been showered with relief. The young nurse who was taking Paul's temperature had smiled at him with his red eyes and told him there was nothing to worry about, he could calm down.

During the next 48 hours, David had watched in disbelief as Paul had burst back to health. Just once, on that first evening, he had faltered and turned grey and the doctors had taken blood, but then he had recovered and continued on his climb. David had pressed to get Paul's blood tested, to see if there was any clue in there, offering to use his company health insurance if that would make it quicker, but Paul just went ahead and recovered. He had not even needed any medication, apart from a drip to cure his dehydration. His colour had flooded back into his cheeks, he was lively and bouncey again, as if the whole episode on Ward Four had been nothing more than a stunt pulled by some invisible trickster, and now it was over and everyone had taken off their masks and gone back to normal.

The whole atmosphere at Queen's Med was quite different to Grantham. The doctors seemed confident; they said they had seen this type of hypoglycaemia before. The nurses came and introduced themselves and offered cups of coffee and talked openly about what the doctors were doing and let the parents read their children's notes. There was even an official hospital rabbit hopping around between the beds in the paediatric intensive care unit. It made Ward Four look like a museum piece.

David had become so desperate with worry that he found it hard to believe that Paul really was recovering, and Paul had only to roll his eyes as he went to sleep or turn his nose up at his bottle to send David chasing down the corridor in search of a doctor. But on Saturday morning, their second full day at Queen's Med, he had seen something in the intensive care unit that finally had convinced him that Paul really was not ill any more. He had seen Brad Gibson being brought in, sunk in a coma, skin like bleach, bleeding wires from every vein, and followed by his tearful parents, Judith and Steve, who hovered uncertainly around him like mourners at a funeral.

Later that day, Kath Crampton had seen Steve, this burly bear with a dark beard, slumped in one of the parents' rooms, crying quietly into his hand. She had tried to comfort him and told him how Paul had got so much better now and she was sure that Brad would do well here too. She found that Brad, too, had been in Grantham and that Steve had been working on a building site at the new Swallow Hotel which was being managed by David. Soon, the two families had become friends and sat watching their children and swapping stories about Ward Four and how they'd never go there again.

The Gibsons had been consumed by grief. They both thought Brad would die in his coma and, despondently, they had talked about how they would try to have another child to replace him. Steve had found Brad's illness impossibly painful, refusing to sit near him in his corpse-like state. He had cried without end and Judith had tried to console him, but he had pushed her away; the only comfort he wanted was to hear that Brad was better. Judith had wanted to spend every minute with Brad—she was not going to feel guilty about leaving him again—and she had drawn great comfort from the nurses who had let her wash him and brush his teeth as he lay there.

She spent hours sitting by his bed, holding his hand, talking to him because the nurses said he could probably hear her voice, staring at his familiar little face just in case his eyes might open. They didn't. On Sunday, the doctors tried to take him off the ventilator which was forcing his lungs to do their job, but as soon as his lungs were left to their own devices, they started to falter and fail. Judith began to lose hope. On Monday, once, his fingers moved in her hand, and she wondered whether perhaps that meant he was coming back to her, but she knew, too, that it might have been nothing more than a nervous reflex. So, she waited. The doctors said on Monday afternoon that they would try once more to see whether he could breathe on his own without the ventilator. They explained that they would take him off the drugs, fentanyl and vecuronium, which were paralysing his body to stop him fighting the machine, and they added in a sombre tone that Judith and Steve must prepare themselves for the worst; Brad might well be damaged, his brain had been starved of oxygen and he might not be the same. The doctors sent them off to get a cup of coffee because they said it would take a while for the drugs to wear off and because it might upset them if he failed again. Barely 20 minutes later, Judith and Steve were coming out of the lift on their way back from the canteen, when someone came running after them.

'He's coming round. Quick.'

Judith and Steve ran back to Brad. And there he was, flailing about, trying to rid himself of all these silly tubes and wires, trying to sit up, eyes open, catching sight of Judith and telling her in a dozy drawl 'I want to go home.'

The next day, Tuesday, he was off the intensive care unit altogether. He was still weak, but he was able to get up and he could walk to the loo on his own, and the doctors were amazed at how quickly he was recovering. As far as Judith could see, he was fine, quite undamaged. Steve was beaming as if he had plums in his cheeks.

The relief which flooded through the Cramptons and the Gibsons was not shared by the doctors at Queen's Med. In the last three weeks they had seen four Grantham children rattle on to the intensive care unit, wrapped in space blankets, bristling with electronic support. And all four had recovered with surprising speed.

When Kayley Desmond arrived at Queen's Med in the early hours of Sunday, 10 March, with Maggie stumbling dazed out of the ambulance behind her, Dr Vibart Noble had examined her, found that she was breathing a little quickly, that her chest was a little crackly but that she was generally pretty well. The truth was that he found it very hard to believe that she had ever been really ill at all, there was certainly nothing that he could see in her condition or her history that should have stopped her breathing, so when he filled in her notes, he had written 'respiratory arrest x 2' and then underlined it several times to signal his surprise. The next day, she had been completely fine and the day after that, they had discharged her.

Then Paul Crampton had arrived, in just the same atmosphere of crisis, only to recover with just the same, baffling speed. All they had done was to ween him off his glucose. Dr Noble had been afraid that his blood sugar might suddenly fall, but it had shown no signs of doing so. And the little Chinese boy, Henry Chan, was equally strange. They had even scanned his brain in search of an explanation for the two violent arrests which he had suffered in Grantham, but there was nothing there to worry them and they had sent him home without any problem. Now, there was the most baffling case of all, Brad Gibson.

Dr Vibart Noble, who had admitted him, had looked carefully at the Grantham notes and at the suggestion that his heart attack had been caused by asthma. Straightaway, he had been surprised to find how easy it was to ventilate him; with an asthmatic child, it was usually very difficult to push oxygen into the lungs, but Brad was easy. He had been curious, too, about the reports that Brad had complained of pain at the site of his drip; he had been unable to see any reason for that. Then he had asked himself the big question: why should a healthy boy with a healthy heart and normal heart rhythms suffer a heart attack at all? There was nothing to explain it, and all of Dr Noble's instincts told him there was something wrong. His colleagues agreed that it was a very strange story and it certainly didn't sound like asthma.

It was Terence Stephenson who came closest to cracking the mystery. He was only 33 years old, but he was already a consultant and impressively bright and he was intrigued by Brad as soon as he saw him on his morning round that Saturday. He agreed with

Dr Noble that this was not a case of asthma: that would have produced a slow deterioration whereas Brad had gone down very fast; and if in the run-up to the arrest, Grantham had not even needed to give him oxygen or any specialized drugs to treat his asthma, it could hardly have been bad enough to stop his heart. No, said Dr Stephenson, this was something else.

It might have been epilepsy, but there was no history of that and no report of his actually suffering a fit. It might be some underlying problem with the heart—and there was just the slightest murmur there—but his blood pressure was normal and the cardiogram gave the heart a clean bill of health. The only other possibility was some sort of drugs mix-up. If Brad had been given the wrong drug, or the right drug in the wrong dose, that might explain it. Stephenson was not sure. But supposing Grantham had taken a common drug like salbutamol which was often used to clear the airways of children like Brad who had bad chests and then, instead of giving it to him in a nebulizer, they had injected it straight into him. That would have hit his heart. He checked Brad's notes. He had indeed been given salbutamol, although the notes recorded that it had been adminstered only in a nebulizer. But supposing that somehow the salbutamol solution had got into his drip. That might even explain this business of the pain in his arm.

Stephenson discussed his theory with Dr Noble and the two of them raised the case at the weekly departmental meeting. The convention was that cases were discussed anonymously, but Stephenson described the history and there was a discussion and it was pointed out that the difficulties which the Grantham Crash Team had had in resuscitating him also suggested the presence of some drug blocking his recovery. At the end of the meeting, the Queen's Med doctors agreed that, given these facts, really the only sensible conclusion was that somehow or other Brad had been given the wrong drug. It was surprising that Grantham had not realized this.

Stephenson's theory became more important than ever on Wednesday, Brad's fifth day on the ward. He told Judith that his legs hurt and that he could not move them properly. The nurses said that perhaps he had been sitting on them and cut off the circulation, but Judith rubbed them and they got no better. When Brad needed the loo, she found she had to carry him from his bed and then it hurt his thighs just to sit there. He seemed to have lost all feeling down the outside of his right leg. That afternoon, when she carried him down to the play area, she watched with a sinking heart as her runaround, rushabout five-year-old son crawled painfully on his hands and knees from one toy to another. The miracle recovery was falling apart.

For the Cramptons, however, the grim adventure seemed finally to be over. Paul was now sitting up in his cot, pulling his toes and behaving like a five-month-old baby should. On Wednesday morning, David went off to work asking Kath to arrange for him to see a doctor. He was happy that Paul was well, but the watchdog in his mind was still prowling, wanting answers to the questions with which he had bombarded Ward Four. The next day, as he left a site meeting in Newark, he picked up a message on his car phone: at 5.30 that afternoon he was to meet a senior consultant at Queen's Med, Derek Johnston, to talk about Paul.

Derek Johnston was a most experienced paediatrician, a doctor of 24 years' standing who had worked in North America as well as the United Kingdom. He specialized in hormonal problems in children. He had been brought into Paul Crampton's case by Nelson Porter who had called him from Grantham after the first two of Paul's hypoglycaemic attacks, to ask for advice. Johnston had done his best over the phone, then when the boy had suffered a third attack and arrived at Queen's Med, he had studied the case more closely.

Derek Johnston told David Crampton a lot about Paul's illness. He said Paul could go home. He said his hypoglycaemia was most unlikely to recur. He said that all their tests had failed to reveal any problem in Paul's health and that he was confident that any future tests similarly would confirm that this was a healthy child. He told him that, by way of reassurance, they should use the BM sticks to check that Paul's blood sugar remained normal.

David Crampton thanked him. He was grateful for some straight information, but he wanted a little more, and in particular, he wanted an explanation for this hypoglycaemia that had come and now gone so suddenly. What about the blood tests? Was there still no result from them? Johnston was afraid that there was not, not yet. So, what did Johnston think the problem was?

'Well, I can't give you any definite answers.'

'Yes, but there must have been something that made it happen. He went into Grantham Hospital with bronchiolitis. Then suddenly he's hypoglycaemic. I mean, something must have happened to him.'

Johnston looked at him. 'Do you mean as a result of the drugs he was given?'

'Well, no,' said David, although he had not forgotten Kath's theory about the cocktail of drugs which Paul received on Ward Four. 'But since you pose the question, perhaps you'd like to answer it.'

Johnston chose his words with obvious care. 'I have no reason to come to that conclusion. All I can say is that I'm pretty sure that there is not going to be another problem.'

David Crampton left the meeting with his brain buzzing. How could they be so sure that Paul's problem would not recur? They must have found out what the problem was. The doctors here were obviously thinking much more clearly than their colleagues in Grantham. And why did Johnston suddenly bring up drugs like that? It had to be because that was what had happened. Some foul-up on Ward Four. That would explain why Paul had got better so quickly as soon as he had left Grantham, and why they were so certain now that he would be all right. There was some kind of foul-up on Ward Four.

It was Thursday afternoon, 4 April. In the department of clinical chemistry at Pilgrim Hospital in Boston, 30 miles east of Grantham, a small perspex vial containing a sample of Paul Crampton's blood was now stored in the freezer. It had arrived by road on Tuesday afternoon and since then the chemist had done his work and tested the blood for growth hormone. He had sent his report back to Grantham.

Of the three samples of Paul Crampton's blood which had now been distributed through different hospitals, this was not the vital one, not the one which contained the chemical bombshell. But it was important, capable of helping Dr Porter to rule out various alternative explanations for Paul Crampton's illness. The chemist had found a growth hormone level of 5.2, which was well within the normal range. But Dr Porter was not to know that.

At some point in its short journey, Paul Crampton's personal details had been wrongly transcribed on to this bottle, and the result of the Boston test was soon completely lost in the bureaucratic undergrowth of Grantham Hospital, and nobody noticed.

Peter Phillips was in a good mood. He was sitting comfortably behind the wheel of £16,500-worth of brand new Audi, the new business he had started custom-cleaning cars was surviving, he had his blue-eyed young wife Sue beside him, and they were on their way to Grantham Hospital to bring home their baby daughter, Becky. He hadn't actually paid for the Audi yet, but he'd fix that. He was good at fixing things—a deal here, a dodge there. That was Peter Phillips, a dodger, living on his wits, always looking for an opening. He was like a mischievous little boy, full of big dreams and little scrapes, striding from scene to scene with high hopes and a cheeky smile, unless things went badly wrong and then he'd scowl and shake his fist at somebody's chin.

He was looking forward to having Becky home again. She'd spent a long time in hospital and so had her twin sister, Katie. They'd been three months premature when they were born at the end of January in Nottingham and they'd weighed barely three pounds each. They were identical, and they were so fragile they looked like a pair of ballet shoes lying there. They were so tiny that they had to stay in hospital for the first five weeks, most of it on the Special Care Baby Unit at Grantham, and even when they'd come home early in March, they were still so small that at the first sign of a problem, the GP had ordered them back to hospital, to Ward Four. Both of them had been having trouble feeding. They'd been 'projectile vomiting', throwing their feed up across the room, and, although Katie seemed to be over it now, Becky had had to go back in again on Monday. Still, they said she was all right again now.

Peter and Sue had nothing but good things to say about Ward Four. They knew people put the knife in to Grantham Hospital—and there were always stories about people being given the wrong operations or having the wrong leg amputated—but, if you asked Peter and Sue, the doctors and nurses on Ward Four were first class. The other day, they had taken the camera down on the ward and taken a whole load of souvenir pictures of the twins with their nurses. They knew there had been some trouble on the ward. They'd seen Paul Crampton lying at death's door and the nurses had told them about some of the other children who had been very sick. But they'd never seen anything to worry them. And if there was anything wrong on the ward, they were all right now. Becky was coming home, safe and sound.

Not all of the staff at the hospital felt as warmly towards Peter Phillips as he did towards them. For some of them, Peter Phillips was trouble. Going right back to the birth of the twins in January, he had created a terrible scene on the maternity ward when he was told that Sue had to be transferred to Nottingham to give birth, and Moira Onions had had to go on to the ward and calm him down and insist that he respect medical advice. He liked to have things done his way. And he was always in the hospital for one reason or another. If it wasn't the little twins with all their problems, it was their three-year-old brother, Jamie, with his constipation, or his teenage daughters from another marriage, Emma and Nicola, going down with one problem and another. It turned out that he and Sue had first met in the hospital, when he was recovering from some murky episode in which someone had taken a baseball bat to his head. But Becky was going home now. Ward Four had done its work.

As Peter and Sue Phillips drove towards the hospital, Becky lay quietly in her cot in her cubicle. On the ward, the ordinary people clattered by. Phones rang, doors closed, pages turned and nobody stopped to watch Becky. She lay alone.

Peter Phillips grinned hallo at the nurses as he and Sue arrived on the ward with their car cot and their carrier bag. The news was all good: Dr Nanayakkara had examined Becky on his round and pronounced her fit. She had fed well, she had not been sick, she had a clean nappy and she was smiling.

No one mentioned it to Peter and Sue, but there had been a hint of trouble the previous afternoon. Bev Allitt had called one of the student nurses, Sarah, into Becky's cubicle and told her that Becky had suddenly gone cold and clammy. Sarah had looked and thought Becky seemed fine. She had decided Bev was just winding her up and told her to stop being paranoid. She wasn't sure what it was about. Bev had mentioned it again today, after she had fed her at noon, trying to make out that Becky was not fit to go home, but no one else agreed with her.

Now Sue and Peter Phillips went to their daughter's cubicle, slid her into the car cot, collected her things and went to the nurses' station to say goodbye.

'Let's hope we're not back in again tomorrow,' said Peter flashing his roguish smile.

Soon they were home, in the semi-detached house in Hawksdale Close, just up the road from the hospital, with the new Audi in the drive outside, and for the rest of that Thursday afternoon, Becky lay asleep, with her twin Katie beside her, the two of them in white cots full of dolls and bears, both of them contented and safe. Beneath her blankets, Becky was warm. Her little belly was full of milk, her blood was rich with sugar and her plum-sized heart pumped steadily, pushing the rich red blood around her body, thumping on, feeding the fuel to her limbs and her nerves and her brain, as if there was nothing strange at all.

When she woke early that evening, Becky cried and she wouldn't feed. Katie was fine, she took her bottle and went back to her cot in the middle of the evening, but Becky cried on alone.

'Oh, God,' thought Sue, 'I'm not going to have to take her back to hospital, am I?'

Becky was doing something funny with her eyes. She kept rolling them right up into her forehead so that all that Sue could see was two white slits, and then they would come back down again. Once, when Peter tried to pick her up, she let out a piercing yelp as if she had been really hurt and then she screamed with all her might so that her whole face was twisted with the effort of it.

Sue didn't want to call the doctor because she was afraid he would send Becky back to hospital, and she had had enough of that. Peter had to walk her up and down for the best part of an hour before she would calm down and even then she wouldn't feed. Eventually he got her to go to sleep, but then the problem was that she was hungry and so she slept only fitfully.

At least she was sleeping. Sue and Peter began to relax; Becky would be better by the morning. Then Sue noticed that Becky's face was twitching in a weird way, as if there were invisible drops of water bouncing into her eyes and cheeks. Sue had never seen her do anything like that before.

'It's like she's having a little fit or something,' she said.

Like it or not, it was time for the GP. Peter called Dr Higgins who came at about 10.30 but, to their relief, he said that Becky's pulse was fine and he was quite sure she was not having fits. There was no need for hospital. He even managed to persuade Becky to drink a little milk from her bottle, and she fell asleep.

'Probably just a touch of colic,' he said.

Grateful for the peace, Sue and Peter laid Becky down in her cot, checked Katie and went off to bed. They slept well, knowing that there was no danger. Soon the whole house was quiet.

Beneath her blankets, Becky was warm, but her belly now was not so full, her blood was not so rich in sugar, and as her heart pumped, filling her limbs and nerves and brain, something else that was strange and foreign spread slowly through her. Her heart, blind to the danger, thumped faithfully on.

It was nearly three hours before the peace was broken. Katie woke, Sue fed her and put her back to sleep, but then Becky woke too and started grizzling. As Sue carried her from her cot, across the landing to her own room, she saw Becky's face in the light and her heart sank as she saw that her eyes were rolling again, and her face was twitching in that same weird way. Her skin was cool.

'Here, Peter, she's not right.'

Sue tried to feed her. Since she'd left the hospital that afternoon, Becky had only had that little drink with the GP and so she must be really hungry by now, but Becky wouldn't feed. It was unusual to get colic in the middle of the night, but Sue popped her up on her shoulder and winded her in case it helped, then Peter sat up and cradled her in his arms and rocked her and cooed to her, until finally she dozed off.

'We'll just lay her down here between us,' said Peter, 'where we can keep an eye on her.'

They turned out the light, Peter rolled over on his front with his arm lying across his baby daughter, and they slept.

For a while, the room was filled with the sounds of night: the breathing of the adults, deep and slow; the rapid panting of the little girl, wheezing slightly; the creak of a floorboard stretching, water running down a pipe, a dog barking somewhere down the road. Something happened. For a moment, or even for a minute, the adults still lay there, still breathing slow, still sleeping deep, but then it reached them, like light in the fog, and Sue woke with a start, instantly rigid with shock, grasping for the words, not finding them, then hearing Peter shout what she was trying to say. 'She's not breathing!' They were up. Crouching on the bed. The light was on. Peter was shouting, 'Oh, God, oh, God' and grabbing the baby and shouting 'Get the phone, get the ambulance' and putting the baby on the floor and trying to breathe into her mouth, and Sue was trying to find the phone and Peter was sobbing now and leaning up from the floor shouting for his daughter Emma 'Help us, Emma. Oh, God. Becky.' Sue dialled 999. 'They're coming,' she said. Peter was still crouched over Becky, blubbering and shaking his head, pulling himself together and breathing into her mouth, slumping back again in tears. Becky just lay there. She was still not breathing. Sue and Peter were both shouting together. 'Get dressed. We got to get dressed. Oh, God. The ambulance. Where's the ambulance? Get Emma. Tell Emma. Where's Katie? Oh, God. Where's that bloody ambulance? What's taking it so long? Get the car. Get in the car.' Sue swept Becky up in her arms. Peter scampered down the stairs, threw himself into the driver's seat and had the engine fired and running by the time Sue and Becky landed in the passenger seat beside him. He skidded out of the drive and hurtled down Hawksdale Close. The hospital was close. Only a minute. Maybe two.

Peter thumped the Audi to a standstill outside the hospital door. He was out. Sue was out, Becky like a rag-doll in her arms. To the door. The door was shut. Find Casualty. Down the side. Running in the dark. Here it is. That's shut, too. Locked. Nobody there. 'Oh, God, for God's sake, open up.' Peter hit the bell and threw himself against the door, hammering it with his fists, sobbing, shouting 'Open the door, open the door,' while Sue stood like a road-side refugee with her baby's body hanging across her arms. The door opened and a nurse appeared like a dream and she must have seen Becky straightaway, because she just grabbed her from Sue's arms and charged back through the door with Sue and Peter running white-faced behind her. The nurse was shouting 'Resus! Resus!' and the whole Casualty area suddenly seemed to be full of doctors and nurses, pouring in from all sides, with bleepers and stethoscopes and trolleys and oxygen cylinders, all swirling into the Resus Room and then they closed the door. Sue and Peter could hear them still shouting to each other 'Defib! Paddles! Bag her! Suction! Stand clear! Everybody clear!'.

Sue and Peter stumbled away, the blue-skinned arms of nurses wrapped around their shoulders, strangers' voices telling them that it would be all right and would they like a cup of tea, and come and sit in here and the doctor will be with you in a minute and it'll be all right, I'm sure they're doing their best. So there they sat with their cups of tea and their well of fear. Peter was still crying but, somehow, Sue knew it would be all right. They'd caught her as soon as she'd stopped breathing and it was lucky they lived so close to the hospital. Once the Crash Team had got her going again, they could get her back to Ward Four and do some tests and find out what on earth was wrong with her. All this illness had got to stop. A sister came in and she said she would try and find out what was happening, and Peter, who had controlled his tears, headed out of the room on her heels.

Down the short corridor, he followed her and into the Resus Room. He was only in there a second and he could barely comprehend what he saw, just a mess of people with their hands on Becky. He noticed that Nanayakkara was in there too, but then the sister saw him and led him out and she didn't say much but when they got back to the little room, Peter burst into tears and told Sue: 'I don't think there's very much they can do.'

Sue knew it would be OK. Peter had a cigarette in his mouth, but he was crying again, so he couldn't suck on it, so he sat down, but he couldn't sit still, so he stumbled out of the door, and off down the corridor and there he saw a young man with a white coat who looked at him and shook his head.

'I am sorry,' he said.

Peter started sobbing and hobbled back to Sue. The sister came in behind him and told her that it was over but by that time, Sue had seen Peter's face and so she already knew, and it was strange, but she didn't feel sad—not right then. What she felt was angry, really, completely angry. In her chair, she raised her fists to the sides of her head and with both of them she gripped her hair and she wrenched at her scalp and threw her head down between her knees and she screamed with fury.

It was just after 3.45 in the morning on Friday 5 April.

The news of Becky Phillips's death flooded out of Casualty and through the corridors of the hospital, carrying with it a foam of rumour and fearful speculation. There were some who said that this proved it. There was something deadly down on Ward Four. They had to close that ward and find out what it was. This was the seventh child to be struck down in less than seven weeks and the third of them to die, and it made no difference that she had gone home for an evening, because she had just spent three days on Ward Four and whatever it was that was doing this to the children had touched her, too. So the ward had to be closed. But there were other voices who said no. After all, Becky Phillips had died at home, hadn't she, so how could that be anything to do with Ward Four? It was just bad luck. That was all.

Dr Nanayakkara was talking to Sue and Peter Phillips. He told them how sorry he was and how strange it was. There would have to be a post-mortem. He asked them to tell him exactly what had happened at home. Sue, who was still iced by anger, told him.

Nanayakkara said he would like to draw some ventricular blood from Becky's heart so that he could do some tests. He was not sure at this stage but it was possible that Becky had been suffering from some kind of infection, and, if that was so, then he was afraid that her twin sister Katie might be at risk as well.

Sue was not going to let that happen. If it was the last thing she did, she would protect Katie. Peter was still babbling with grief and so Sue left him behind, walked quickly out of Casualty to the car park, and drove off through the half-light to find her remaining baby daughter. There was no time to lose. If Katie was in danger, Sue was going to save her, by moving her right now to the one and only place where she could be sure that she would be safe, where nothing could harm her. She would take Katie to Ward Four. Now.

From the moment that Katie Phillips arrived at the hospital, she was surrounded by helpful hands. As far as anyone knew, there was nothing wrong with her. She was only there for tests, but from Casualty, where Sue handed her over to a sister, to Ward Four, where Dr Joshipura admitted her, she was never alone. They put her in the second cubicle, within sight of the nurses' station, with Mr Nosey on the door. There, the hands fluttered all around her. Kind, attentive, caring hands. They took her temperature and her blood pressure, they tested her blood and her urine, they topped her up with vitamins and iron, they fed her antibiotics through a drip, they strapped an apnoea monitor to her abdomen. Once, her eyes rolled, and a doctor's hands were instantly running all over her body, prodding and pushing. Dr Porter's hands came and probed her, carried out a lumbar puncture. It revealed nothing. Then Dr Nanayakkara's hands came and carried out another lumbar puncture. It revealed no more. From time to time, her parents' hands reached down and touched her, just to reassure themselves that she was real, that she was still there. All through the morning, a nurse called Mandy Poole sat with her, until lunch time when Bev Allitt took over. She was never alone. At least, not to begin with.

While Katie lay in the cubicle, her parents drifted through a fog. A nurse gave Peter whisky, to stop him crying. Sue went to see Becky, to say goodbye. They went home and sat, dazed, on the sofa, trying to make sense of what had happened. They drifted back to the hospital, as if they were addicted to the pain it brought them.

A sister asked Sue if she would like to see Becky one more time before she was taken down to the mortuary, where the post-mortem was to be performed. Sue said yes, and the two of them set off from Ward Four and turned off the long central corridor down towards the operating theatres and Casualty, where Becky still lay in a side room, but as they walked, in silence, Sue noticed a figure approaching them from the end of the corridor, a young man with a long stride. She was not sure who it was, but the sister stopped her.

'Would you like to just step in here a moment?' she said, opening the door to a side room off the corridor.

'Why? What's wrong?'

The sister glanced up to the figure who was still approaching, and, at first, Sue didn't see, and the sister was trying to move her into the side room, but then Sue looked again and she understood. It was a porter and he was carrying a basket, a child-sized mortuary basket. He was heading into the Casualty department and as he went he was whistling loudly and beating the rhythm of his song by swinging the basket gaily in his hand.

'Do you want to go on?' the sister asked.

'No,' said Sue. 'Not now I've seen that.'

They sat by Katie's cot, trying to make conversation with Bev who sat there, too. There was nothing to say. Katie lay quietly, oblivious to her own bereavement, surrounded by wires. Peter watched her, barely willing to believe that each new breath was not her last. Suddenly, there was chaos. A shriek of alarm. Nurses ran from all directions. It was her apnoea monitor. Peter was aghast. 'She's stopped breathing.' But she hadn't. It was just that her apnoea monitor had slipped.

Their GP, Dr Higgins, came. He was upset and Sue told him not to be, they knew it wasn't his fault. He had been to the post-mortem and he told them the result. Becky had died of Sudden Infant Death Syndrome, a cot death. Sue told him she didn't believe him.

The truth was that she didn't want to believe him. A cot death was so vague. If Becky had to die, she wanted to know that at least she had a real illness, a real cause. The GP agreed that there was one odd thing—her heart seemed to have been blistered, which was unusual—but the pathologist seemed pretty sure of his conclusion.

Bev was in the cubicle again. She seemed rather stand-offish, but when she heard the result of the post-mortem, she opened up a little.

'I'm ever so sorry about what's happened to Becky,' she told Sue.

Sue nodded. Bev went on: 'But don't worry about Katie. She'll be all right. I'll make sure of it.'

Sue smiled at her. 'You don't have to say sorry. It's nobody's fault. You can't do anything about a cot death.'

Around 3.00 on that Friday afternoon, Sue and Peter went home for a while. They had to think about a funeral for Becky. Katie lay in her cot. She was asleep and now, at last, she was alone. With a stranger's hands.

Quietly now, like a film in slow motion, the crisis breaks. It is Bev who spots the trouble and calls across that Katie has gone blue, and it is Betty Asher who contemplates the nightmare and has to tell a student nurse to call the Crash Team—yet another 222—and then Betty runs, as fast as she can manage, and makes it to the cubicle and somehow has a moment in her mind to question why Katie's cot is twisted all across the room at such a funny angle before she hears Bev's voice again saying 'Cardiac arrest, Betty.' Now, the oxygen tap won't work, and Mandy Poole comes and she and Bev pick Katie up and slip the plastic Ambubag across her tiny mouth and as they squeeze the first few drops of air between her lips, the Ambubag collapses in their hands, just falls to bits, and they have to carry Katie to the Treatment Room and work with oxygen and desperation—Betty and Bev and Mandy together—and when Katie starts to breathe again, it feels like a miracle.

Now, more than ever, Katie could not be alone. There were not enough nurses on the ward, so Jean Savill, the night sister, came in early and sat with Katie. She seemed very concerned. Even when Bev Allitt offered to relieve her several times, she refused and stayed sitting by the baby girl's cot. Dr Porter came and did his best to diagnose the problem. He ordered an X-ray of her chest and thought perhaps the trouble had been caused by vomiting and choking. Someone called the Phillips at home and told Peter that there was nothing to worry about, but Katie had been having trouble breathing. Very fast, he went back to the ward. Sue followed. All that night, Sue slept in the cubicle, right by Katie's side. Peter slept in the parents' room, although he hardly slept at all and kept padding down the corridor to make sure that Katie was still breathing. All next day, Saturday 6 April, they stayed by her side. Never mind the business. Never mind anything. Just stay here and watch Katie, try to see what's going wrong. Somehow fix this thing. Full of fear that she would die, they arranged for her to be baptized. The hospital chaplain, Ian Shelton, came with his silver bowl and his holy water and baptized her Katie Sue Phillips and he said some prayers, and Sue said them with him. Then afterwards, she told him that she didn't think much of his God that he believed in, and he told her that he knew what she meant. That Saturday night, Sue stayed with Katie again and Jean Savill, the night sister, who had four wards to look after, came and sat with her again. She, too, seemed determined that Katie must never be alone.

But by Sunday morning, Dr Nanayakkara said that Katie was so well that she could come off most of her electronic monitors.

They would keep the apnoea there, just as a precaution, but he could not see any cause for alarm. Indeed, he thought, she could probably go home in a day or two. Peter and Sue relaxed and on Sunday afternoon, at about 3.30, they felt so much better about Katie, so sure that she was in safe hands that they went off together to the canteen.

Katie was alone again. A minute passed. Maybe two. There were hands near her again. She was crying.

Bev Allitt picked her up. At the nurses' station, Lynn Vowles heard the cry and looked. Bev was holding Katie, beckoning with one finger, hooking in the air. Lynn thought that maybe she might need a dummy. So she stopped to look for one. Katie was still crying. Lynn just couldn't find the dummy anywhere and Bev was still beckoning to her and so Lynn went and as soon as she got to the cubicle door, she saw that Katie's face was a terrible red.

The two nurses raced through the ward to the Treatment Room. She had no pulse. Lynn Vowles tapped her firmly on the chest with one finger, trying to trick her heart back into life. Bev Allitt poured oxygen down her throat. The Crash Team came, Dr Nanayakkara came. They needed more equipment. They had no staff to fetch it. The chaplain was there, trying to comfort Sue and Peter. They sent him running round the hospital to fetch the equipment for them. Nanayakkara was afraid he was losing the child. Her heart was struggling and now both her lungs were leaking air. He guessed this was from the force of the ventilator pushing oxygen into her chest. He started fitting drains to both sides of her chest, a complex and most demanding job. For 40 minutes, they worked on her, but she had faded. All of the monitors that were hooked into her body told the same story on their electronic dials. Katie had no life in her. She had succumbed, like her sister before her.

Outside the Treatment Room, Sue and Peter Phillips waited for news. Inside, the doctors and the nurses stopped their work, and pulled off gloves and put down tools and sighed.

Someone said: 'Right. So, who's going to go out and tell those people that they've lost another daughter?'

No one answered.

Katie lay breathless and still on the table. A monitor blinked.

Every eye in the room turned down to the baby's body. The monitor blinked again. She'd brought herself back. She was alive again. The Treatment Room exploded in activity.

At 4.30, Dr Nanayakkara went to telephone Nottingham City Hospital, where Katie had been born, to ask if she could be transferred there. Lynn Vowles and Bev Allitt were looking after Katie in the Treatment Room. There was an accident; Bev sprayed an ampoule of medicine into Lynn's eyes and she had to run out to a sink in the six-bedroom area. Five minutes later, Katie broke into a rapid series of fits, turned deep blue and then stopped breathing. Her body was rigid. Bev Allitt gave her oxygen. Dr Nanayakkara raced back to her.

Now, Katie's life was ebbing away again. There was nothing they could do for her on Ward Four. All that mattered was to get her to Nottingham as fast as possible. Nanayakkara called for the Flying Squad, a high-speed ambulance with a police escort and, minutes later, Katie was wrapped into a space blanket and strapped into the back of an ambulance which screamed through the outskirts of Grantham and burst out on to the Barrowby High Road with one police car slashing through the traffic in front of it, and another bringing up the rear, all of them with sirens wailing and lights flashing, as they careered on to the A52 for Nottingham with Katie cradled in the back.

With Sue beside him in the Audi, Peter Phillips tried to catch them and he reckoned they touched 140 miles an hour as they swooped along the A52 but he never got close and, even though he covered the 25 miles to City Hospital in only 17 minutes, by the time he slid to a halt in the hospital car park, Katie was already out of the ambulance and being strapped into a life support machine on the children's ward.

In a brown manila file, tucked in amongst the nursing notes and fluid charts that traced the history of Katie's stay on Ward Four, there lay an X-ray.

It had been taken on Friday afternoon, when Dr Porter was examining Katie in the Treatment Room after her first arrest. It showed all the detail of the inside of Katie's upper torso: her lungs with their dark clouds, her ribs like devil horns, a foggy swirl of heart and vein.

The doctors had looked at it already when Katie was still lying in the Treatment Room and they had seen nothing to help them in their diagnosis. But they were tired and they were busy and they were only ordinary doctors.

They never saw the wrinkled lines that spread through Katie's ribs like cobwebs. They should not have been there. They were fracture lines. Katie's ribs had been broken, splintered at the front and back. Even though her nine-week-old bones were as soft and spongy as plastic, someone had squeezed them so hard that they had snapped. It was a clue. But no one saw it.

The clue was hard to see. Ordinary doctors might easily miss it. A specialist might do better. But, in spite of all the bureaucratic safety nets and all the procedures which were designed to ensure the discovery of all the elusive little clues which were hidden in the shadows of an X-ray, no specialist was shown it. The clue remained unseen.

Two hundred miles away in the University Hospital of Wales in Cardiff, a small perspex bottle containing the blood of Paul Crampton lay in a refrigerator in the biochemistry lab. This was the bottle that contained the chemical key to the mystery on Ward Four.

After spending five days lying in the path lab at Grantham, it had been dispatched to Cardiff by ordinary road link instead of an emergency courier and so it had taken two more full days to make the journey. It had arrived in Cardiff finally on Thursday 4 April—on the day that Becky Phillips was discharged from hospital, apparently healthy and well—exactly a week after it had been taken from Paul's groin and sent for urgent analysis.

The lab at Cardiff had the capacity to test an urgent sample immediately and to produce a result on the same day. But by the time that Paul Crampton's blood sample reached them, the idea of its being urgent had been lost somewhere along the route. Nobody told them that there was anything unusual or important about it. Nobody called them at all. So, they put it into storage in the lab refrigerator to wait its turn in the long queue of samples awaiting routine analysis. It might wait a week or even ten days before its turn came round.

And so, as the Crash Team clattered blindly through Ward

Four, the little perspex bottle lay in the fridge, undisturbed and unseen.

On Ward Four, life chugged on as usual.

5

Six and a half weeks now had passed since Joanne Taylor had carried her baby son Liam into Ward Four to cure his heavy cold. In that time, eight different children on the ward had suffered a total of 14 respiratory or cardiac arrests, an average of one arrest every three days. The Crash Team, who normally would expect to visit the ward only once or twice a year, had been called in on ten occasions. Three children—Kayley Desmond, Paul Crampton and Henry Chan—appeared to have recovered; two—Brad Gibson and Katie Phillips—were still suffering, and three children—Liam Taylor, Tim Hardwick and Becky Phillips—were now dead.

The hospital was boiling with talk about the trouble on the ward. But the more they talked, the less they seemed to do. All kinds of people—from cleaners to consultants—were wondering about it, but all of their anxiety and speculation simply fought its way to the surface and then disappeared in tiny bursts of hot air.

Some of those who worried were too far from the ward to make a difference. Brad Gibson's GP, Dr Sarah Parker, was dumbfounded to hear that the boy she had sent to hospital so that he could take his antibiotics on a drip had had a heart attack and died for 32 minutes. The path lab technicians could make no sense of the strange test results they had been getting from Ward Four, although they had still not alerted the Control of Infection officer. Jenny Starling, the physiotherapist who had visited Liam Taylor on his last night to clear mucous from his tubes, could not believe that the same baby had died only an hour later. In Nottingham, the registrars were swapping theories about the puzzling cases they were getting from Grantham, but their ideas were never relayed to the doctors on Ward Four—even their belief that Brad Gibson must have been given the wrong drug never bridged the gap between the regional powerhouse of Queen's Med and the doctor whose patient he had been. Dr Porter still thought Brad had been struck down by asthma.

Others were stymied by procedure. Members of the Crash Team, for example, who had seen the crisis at first hand, were particularly worried. But the Crash Team was not a permanent group; it simply consisted of the half-dozen senior nurses and junior doctors who were carrying the cardiac arrest bleepers on any shift. There was no permanent team who could collate all the information from the ten 222s and try to draw conclusions. There was, however, a procedure. After every 222, staff had to fill out a Resus Report to record all the details of the incident. The reports were passed to a clinical services manager who presented them to the monthly meetings of the Resus Committee, a group of four specialists who met in order to review the work of the Crash Team, to collate all the information on the latest arrests, to spot shortages of equipment, to learn lessons. This committee, however, was out of action.

Its chairman, a physician named Alan Henderson, had left the hospital. His vacant post had become tangled up in the cost-cutting surrounding the new link with Newark and, a year later, he had still not been replaced. So the committee which he had chaired was out of action, and the Resus Reports from Ward Four gathered dust in a drawer in the clinical service manager's office.

There was a similar problem in the mortuary. The consultant pathologist who was responsible for carrying out post-mortems, Dr Spencer, had suffered a heart attack and died just before Christmas the previous year. The business of replacing him had then been sucked into a bureaucratic vacuum which frequently swallowed consultants' posts when they fell vacant. They could not be filled without the approval of one of the Royal Colleges. In this case, the hospital contacted the Royal College of Pathologists, who then hired an expert to review the terms and demands of the job; the expert did his work and reported back to the College, who then considered his work and reported back to the hospital. The vacancy was lost somewhere in this bureaucratic pipeline. Even when the Royal College had finished, the hospital would not be able to start hiring. According to procedure, a consultant could be hired only by the Regional Health Authority, so the hospital then had to contact the Region with the job specification; the Region had to advertise in the medical press, liaise with the hospital, set up interviews, and finally choose their new pathologist. More months would pass. It could take two years to fill the post. The result was that all of the post-mortems in Grantham Hospital at this time were being carried out by Dr Terry Marshall, a 'locum' consultant, who might be fully qualified on paper but who had no experience of the established pattern of death on the children's ward.

On Ward Four, where staff were protected by neither distance nor procedure, there was a grim game of blind man's buff in which nurses and doctors seemed to have their eyes bandaged into the darkness by fear or complacency or fatigue or sheer confusion, so that they stumbled from one crisis to another, fumbling clumsily to identify the cause before crashing on through the dark, grabbing at another half-discovered explanation, rejecting it, and staggering on.

There was no explanation. Some of the staff still claimed to believe that this was nothing more than a run of bad luck, and they clung to their theory like a haunted child hugging its pillow in the night. But most of them admitted there had to be a cause. There was a virus in the town. There was an infection on the ward. There was something that no one could see, that no one could understand. But it killed children. It could be anything. Maybe it was something the children were eating or drinking, or something they were touching. It happened when they were sleeping. It happened when they were alone. It was in the plumbing, or in the ventilation ducts, or in a bad batch of drugs. All the commonplace dullness of Ward Four was suddenly full of danger. It could be anywhere. Some of the nurses were so frantic to find the enemy that they began to blame themselves. They thought they must be carrying some kind of plague. Here they were— nurses, who had spent years of their life just caring for children, and now the children were dying in their arms. The nurses needed help. The doctors could not solve the mystery any more than the chaplain could, running round the ward with his crucifix and his holy water. They turned to their managers.

They asked for more staff, for more equipment, they asked for swabs and tests. They got nothing. Their night sister, Jean Savill, tried to help. She had never been afraid to fight. She was always asking for more staff. Just recently, she had stood up and insisted that the lone night porter be given a bicycle so that he could cover the hospital more quickly. The management had refused, so she had bought him one herself. But now she went further. This was not just about a hospital being tight with its funding, this was about innocent children and helpless nurses who felt trapped and abandoned. Jean Savill was feeling it herself. She was on the ward regularly filling holes in the rota. She had seen Brad Gibson drained of life. She had watched Katie Phillips being dragged back from the brink. She told Sister Barker that she had got to the point where she was afraid to pick up a child in case it stopped breathing. So now, although she was technically a member of the management herself, Jean Savill changed sides. She went to the hospital unions to help them fight for Ward Four, and then she sat down and wrote a letter to Moira Onions.

'Once again, I find it necessary to express my concern about the staffing levels on Ward Four during the period of night duty,' she wrote. She explained that the remedies which had been offered before were no good. They could not call in bank nurses in the middle of the night when there was a sudden emergency. A single trained nurse alone at night was being faced with an impossible choice when a child collapsed: whether to leave the child and fetch help, or stay with the child and risk disaster. 'I am sure you can appreciate the dilemma this poses for the staff and the emotional stress this causes. There have been seven cardiac arrests on Ward Four during the last three months.'

Staffing was not the only problem, she said. The defibrillator had to be brought from Casualty, which meant that the porter had to be found and sent on his way, while vital minutes were lost. The ward's own resuscitation equipment was inadequate. 'It does not comply with minimum recommended standards for safe practice,' she added.

She pulled no punches in her conclusion. 'As the night duty manager, I feel very distressed about the situation on Ward Four and I feel most strongly that being professionally accountable for these children in our care, I must voice my concern in the sincere hope that an early solution may be implemented before a tragedy occurs.'

Sister Savill sent her letter to Moira Onions and to both the consultants and to the hospital manager, Martin Gibson. Moira Onions relayed a copy to Hannah Newton in Boston. But the letters disappeared into the darkness.

They did provoke a little activity. Miss Newton came to Grantham and met Mrs Onions. They both met the deputy manager, Peter Flood. He tried to find some spare nurses from adult wards to work with them temporarily. He managed to get them some child-sized paddles. But there was no defibrillator—that would cost £6,000 and they didn't have £6,000 to spare—and there were no permanent extra staff. There was no answer to Sister Savill's cry for help.

Sister Savill felt that she had stepped out of line and made herself some enemies. In private, some of the managers started to wonder out loud about her. She was rather tense, they said, a worrier. She seemed to exaggerate things, especially where death was concerned. She was definitely odd about death, they said. She was always volunteering to sit with the terminal cases and she had applied to be a Macmillan nurse, specialising in the care of the terminally ill. If one of the Macmillan nurses was on holiday, she would come in during the day to take on her work. The management were not sure what to make of her concern about Ward Four, and they said they would see what they could do. The best they could offer while they made up their mind was the prospect of a bereavement officer whom they were planning to appoint to look after the relatives of those who died in the hospital.

Without extra staff, Moira Onions had to turn to the British Nursing Agency to ask for casual nurses to help out on Ward Four, but their response was not what she had expected

'Would you take one of your own?' they asked her.

It took her a moment to realize what they were saying—that one of her own Ward Four staff was moonlighting with the BNA. She asked who it was, but they refused to tell her. Moira Onions said she would not take anyone who was working their nights or days off as well as their full shifts on Ward Four—they would be too tired—and she went and asked Sister Barker who this person was. She said she didn't know.

Ward Four staggered on. Then another child suffered a heart attack.

A six-year-old boy called Michael Davidson had been brought

in on the Sunday that Katie Phillips was transferred to Nottingham, 7 April. He needed minor surgery to remove an airgun pellet from his chest, just below the sternum. He had been shot by accident; his uncle had heard a prowler and used his airgun to scare him away and then left the weapon lying around loaded on the pool table, where a lodger had picked it up and accidentally triggered it in young Michael's direction. The boy had lost a little blood but they had operated as soon as he had arrived on Sunday afternoon and he had been recovering well, at least until this Tuesday afternoon, 9 April.

A junior doctor from a surgical ward, Karen Bradshaw, who was looking after Michael, was transferring his I/V drip from his left arm to his right. She had punctured his skin with the point of the cannula and she was just starting to inject antibiotics through its open end when Michael went rigid and stopped breathing, quite suddenly and dramatically. His face was black blue and his back was arched stiff, clear off the bed. Dr Nanayakkara came running and pumped his chest and by the time the Crash Team arrived, Michael was breathing again. Everyone on the ward said that it was a most unusual incident. But Dr Nanayakkara had an explanation.

He decided that the boy had been so terrified of the needle going into his skin that he had hyperventilated and gone into a carpopaedal spasm, a kind of fit where the patient's hands curl up into claw shapes. In other words, Michael had literally almost been frightened to death. Dr Bradshaw disagreed. Michael had already had five injections in the last 48 hours and, although he had grizzled a fair bit, he had shown no sign of terror. More than that, she had been with the boy when it happened: he had not been hyperventilating at all and he had certainly not been hyperventilating long enough to go into a carpopaedal spasm. Dr Nanayakkara showed no signs of changing his mind. But when he saw the results of Michael's blood tests, he was forced to. His calcium level was rock-solid normal. If he had been hyperventilating, it would have fallen fast. But the commotion was passed now, Michael was back on the road to recovery, and there was obviously no link to any of the other incidents.

Still it caused a bit more of a commotion on the ward the next day, when Michael Davidson's mother, Fay, a forceful woman, cornered a doctor and demanded an explanation for her son's sudden illness. She complained that she had been told that he had suffered a convulsion which had been brought on by his fear of needles, but she'd never known him to be afraid of needles and overnight she had talked to a friend of hers who was a nurse who had told her that it sounded more like a cardiac arrest.

'I want to know the truth,' she demanded. 'Did Michael have a cardiac arrest?'

'Well, to be honest,' she was told, 'yes, he did. He had a brief cardiac arrest, and he did stop breathing.'

'Well, why on earth didn't you tell me?'

The doctor said that they had not wanted to frighten her, some parents found it hard to cope with that sort of information.

'Well I'd rather be told the truth than find out by beating about the bush.'

And with that Mrs Davidson had let the doctor go, wondering out loud to herself why doctors kept secrets from parents and whether they really expected her to believe all that stuff about Michael being afraid of needles.

The two consultants, Dr Porter and Dr Nanayakkara, at last were confronting the mystery. But they could not explain it. Instead, they played like a pair of pantomime dames beseeching their audience to tell them where the trouble was. The answer was screaming at them. The consultants flounced their dresses and swore they could not see it. The answer came screaming back again—the boy who died of epilepsy when he wasn't having a fit, the baby who had a heart attack when there was nothing wrong with his heart, the air bubbles in a little girl's armpit, the baby with the broken ribs. But the two old dames looked slowly around them and insisted there was nothing there. What about the blood samples scattered in a bureaucratic swamp? No, said the consultants, they couldn't see the trouble.

Jean Savill spoke to Dr Porter about the problem and he agreed to check his notes to see if he could find any common factor. Moira Onions spoke to both consultants and to Sister Barker. None of them agreed to do anything to tackle the problem. They wondered whether perhaps they should stop taking new patients for a while—Moira Onions had had to stop admissions to the ward twice in the last few weeks because they were so short of staff—but they decided not to.

The two consultants were still trapped in their unhappy marriage. They met at the weekly doctors' meetings, at the monthly paediatric divisional meetings; they met on the ward and in the corridors of the hospital; but they never sat down together to solve the mystery. Each man reacted alone. Dr Nanayakkara had never told Dr Porter of his experience with Tim Hardwick or Kayley Desmond. Dr Porter had never told Dr Nanayakkara about Brad Gibson or Henry Chan. Dr Porter was not sure that there was any connection at all between the incidents, although he was beginning to wonder. Dr Nanayakkara was convinced that there was a simple medical explanation and swept from one angry clash to another in his efforts to make the point.

He had a row with the surgeons who had operated on Michael Davidson. When he called them to say that he couldn't understand what had happened to the boy, one of them told him he was over-reacting.

'Do you really mean this?' asked Nanayakkara, his pride ruffled. 'In that case, don't send your bloody patients here.'

He had received his copy of Jean Savill's cry for help, and he had taken it as a personal attack. Why was she writing to managers without asking him first? Was she saying it was his fault that there was a lack of equipment on the ward? He complained to her most bitterly and mentioned it to the hospital manager as well.

He continued to argue with Dr Porter about the diagnosis of children on the ward. During Katie Phillips's brief and traumatic stay on Ward Four, he had noticed that Dr Porter had written in her notes that her twin sister, Becky, might have died of meningitis. Dr Nanayakkara said nothing to Dr Porter but scribbled two question marks on Porter's notes and wrote a firm 'no' against his opinion. He also continued his struggle with the locum pathologist, Terry Marshall.

His partial victory after the death of Liam Taylor, in persuading Marshall to send Liam's tissue samples for a second opinion, had yielded no clues. In fact, Nanayakkara had heard nothing. He assumed that Liam's samples were being analysed elsewhere and that the mystery would soon be solved. Five weeks passed. No result came through. So Nanayakkara started to put some pressure

on the pathologist and on Wednesday 10 April, he finally received
a copy of Marshall's full report to the coroner on Liam's death.

Dr Nanayakkara was shocked to discover that the report did
not even mention Liam's blood and tissue. If they had been sent
off, there was no sign of any result. As far as Nanayakkara could
see, the entire mystery of Liam's heart attack had been shelved.
If anything, the mystery was made deeper. In his full report, the
pathologist suggested for the first time that Liam's heart had been
dying over a period of 48 hours before his death. Nanayakkara
was sure that that was not right. He had been dealing with the
child all through those 48 hours. And Nanayakkara's frustration
turned to anger when he saw that the report was dated 28 February—it had taken Marshall six weeks to send it to him. Nanayakkara was furious. He wanted to protest in the strongest terms
to the pathologist. But he couldn't. Dr Marshall had ended his
temporary stay at Grantham Hospital on the day that he finally
sent Nanayakkara his report. He was going off to a new job—in
Australia.

Even as Marshall packed to leave, Nanayakkara was pursuing
him. This time, the quarrel was over Becky Phillips. Nanayakkara
had received a series of phone calls from Nottingham, from Terence Stephenson, the young consultant who had worried over
Brad Gibson's collapse, who was now trying to make sense of the
series of arrests suffered by Becky's twin, Katie. Stephenson was
groping for an answer. It was reasonable to assume that the two
twins had been struck by a common problem. But what? He told
Nanayakkara that there was no sign of any infection. There was
no evidence of any inherited disease. But whatever the answer
was, it was clear that the explanation of cot death which had been
offered for the death of Becky was inadequate as an explanation
for Katie's suffering. Stephenson told Nanayakkara that they must
do more tests. Nanayakkara took a bold decision: he would try
and stall Becky's funeral, which was due to take place the next
day, to allow for a second post-mortem.

That afternoon, Wednesday 10 April, in the central corridor of
the hospital, he bumped into Peter and Sue Phillips who were
visiting staff on Ward Four to thank them for their help with
Katie. He beckoned them into the nearest private room, which

happened to be the hospital chapel. The chaplain, Ian Shelton, hovered as they spoke.

'I'm glad I've caught you,' Nanayakkara said. 'I want a word. I think you are going to have to put off the funeral.'

Peter and Sue protested. Everything was arranged and they wanted to have their mourning.

'Do you want to help Katie?'

'Of course. We'll do anything to help Katie. Anything at all.'

Nanayakkara said he would call the funeral director and ask him to delay the funeral. In the meantime, he would arrange for a paediatric pathologist at Queen's Med to perform a second post-mortem.

Bewildered and upset, Sue and Peter Phillips went home and spent the next 24 hours ducking a cross-fire of phone calls. The funeral director said he had never come across such a request in all his years in the business. Nanayakkara would not say exactly why he wanted this second opinion. Eventually, Nanayakkara emerged with another compromise: the funeral would go ahead as planned on Thursday afternoon, but Becky's brain, liver, lymph nodes, gut mesentry, trachea, thymus and ventricular blood would all be held back and sent to Queen's Med.

Terry Marshall flew to Australia.

For all his doubts about some of his colleagues, Nanayakkara still held fast to his view that these children were suffering from an assortment of identifiable medical problems and that there was no underlying problem on the ward. A consultant anaesthetist, Jean Breckenridge, tried to bridge the gap between Ward Four and the Crash Team, for which she was nominally responsible, by going to see Nanayakkara and by writing him a letter, expressing concern about the soaring number of arrests. Nanayakkara wrote back to assure her that all was under control.

Finally, on the afternoon of Friday April 12, the answer was bellowed out once more, and this time, one of the pantomime dames began to listen.

The warning now came in a phone call from the chief medical laboratory scientific officer at the Department of Medical Bio-chemistry at the University of Wales in Cardiff. His name was Robert Henley, and, at 5.30 that Friday afternoon, he called the Grantham Hospital path lab, found there was no one in and asked to be connected to Dr Nelson Porter on Ward Four. This was not normal procedure. But after eight days in the queue, Paul Crampton's blood sample had finally been tested that day and Henley realized that it would not be good enough simply to put the result in the post in the usual way.

When Dr Porter came to the phone, Henley told him that he now had the results of the insulin test on the blood which had been taken from Paul Crampton's groin 15 days earlier on 28 March, and the short answer was that the insulin content was so high that they could not measure it accurately. All he knew was that the insulin level was more than 500 milliunits per litre. The normal, healthy level was 15. So Paul Crampton's blood contained more than 30 times the normal level of insulin, possibly even more. And that was not all.

Henley's department had conducted a second test, to measure the level of C-peptide in Paul Crampton's blood. C-peptide is produced by the pancreas at the same time and at the same rate as it produces insulin. If this huge quantity of insulin in Paul's blood had been produced by some malfunction in his pancreas, the C-peptide would have soared to an equally high level, indicating that his pancreas was terribly flawed. But, if the C-peptide was low, it meant that this flood of insulin could not have been produced by Paul; it would have to have come from outside him. Robert Henley told Dr Porter that the C-peptide level was 0.16 millimols per litre. That was low.

Henley asked whether Paul was being treated with insulin. No, said Dr Porter. Henley expressed his concern. Dr Porter dismissed him. The result must be wrong, he said: there must have been a lab error. For Henley, it was a familiar reaction. If ever a doctor got a result he didn't expect, he blamed the lab. Henley politely agreed that an error was always possible but, at the very least, they should find another sample of this baby's blood and check the test. Dr Porter tutted and sighed and finally agreed that he would call Queen's Med and ask them to send one of their samples of Paul's blood to Cardiff so that they could be put through the same tests. Henley thanked him.

Porter called Queen's Med and spoke to Vibart Noble there, who said he would arrange everything. The two doctors discussed the result. A lab error was always possible. But by the time their conversation was ended, the two doctors had agreed that on the face of it, the meaning of Robert Henley's news was clear. Somehow, someone had injected Paul Crampton with a very large amount of insulin.

The pantomime shout was louder than ever. 'There's a killer on the ward'.

Dr Porter was not sure. Everyone who ever dealt with Nelson Porter agreed that he was an intelligent man, highly intelligent some of them said. But his mind seemed to move like a bat in flight, darting from one idea to another, flitting and diving, fluttering forward then hurtling sideways as if to escape some unseen obstacle, and almost always in the dark. And so, although everyone always agreed that he had great intelligence, they often added that he was perhaps a little pedantic, that he lacked common sense.

But it was coming clear now. Paul Crampton had been injected with insulin. That was the clear implication of this result. Porter could see that. That was certain. Undeniable. But how had this injection come about? Surely not a deliberate act.

Could it have been an accident? Unlikely. The insulin was kept in the fridge, and the fridge was locked. It was not as if it was just left lying around in the same box as the antibiotics. It must have been deliberate. But no, there must be another explanation, some other way out.

Could it have been a contaminated batch of drugs? Possibly, possibly that was it. But no, that did not fit. Paul Crampton's drugs had changed completely from the weekend of his first two attacks, when Dr Nanayakkara had taken over, to the Thursday of his third attack, when Porter himself had been in charge again. There was no one drug that he had taken before all three incidents. There must be another explanation.

Dr Porter was not sure. On the face of it, this might be evidence that there was a poisoner on the ward. But what should he do? He would have to tell someone. That was obvious. Dr Nanayakkara would have to know. And Moira Onions, too. And Sister Barker—no, Sister Barker had finally gone on holiday—he would have to tell Margaret Geeson instead. She was acting sister. She would have to know, too. But what could he tell them? What should they do?

He could ask an outside expert—perhaps someone from

Queen's Med—to come to the ward as a matter of urgency to help solve the problem. He could organize urgent tests to check for poison in the blood of any child who now suffered an arrest. He could try and find blood samples for children who already had suffered arrests and test them—perhaps he should have done that already, especially as Katie Phillips had been given a BM stick on her first night which showed her blood sugar to be down on the floor, at only 1.7. But Dr Porter did none of these things.

He could contact Paul Crampton's father. After all, he had promised him repeatedly that he would tell him the results of this blood test. He could call all the Ward Four doctors together for an emergency meeting to pool their thoughts. He could contact all ward staff and hold a meeting to discuss events, to come up with a plan, at the very least to warn them all. But he did none of this.

He could go straight to the general manager of the hospital, Martin Gibson, and ask him to close the ward until they sorted this out—there seemed to be something very dangerous happening on Ward Four. Whether it was malice or mix-up, it was certainly dangerous. The general manager might decide to contact GPs to ask them not to send children to this place, or even call a press conference to alert the public, who paid for the hospital and who trusted and used it and continued to send their children there. If it was true, as the evidence now suggested, that there might be a killer on the ward, Martin Gibson could call in the police. Indeed Dr Porter could simply go straight to the police himself and tell them that he had reason to believe a serious crime might have been committed.

All of these moves were possible. But Dr Nelson Porter made none of them. He would have to tell Dr Nanayakkara and Moira Onions and Margaret Geeson. But he would tell them to do nothing. He would tell them to say nothing. After all, it might just be a lab error.

So Dr Porter solved his problem and went home.

It was the next day, Saturday afternoon, 13 April. Sitting in cubicle number two, with Mr Nosey on the door, Belinda King could hear a commotion. She tried not to look concerned, to concentrate instead on comforting her baby Christopher, who was feeding badly, and on talking to her parents, who had come to visit.

Belinda King was used to hearing commotions on wards. She was a nurse herself and had been for eight years. For the last five years, she had worked in this same hospital, down the corridor in the Casualty department and then in the fracture clinic.

She had only been on Ward Four for 48 hours—since Christopher's coughing and vomiting had got so bad on Thursday—and she knew that nurses were notoriously hard to nurse, always asking too many questions, thinking they knew best, but even so, she was surprised to discover the way they ran things here. It was not at all what she had expected. The truth was that she felt that this was a rotten place.

There were simple, silly little things that annoyed her. None of the nurses ever told her their names, or bothered to tell her anything about Christopher. And they had all these ridiculous rules. Like with the television in the play area—only children could watch it. Even if the play area was empty, parents were not allowed to sit there. Or about cups of tea: Belinda was allowed to use the ward kitchen to make one cup—and only one cup—of tea per day; if she wanted a second cup, she had to leave Christopher and traipse all the way up to the canteen to get it; her husband, John, was banned from making any cups of tea at all, because he was not a resident; and wherever they managed to find their tea, neither of them was allowed to take a cup of anything at all into Christopher's cubicle. They had to stand in the corridor to drink. They were only silly little rules, but, as a nurse at the same hospital, Belinda King found them all pointless. They all added up to the conclusion that as a parent, she was getting no support.

There were more important things, too. Perhaps it was just that she was over-anxious but she felt that the nurses were not really interested in Christopher. One of the other parents had told her that Christopher had been left crying for ages on Thursday night when she was at home. Belinda had complained and they had told her it wasn't true. Then she had been very put out when she heard an auxiliary talking to a nurse who was coming on duty, telling her: 'You can take your pick of this lot. They're all whingers.' On Friday night, Christopher had been grizzling for a bottle and the Chinese staff nurse, Catherine Morris, had said he couldn't have one because he had just been sick; Belinda had insisted that if he was hungry he must be fed and she had ended up having a furious row about it. Then, when she had complained that Christopher was not getting enough care, they had tried to tell her that she was just suffering from post-natal depression, which might even have been true but it didn't change the fact that Christopher was only five weeks old and he had spent most of his short life coughing and throwing up. On Friday morning, he had choked so badly that they had had to give him oxygen.

Today, Saturday, Belinda's parents had arrived on the ward to visit her and after sitting with her for an hour or so, her mother had turned to her and said 'Do the children here cry all the time?'

They did, and no one ever seemed to cuddle them. So far as Belinda could see, on Ward Four, there was not enough experience and not enough warmth. She was sure they did better in Casualty.

The commotion outside on the ward was getting louder. It was coming from the cubicle next door, the one nearest the nurses' station, with Mr Funny on the door. Belinda's mother obviously could not understand it, but Belinda knew exactly what was happening: the sudden flutter of panic, the wheels of the Resus trolley hurtling across the ward floor, the muffled urgencies of the Crash Team at work. Someone was having an arrest. Belinda was about to explain to her mother, when they heard a sound which made that unnecessary.

It was a terrible wailing cry which filled the air and smothered every other sound and slowly formed itself into one long word. 'No!'

Belinda saw her mother's face drop. 'Someone's having an arrest,' she told her and got up to close the cubicle door. 'It'll be all right. The Crash Team's there.'

The woman's voice leaked through the flimsy wall again, repeating one plea: 'You've got to bring him back . . . You've got to bring him back.'

This chorus which haunted the ears of Belinda King and her parents was coming from Creswen Peasgood. In the cubicle next door to Belinda King, Creswen was standing now at the end of her baby son's cot, gripping the bars and pleading for his life.

Creswen was a tough woman. She often looked as though she

had just woken up from a bad night on a strange floor: a voice full of old smoke, tangled hair, eyes bruised with tiredness. She was rough and usually ready for a fight and, at the first sign of trouble, she'd let fly with a volley of curses. But like a lot of fighters, she had been beaten up inside and, in a life full of blows and bitter disappointments, the worst thing that had ever happened to her was coming back to haunt her.

Eighteen months ago, her baby daughter Michelle had died in her cot. She had been Creswen's only pleasure. She had been born after an apparently endless series of failed pregnancies, which had taken Creswen through nine miscarriages. Then, one cold night in November 1989, Michelle had died in her cot. And Creswen had carried her from her home to the back of the ambulance on a futile ride to hospital, and all the way she had stared down at her Michelle, blue with death and all limp. It had been the end of everything for her. Nothing that had happened to her before— being given up for adoption by her own parents, busting up two marriages, living on the dole in a dead-end estate—nothing had ever hurt so much. Her only consolation had come this February when, after nine months lying in a cradle of drugs, she had succeeded in delivering a new baby, her son, Chris. And now she stood here, at the end of her eight-week-old son's cot, and she looked down at him and all she could see was Michelle's face, just the same, the same colour, the same limp body, the same terror in Creswen's heart. So she sobbed to the doctors, quieter now. 'You've got to bring him back, you've got to bring him back.'

The doctors carried Chris to the Treatment Room. Some nurses led Creswen away, and one of them took her quietly down to the parents' room and sat with her arm around her and told her not to worry.

'He's in the best place, here,' the nurse said.

Creswen refused to be calmed. She didn't understand what was happening. Her GP had only sent Chris to hospital to reassure her, because she was so cut up about Michelle. He hadn't been very ill, just chesty, and he'd looked fine half an hour ago when she'd gone out and found a nurse and asked her to come and feed him. It was a stocky girl called Bev. And she must have thought Chris was all right, because she had told Creswen to go off and have a smoke.

Creswen paced and smoked and swapped nightmares with her mother. Eventually, they let her back to the Treatment Room where, for a while, it appeared that Chris was going to be all right. The doctors said they thought he had choked milk into his lungs, although the physiotherapist said she had checked his mucous and there was no milk in it at all. In any event, Chris had started breathing again and his colour had returned, but Creswen listened gloomily as she was told that there was no explanation for the problem and they could not be sure that he would be all right. The nurses suggested that the chaplain should come and give him an emergency christening.

Creswen slumped down on a chair in the play area with her husband Mick, and her mother, blank with shock, trying to understand, and while they sat there they heard the monitors starting to shriek in panic and the doctors and the nurses clattering across the ward and, as the door of the Treatment Room slammed behind them, Creswen turned to her mother and told her with surprising calm that Chris was dead, they had lost him.

The doctors still struggled with the little boy's lungs. The chaplain arrived and, hastily, he took out the contents of the emergency baptism box and blessed the baby boy and named him Christopher William Steven Peasgood. They asked Creswen if she had any photographs of her son, and she said she didn't think so, and the chaplain used a polaroid to take two pictures of the little boy's face with its halo of wires. Then a doctor told Creswen that there was not much hope—Chris was failing to breathe properly on his own and they did not have the right equipment on Ward Four to help him. They wanted to move him to Queen's Med, but, if he had another arrest on the way, they would lose him. Whether he stayed or went, he was at great risk. The doctor told Creswen that it was up to her to decide what to do.

Creswen had never been afraid to speak her mind. She'd been a shop steward in the clothing factories around Newark where she'd worked for a while after school. She was afraid of no one. But what could she say? She wasn't a doctor, she'd never learned about medicine, she didn't know.

As she stood with Mick and her mother outside the Treatment Room, she could hear someone arguing inside. There were two nurses and, although Creswen could not quite make out what they were saying, she was in no doubt that they were having a go at each other. Then the door flew open and the staff nurse who had been looking after Chris paced out, with her face flushed. She was tall and thin and perfectly poised, rather like Princess Anne to look at. Her name was Clare Winser and Creswen stopped her.

'What we going to do?' she asked her. 'We're not doctors. How are we supposed to know?'

Clare looked straight at her. 'Send him to Queen's Med,' she said. 'Move him. If you don't, he'll be dead before morning.'

For once in her life, Creswen was lost for words. She had not expected anything so blunt. She didn't know how this nurse could be so sure or what she was thinking at all, but it took her only a second to decide that she would take the advice. The Treatment Room door opened again and Bev walked out, still flushed like Clare before her.

Inside her cubicle, where she was still sitting with her mother, Belinda King had heard Bev saying that she wanted to go in the ambulance to Nottingham with the baby who had just arrested. Belinda had noticed that Bev had a practical streak that was missing from some of the other nurses on the ward. On her first day, Belinda had watched a couple of nurses twittering over Christopher's bottle, trying to decide how to enlarge the hole at the top of the teat to make the milk flow better. They were never going to make up their minds, but Bev had bluntly interrupted and said 'For God's sake, stop messing around, get some sterile scissors and cut it.'

Now, as Bev left with permission to escort Chris Peasgood in the ambulance to Nottingham, Belinda was left feeling very isolated. This whole business had gone badly from the start. At home, when they had first tried to call the GP to come and help them with Christopher, they had rung and rung and found it was engaged for three-quarters of an hour. Things had gone downhill ever since.

Belinda talked to her husband, John, and they agreed that the only way to get anyone to pay any attention to Christopher was to go home for the night, so that these nurses would have to look after him instead of leaving it all to them. Belinda did not like much about the ward, but she never doubted that they would care for Christopher. She trusted them completely. And since she had been away on maternity leave, cut off from all news about the hospital and the strange illnesses among the children, she had no reason to be worried about the ward. Nobody warned her. So she went home.

On Monday morning, 15 April, Dr Porter arrived to find Ward Four recovering from the trauma of Creswen Peasgood and her son, Chris. Dr Porter, who had been called in from his home on Saturday afternoon to deal with Chris Peasgood's first arrest, was fairly sure in his own mind that there was nothing untoward about this particular incident. This was a very poorly little boy with a lot of mucous in his tubes, and it seemed clear that he had simply become blocked up. The physiotherapist who had been dealing with Chris, Alison Gibson, did not see it that way at all. She had cleared Chris's tubes after his first arrest and was most surprised to be called back that same afternoon to find him blue in the face and barely alive. But Dr Porter was satisfied that this was not a suspicious incident. Just as his colleagues were equally satisfied that there was nothing suspicious about Michael Davidson, whose heart had stopped last week, apparently at the sight of a needle, even though his mother said he had often been injected and never shown any fear at all. And so it was that while he was examining the boy, he never told any of the other nurses and doctors of his fears about a poisoner being at work on the ward.

Over the weekend, he had realized that there might be an innocent explanation for Paul Crampton's insulin overdose—if there was some other patient who was supposed to have it, some child with diabetes who needed the insulin, if there had been some terrible misunderstanding and if a nurse had given it to the wrong child. That would explain it. That was a possibility. And hadn't there been a diabetic child on the ward? Leah Featherstone! She was diabetic. She was on the ward at about the right time. That could be it. Someone could have taken Featherstone's insulin and accidentally given it to Paul Crampton. They would have to have done it three times, though. Paul Crampton had had three attacks. Heaven only knew how it could have been done three times. But that could be it. An accident. Not attempted murder. Not on Ward Four.

Dr Porter spoke to Moira Onions and asked her to check her

files to see whether this Featherstone girl, or any other diabetic child, might have been on the ward at the same time as Paul Crampton. He asked her, too, to try and find out how much insulin had been sent up to the ward by the pharmacy, whether an excessive amount had been used over the last few months. And no one must know. Moira Onions said she would do her best.

The rest of Monday passed. Nobody's heart stopped. Belinda King watched the ward and longed for Christopher to get better so that she could get out of this dreadful place. She had gone home on Saturday night to get away, but when she and John had returned on Sunday morning, they had found the ward as slack as ever.

A staff nurse had told her that they had had to bath and change Christopher early on Sunday morning because he had had a very big bowel movement, but she didn't seem to know why and she even seemed to think it was funny, and Belinda felt that, as usual, the nurse was not about to tell her any more than she had to. Later on Sunday morning, she and John decided to go up to the canteen for lunch and they were told that that was fine, because the nurses would be keeping Christopher under close observation. But when they came back, 40 minutes later, they had found him all alone in his cubicle, soaked in fresh vomit and crying, while a group of nurses sat together talking at the nurses' station. Christopher was obviously not getting any better, he had been violently sick three times on Monday morning, and since Belinda understood the language that the doctors were speaking, it was obvious to her that they were quite unable to make up their minds about the reason.

Dr Porter was afraid that the trouble might be a tumour. He had felt Christopher's abdomen with his hands and once or twice he suspected there might be something there, but in the end he couldn't be sure. He had prescribed Carobel. Dr Nanayakkara, however, had also felt for a tumour and he was in no doubt that he could certainly feel one. He had cancelled the Carobel.

Dr Porter suspected that Christopher's stomach was rejecting his food because the muscle at its exit was too tight—a condition which Belinda knew as pyloric stenosis—but when he had given Christopher two test feeds, both of them had been negative. Nanayakkara gave him another test feed and this time he got a positive result, but when they followed that up with an ultrasound scan, the result was negative again.

By noon on Monday, Belinda was crying tears of desperation, and Christopher was still vomiting his heart out. Dr Nanayakkara decided that regardless of the muddle in the test results, Christopher should have surgery on his stomach that afternoon. As Monday night fell, Belinda stayed with Christopher, full of hope that the operation had cured his problem, that her troubles were over.

On Tuesday morning, at 8.20, Dr Porter was telephoned at home. There was more trouble on the ward. One of the children was looking very grey, his oxygen saturation was down to 77 per cent and his heartbeat was fast, at 130. The child was Belinda King's son, Christopher.

The staff on Ward Four had been shocked by Christopher's sudden deterioration, but not as shocked as Belinda had been. The staff, at least, knew that he had had a respiratory attack on Sunday morning—suddenly deteriorated without reason, and gone dusky and pale, and blue around the eyes, so that they had called the doctor who had ordered close observation. But they had not told Belinda, even though she was a nurse, even though she was his mother, even though she had asked quite clearly to be contacted if Christopher was upset by anything.

Over the phone now, Dr Porter prescribed antibiotics and ordered them to take blood for a full count, gases and culture. And one more thing—a BM stick to measure the blood sugar. He told them he would be right there.

But by the time he got to the ward some ten minutes later, Dr Porter found that his colleague, Dr Nanayakkara, had already arrived and taken over the case. Christopher King seemed to be recovering and Dr Porter's advice on the case was not needed.

In one sense, this suited Dr Porter. The truth was that he had a long-standing engagement that morning—to go to the annual conference of the British Paediatric Association at the University of Warwick outside Coventry. He had arranged for a temporary locum consultant named Charles Livingstone to stand in for him while he was away. Livingstone was already on the ward and Porter now spoke to him, giving him a rough guide to his patients, showing him the ropes and as they walked, Dr Porter mentioned that he had received a rather worrying test result which seemed to suggest that someone had injected a child with insulin and it was probably worth testing blood sugar levels if there did happen to be any problems, but he hoped it would be all right. While they were speaking, Livingstone was bleeped urgently. Christopher King had had a relapse; he was in distress, fighting for breath. Livingstone darted off. Porter bade him farewell, picked up his case and headed for the station. If he was quick, he could still catch his train and be off to Warwick for two days, leaving Ward Four and all its mysterious headaches behind him. Nelson Porter headed for the station, where the bill boards of the local paper advertised the fact that in Grantham this week, it was Crime Prevention Week.

On the ward he left behind him that Tuesday morning, Belinda King was in tears, while her child's life fell apart in the doctors' hands.

She had been hoping so desperately that Christopher would get better and now it had all gone wrong. She had spent the night sleeping fitfully and watching Christopher and he had seemed to be recovering from his operation with his drip feeding dextrose into his arm. They had found no sign of a tumour, despite Nanayakkara's prediction, only a slight thickening of the gut. She had slept so little that when Bev Allitt came into the cubicle just before 8.00 in the morning and offered to watch Christopher while she went up to the canteen, Belinda had been happy to accept and get away for a moment. She had popped up to the canteen for a cup of tea and a cigarette and had begun to enjoy the feeling that the trouble was all over, that the operation had done the trick. Twenty minutes later, she had walked back into Christopher's cubicle and found Bev giving him emergency oxygen.

'I was just about to give him a feed and he went off on me,' she said, pointing to a bottle of milk she had prepared.

For a moment, Belinda had been confused. Christopher was on a post-operative diet of water only. Why had Bev given him milk? But there was no time to ask Bev what she had been trying to do, Christopher looked terrible. His face was completely grey. Belinda felt that he was dying

Someone had said that Dr Porter was on the way. Belinda had hurried out of the ward, looking for a phone. She wasn't allowed to use the one on the nurses' station—she was only a parent—but she found a payphone on the main corridor and called John, who was asleep at home.

'You'd better come straight away. He's not well.'

John had been caught by every traffic light between home and the hospital. Belinda stood in tears outside the Treatment Room, now quite sure that Christopher would die. She watched the commotion around Christopher's cubicle, understanding everything only too well: the radiographer running into the Treatment Room to X-ray Christopher's lungs, the orders for more blood tests. By the time John arrived, Christopher was recovering and they limped off to the parents' room to get a cup of coffee.

Belinda and John arrived back on the ward to find a new storm of activity around Christopher in the Treatment Room. This time, he had been in the Treatment Room with Bev Allitt when she had called for a doctor. When Dr Livingstone, the locum consultant had arrived, torn away from his conversation with Dr Porter, he had found Christopher struggling for air. Belinda and John took shelter in his cubicle. Christopher recovered. The nurses and the doctors withdrew. Bev Allitt stayed with him to make sure he was all right. But the calm lasted for only 15 minutes before his breathing faltered and threatened to stop and his heart started lumbering, and Bev had to give him oxygen and raise the alarm, and, in the cubicle, Belinda saw the signs of crisis: a student nurse hurtling in looking for the oxygen saturation machine; a fast bleep going out, the type she knew they used only for real emergencies; a phone call to the Special Care Baby Unit for a neo-natal ventilator, small enough to force the lungs of a five-week-old baby, and finally the decision to transfer him to Nottingham.

John drove. Belinda sat beside him, her thoughts knotted into an impossible tangle about Christopher's funeral. It was obvious he was going to die, so then they'd have to bury him, but where would they do it? John's family lived in Birmingham, Belinda's family were miles away in Northamptonshire, she and John were living in Grantham, but for all she knew, they would move. She couldn't sort it out. One thing she knew. If Christopher survived, she was never taking him back on to Ward Four. She might work at the same hospital but that didn't make any difference. That ward was a rotten place. They didn't even have the right emergency equipment. If Belinda had known that, she would never have let them operate on her child. And the doctors didn't seem to know what was wrong. One of them was trying to say that Christopher must have a bad heart. Another one was saying he must have an extra bit of tube between his oesophagus and his trachea. Another said it was congenital. They didn't know what it was. Christopher's only chance was that he would get better care at Queen's Med.

A few hours after Christopher King was hustled out of Ward Four, Chris and Joanne Taylor walked down the central corridor and through the double doors for the first time since Liam had died there. They had come to see Dr Nanayakkara, to find some answers to the questions that had continued to trouble them. Joanne felt very daunted by the ward, and when no one was there to meet them she hung back and stared at a picture of James the Red Engine, while Chris had to go round the corner on to the main part of the ward to find someone.

They were still trying to understand why Liam should have had a heart attack. They had seen the death announcement of Becky Phillips in the *Grantham Journal*, they had heard from Joanne's mum, Shirley, who was still working as a tea-lady at the hospital, how there were so many very poorly babies on Ward Four. They had talked about it all at home and they thought there must be some connection, perhaps a new virus that no one had ever come across before that had got into the ward, but it couldn't just be coincidence.

Nanayakkara wanted to talk to them about grieving. He explained that they would go through periods of anger and of guilt. Chris and Joanne asked about their decision to withdraw drugs from Liam. It was beginning to eat at them, but Nanayakkara reassured them that it had made no difference to the end result.

'He still would have died.'

They started to ask him why and then they found that Nanayakkara had more complaints than answers. The pathologist, he said, had failed to give him information. Liam, he was sure, had not died of a heart attack at all. That was a mistake by the pathologist. The procedure of resuscitation could easily produce symptoms in a child that looked very similar to those of a heart attack. That was surely what had happened in Liam's case, but the pathologist had failed to see that. There was nothing at all in Liam's history to suggest any reason for his suffering a cardiac arrest. Chris and Joanne started to lob their questions.

'So what do you think it was?'

'That is what I am unable to establish.'

Joanne said: 'We've heard that there have been some more poorly babies.'

'We have had a lot of problems. We have never had so many cot deaths and we have a case that might be meningitis.'

'But is it right that they've had the same symptoms as what Liam had?'

'Well, not really, they have been very sick but their symptoms have not been the same as Liam's.'

'So what do you think it was?'

If he could look at the slides and samples, he said, he might be able to solve the mystery, but this pathologist had failed to hand them over.

Chris pressed. 'But we want to know why. If we said we wanted you to have a look at 'em, wouldn't they give 'em to you then?'

'I'm afraid not.'

'But can't we say that this is our son and we want these slides?'

'No,' said Nanayakkara. 'I'm afraid you have no rights whatsoever.'

Chris and Joanne left. Nanayakkara fired off a letter to Dr Marshall, pulling apart his report: ' . . . totally not in keeping with the clinical presentation and the course of his stay . . . quite inconsistent with the diagnosis . . . very disturbing . . . not only a mystery but unexplained and highly improbable.' He received no reply.

David and Kath Crampton were struggling, too, to come to terms with what had happened to Paul. They had tried hard to accept the easy reassurance of Derek Johnston at Queen's Med, that Paul would suffer no more hypoglycaemic attacks, but it was hard.

Each night, they put Paul to bed and then they tried to sleep themselves and sometimes Paul would yell and scream and keep them awake. Before he had gone to Ward Four, he had been sleeping through the night, but not any more. On some nights, he would wake them half a dozen times, as if he was having some sort of recurring nightmare. But the other nights were even worse, when Paul lay in his cot without a sound, and David and Kath lay in their bed in their room, staring at the ceiling and wondering why he was so quiet, and whether he was going grey and clammy and cold again and, sooner or later, one of them would have to get up to make sure that he was still alive.

They had heard nothing from any of the doctors. For days after Paul was discharged, David had been impatient to hear the result of this blood test. He wanted the truth. For all he knew, Paul was suffering from some kind of problem that was going to affect the rest of his life. The blood tests should tell them. Then they could get on and deal with the problem, whatever it was. And they might even be able to sleep at night. But there was no word from the hospital. No one told them a thing.

No one told Peter and Sue Phillips about what had gone wrong with Katie. When she had left Ward Four on that terrible Sunday afternoon, she had been hovering on the brink of death. Sister Savill had gone with Katie in the ambulance and Peter and Sue were full of gratitude to everyone on the ward for saving Katie for them. At Nottingham, Peter and Sue continued to live by her bedside, while Peter's business ran down the drain. After ten days, Katie had been well enough to leave intensive care and they had been happy to bring her back to Ward Four and they wanted to find some way to show their thanks to the ward and their faith in the staff, and so, back on Ward Four again, they decided to make a very personal gesture to one of the nurses. They had chosen the young nurse who was now specialing Katie every time she was on duty. She was Bev Allitt and when Sue and Peter asked her, she agreed to be Katie's godmother.

Judith and Steve Gibson were still in Queen's Med, watching Brad as he struggled to enjoy life with legs that slumped and slid from under him. It seemed that his heart attack must have cut off the oxygen to his brain for some minutes and done lasting damage to him. He seemed very upset. He refused to talk to any of the nurses; for some reason he turned his head to the wall if any of them came close to him. Sometimes, in bed, he howled with pain because his legs were hurting him, and, to make matters worse, he had lost control of his bladder and bowel. It grieved them to see their proud little five-year-old reduced to the baby life of nappies. A registrar with a sour face told Judith to face facts— 'he'll never walk properly again'. Judith hated her for saying that, but she feared it might be the truth.

Brad had been doing his best to carry on. On the Saturday when Chris Peasgood was arresting on Ward Four, Brad was visited in Queen's Med by his friend Hugh, who took one look at the bright red and yellow plastic bubble cars standing in the play area at the end of the ward and went racing. Brad watched round-eyed from his bed and said he wanted to do that, too. Judith knew his legs wouldn't be up to it—he couldn't even get himself into the car, let alone push it round the floor—but she thought it was better for him than just sitting on his bed watching.

So Brad spent Saturday afternoon, crouched in the little yellow car, flapping his stiff legs on to the floor and, despite losing every race, enjoying himself. Then Sunday was the same.

They were visited by Judith's friend, Nadine, who happened to be an auxiliary on Ward Four. She brought along her two small boys and, within minutes they were in the cars and roaring around like maniacs, and Brad was trying to join in again. Judy told Nadine about the doctors' diagnosis, that Brad would never walk properly again, he had been crippled by this mysterious attack. Nadine said it was terrible and she added in passing that they had had a bit of a rush on recently on Ward Four.

'It gets like that sometimes,' she said with no hint of alarm.

As they talked, Nadine's boys were travelling so fast that Brad was becoming frustrated and he was putting more and more effort into flipping his feet behind them and, after a while, he developed a technique for shuffling his car along quite fast. He was whooping with joy at his success and spent the whole day roaring around the play area.

On Monday morning, when the physio came to put Brad through another session of painful therapy, Judith stopped her on a hunch and said: 'I could be wrong about this, but I think he might have got a bit better.'

She explained how well he had done in the little red and yellow car, and the physio said: 'Well, fine, let's see what he can do.'

Together, they rolled back Brad's blankets, put their arms

around his back and under his armpits, lifted his dead-weight to the side of the bed, balanced him upright on his feet, slowly let go of him and stood and watched, and as they watched, he tipped forward and started to totter towards the bright light of the window, one shaky step after the other, spreading his arms for balance, staggering unevenly, but staggering all the same and, by the time he lurched on to the window sill and turned to give them a triumphant grin, Judith was whooping for joy and trying not to cry in case it upset him.

For the doctors at Queen's Med, Brad Gibson's new recovery only fuelled their concern at the Grantham mystery, which deepened with every child they saw. Creswen Peasgood had arrived in the ambulance with her son Chris, and just like the others before him, he lacked any symptoms to explain the arrests which he had suffered. One of the doctors, Stephanie Smith, had gone out to see Creswen who was crouched in tears outside the intensive care unit.

'Why have they sent him?' Dr Smith asked.

'He's had two arrests,' said Creswen.

'Arrests?'

'They said he needed a respirator.'

'Well, just now he's screaming my unit down. He certainly doesn't need a respirator.'

Two days later, he was discharged and sent home.

Now Christopher King had arrived. Belinda was desperate. She felt that somehow she had let him down, that she had failed as a mother. She found the sight of him, still weak and hooked up to monitors, so painful that she could not bear to touch him, not even to kiss him goodnight at the end of the day. The thought that he was going to die was beyond her. She put up a shield, and in her mind, she told him: 'If you're going to die, boy, go on and do it, just don't expect me to watch.'

But Christopher King did not die. He, too, recovered. And the doctors at Queen's Med decided that there was something very odd going on at Grantham, that they were looking at a pattern here.

At the University of Warwick, the annual conference of the British Paediatric Association was running smoothly. But Dr Porter, who had arrived from Grantham on Tuesday morning, was haunted by events on Ward Four.

It was not just that he had still to puzzle over Paul Crampton's blood, but that, even in the calm and academic surroundings of the university, the crisis pressed itself upon him. On Wednesday, his first full day at the conference, he found himself listening to a paper which was being given by a distinguished paediatrician, Dr David Southall from the Royal Brompton Hospital in London. It was titled 'Parentally Imposed Upper Airway Obstruction' and it discussed a most striking possibility, that numerous cases of respiratory arrest in children might have been caused deliberately by emotionally disturbed adults.

Dr Southall described in detail how doctors in Chelsea had studied 14 separate cases over a five-year period where children had been suffering from unexplained breathing problems. The doctors had become suspicious, called in social services and the police, and then set up hidden video cameras in the hospital ward. In all 14 cases where this was done, they discovered that an adult relative, usually the mother, was secretly suffocating the child. The reason for this appeared to be that the relative was suffering from a little-recognized emotional disturbance, known to psychiatrists as Munchausen Syndrome By Proxy: they were desperate for attention and sympathy, they had previously found it for themselves as patients in hospital, and now they sought it again by making their children patients. Dr Southall urged his audience to consider that if they faced a series of respiratory arrests and if it seemed that the arrests always occurred in the presence of one individual, they should use covert video surveillance.

Nelson Porter listened carefully.

At the conference, he also came across Professor David Hull, one of the most respected paediatricians in the country—and the man in charge of paediatric services at Queen's Med in Nottingham. As the conference ebbed and flowed around them, Dr Porter confided his fears to the professor—Ward Four might be harbouring someone with Munchausen Syndrome. Hull's advice was clear: if there was evidence of a crime, call the police.

But Dr Porter did not. He was not sure what to do. On Wednesday night, he left his conference in an agony of indecision.

In his absence, the staff of Ward Four were struggling to survive like sea-sick travellers, holding on tight as they lurched from crisis to crisis, desperate to find solid ground again but able to do nothing more than to cling on and hope the end was in sight. The hospital management had agreed finally that Ward Four could have its own defibrillator as long as they did not have to pay for it out of hospital funds; they were asking the League of Friends to pick up the bill for £6,000. Until the League made a decision, Ward Four could not afford to buy the equipment.

The strain of coping with the arrests was beginning to trouble some of the nurses. Bev Allitt, for example, seemed to have had to deal with every single one of them, and some of the nurses laughed about it with her and teased her about how bad luck seemed to follow her around. Bev didn't seem to mind. She said she must have a jinx. But not all of them thought it was funny. One of the night nurses said Bev must have some kind of resistant bug; everywhere she went, she made the children die. Joan Cottam decided to mention it to Sister Savill, who agreed that it was worrying. She wrote a letter to the management pointing out that this young nurse had been involved in more than 20 arrests in less than two months and asking whether they would pay for her to have some counselling to help her cope.

Joan Cottam warned Sister Savill that there was a little friction around Bev. Evidently, she had been saying bad things to Mr and Mrs Phillips about Catherine Morris, claiming that Catherine panicked and dropped things when there was a crisis. Sister Savill did not like the sound of that. She checked with the Phillips and decided to speak to Bev Allitt, but she was busy and asked Margaret Geeson to do it for her and she never had the time to find out whether Margaret did.

The truth was that this was not the only friction around Bev. Betty Asher had begun to harbour serious doubts about that girl. It seemed to her that in some way, Bev rather enjoyed the arrests, not that she enjoyed the suffering of the children, but that she seemed to be excited by the drama of it all, the sudden panic and rush. Somehow, she always seemed to manage to turn up at the centre of things, helping the Crash Team, going on escort in the ambulance. And she had this odd way of smiling to herself when other people were talking about their problems. Betty wasn't sure what it meant, but she didn't like it. It wasn't right. Still, she had no evidence, no proof of anything improper, and so she said nothing.

Clare Winser did not like Bev at all. She had no proof that she had done anything wrong, but there was something strange about her, something cold. Back in February, just after Bev had qualified and been given her access code to the hospital computer, Clare had noticed her playing with the terminal on the nurses' station, flicking through the personal details of patients on the maternity wards. She had asked what she thought she was doing and Bev had just muttered something about looking for some friends. Clare didn't know what the truth was, but it had left her feeling a little uneasy about her. And Bev always seemed to be around when these children became ill. Sometimes she seemed to enjoy the drama of it, so that she would stand and watch as if she were a spectator, instead of a nurse. Clare had made a barbed remark in front of Bev, saying that there were always arrests when she was on duty, and Bev had flared up and threatened to walk off the ward. Clare had had to calm her down. But that didn't mean she liked her. She had ended up saying something even more direct, more or less on the spur of the moment.

It was on Saturday evening, when Chris Peasgood was in the Treatment Room recovering after his first arrest. Clare had been looking after him. She had only just recovered herself from the shock of that arrest—she'd been so surprised that she'd dropped a syringe full of medicine on the floor and then been completely confused to find Bev Allitt standing over the baby's cot with the apnoea monitor wailing and doing nothing about it. Now, she was watching him closely as he recovered in the Treatment Room. Bev had come in and asked if she wanted to be relieved. Clare did want to go to the Ladies, so she had said yes, thanks. And then, just as she was going, she'd said it, almost before she had had a chance to think about it.

'Just you behave yourself while I'm away.'

Bev had just stared at her. Clare had gone to the Ladies and then, unbelievably, she had returned to find that Chris was having a second arrest and Bev had called out for help. She'd looked at Bev.

'I can't leave you alone for five minutes, can I?'

There was all sorts of chaos with the child being revived and then being given an emergency baptism and Clare had had no chance to say anything else. Then, to make matters worse, Bev had started insisting that she should go with the baby in the ambulance to Queen's Med. Clare had protested. This was supposed to be her patient. They had ended up having a blazing row in the Treatment Room. Clare had stalked out and bumped straight into the baby's mother and when she'd asked her what to do, she'd had no hesitation in telling her to get her child out of there or he'd be dead before morning.

Clare was certain now that she did not like that girl. But that was not enough. She was tempted to say something, but she was not sure that she could.

The next day, Thursday 18 April, a seven-week-old boy named Patrick Elstone lay alone in his cot in cubicle number six on Ward Four, the one with Mr Silly on the door. He had been admitted on Tuesday evening with gastro-enteritis. He was a nice-looking little boy with big brown eyes. He had an identical twin brother, Anthony. Their parents, Bob and Hazel, were short of money and Bob was out of work and worried about it, but they were full of excitement about their twins. Bob Elstone, who was a small wiry man with a genius for darts, had this dream that both boys would grow up to be sportsmen. Maybe they'd be footballers or runners. He wasn't sure, but he was excited at the dream of it all. Bob and Hazel had visited during the morning and been a bit worried to find a mysterious bruise on Patrick's head, but now they had gone back home with Anthony to the little terraced house they rented near the railway line. And the doctors had decided that Patrick might have some kind of infection, so they had isolated him from the other children, in the cubicle, all alone. Time passed.

Somebody on the ward was looking for a victim. They were looking for someone who wouldn't complain. That was easy. There were plenty to choose from. It hardly mattered who. Pick this little girl with the blonde hair and the wheeze? No. Pick this boy with the brain damage? He's two but he can't even speak. No. Pick this one—this baby boy with brown eyes like olives. Pick him. He's on his own. No one can see. Do him. It's easy, as easy as pulling petals off a daisy. Pick Patrick Elstone.

It was just before 4.00 that Thursday afternoon when Bev Allitt raised the alarm. First she fetched Nadine Shelbourn, the auxiliary, and she followed Bev into the little cubicle and she agreed that Patrick didn't look well. So then Bev went off to get Mary Reet, the staff nurse, and she told Mary that she'd had this feeling that Patrick might be in trouble and so she'd gone to have a look and found him like this. Mary looked and saw that Patrick Elstone was pale and grey and his breathing was shallow—but at least he was still breathing. Mary called for a doctor and tried to give him oxygen but the oxygen tap wouldn't work, so she asked Bev to carry him to the Treatment Room and there, within a few minutes, they were bringing back the colour to his cheeks, and his breathing settled and became a little deeper.

The doctors took blood for tests. Mary Reet said she would special him. She was not going to take any chances. She sat by Patrick's bed and watched him and was relieved to see that he was fine. At 7.00 one of the junior doctors came and examined him and agreed with Mary that he was fully recovered now.

'There's no need to special him any more,' he told her. 'You can leave him now.'

Mary was still determined to take no chances. Back in his cubicle, she fitted an apnoea monitor to Patrick's torso and hooked him up to an oxygen saturation monitor, so that they could hear and see immediately if he was having any kind of respiratory problem. Then she left him, all alone.

Somebody on the ward was looking for a victim again. They saw Mary Reet leave the cubicle. It didn't take long. It was easy—to walk round, slip into the cubicle, kill the apnoea, switch off the oxygen monitor and do him again, as easy as knocking blossom off a tree.

This time, Patrick Elstone stopped breathing.

By the time that Bev Allitt raised the alarm again and Mary Reet ran into the cubicle, the monitor was showing that his oxygen saturation was down in the low 70s and Patrick had gone blue around the mouth. Mary Reet was horrified. She also could not understand why the monitors had not gone off. But there was no time to stop and think. They had to whirl Patrick out of his cubicle, round the corner to the Treatment Room and pump him back to life.

The Crash Team hurtled on to the ward again and, as they

worked on him, Bob Elstone came through on the phone at the nurses' station, just to make sure that Patrick was all right, he said. The nurse who answered fetched the night sister, Jean Savill.

'I'm glad you've called,' she told him in her slightly anxious way. 'I want you to come to the hospital straight away.'

'Why, what's up then? What's the matter?' asked Bob, who had had to leave the house to use the phone at the bus station because they hadn't got one at home. He wanted to get back to watch 'The Bill'. 'Is he playing up then? Can't you get him to sleep?'

'Please, just come to the hospital straight away.'

By the time that Bob and Hazel arrived at the hospital, clutching Anthony, the sister was ready to tell them that Patrick was very seriously ill and they were not sure whether he would survive.

That night, they transferred him to Queen's Med, where Bob and Hazel sat in a daze with Anthony, while Patrick lay lifeless and the monitors bleeped and a priest came and baptized both boys.

Bob and Hazel Elstone were left bewildered by Patrick's arrest. They felt that no one really had told them anything. They were only Patrick's parents, but nobody at Grantham had told them that Patrick had had two crises during the day, that while they had been away from the ward during the afternoon—going home and taking Anthony to the GP to make sure that he was all right—his breathing had suddenly become so weak that he had needed emergency oxygen. They had not been told—any more than Belinda King had been told about Christopher's crisis on Sunday morning, or Fay Davidson had been told that her boy, Michael, had suffered a heart attack and not just a fit when he reacted badly to the sight of a needle.

Dr Nanayakkara had no opinion at all about Patrick Elstone. He did not look into the incident. That morning, he had gone off, leaving the mysteries of Ward Four behind him, to attend the final two days of the paediatric conference at the University of Warwick. No one thought to tell him that Patrick Elstone, who was officially one of his patients, had been rushed away in an ambulance, half dead without an explanation.

Dr Nanayakkara had begun to listen to the sounds of alarm on the ward. Sister Savill had finally made him hear when she had gone to him and apologised for firing off her cry for help without

consulting him. She had calmed him down and he had begun to
see for the first time that the real significance of her letter was the
underlying pattern—seven arrests, she had mentioned. He had had
no idea about several of them. No one had told him. And there
had been more since then. He didn't know how many: it was
only by chance that he had heard about Chris Peasgood being
transferred, even though he was one of his patients. None of the
doctors had told him. One of the nurses happened to mention it
in passing. Dr Nanayakkara began to worry.

Dr Porter had told him about Paul Crampton's blood result
and urged him to do nothing and to say nothing. Nanayakkara
had not liked the plan at all.

'Oh, my God don't tell me that,' he had said. 'This is bloody
nonsense.'

Then they had had an argument. Nanayakkara couldn't see why
all this had to be such a secret. Porter had insisted that they should
watch and do nothing. Nanayakkara had objected.

'If everybody is watching everybody else, how can I work in
this unit? If I have to suspect everyone?'

Porter said he wanted to check the result. Nanayakkara thought
he just wanted to crack the mystery on his own. But in the end
he had given in and left him to it. He said nothing about it to
anyone else. Still, he worried. He decided to try and gather
together the notes of some of these children, so that he could
write a report. Surely, there was a medical explanation for all this,
but he found himself dwelling on the subject. And, as he thought
about it all, a particularly horrible idea formed slowly in his mind,
an idea that contained within it several of his deepest fears. He
knew he was not always popular. He was a strong character and
he did argue with people. He had enemies in the hospital, he had
no doubt. More than that though, deeper than that, he was not
English. He was Sri Lankan, a foreigner. Perhaps this was all an
attempt to discredit him. Could that be it? Could somebody be
attacking his patients to make him look foolish, to make him look
bad? It was with this painful fantasy in mind that Dr Nanayakkara
had left the ward that Thursday morning to travel to the conference in Warwick.

Dr Porter was back in the hospital. He was on the ward when
Patrick suffered his first arrest. He believed that this was possibly

meningitis. At any rate, it was not suspicious. Any more than Michael Davidson was suspicious; that was possibly fear of needles. Or indeed Chris Peasgood; that was possibly mucous. Or indeed Christopher King, which was possibly a lot of things. No, this Elstone case was no cause for alarm, he was pretty sure about that.

Moira Onions had been busy trying to track insulin through the ward, but she could find no evidence of excessive use. She also had checked her files to see whether it was possible that Paul Crampton had been given insulin by mistake. And yes, she found, Leah Featherstone had been prescribed insulin. But no, the dates did not fit. Leah Featherstone had not arrived on the ward until 3 April, a clear six days after Paul Crampton had left. The two children had never been on the ward at the same time. There had been two other diabetic children on the ward recently, Stephen Birks and Katie Woods, but they had both left well before Paul Crampton arrived. No one could have given Paul Crampton an insulin injection meant for another child. It was not possible.

Mrs Onions was worried. She and Dr Porter had agreed to keep this business a secret—and she had been pretty sure there was an innocent explanation—but now she needed to tell him what she had found. She arranged to see him on Friday afternoon at 5.30. She gathered together the paperwork, rehearsed her conclusion, set off for his consulting room at the side of Ward Four and then found that he was nowhere to be seen. She waited. No sign of him. She waited some more. Still, there was no Dr Porter. Eventually, she gave up and went home.

Dr Porter was busy. He had come back from Warwick ablaze with anxiety, fumbling with the fragments of the truth—Munchausen Syndrome, blood samples, unexplained attacks. He had still not acted. He had spent Thursday night puzzling and he was still not sure what to do when, late that Friday afternoon, Dr Charles Livingstone, the elderly locum consultant who had been standing in for him and Dr Nanayakkara during the week, asked him if he might have a word.

The two men had not spoken at any length since Tuesday morning when they had been interrupted on a tour of the ward by Dr Livingstone's bleep calling him urgently to the lifeless Christopher King. Dr Livingstone had felt a little irritated at being abandoned with such a sick child and he had had no idea what to make of Dr Porter's muttered last-minute warnings about a strange blood test result. But in his four days on the ward, Dr Livingstone had developed a grave suspicion. It involved Christopher King. He had considered all kinds of explanations for that baby's frightening series of respiratory attacks. None of them was convincing. He had looked at it from every point of view, and he had remembered Dr Porter's warning and, almost reluctantly, he had concluded that there was only one explanation: Christopher King had been asphyxiated. With a heavy heart, he told Dr Porter what he thought and advised him that he must inform the hospital management.

Alone again, Dr Porter played hide-and-seek with the facts, dodging in, and out of the truth. Eventually, there was nowhere else to hide. He was forced to believe the unbelievable. Late on Friday evening, 19 April, he picked up his phone and made a series of phone calls: to Queen's Med where he warned a registrar to test Patrick Elstone's blood for insulin and was told that the registrar would say something to Professor Hull; to the manager's office, where he spoke to the duty manager, Stuart Jackson, an affable man who was in charge of finance and planning and who knew nothing about the chemistry of insulin and the significance of C-peptide; to Moira Onions who spent nearly an hour on the phone with him at her home, trying to see through his excitement to make sense of what he was saying; and finally to the hospital manager, Martin Gibson, who was at home preparing to celebrate his 44th birthday that weekend. With all of them, Porter started to stammer his way into the story. He weaved in and out of the normal level of arrests on the ward, this very high rate of arrests since the middle of February, the clinical pattern and the various indications of the possibility of Munchausen Syndrome By Proxy. And Paul Crampton. The results of his blood test were crucial. And the point was that he wanted to install hidden video cameras on Ward Four.

Moira Onions told him she would call the ward immediately to warn them to improve their security. As a result, they locked one of the doors on the race-track corridors, so that anyone who tried to approach the cubicles would have to walk past the nurses' station. But that was all. Nelson Porter had suggested they should close the ward and maybe even call in the police, but Moira Onions and Stuart Jackson both agreed that if he wanted to take any more serious action, he would have to speak to the manager.

Nobody who had worked with Martin Gibson ever doubted that he was a decent man. He was not the sort of manager who threw his weight about or shouted or bullied in any way. Indeed, he was a most unthreatening character, a small, diffident man, unfailingly polite and habitually shy. He had managed the hospital for nearly six years now. Most men of such mild temperament rise no further than the middle ranks, but Gibson had worked hard to reach his limits. His soft manner sometimes exasperated colleagues who found themselves waiting for days for decisions which should have been made in minutes, but they soon discovered that he had a streak of determination in him which meant that there was no point in trying to hurry him and not much point in trying to change his view once he finally did make up his mind. When he first came to Grantham from Boston, he found some staff were pilfering from the stores and acted with such severity that he earned himself the unsuitably aggressive nickname, the Boston Strangler.

In all his years in the health service, Gibson never before had been confronted with a request for covert video surveillance on one of his wards. He started to tell Dr Porter that it was rather difficult to make a decision like that at 9.00 on a Friday night. Porter stammered onwards with his argument. Then Martin Gibson wondered what Dr Nanayakkara had to say about all this.

Dr Porter confessed that he had not actually discussed this with Dr Nanayakkara. In fact, he had not mentioned it to him at all. Gibson asked him if he would please do that and then come back to him and they could talk about all this properly. The conversation ended. The urgency faded into dusk. On Ward Four, seven days after the result of Paul Crampton's blood tests came through, still nothing had changed.

Nelson Porter was now deeply troubled. Despite the advice of Professor Hull, he still resisted calling the police. But, intellectually, he was now sliding unstoppably into the truth.

That weekend, he studied the notes and files of the children who had suffered arrests. He combed through them, looking for clues and, in his scrupulous fashion, he listed carefully the points which worried him. There were too many arrests to be explained by chance. Most of the children had not been seriously ill before their admission to the ward; yet they became so. Some children had suffered respiratory arrest, even though they had not been suffering any respiratory illness. One of them had been proved to have received at least one exogenous insulin injection. Another of them had complained twice of pain at the site of his I/V drip, possibly indicating potassium in the drip.

The children showed a similar clinical pattern: they became pale and they shut down, their respiration became shallow, they then recovered only to collapse further, a pattern which was consistent with their having been administered some toxic drug. This would make them ill and then trigger the body to shut down; that, in turn, would prevent further circulation of the toxin and so the child would start to recover; but at that point, its normal circulation would resume, the toxin would spread once more and the child would collapse again. Most of them were babies in isolated cubicles.

The more he studied the files, the more clear his suspicion became. By Sunday night, his intellect had forced him deep into the truth: not only Paul Crampton but perhaps as many as 12 other children had all been attacked by a poisoner. And there was no outsider who had ever had access to that many of the children. If he was right, it was one of his own staff who was killing the children.

But he was still not sure what he should do.

On Monday morning, 22 April, at 9.00, Moira Onions sat down with the two consultants from Ward Four and asked them what action they were going to take. Dr Porter repeated his demand for cameras and for more security. Dr Nanayakkara, who had been phoned by Dr Porter at the weekend, disagreed. In his view, Dr Porter was going too far. The incident with Paul Crampton was certainly very worrying, he agreed, but that was only one isolated case. That did not prove that they were dealing with something deliberate in all these cases. Dr Porter wondered whether they might hire someone disguised as a time-and-motion surveyor to monitor everyone's movements. The two men started to argue. Moira Onions could see that they were never going to agree. They were getting nowhere, and Martin Gibson was waiting to hear their decision. In the end, Nanayakkara exercised his stronger personality. He would look at the 13 cases which Dr Porter had identified and he would write a report on them for the manager. In the meantime, they would sharpen up their procedure for dealing with emergencies, buy a new incubator and try and make sure that there were enough adequately trained nurses on hand. No cameras. No extra security. No policemen.

On Monday afternoon, at about 4.15, Claire Peck came to Ward Four. She was a very pretty little girl, aged 15 months, with wavy blonde hair and a cheeky way of blinking both eyes when she laughed, full of new words and new sounds she liked to imitate—ducks and dogs and cars—and she was beginning to walk, though she still fell over if she had nothing to hang on to.

Claire was carried through the double doors by her mother, Sue, while her father, David, strode beside them with her bag of bits and her small brown bear. Both of them were worried. Claire had had quite a few problems with her health. She had had to spend five days on Ward Four in January with febrile convulsions, and all this month she had been having trouble with her breathing. They said she was asthmatic, like her mum. Last week it had got so bad that on Thursday afternoon she had had to come in to Ward Four to be put on a nebulizer. As soon as she had started inhaling the salbutamol in the nebulizer, she had improved and on Saturday, she had been sent back home. But yesterday afternoon, she had started to have trouble breathing again. It had got worse and worse and even though the GP had come out this morning and given her two steroid tablets and a nebulizer, she had been having such trouble this afternoon that the GP had sent her back to Ward Four. Now, Claire was lying in the arms of her mother, Sue, heaving her chest in search of air.

Sue knew that this was a bad attack, more severe than Claire had ever had before. But the GP had said that as long as they got her to hospital, she would be all right. In fact, he had said that within 24 hours she should make a remarkable recovery. And so, as she reached the nurses' station, Sue Peck felt relieved. She sat down in the four-bed area with Claire on her knee and David standing beside them, while the nurses gathered round.

No one told them that there was anything to worry about on

the ward. No one mentioned anything about the 24 occasions when the hearts or lungs of children on the ward mysteriously had ground to a halt in the last two months.

A junior doctor put Claire straight on to a nebulizer, but unlike last week when the salbutamol had immediately opened Claire's tubes, this time there was no improvement. Someone said they would check her blood pressure and they strapped her arm to a machine and talked among themselves, until Sue stopped them.

'Excuse me,' she said. 'Her arm's gone blue.'

'Oh, I'm sorry,' said the nurse. 'It must be the machine's gone wrong. It should have switched itself off.'

The nurse went off to fetch a heart monitor instead. Claire lay wheezing on Sue's lap while the nurse attached her to the monitor which started to bleep erratically.

'Oh dear,' said the nurse. 'We're not having much luck today. This machine's had it, too.'

Claire was still wheezing. The nurses were obviously unsure what to try next, so they called Dr Porter. He would know what to do.

When he appeared at about 5.10, Dr Porter said he would like to X-ray her chest and he would take her to the Treatment Room and try to get a tube down her throat so that she could breathe through that. Someone asked Sue and David if they wanted to come and watch.

'No, I don't think so,' said Sue.

'We'll only be five minutes.'

Sue and David turned to go to the parents' room. A nurse with dark hair picked up Claire and took her to the Treatment Room. A second nurse followed them in. It was Bev. Sue had seen her as soon as they came on the ward, sitting at the nurses' station. She didn't know her name—she called her 'the chubby one'—but she knew she didn't like her. She thought she was surly and cold. When Claire had been in hospital in January with febrile convulsions, Sue had needed some nappies and she had asked Bev, who had looked all sour, and eventually, when she brought them, she had just slapped them down on the table without a word. Then last week, when they had been on the ward, Sue had taken Claire for a bath, because she loved playing in the water, and some of the nurses had been standing around and Claire was happy and smiling at them and they were all smiling back, and this chubby nurse had just stomped by the door without even a glimmer of a smile and Sue had said to Claire—loud enough so that Bev would hear: 'We don't care if she doesn't talk to us, do we, sweetheart?'

Sue and David sat in the parents' room. In the Treatment Room, Dr Porter decided to attack Claire's asthma head-on with an injection of aminophylline. That certainly would cure it, but it was a delicate operation. The injection had to be done slowly over 15 or 20 minutes to avoid harming her heart, and he would need to be very precise about the dose. In preparation, he inserted an I/V cannula into Claire's right arm; then he and the junior doctor went off to calculate the dosage for her. In the Treatment Room, Bev and the dark-haired nurse fussed over the little girl on the Resuscitaire, and then the dark-haired nurse decided to go and see if Claire's parents were all right. When she got back a few minutes later, Claire's face was dark blue, her back was arched up off the sheet, and she was not breathing. Bev was standing alone beside her.

The nurse called to her: 'Get some oxygen suction!'

Bev didn't move. The dark-haired nurse turned Claire on her side and started slapping her back. Dr Porter came in.

In the parents' room, Sue and David wondered how much longer it would be. Sue's mother and father had joined them. Sue was pacing up and down.

'What's going off?' she was saying. 'What ever is going off?'

In the Treatment Room, Dr Porter fed oxygen into Claire's lungs through a face mask and she started to breathe again. He attached a syringe of aminophylline to her cannula, and slowly started to press the plunger. He was being extremely cautious because he knew that if he injected too fast, he could stop her heart. Watching the ECG machine out of the corner of his eye, he took 20 minutes to ease the aminophylline into her body. By the time he had finished, her breathing was stronger and clearer. He gave her hydrocortisone steroids and was relieved to see her oxygen saturation climb up to 96%. Leaning over her, he could hear the air now flowing in and out of her lungs. She looked better. He ordered a new nebulizer, X-rayed her chest, took a blood sample and went off to tell Claire's parents the news. The

five minutes which he had said it would take, had turned into
more than an hour.

Dr Porter was leading Sue and David along the corridor in front
of the isolation cubicles with Sue's parents behind them, explaining
that Claire was stable now and that if she remained stable for the
next 20 minutes, they would transfer her to Queen's Med. It was
a little before 6.30. Sister Barker was with them and they had just
reached the nurses' station, when Bev Allitt suddenly appeared at
the door of the Treatment Room and ran towards them, crying
'Quick, quick, she's gone blue again!'

Porter scampered away. Sue and David felt themselves physically grabbed by the hands of several strangers. They barked out
questions but no one would answer, they pressed to reach Claire
but no one would let them. Together with Sue's mother and father,
they were hustled back to the parents' room.

Porter ran through the door of the Treatment Room to Claire
and saw within seconds that she was dead. She was as blue as a
bruise. She was not breathing. Her oxygen saturation had slumped.
Her heart had lumbered to a halt. Porter threw himself into an
effort to bring her back with all the desperation of a grieving
parent.

Sister Barker went back to the parents' room and told them
Claire had had another attack. Sue stood up and asked her if Claire
was going to die.

'I sincerely hope not,' the sister said.

Dr Porter was pushing 100 per cent oxygen down the airway
in Claire's throat. He took blood from her groin for urgent tests.
The Crash Team arrived with the defibrillator and ran a rapid
series of electric shocks through her chest. Porter fed sodium
bicarbonate and adrenalin into the cannula in her arm. He could
hear the oxygen in her lungs. He could feel a faint pulse in her
groin. At one point, her eyes flickered open and her heart staggered slowly into life, but then it was still again and her eyes were
closed. Dr Porter started to inject the adrenalin directly into her
heart in half-millilitre doses. Four times, he did it. Her oxygen
saturation was now up to 85 per cent. Everything that Nelson
Porter had ever learned told him that by now her heart should be
beating again. But it wasn't. He gave her two more doses of
adrenalin. He gave her calcium chloride. He thought of Paul

Crampton and boosted her blood sugar with an I/V drip of glucose and 50 per cent dextrose. Nothing worked.

In the parents' room, Sue and David sat with Sue's mother and father. A nurse sat with them.

Sue asked her: 'Is she going to die?'

'I don't know,' said the nurse. 'I've only just come on duty.'

For an hour and a half, Nelson Porter and the Crash Team struggled to find life in the little girl. Porter felt that there was something fighting him. In another age, he would have guessed that Claire had been possessed by some demon which was determined to have her soul. But this was no demon. He knew better than that. It was something just as vicious, just as powerful. It was poison. He could feel it blocking them.

It was nearly 8.00 when Dr Porter trailed out of the Treatment Room to find Sue and David Peck.

'Things do not look good,' he told them. 'We are still working on her.'

Sue composed herself. 'If she is going to die, I want to be with her.'

'Perhaps you should come and see us working on her.'

Pale with fear, the parents followed the doctor back past the little cubicles, round past the nurses' station and into the Treatment Room. As they walked in, the doctors and the nurses there stood back from Claire, and David understood the gesture: they were trying but they knew there was nothing they could do now except to show the parents some respect. He knew then that they had lost her. She looked so dead. David and Sue leaned over her, touched her limbs, stroked her wavy blonde hair, kissed her.

As Dr Porter led them back to the parents' room, he told them he would go back and try once more.

Sue found herself pleading with him. 'No, stop it, stop it now, she's had enough.'

And Porter spoke to her with a vehemence she could not understand. 'You can't tell me that. You can't tell me to stop. I have to decide.'

But this time, when he disappeared into the Treatment Room, it was only five minutes before he returned and confessed that it was over. David stayed, slumped in his chair in the parents' room, but Sue wanted to go back. Her father went with her.

'I want to hold her,' she said, and the doctors released Claire from the grip of their machines and lifted her and sank her gently into her mother's arms.

Sue had no idea how long she sat there with her, hugging her and stroking her hair. Perhaps it was not long. Although she was all full of grief, in a strange way, she felt nothing, only the lingering warmth of Claire in her arms. Once, she looked up at the room full of anxious faces and her eye was caught by the chubby nurse, who was standing against the wall with her arms folded across her chest, staring at her.

Sue thought: 'My little girl is dying and all she can do is stare at me.'

At about 8.25, Sue gave Claire back to the doctors and she and her father stumbled outside. A few minutes later, Dr Porter came to the parents' room. His face and beard were bright with sweat, he looked haunted and when he started to speak, Sue could hear that he was close to crying.

He sat down in a chair and shook his head with a terrible sadness, and Sue heard him say: 'This should never have happened.'

6

When Nelson Porter left Sue and David Peck with their tears in the parents' room on Ward Four, he was ablaze with emotion but he was determined to behave like a scientist. He had told the Pecks that he believed Claire had been killed by asthma, that the chances of her failing to respond to the treatment which he had given to her were a million to one—she had just been terribly unlucky. But he did not believe that.

He went straight to the Treatment Room where he drew blood directly from the heart of the dead child and then began to dismantle the I/V drips, tearing the tubes and bags from their metal stands at the side of the Resuscitaire. Sister Barker saw him. She had never seen a doctor do this before and she challenged him.

So he told her openly and with some passion that he believed that one of the nurses had been tampering with the children, that this nurse had just murdered Claire Peck, that that meant there might have been 14 victims now and that the evidence might be in the I/V bags. Or in this blood sample.

Sister Barker did not know what to think. She had just come back from a ten-day holiday that morning and she had heard from Margaret Geeson what Dr Porter was saying about Paul Crampton's blood test. She had found that hard to believe. But this was unimaginable.

Porter sent his evidence off to the path lab and asked for an immediate result on the blood tests.

Alan Wills was the duty scientific officer for the path lab that night, and already he had had a difficult evening. He had been called in by the hospital switchboard at 6.50 and told that he was needed for blood gas tests on a child in Ward Four. It had been 7.30 by the time he sat down in the lab with the clot of blood from the ward and started to analyse it on his Technicon.

While he was working in the lab, Dr Porter and the Crash Team had been struggling still to bring Claire back to life in the Treatment Room on Ward Four. Wills had run a series of tests. The results of one of them were very unusual. When he had tested for potassium, the reading had gone off the top of his gauge. He had found it hard to believe that this patient could have more than 9.99 millimols of potassium for every litre of her blood. So he had run the test again on a different machine, a Flame Photometer. He had got the same result. He had wondered whether the plasma could have been contaminated in some way, so he had found the watery serum from the original blood sample and tested that on the Technicon. The result was still the same. Alan Wills had recorded it in the computer, kept the print-out from the Technicon, and phoned the result through to Ward Four. At least, he said he had phoned it through.

Now, at 8.45, the switchboard was calling him again to do more tests for Dr Porter, and Dr Porter was insisting that no one had ever told him the results of the first lot.

Alan Wills went through the tests again with the new sample of blood and once more he recorded a potassium level that went off the gauge of the Technicon. At 9.15, he made sure that he not only phoned the result through to Dr Porter but followed it up in writing. By this time, however, it was too late to make any difference to Claire Peck.

Dr Porter arrived at the hospital the next morning, Tuesday 23 April, convinced that there was a murderer at work on Ward Four. He went to the path lab and told Alan Wills that he believed they were dealing with a crime and that he must keep all the blood samples and I/V equipment which he had collected the night before. Wills agreed. Shortly afterwards, they discovered that they had lost the Technicon print-out from the potassium test on Claire's first blood sample. Wills said he had definitely not thrown it away and he was sure he had given it to Porter. Just as he was sure he had phoned the ward with the result of the test. Porter said he was sure that he did not have it. Just as he was sure that Wills had never called him. In any event, it was gone.

Porter also went to see the pathologist, Dr Klaus Chen, a temporary stand-in, who had replaced Dr Terry Marshall, the previous temporary stand-in. Porter explained to him that he must look for evidence of crime, and Dr Chen agreed.

The pathologist conducted the post-mortem that afternoon. Dr Chen conducted all the routine tests and, despite the quantity of potassium in Claire's blood, he said that he could find no evidence of crime. The potassium might well have occurred naturally in her blood as a result of death, which always caused the red blood cells to leak potassium. But normally, this did not happen for two or three hours after death. And the blood which was showing high potassium had been taken from Claire's body only half an hour after her death. Nevertheless, Dr Chen decided that she had died a natural death and ruled that she had been killed by asthma. He signed a death certificate. The coroner, T. J. Pert, approved it. Claire's body was then released to her parents who—entirely unaware that there was any suspicion around her death—arranged for her to be cremated 48 hours later, thus destroying the bulk of the evidence on which Dr Porter was trying to construct his case.

Dr Porter had no suspect. If anyone would listen, he talked almost with enthusiasm about Munchausen Syndrome, this dangerous deformity of the personality, this addiction to hospitals, this deadly yearning for attention and sympathy. But despite running around the hospital, raising the alarm with the path lab, the pathologist, Dr Nanayakkara, Moira Onions, Sister Barker and Martin Gibson, insisting to all of them that they were dealing with a murder, Dr Porter did not tell the police. He had had to inform the police of Claire's death. As the doctor in charge, it was his legal duty to inform the coroner's officer of the death of a patient who had been in hospital for less than 48 hours. He did his duty and made sure that the police knew of the death, but he did not tell them that he believed she might have been murdered. Soon, his daily routine enveloped him again—meetings, tutorials, clinics, rounds. He believed he had done all he could. He had called for help. Now it was up to others to act.

In the meantime, Dr Nanayakkara was writing his report for Martin Gibson. He had been trying to collect children's notes since Sister Savill's letter had alerted him to the problem, but he found they were scattered all over the place between Grantham and Nottingham. He had overcome his private anxiety that he was the victim of some kind of racist campaign and now he was finding

Dr Porter's attitude hard to understand and the two of them had clashed on Monday night when Dr Porter had called him at home to tell him about Claire Peck's death. Now, in his report, he offered no support for Dr Porter's worst fears. He insisted, as a scientist, that they should keep an open mind about these events. He conceded that Paul Crampton probably had been wrongly injected with insulin. 'This was an extremely serious episode and the culprit must be identified,' he wrote. But his report to the manager contained none of the other clues which Dr Porter believed he had found: the sheer number of arrests which defied being explained by chance; the respiratory arrests in children with no respiratory illness; the high incidence of arrests among babies who were alone in one of the little cubicles; the pain which Brad Gibson had felt at his I/V site. He did not mention any of his own worries about the cause of Liam Taylor's death nor the puzzling over Becky and Katie. Dr Nanayakkara reported to the manager that, apart from the incident with Paul Crampton, 'we have not yet found any other suspicious circumstances ... Whether this is something unexplained but natural or whether it is something deliberate and intentional is not clear.'

Dr Nanayakkara worked hard on his report. However, he was busy, too, with his normal work on the ward. Even after he had written it, it had to be typed; even after it was typed, it had to be signed; even after it was signed, it had to be delivered. Days passed.

Moira Onions did not know what to make of it all. Once, after being confronted by Dr Porter with his theory about Munchausen Syndrome, she had wondered briefly about Peter Phillips. He seemed to spend an inordinate amount of time in Grantham Hospital with one child or another, he was always at the centre of attention and he had been at home with Becky when she became ill. But he was nowhere near the ward when most of the children collapsed. He was obviously a victim and not a suspect. She was baffled. She had, at least, got to the bottom of one lesser mystery by finding the identity of the nurse who was moonlighting with the BNA nursing agency.

She had discovered the truth by chance when Clare Winser came to see her to complain bitterly about the way she had been treated by Bev Allitt. She explained that she had been specialing

Chris Peasgood and that she had helped him through the two arrests which he had suffered and naturally she had expected to go with him on escort in the ambulance to Queen's Med. She felt that Creswen, the mother, trusted her. But Bev Allitt had over-ruled her, insisted that she should go instead. Bev was only an SEN, while Clare was a fully-trained staff nurse, but Bev had said that she took precedence because she was full-time while Clare, who had young children at home, was only part-time.

Moira Onions reassured her that she was senior to Bev but as they talked, Clare let slip—apparently by accident—that it was Bev who was moonlighting.

Shortly afterwards, Moira Onions saw Bev Allitt on the ward, and she had the strangest feeling. As soon as she saw her, she was struck by how pale and tired she looked. She guessed that was the result of the moonlighting.

'Are you all right, Bev?'

'Yeah,' she shrugged.

Bev turned to walk away and just then, just for a moment, something painful brushed through the back of Moira Onions' mind so gently that she barely felt it, and, just for a moment, she had the terrifying hint of a thought that there was something very odd about this girl and that perhaps she might know something about these arrests which were upsetting Nelson Porter. For a moment, she was going to call her back. But the moment passed—well, what could she say?—and Moira Onions walked away. She said nothing. It was all very mysterious, but for Moira Onions there was nothing more to do. She had some annual leave booked and so now, three days after Claire Peck's death, with the mystery unresolved, she left Ward Four to go to a wedding in the south of France.

The ward was quiet. Since Claire's death, there had been no more arrests. Perhaps the hue and cry which had been raised by Dr Porter was enough to warn the killer to lie low. The nurses did not know what was happening. They were still living in fear of the next disaster, most of all Margaret Geeson who had been left reeling from her week as acting sister. She had been instructed by Dr Porter and by Moira Onions to say nothing to anyone about Paul Crampton's blood sample and she had been compelled to stand by in silence while more children collapsed and then

Claire died. It had been the longest week of her life. Now the ward was quiet again and she waited—like the other nurses and the doctors and the managers. They all waited. It was as if the whole hospital was in spasm. Nothing happened.

While Grantham Hospital was stalled, the doctors at the Queen's Medical Centre in Nottingham were beginning to move. The group of young registrars who had been working on the paediatric intensive care unit decided to meet to discuss the Grantham children. Vibart Noble talked about the results of Paul Crampton's blood tests, and about Brad Gibson, whose heart attack had been so odd that at the time they had wondered whether he had been given the wrong drug. Stephanie Smith recalled the bizarre and unexplained arrests which had been suffered by Chris Peasgood and Christopher King. They talked, too, about Patrick Elstone, the most recent arrival. They had questioned his mother, Hazel, very closely in search of clues and found no decent explanation for his illness. By the time they had finished talking, the registrars were firm in their view that there was real cause for concern at Grantham. One of them, a young Australian doctor named Annie Moulden, who was particularly determined that action should be taken, said that she would go to see Professor Hull.

On the afternoon of Friday, April 26, Annie Moulden relayed the fears of the registrars to Professor Hull. On Monday, armed now with the minutes of the registrar's meeting, the professor called Nelson Porter in Grantham and spoke in terms that were polite but unmistakable: if Grantham did not call in the police themselves, he would do it for them. It was an ultimatum.

At this moment, a stranger's hand intervened. With fire.

The flames burst suddenly out of the mattress of a cot on Ward Four. There was no child near and, after the first flurry of panic, it was obvious that there was no danger and the flames were quickly doused. But when the hospital's fire officer examined the cot, he was very clear about one thing. This fire had been set deliberately.

On Monday, 29 April, when Dr Porter heard the ultimatum from Professor Hull, he went to see Martin Gibson. The fire in the cot he said, was further proof of a malicious hand on Ward

Four. They must call the police. Before Professor Hull did it for them.

For ten days now, Martin Gibson had pondered the meaning of Dr Porter's fears and he had wondered and he had waited to receive Dr Nanayakkara's report and he had taken no action. Because he was a decent man, Martin Gibson also liked to consult. He believed in open management and so now he spoke to his deputy, Peter Flood, who was responsible for all the adult wards in the hospital, and asked his opinion. Flood, who unlike most managers had trained as a nurse, said simply that they should close Ward Four until they had explained the mystery. That was the safe option, he argued, which would protect the children regardless of what the problem turned out to be. Gibson was not sure, so he did what he regularly did when he had a problem. He called the Trent Regional Health Authority and asked them to decide.

The choice was clear. On the one hand, they knew there was a problem and they had to take action to protect the children. If another child died, Flood pointed out, it would be Martin Gibson's head on the block. But on the other hand, there were the new rules of the National Health Service. The hospital was no longer simply an institution. It was now a provider unit in the internal market of the National Health Service. This year it had to earn £17 million from patient referrals and at the moment, it had overspent by £200,000. It was a tiny fraction of the budget, but the money had to be found and the hospital could not afford to go creating a public panic, driving valuable patients away. Martin Gibson could see a terrifying domino effect: if they closed down Ward Four, they would not have the income from patients to pay for the two consultants, Dr Porter and Dr Nanayakkara; if they lost the two consultants, they would not be able to run the Special Care Baby Unit; if they lost that, they would not be able to run the maternity wing; and if they lost that, they would have lost one of their 'core services' and they would then lose their status as a District General Hospital. In other words, in the brave new world of the NHS market, if they created a public scare when none was necessary, they could lose the hospital. Martin Gibson waited for the Region's verdict.

The next day, Tuesday April 30, Dr Nanayakkara's report, dated April 23, finally found its way to Martin Gibson's desk.

Gibson was clear in his own mind that the police must be called. He had dealt with them before—that was how he had earned his title as the Boston Strangler, by calling in the police to deal with petty theft by staff—and now, although Dr Nanayakkara cast doubt on almost everything that Dr Porter said, he did at least agree that there had been a serious incident involving Paul Crampton.

In his office, Martin Gibson had a direct telephone link to the Region's headquarters in Sheffield. He used to call it the Batphone. Sometimes, when he used it, the Region would leave him waiting for days for a reply. This time, when the waiting ended, the message from the Region was clear: call the police but keep the ward open; do nothing that would undermine public confidence. For all Gibson knew, there might have been furious debate within the Region but later the message was repeated: if they closed the ward now, they might never get it open again. Gibson accepted their verdict. And so, on the afternoon of April 30—11 days after Dr Porter first told him he thought there might be a killer on the ward—the hospital manager finally lifted the phone and spoke to the CID at Grantham police station.

But beyond the walls of the hospital, no one was any the wiser. The killer might know that the alarm had been raised, but for the outside world it was a secret. There was no press conference to warn the public that there was something deadly on the ward and no urgent memorandum to local GPs alerting them to this unidentified danger. Inside the hospital, there was no new security on the ward door, there were no extra staff allocated to the ward, no new precautions about the handling of poisons—and no video cameras. In Grantham and Newark that week, GPs still thought Ward Four was a safe place to send sick children; parents still led their reluctant offspring down the long corridor and through the double doors, coaxing them forward with the promise that the nurses would look after them; staff on the ward waded through another week of anxious desperation, waiting for the next nightmare to break.

And this inaction was no longer the result of human error or muddled thinking. This was a deliberate decision an instruction handed down to the hospital from the Regional Health Authority.

*

Detective Superintendent Stuart Clifton looked, at first sight, like the very model of a modern police officer. He spoke well, he dressed well, he could talk to social workers or community leaders without putting his foot in his mouth, he handled press conferences and legal seminars and he could deal with a computer without breaking into a sweat. In some ways, he was typical of the new breed of police officers who had swept into the senior ranks of forces all over the country during the 1980s: born at the end of the war, reared by the new welfare state, better educated, more confident, better trained and better paid than their predecessors. But Stuart Clifton did not quite fit the mould.

The difference was probably rooted in nothing more complicated than the fact that he had grown up in North Yorkshire and spent most of his working life in Lincolnshire. His counterpart in the big cities was likely to be more ambitious, more arrogant, a touch flash. Clifton had a simpler approach. He liked being a detective because he wanted to pit his wits against criminals. He had no dreams of writing thoughtful features for *The Times* or telling the Home Office how to draft new laws. It was not that he lacked the intelligence—in between murder inquiries, he was burning the midnight oil to finish an Open University degree—it was just that he was not interested. When he was younger and playing football for Rotherham Boys, he was never a death-or-glory forward, he played wing-half, solid, reliable, vital. If he was working on a degree, it was for his own satisfaction, for the sense of achievement. If he had a crime to solve, he'd put in very long hours until he got through it, and then he'd put it behind him and go home. A little way beneath Stuart Clifton's modern exterior, there was an uncomplicated, unflappable detective of the most traditional kind.

It was Wednesday morning, 1 May, and Clifton was driving from force headquarters in Lincoln down to Grantham, to the hospital. At this exact moment, he knew very little of what had been going on there. The little he did know had come from a confused phone call which he had taken the previous evening. He had been over in Walcot working on a murder inquiry and he had spent most of the day supervising a dig in a desolate council house garden, which had revealed the body of a dead baby. The father had confessed to killing the child and Clifton had been in the pub with the Home Office pathologist, tying up a few loose ends, when his bleeper had gone off.

The call was from a detective sergeant in Grantham, who explained that he had been called into the hospital that afternoon by the manager, Martin Gibson, and told that there might be a problem there on the children's ward. The manager had had two consultants with him, and he had handed over a report from one of them, Dr Nanayakkara, which suggested that there was very little evidence of crime at all, just a series of medical problems which had affected 14 different children. But Gibson had asked him to look at it.

'There may be nothing in it,' the sergeant had said, 'but if there is, it's bloody horrendous.'

Stuart Clifton had agreed to have a look. In between completing his log and wrapping up the loose ends of his murder inquiry in Walcot, Clifton had asked the sergeant from Grantham to set up a meeting at the hospital for the next day.

Now, this Wednesday morning, as he drove his red Cavalier down to the meeting, Clifton felt curiously apprehensive. He had dealt with a lot of murders. He had been an officer for 25 years and although he had started out as a village bobby in Kirton in south Lincolnshire, he had soon transferred to become a detective constable and gone on to be promoted through every rank in the CID. Now he was operational head of CID for the whole county. He had seen the emotional and physical results of every kind of violence, with every kind of victim, and he was not about to be surprised by anything, but there was something wrong about this one.

From what the sergeant had said, it seemed that even the hospital was not saying that there was a crime here, and Clifton had an uneasy feeling that he might be being hired as an unofficial janitor—to clean up someone else's mess and lock up before he left. But on the other hand, if this did turn into something 'bloody horrendous', he wanted to be prepared and so he had asked for half a dozen different people to come to this meeting: Martin Gibson; any of the doctors who knew what this was about; an independent medical expert who could stand back and sort it all out; and the force press officer, Tony Diggins, who was in Clifton's front passenger seat now and who would need to hold the line against the world's press if it turned out that someone really was attacking children in the hospital. Clifton decided that this was the sort of meeting where it was best to let the others do the talking.

Clifton turned into the hospital car park. He knew the place a little. His wife had been brought in once as a patient when a horse had got the better of her and thrown her on her neck, and during the three years when he had run the local CID office at Grantham, he had had to come in from time to time for post-mortems. It still looked the same.

As Clifton and his press officer got out of his car, half a dozen men were waiting upstairs on the first floor in a small, slightly shabby room with the appearance of a provincial businessman's office. There was a large, untidy desk with a pseudo-teak finish whose surface was littered with several piles of unkempt papers, plastic filing trays, a push-button telephone that had looked new in the 1980s, a blotter and a Desperate Dan coffee mug. The walls were plastered with pinboards full of internal bulletins and the occasional child's painting. On the window sill, a dessicated plant stood, still wearing the plastic display badge which named it Radermachera Sinica. Next to it was a six-inch diameter badge with the words 'Keep Smiling—the boss loves idiots'. The office belonged to Martin Gibson, who sat now at the desk with his tight smile and his nervous blink.

Martin Gibson was proud of his job and of his hospital and if he was nervous now, it was because he had spent the last 11 days, watching everything he had worked for start to shudder and crack. He did not believe there really could be a crime like this in his hospital, and he had handed the police Dr Nanayakkara's report in the confident hope that he would turn out to be right, that his hospital was prey to nothing more than an unlucky streak of sickness.

Now he sat quietly in his office with Dr Porter, Dr Nanayakkara, several officials from the Regional Health Authority, and Professor David Hull from Queen's Med who had agreed to play the role of the independent medical adviser requested by the police.

The door opened. Stuart Clifton came in. The meeting began. Martin Gibson cleared his throat and made some introductions.

Clifton scratched his chin and watched as Gibson began talking without saying very much. The officials sat like sentries. It was Dr Porter who got to the point.

The number of arrests among children on Ward Four was inexplicably high, he said, far higher than the established average. Chance could not explain this. Porter paused. It was a mistake. It gave Dr Nanayakkara an opening to speak, and he used it to disagree. Porter persisted and, speaking without notes, began to list the causes of his concern.

From time to time as Porter spoke, Nanayakkara interjected. He disagreed. Porter persisted. Nanayakkara disagreed again. Clifton watched the friction fizzle between the two of them. Nanayakkara was glaring at Porter, while Gibson, who was now as nervous as a fawn, tried to soothe them with neutrality. Clifton began to worry about both men. Nanayakkara struck him as arrogant and Porter as a pedant.

Porter struggled to press his case for a murder inquiry, his voice rising with urgency as he spoke. He believed that these arrests were the result of foul play, he said, whether by an outsider coming on to the ward or, even, as he suspected, by a member of hospital staff with Munchausen Syndrome By Proxy. He believed that three children had been murdered and that 11 others had survived attempts or, in some cases, a series of attempts to murder them. Porter mentioned Brad Gibson—the pain which he felt at his I/V site strongly suggested the use of some toxin in his drip. Clifton saw a thunderous look on Nanayakkara's face. Then Porter played the one strong card in his hand—Paul Crampton. There was no doubt in his mind, he said, that tests on this boy's blood proved that he had been injected with insulin. Porter said he had made his own enquiries and was unable to establish any circumstances which could explain this and, therefore, he concluded that the boy had been attacked.

Nanayakkara pointed out that the presence of an abnormal quantity of insulin in the blood might have a medical explanation. Porter countered that the quantity of insulin was too high for that. They wrangled on, with Nanayakkara conceding that in this one case there did seem to be grounds for concern and Porter insisting that they should install video cameras on the ward. But if Porter was looking for support, he received none. Neither Martin

Gibson nor Professor Hull would enter either side of the argument. Clifton had heard enough.

He proposed that Professor Hull should take the medical files of all 14 children and 'audit' them in order to see whether there really was anything suspicious about any of them. Hull would report back to him. In the meantime, the police would handle any publicity and he was grateful for any help the hospital could give him. Martin Gibson agreed to co-operate in every way. The meeting ended.

Clifton took the names and addresses of the 14 children Porter was interested in. He was not allowed to take their files until he had permission from their parents. As he walked back to the car, he was thoughtful.

Either this was the biggest crime he had ever come across, a case of multiple murder and attempted murder on a scale and in a fashion that would command pride of place in the Chamber of Horrors, or else there was no crime at all, just a daft doctor with a panic attack. Clifton was worried. A detective likes a mystery, just like a journalist likes a story, but with this one, he didn't even know whether there was a crime at the bottom of it at all, let alone who the criminal might be; he had no hard evidence, no solid ground, nothing more than suspicion and doubt to work with, and to make the mystery even deeper, he was being led far away from the familiar beaten track off into the strange and uncharted world of doctors and medicine.

He also still had the uneasy feeling that the hospital was trying to use him. It was only a hunch but he was pretty sure that, whatever Dr Porter might think, he was expected now to go off and spend a couple of weeks looking into this and then to report that all was well, that there was no sign of crime and that the hospital was in the clear. He didn't relish that job.

As Clifton's red Cavalier pulled away from the front of the hospital, it swept past a row of clear glass windows, each hung with faded white curtains blotched with blue flowers. Beyond them, in blurred outline, elderly men and women shuffled slowly in their slippers and sat crumpled in bedside chairs, their parched faces peering at the world passing by. This was the geriatric ward.

On this particular morning, on a steel-framed bed in the far corner of the ward, tucked well away from the bustle of bedpans and walking frames, an old lady lay sleeping deeply. She was 73 years old, she was almost blind, she was diabetic, and she was now so senile that she barely recognized her own name. According to the notes on the clipboard at the foot of her bed, she was Dorothy Lowe, or just plain 'Dot' to the friends she used to know.

She had lain there now for four days, hovering always on the brink of unconsciousness, life glimmering into her from a drip at the head of her bed. She seemed to be holding her own but four days ago, when she was rushed into the hospital, she had been very close to death. She had been brought by ambulance from an old people's home in Waltham on the Wolds where, quite without warning or explanation, she had suddenly sunk into a coma, her body had gone cold and become clammy with sweat, her dried old skin had drained to grey, she had been unrousable. No one was too sure what had happened. It was true she was mildly diabetic but her condition had been stable for years, held in check with a regular injection of insulin every morning, and yet all her symptoms pointed to one explanation: despite her regular medication, she had suffered a severe attack of hypoglycaemia. Her blood sugar had simply melted away.

It was only quick action by a sharp-witted GP in Waltham on the Wolds that had saved her. He had immediately hooked her up to a glucagon drip and dragged her slowly back out of the coma. On the geriatric ward in Grantham, the staff guessed that Dot must have missed a meal so that her normal insulin injection had burned through her veins without encountering any opposition and devoured her vital blood sugar as it went, or else she had accidentally been given far more insulin than normal. The old people's home was short of staff and used a lot of temporary nurses who were moonlighting from places like Grantham Hospital; they said they couldn't understand it. Dot herself, blind and confused, was oblivious to all that had gone on and could tell the doctors nothing of what had happened to her. Still, whatever the cause, she seemed to be on the mend now. Everyone on the geriatric ward seemed pretty sure that there was nothing to worry about.

The red Cavalier turned right out of the gate and swept down the hill into Grantham. In the front seat, Stuart Clifton gripped the wheel and wondered.

*

Clifton had no idea how long Professor Hull would take to finish his audit of the children's files. He knew, too, that the whole affair might prove to be a lot of nonsense, but he decided it would do no harm to have a little look, see what he could turn up. So on the day after the meeting at the hospital, Thursday 2 May, he persuaded the Detective Chief Inspector at Grantham, Alan Smith, to give him some space in his office and to let him use the team of five Family Service officers who dealt with child abuse and who, Clifton thought, might have the right sort of light touch to deal with bereaved families and frightened kids. Then he started to spin a few wheels.

If Nelson Porter was right—and Clifton could not forget that urgent voice—then three of these children had been murdered, Liam Taylor, Tim Hardwick, Claire Peck. They had to be the starting point. In a case without evidence, here were three small bodies, three small reservoirs of reliable fact, all of which would have been recorded in the post-mortem reports and other paper-work filed at the time of their death. Clifton dispatched a car to the coroner's office.

But the children who had died were only part of the story. Dr Porter had identified 11 others who had survived what he believed were attempts to murder them. Clifton decided to fish a little, to try and talk to patients, parents, doctors, nurses who knew about these kids. He'd start with Paul Crampton and Brad Gibson since their names had come up the strongest at the meeting. And since any of these people they were talking to might turn out to be a multiple killer, he asked for a PDF, a personal description form, to record the biographical details of each one of them. And, while they were about it, they had better try and find blood samples taken from some of these other children while they were ill. For all Clifton knew, they might all have had too much insulin.

With his small team sent off to different corners of Grantham, Clifton went looking for some back-up. The permanent incident room at Grantham was not being used, so he booked it. That gave him a nice big airy room with 12 computer terminals and a stack of telephone lines. The problem then was to beg or borrow some staff to run it. He needed an office manager to take charge, a receiver to handle all incoming information, a statement-reader to collate and analyse it, an action-allocator to farm out work to detectives and he would also need typists. He managed to recruit just two uniformed constables, only one of whom knew his way around the computer system, because he trained others how to use it. For the moment, it was the best he could do. Clifton decided to take a break and go and have a look at what all the trouble was about.

He walked on to Ward Four unannounced and unchallenged, wandered around the race-track corridor, past the play room and the six-bed area, poked his head into the Treatment Room, strolled past the four-bed area and round past the cubicles, pausing only to glance through a window at the interior of one of them. He sauntered back, wondering how you could ever cover a four-cornered, four-sided, multi-chambered area like this with security cameras, and concluded that he would fix one camera over the main double doors to see who was coming and going and hope that that did the trick. Then he wandered out, still unchallenged and apparently unremarked.

Soon the first results of Clifton's inquiries began to flow back to the incident room at Grantham police station. They were confusing.

The post-mortem reports revealed no hint of foul play: Liam Taylor had died of heart failure, Tim Hardwick of epilepsy, Claire Peck of asthma. Tim Hardwick had been buried, but the other two had been cremated. The medical evidence clearly indicated that all of these deaths had natural causes. No sign of foul play. No need to look any further. But Clifton did and for one very clear reason.

The officer who had collected the post-mortem reports explained that the elderly coroner, T. J. Pert, had been hatching a few worries of his own. Pert knew all there was to know about death in south Lincolnshire and he said there was something wrong here. Nothing he could put his finger on. Nothing he had wanted to make a fuss about. But, still, there was something odd. Put at its simplest, T. J. Pert was afraid that there were too many dead children on his patch. On the face of it, there was nothing suspicious about any of them—which was why he had held no inquests—but taken together they worried him. So Pert had handed over the post-mortem details of five other children who had died in the area in the first few months of the year. He was not saying that there was anything wrong with any of these five deaths, just that he sensed that something was wrong. Clifton felt the force of Pert's anxiety.

He scanned the five new files. Like the three dead children on Nelson Porter's list, all were said to have died of natural causes, and, at first sight, these five had nothing to do with Ward Four. Unlike the three on Porter's list, the five provided by the coroner had all died at home—two babies who had been dying slowly since birth, a seven-year-old girl who had suffered all her life from cerebral palsy, a baby boy who had died in his cot, and a little girl who had died in a cot death at home after spending some time in the hospital. Her name was Becky. It was hard to see how any of them could be linked to events on Ward Four. But Clifton thought he would look a little deeper, because the fact was that he understood the infant doubt that had nagged at T. J. Pert; he could hear the same small cry of alarm in his own mind.

Now he had 19 potential victims—eight dead and 11 surviving—and no evidence. The only way to deal with confusion was to get more information. Were these post-mortem reports reliable? What else could they find on the dead children? How many of them had been treated on Ward Four, how many had died there, or if they had been discharged from the ward, how much time passed before they died elsewhere? What kind of drugs might have been used? And who had access to them? Clifton briefed his officers, who went out looking for answers and who then returned to the incident room with more confusion.

Since he was sharing his office, Clifton had appointed the local DCI, Alan Smith, to be his deputy on the inquiry. Smith had been to see Martin Gibson at the hospital and tried to find out more about insulin. Gibson had explained that all of the hospital's insulin was produced from human cells. None of it was manufactured synthetically. Alan Smith said he understood. Then he talked to a police surgeon who said that human insulin was very different to the manufactured type and would cause an immediate coma, not the kind of drowsy decline reported with Paul Crampton. If that was right, Smith reasoned, then somebody must be bringing manufactured insulin into the hospital from an outside source, in which case the tracing of that source would be a crucial part of the inquiry. Smith decided to double check and spoke to Professor

Hull at Queen's Med, who said that Smith's information was entirely wrong: both types of insulin produced exactly the same symptoms. The lead took them nowhere.

The officers who had been to see the parents of Paul Crampton and Brad Gibson reported back. They had spoken at length to David Crampton and to Judith Gibson. They had been very helpful and very intrigued and they confirmed the general air of confusion and mystery around their children's illness, but they had no more idea of what had really happened than anyone else. The interviews led nowhere.

Clifton was having trouble finding blood samples for any of the other children. He was also having trouble staffing the incident room. In the old days, a senior detective would launch an inquiry and grab whatever men he needed. Now, everybody had a budget; every department and every operation had to justify its use of resources; and there was hell to pay for anyone who wasted anything. At the moment, he couldn't even get enough typists, let alone extra detectives.

Still Clifton pushed forward. On Friday, he sent officers back to Grantham Hospital. One went to Ward Four to find out about insulin—how much was held there, where it was stored, who had access to it—and another went to see Martin Gibson and asked for a list of all staff who had access to Ward Four. Martin Gibson said he was anxious for the hospital to co-operate in every way and he understood the importance of this list, but he was afraid that he could not do very much now. There was a bank holiday. The hospital offices would be closed until Tuesday. For four days now, he could not help.

If Nelson Porter was right, if someone was murdering children in that hospital, Clifton only hoped that the killer took a rest as well.

David Crampton was beginning to understand. A month had passed since Paul had been discharged without explanation from Queen's Med. At first, he had been bursting to discover the truth but then, as the days passed and he heard nothing, he began to shelter behind his ignorance. There was something comforting about not knowing too much; it was a relief to pretend that life was normal again. Still, it was not long before his character asserted itself and he and Kath felt strong enough again to want an answer. Kath went to see her GP and asked for the truth—what was wrong with Paul? The GP said he thought that he might have a bit of a squint. Kath persisted. She could see that the GP had Paul's file open on the desk and she could see a letter from Queen's Med, but the GP wouldn't show it to her. This made David angry, ready to start thumping tables again in search of the truth.

Then he had a call from the police, and at 11.10 on Friday morning, May 3, Detective Sergeant John Osbourne walked into his office at the construction company and told him that they were inquiring into the possible maladministration of drugs at the hospital.

'Well, that would explain a hell of a lot,' said David.

He and Osbourne then talked for five hours, at the end of which David had disclosed every tiny fragment of fact which he could recall about Paul's time on Ward Four, while Osbourne had revealed almost nothing.

That night, David talked to Kath. This was obviously something to do with insulin. That much had been clear from the sergeant's questions. They went back to their suspicions all those weeks ago that the hospital had somehow made a mess of the drugs which they had been giving Paul. But why call the police to deal with that? David decided to go back to the hospital and thump a table or two there.

Before he had a chance to do that, he was called by Judith Gibson. The two families had swapped phone numbers in Queen's Med and had said they would stay in touch. Brad finally had been released from Queen's Med and declared fit and well. The *Grantham Journal* had made a big fuss of the 'miracle boy' who had died on Good Friday and then come back from the dead, and the hospital had basked in the reflected glory when a couple of national papers picked up the story. The truth was that Brad was not really so well. He still had pains in his legs and he was having terrible nightmares. Judith was not sure what to do and a child psychiatrist suggested that she ask Brad to make a drawing of the dreams. And he sat down and painted himself, lying in bed with huge monsters rising over him, trying, as he put it, to gobble him up.

Judith called the Cramptons now to tell them that she and Steve had had these strange visits. The first was from the police, two women officers who had been so discreet that they might almost have been on a training exercise. Then they had had a second visit, from two of Martin Gibson's assistants at the hospital, who had absolutely refused to explain what was going on but kept insisting there was nothing to worry about.

'We've just come to reassure you,' one of them said.

'About what?'

'About this police inquiry. We're quite sure it will all blow over in a couple of days, and there is absolutely no reason to worry.'

'About what?'

They wouldn't say, but when they had gone, Judith and Steve wondered whether the Cramptons had heard anything, so Judith called and together they started piecing together the clues, detecting the detectives.

The other families were still alone. Chris and Joanne Taylor were now so confused about the cause of Liam's death that they had begun to suspect themselves. They had gone to their GP and asked for tests to make sure that they were not suffering from some genetic fault which might destroy their surviving son, Jamie, or any other children they might have in the future. The GP said they were fine. Joanne was back at work now in the hairdressers, and chirpy again with her customers. Except for one day when someone brought in a copy of the *Grantham Journal* whose front page was full of the story of a miracle boy who had come back from the dead. Why couldn't Liam have come back? The thought pierced her heart and suddenly she found herself crying in front of everyone.

Belinda King had decided that she could not just go back to work in the hospital and ignore all the faults she had found on Ward Four, so she had gone to see Dr Nanayakkara and told him how disgusted she had been and, in particular, how worried she had been at the lack of emergency equipment. Dr Nanayakkara said he would write to Moira Onions, who would contact Belinda to discuss this. But Belinda never heard another word.

Sue and David Peck were still in pieces. David had accepted Dr Porter's word that Claire had died from asthma and that it was a freakish million-to-one chance that the medicine had not saved her. But Sue's dad was suspicious. He was not sure why, but he wanted to hire a solicitor and sue that hospital. As he and Sue were leaving the Treatment Room, with Claire dead on the Resuscitaire behind them, he had heard a nurse say 'Oh, no, not another one'. In some way he was sure that it was the hospital's fault. Sue Peck didn't feel like hiring lawyers, but she knew what her father meant. They put a message in the newspaper about Claire's death and she knew that it was normal to thank the hospital for all their efforts but somehow, instinctively, she knew that that would be wrong, so she wrote an announcement that deliberately left out Grantham Hospital.

On Ward Four, all the children who had suffered arrests were home now, except for Katie Phillips, who still came back on to the ward each night for observation. She was still being specialed by Bev Allitt, who had agreed to be her godmother and had become a close friend to Sue and Peter Phillips. She would go round to their house to visit or come into the ward on her day off with a gift for Katie, and this bank holiday weekend, just for a treat, she was taking Katie off to Skegness for the day, well away from the hospital, well away from everyone, the two of them together.

The deputy manager, Peter Flood, was trying to get to grips with the mystery. He happened to bump into the Control of Infection Officer in the corridor and he explained the problem and wondered whether they could be dealing with an infection, possibly Legionnaire's disease, which was being carried into the ward through the ventilation. He asked for some swabs. A few days later, he got the result. Negative. Then he discovered there had been a misunderstanding. The swabs had not been taken from the Ward Four ventilation shaft at all, but from the ventilator in the Treatment Room, the machine which was used to help sick children breathe.

Flood had another idea. If Dr Porter was right, the children on Ward Four were virtually defenceless and so, in secrecy, he approached a handful of nurses from other wards and asked them to work shifts on the children's ward. As far as the Ward Four staff knew, the extra nurses were there to help them deal with the crisis, but Peter Flood had something else in mind: the outside nurses were there to watch and if they saw anything suspicious they must tell him. More than that, if they saw any nurse going into one of the cubicles alone, they should find an excuse to follow. Flood was careful to choose nurses he could trust; one of them was his own wife.

The ward staff huddled together under their familiar routine like campers in a storm. In all the weeks of anxiety, they had never imagined they were dealing with murder. The police had been called in? Ridiculous. What do the police know about medicine? Calling in the police was just ridiculous. They'd just upset everybody. They'd gone and installed this ugly camera over the double doors. Bev and Nadine giggled at it, and Bev cracked some joke about Big Brother. And they'd gone and put an alarm bell on the Treatment Room door so that no one could walk in there without upsetting everyone on the ward. It was all so ridiculous. Most of the staff ignored it all, got on with their work and tried to pretend that nothing so silly was happening.

So it was that just before the bank holiday, when a young policewoman came to the ward to ask about insulin, she was told everything she could possibly want to know: all about the different types of insulin that were kept there, and the 10 ml vials they were all stored in, and about the fridge behind the nurses' station where the insulin was safely locked away so that it could be reached only by using the key that was held at all times by the nurse in charge. However, no one told the officer that on 14 February, just before the first of the children fell ill, the key to this fridge had gone missing and never been found again.

And Sister Barker did not mention that now something seemed to have gone missing from the nurses' station. It was the allocation book, in which she listed the particular children who had been allocated to each nurse on each shift. It had vanished, but she did not tell the police. She thought maybe they had taken it, or else it was not important.

As soon as the bank holiday was over, on Tuesday morning, Stuart Clifton dispatched officers to the hospital to start digging out work rotas and tracing nurses for interview. In the incident room, he sat down to read Professor Hull's report on his audit of the 14 children's medical notes, which had arrived that morning, earlier than he had dared to expect.

The report hindered at least as much as it helped. On the face of it, Hull was joining Dr Nanayakkara and the pathologists in demolishing Dr Porter's fears. Having read the hospital notes, Hull was saying that they contained no evidence of anything suspicious about most of these arrests. On the evidence of the hospital notes alone, they could be explained by natural causes—inhalation of vomit, build-up of mucous, sick children becoming sicker. But there were three cases—Paul Crampton, Brad Gibson and Patrick Elstone—where he signalled some worry, saying he thought there might have been 'unexplained events'. Even there, he was tentative, volunteering that the arrests of Brad and Patrick might yet be shown to be natural. It was only Paul Crampton who really worried him. Here, he said, the notes did contain 'evidence of an untoward act'. For Stuart Clifton, scratching his chin as he flipped backwards and forwards through the report, this was not enough to mount an inquiry. Indeed, the report was so vague that, in evidential terms, it was nothing.

Still, Clifton was moved more and more by a feeling, which he could barely explain and which he could certainly not justify, that he had to pursue this thing. So strong was this feeling, that he spent the morning spreading his feelers through four different subdivisions of the force calling in old favours to poach eight more detective constables for his inquiry with the bonus of a detective inspector for office manager, bringing his team up to a total of 18, though he still couldn't persuade anyone to lend him enough typists.

On Wednesday, Clifton drove to Nottingham to see Professor Hull and Derek Johnston. For two hours, he wrestled with the technicalities of body chemistry, and insulinoma. He learned about blood sugar—'the fuel of the central nervous system'—and about how it was supplied by food and controlled by the pancreas which pumped out insulin to destroy it if it started to rise too high. A pancreas could develop faults. In some people, this meant that it failed to pump out the insulin when it needed to, with the result that they overdosed on blood sugar; these people were diabetics and had to be injected with insulin. Other people might have the opposite problem: the pancreas would churn out insulin when it was not needed, destroying blood sugar and throwing them into a hypoglycaemic coma.

Clifton tripped and stumbled through the unfamiliar terrain but he kept going—insulin could not be taken orally, only by injection, it faded quickly in the bloodstream but it could be preserved outside the body by freezing, just like milk—and finally, after skirting through the signs of foul play on the 14 children, he arrived at a clearing. If you took Nelson Porter's fears and you attacked them with the greatest possible scepticism, then at this stage you could say that there was no hard evidence that any child had been murdered; you could say that there was no proof at all that ten of the 11 surviving children had ever been attacked by human hand; you could say that in the case of the eleventh child, Paul Crampton, there was a remote, theoretical chance that his first two hypos could have been caused by a natural flaw in his pancreas aggravated by clumsy treatment; but when Paul Crampton suddenly plummeted into his third hypoglycaemic attack, at lunch-time on Thursday 28 March, when his insulin level suddenly soared up above 500, at that moment, there was clear evidence that someone had stuffed that little boy full of unprescribed insulin. It was the only available explanation. Stuart Clifton was sure he had now found some firm ground to stand on.

Working on Professor Hull, Clifton now came up with a time frame. The blood sample which proved that Paul had been attacked had been taken at 1.30 on 28 March. Hull believed that the attack had taken place only 20 or 30 minutes earlier but it was just possible, if Paul had been fed in the meantime and the food had temporarily built up his blood sugar, that it might have happened earlier, possibly as much as three hours earlier. Playing safe, Clifton sectioned out the four hours from 9.30 that morning until 1.30. At some point in that time frame, the attacker had got to Paul Crampton. Clifton now threw his whole team at this one point.

That afternoon he issued a volley of orders. Target anyone who had access to Paul in this time frame, and TIE them—Trace, Interview and Eliminate. They all have to give their movements, and everyone else's movements, too. Then cross-check them. That means consultants, junior doctors, nurses, visitors on the ward and the boy's parents, too. Take a look at them—could they have done it, are they really that happily married? Contact the labs in Cardiff: check this blood test they did, get more detail, send someone down there to talk to them. Contact pharmaceutical companies: check the effect of insulin on a five-month-old boy, find out the drug's exact rate of decay, check whether you can be sure it has been injected and not produced by the pancreas. Draw up a chart with everything we know about Paul Crampton's blood sugar—feeding times, medications, blood sugar levels, everything. Get an expert to graph the time he was given the insulin. Get a new sample of the boy's blood, check his sugar level when it's normal. And where did this insulin come from? Find out how much insulin has been supplied to Ward Four and can they account for all of it? Is there a local registry of insulin users? Find it, get all the names. And how was he given it? Could it have been in the nebulizer? Get it and examine it. And somebody get hold of more typists.

Clifton's team was soon staggering through a blizzard of detail. There were times when they seemed to see a shape emerging, only to find it blown away in the next swirl of information. At other times, they wandered off and hit dead ends, but they kept coming back to their original track, to the insulin in Paul Crampton's blood.

Working in pairs, detectives started to trawl through the recollections of everyone who had worked on Ward Four between 9.30 and 1.30 on 28 March. Trace, interview, eliminate. They questioned Dr Porter and Dr Nanayakkara. They found the nurses who had cared for Paul, Kate Lock, Bev Allitt, student nurse Moore, Betty Asher, Sister Barker. They started looking for other parents whose children had been on the ward that day. They looked, too, for outsiders. There was no perimeter security at the hospital. Anyone could walk through the main door and down the long central corridor to Ward Four. If it was visiting time, anyone would have a good chance of wandering on to the ward and mixing with the children.

In Cardiff, Detective Inspector Newmarch confirmed the results of Paul's test, that it had registered 500 milliunits of insulin per litre of blood and then gone off the gauge, while his C-peptide had stayed low, and he came away with a new thought, something which was obvious in hindsight. If they took Paul's blood sample to another lab with different facilities, they could complete the test and discover exactly how much insulin was in his blood.

Officers went back to David and Kath Crampton and discreetly took each of them aside to ask whether there was anything wrong with their marriage, or to put it another way—and the officers said they were sorry to have to ask this—but was there anyone else in their life? Each of them said there was no one. The detectives asked for the records of David's car phone and used them to check the Cramptons' account of their movements. They went up to the canteen and seized hundreds of feet of old till-roll so that they could look for a record of the cardboard Cornish pasty which David said he had bought at lunch-time on 28 March.

Back at Grantham station, they soon found the date and time on the till-roll, but there was no sign of anyone buying a pasty. David was led into an interview room. Stuart Clifton followed him in. David sensed that he was a suspect as well as a witness. It gave him a creepy feeling. He sat in one of the chairs and leaned back, trying to look relaxed. He wondered about the Guildford Four. He hoped Clifton knew what he was doing. And why the heck wasn't there a record of him buying his lunch? The door opened. Two young policemen in uniform approached him. They stopped in front of him, one at each arm.

'Mr Crampton,' said one.

David stared up at them in shock. 'Yeah?'

'Would you mind moving? You're leaning against the emergency buzzer.'

It seemed to take ages to sort out the till-roll, but eventually they discovered that the clock in the till had slipped and it was exactly 14 hours and 51 minutes slow and so, at last, they found the pasty and it was confirmed that David had been in the canteen by 12.52 that day.

For David and Kath, all this investigation did little to help. Both of them had now been interviewed repeatedly and at exhausting length, and there was now no doubt in either of their minds that the police believed that someone deliberately had poisoned Paul with insulin. But who? And why?

They knew that Judith and Steve Gibson had been visited by the police, but they had not been through these kind of interviews. They guessed that the police had spoken to the Gibsons only because they might have known something about Paul. But why would Paul be singled out for attack by this poisoner? At home at night, David guessed it must be someone with a grudge against the family. And if it was, surely they were liable to attack again. Night after night, he woke in the darkness and went padding round the house, following sounds, checking the doors and windows, noting the whereabouts of usable weapons in case he needed to defend the family. He warned Kath that they would have to be careful. When she collected the children from playgroup and school, she was looking over her shoulder in case she was being followed, checking parked cars and pedestrians in case there was a strange or hostile face. If she stopped to go into a shop—even if her car was parked right outside the shop door—she took all three children in with her. But there was never any clue. Everyone was suspect. Once or twice, David and Kath even suspected each other, suddenly caught themselves thinking the unthinkable and then quickly chased the thought away and told themselves to take it easy.

Clifton had to juggle his resources. He wanted to concentrate on Paul Crampton, but his officers kept stumbling into other leads. Professor Hull told them that, from his conversations with Nelson Porter, he knew that Porter had found some traces of insulin in Claire Peck's blood and that he also suspected that there might have been insulin in a batch of sodium bicarbonate which he had been feeding into Claire's I/V drip. This would change everything—if they were dealing with a contaminated batch of sodium bicarbonate, and not a crime at all.

Clifton sent officers to Ward Four to seize a dozen samples of sodium bicarbonate and to the path lab to seize the blood which Porter had drawn from Claire's heart immediately after her death. He sent them straight off to Cardiff for analysis. He called Martin Gibson and warned him to withdraw sodium bicarbonate from all over the hospital until Cardiff had finished their tests. He contacted the Medicine Control Agency, in case this turned into a national problem, and they agreed that they would be on standby when the test results arrived. DI Newmarch travelled back down to Cardiff to get the results as they came through. But he hit a dead end. The sodium bicarbonate was clean. Claire's insulin count was high—it was up to 161—but her C-peptide was also high: she had manufactured the extra insulin herself. The doctors explained to the detectives that Dr Porter had pumped glucose and dextrose into her, thus raising her blood sugar, and that her dying pancreas had behaved as it should have done and poured out extra insulin to reduce her sugar level. Still, there was one curious loose end here—Nelson Porter. Why had he never told the police that he thought there was insulin in Claire's blood and in the sodium bicarb? Was he trying to hide something?

Porter was summoned to Grantham police station. For several hours, the man who finally had insisted that the strong arm of the law be brought into the hospital found himself clutched in its grip. He explained that on the very day that Stuart Clifton had first come to the hospital, he had sent off samples from Claire Peck's blood and I/V bags to Cardiff. He had not told the police. He did not know what the tests would show. Even when he got the results, by phone two days later, he had still not told the police because he could not find them and he was not sure what the results meant. Then he was released, shaken but clearly not guilty of anything other than his normal scattered thinking.

There was one final point. Dr Porter's suspicions about Claire and her sodium bicarbonate had been proved to be wrong and the episode appeared to confirm Professor Hull's view that there was nothing suspicious about the death and illness of most of these 14 children. But Clifton now recognized that if this case amounted to anything, it would be because doctors were fallible. He asked his officers to look a little further in their search for blood samples for all these children.

From time to time in his career in the CID, Stuart Clifton had been sent off to the police college at Bramshill in Hampshire to learn about murder inquiries. But all he had been taught there was about computer software and man management. The business of detection he had learned on the ground. As far as he was concerned, there was nothing magical about police work. There were a few good rules of thumb: keep it simple, follow your leads, don't fly off after fancy theories, don't look for luck, and don't give up until you reach the end, at least for as long as the manpower lasts.

He covered his back, ruling out every last alternative explanation for Paul Crampton's illness. Like Nelson Porter before him, he found that no one on that ward on 28 March should have been given any insulin at all. After learning how Claire Peck had produced excess insulin to deal with all the glucose she was being fed by Dr Porter, he wondered whether Paul Crampton might have done the same. He made a rough chart linking his feeds and his medication with his BM stick results, and he took it to Nottingham to show to Professor Hull.

Hull looked at it and tutted. 'I wish I could get my medical students to do work like this.'

Clifton accepted the compliment. 'But is it feasible? Could this be the explanation for the boy's hypoglycaemic attacks?'

Hull said he would look at it and produce a more detailed chart, but when he did so he concluded that this could not possibly be the explanation. The only other possibility was that there was something bizarre about Paul's blood and its normal day-to-day insulin reading, so Clifton asked the Cramptons if he could have a sample and send it down to Cardiff to be tested. And whereas the hospital had taken 15 days to get a result, the police now arranged for the blood to be taken at 9.00 in the morning, labelled at the police station at 9.30, biked to the hospital at 10.00, spun in the centrifuge there at 10.50, frozen at 11.10, returned to the police station at 11.30 and couriered down to Cardiff at 11.40, in time for it to be tested that same day. The result that afternoon showed that there was nothing unusual about the insulin in Paul Crampton's blood. The more Clifton checked, the more certain he became that he was investigating an act of malice.

His detectives struggled to find their way around the world of science. Clifton sent two of them to London to track down a sample of blood which had been taken from Paul Crampton on Monday 25 March, the day after his second hypoglycaemic attack. The Grantham path lab had been asked to send it off for insulin tests at the time, but after a preliminary test they had decided not to. Weeks later, on the advice of Queen's Med, it had been sent to the lab at Hammersmith Hospital in London who now reported that the insulin level in this sample was only 33. Clifton was puzzled. If his gut feeling was to be believed, each of this boy's arrests was the result of an insulin overdose, yet this lab result completely contradicted the theory. Perhaps the insulin had been flushed out of Paul's system before the blood was taken to be tested. It was a day or two later that Clifton discovered that the London lab was measuring its insulin in different units to Cardiff, and the London numbers needed to be multiplied by 7.5. In other words, on 25 March, on the day after his second hypo, Paul's blood had contained 250 units of insulin—not nearly as high as on 28 March, but high enough to be most suspicious.

Clifton pressed Cardiff to produce the 28 March sample so that it could be sent off to a different lab to discover how far over 500 it would register. Cardiff apologized: they had exhausted the sample.

On Ward Four, too, the detectives were struggling to penetrate the secret and mysterious world of medicine. The nurses all said it was impossible to remember exactly what they had been doing on the morning of 28 March. The detectives understood that, but they knew there was more to it than that. The nurses felt threatened. They knew that Martin Gibson had handed over a computer print-out listing the names of all the staff in the hospital, broken down into four groups according to their ease of access to Ward Four. The nurses knew that they were all prime suspects. They were nervous of saying something that would get them into trouble or, just as bad, that would get a colleague into trouble, and some of the bolder nurses made no secret of their insistence that there was nothing criminal here. They made it very clear that they resented the whole inquiry and when officers went down to the ward to seize drugs or to find staff for interview, they some-times felt like trespassers. Whatever the reasons, the nurses found it hard to be forthcoming.

Two days after she noticed that the allocation book was missing, Sister Barker discovered that someone had cut out a sheaf of pages from the old diary which she habitually carried with her on doctors' rounds and where she noted down their instructions and also recorded which nurse was allocated to each child. This meant that she no longer had any central record of the staff allocations for most of the period when children had been suffering arrests. But she did not mention it to the police.

No one expected the police to find anything. One afternoon early in the inquiry, a student nurse called Sarah Biggs was talking to Bev Allitt about it. Sarah was saying that she'd heard that the Royal College of Nursing was finding a solicitor to sit with nurses during their interviews to give them advice. Bev said she'd already been interviewed once and she didn't think the RCN were a very good union and anyway, she added, the police were never going to be able to prove anything because they would never find the syringes that had been used.

'They've already been disposed of,' she said.

Sarah wasn't sure what she meant by that.

Stuart Clifton realized that, if this inquiry ever led anywhere, they were going to have to come back through most of these people and ask them not just about Paul Crampton on 28 March but about all the other children and all the other incidents. He decided that they should draw up a chart, logging all of the children they might be interested in and all of the doctors and all of the nurses who had been at work when they suffered arrests. That way, they could use each interview to cover all of the children, try and save themselves some time and some pain.

During the second week of the inquiry, the local press blew the detectives' cover, reporting that police had been called to the hospital to investigate the possible misuse of drugs. The hospital masked the crisis with a misleading press statement which pretended that the police had been called in as the result of one routine blood test result, and news failed to travel beyond Lincolnshire. Even the parents of children who had suffered arrests failed to understand the significance of the two-paragraph story in the *Grantham Journal*, headlined 'Police Probe Drug Error'.

By the time the inquiry moved into its third week, the process of cross-checking and elimination was beginning to narrow the field. It reminded Clifton of a murder he had handled once, when a child had been found dead at home. The killer clearly knew his way around the flat. So he had been there before. The trouble was that the child's mother was a prostitute and Clifton had had to work his way through a thick address book full of possible suspects before he finally found his culprit. But he had got there.

By this time, he was convinced that the Cramptons were innocent—they had no motive and neither of them had been with Paul for four hours before his first hypo, on Saturday 23 March—so it was a fair working assumption that the attack on Paul had taken place when neither of them was with him. This idea blocked out a large area of the time frame he was looking at. Kath Crampton had gone into the cubicle at 8.30 that Thursday morning, and nurses, doctors on their rounds, visitors and other parents logged her presence there until 12.17 when David had arrived to take over from her. Kath had left at 12.20, a time which showed up on the records of the car phone which she had used to call the school where the eldest Crampton child, Louise, was ill. David had stayed in the room until 12.45 when he had gone off for his pasty, which had finally shown up on the canteen till-roll. He had returned at 1.15. While he was away—for that critical 30 minutes— Paul had been unguarded. In that short time, only a handful of people had been seen in Paul's cubicle. They were now the shortlist of suspects. In all probability, one of them had tried to kill him. Clifton sent his men out to interview the names on this shortlist for a second time.

He was still trying to stay on top of leads involving other children and he needed more men. He knew there were senior officers who were griping that he was wasting everybody's time but, with a combination of political clout and good humour, he drafted in reinforcements so that he had more than 30 officers on the inquiry. He was now sure in his own mind that he was dealing with a child-killer. All he needed was one good break. He was beginning to work very long hours, starting by 8.00 most mornings, returning home around midnight. He was also under pressure with the Open University whose rules permitted him to miss only one essay assignment, which he had already done. On some nights, he was returning home from the incident room and going straight to his textbooks, working on social studies until dawn and then returning to the incident room without sleep.

In the third week, the pressure began to pay off. First, he got a small break. A detective constable had gone to Pilgrim Hospital down the road in Boston to see if there was any blood there from any of the children who had suffered arrests. And there, in the freezer, he had found a small bottle containing blood taken from Paul Crampton at 1.30 on 28 March. It was the blood that had been lost in the system because of an error on the bottle's label. Its discovery meant that even though Cardiff had exhausted their supply, this could now be sent to a lab with different facilities so that they could come up with the whole truth about the amount of insulin which had been injected into Paul Crampton. The constable went back to Grantham triumphant.

Then Stuart Clifton got the big breakthrough he had been waiting for, and when it came, it arrived from an unexpected direction. As Clifton checked and rechecked the exact movements of every individual around Paul Crampton's cubicle between 12.45 and 1.15, PC John Griffiths was putting the finishing touches to a sprawling wall chart in the incident room. For several days he had been trying to log every arrest of every child on Nelson Porter's original list and cross-refer them to columns displaying the names of doctors and nurses who were on duty in the ward at the time of the arrests. Clifton had asked for it, just in case it told them something and because, at the very least, it would be a useful guide for interviews. But it was a complex job: 14 children, a couple of dozen different arrests over a period of months, several dozen different staff members, some of them permanent, some of them temporary, coming and going on different shift patterns, calling in sick and swapping jobs at the last moment.

Eventually, PC Griffiths managed to assemble all of the data and organize it into a chart, and as the young constable carefully listed all of the names for all of the incidents in tidy columns, finally, on Monday 20 May, 19 days after Stuart Clifton first drove to Grantham Hospital to begin the inquiry, nearly 13 weeks since Liam Taylor first arrived on Ward Four, there it was—one word, over and over again, against the name of every child, against the time of every arrest, one word, one name, one answer.

Allitt.

Part Two

Light

Like a bird on the wire,
Like a drunk in a midnight choir,
I have tried in my way to be free.
More like a baby, still born,
Like a beast with its horn,
I have torn everyone who reached out for me.

(Leonard Cohen, 'Bird on the Wire')

7

Bev Allitt was nobody special.

She was born in a little village called Corby Glen which lies in the hills about ten miles south-east of Grantham and looks as though it was thrown together by a drunkard in the dark. It is an ancient tumbledown jumble, all covered in ivy, with narrow lanes that totter uncertainly from one door to another and lots of elderly buildings which seem to be leaning together with their arms slung round each other's shoulders for support. The fields around Corby Glen are full of cows and rabbits and pheasants, and the people you meet in the pubs there often have the same surnames that you can see carved under the moss on the old gravestones up in St John's churchyard. It is a fragment of old England.

Bev Allitt's father, Richard, was born in the village, a sturdy, solid country man, thick set with green eyes and coarse hands. He left school when he was 15 and worked for 22 years in a tractor factory down the road in Essendine until Fiat bought it and closed it down and put half the men in Corby on the dole. Since then, he has driven a delivery van for Jeremy Marshall Roberts, an amiable entrepreneur in the mould of Jeffrey Archer, who sells fine wines and picnic hampers from a converted barn near the church.

Bev Allitt's mother, Lillian, was born five miles away in Castle Bytham, the youngest of eight children in a family that never starved but never had money to boast of. She met Richard when she was only 15, when a friend took him out in his car for a driving lesson round Castle Bytham and they stopped to chat her up. She started going out with him and got pregnant and married him when she was 18. She has always worked, and her hands are worn and red-knuckled. She used to do industrial sewing, stitching sports clothes on a big old sewing machine in the front room, and she has been a cleaner and a school dinner lady.

Bev was born in the council house on the little 1960s estate in the middle of Corby Glen where Richard and Lillian moved after sharing his mother's house for the first couple of years of their marriage. It was an easy birth. At 6.30 on a sunny morning, Richard went off to fetch the nurse, whose name was Mrs Love. He took their daughter, Donna, who was three, round to her granny in Castle Bytham, stopped to tell her the news and then drove over to Essendine to tell them he'd need a bit of time off and, by the time he got back home at 9.30, it was all over. They say second babies are like that; they just can't wait to get out in the world. Richard and Lillian decided to call her Beverly Gail, Bev for short. It was 4 October 1968.

Bev grew up and played in the street with all the other kids on the estate. Most of the families there seemed to have young children—the Skerritts, the Curtises, the Footitts, the Joyces, the Coxes—and Bev spent most of her time running from one front garden to another with mucky fingers, screaming and yelling with the rest of them. She and Rachel Skerritt used to play mothers and babies for hours on end. Just before her fifth birthday, she started at the primary school and every morning she set off to walk across the estate, round the corner by the Fighting Cocks pub, across the bottom of the market square to the Victorian red-brick schoolhouse. She had assembly every day with Mr Holman, then went to Mrs Robinson's class with the other infants, cutting and sticking and drawing. She was a popular little thing, bubbly and pretty and very well-behaved, always volunteering to put round the pencils, not like her little sister Alison, who had such a row with her teacher one day that she turned on her heel and walked off home in a huff. Bev went off on day trips to Sherwood Forest and the fire station and, at Christmas, she played the recorder in the school concert and acted in the nativity plays that were written by the deputy head, Mr Holt.

The village was not as lively as it once had been. The motor car had seen to that. Everyone went off to Grantham or Bourne if they were looking for entertainment. There were only three shops left open now, where once there had been 20: Doggett the baker, Smedley the chemist, Tomlinson the grocer, Brown the bootmaker and most of the others like them had gone. But there was still life there. There was the football team and the bowls club; Bev's dad was keen on both of them. There was cricket, with tea by Mrs Podham; Friday night youth club in the Church rooms; and Brownies, too. Some of the old village traditions still survived: Plough Monday at the beginning of the year; May Day when the children took garlands round the village; and, most of all, Corby Sheep Fair, every October, when farmers came from all around to sell their sheep and everyone joined them to drink till they drowned for three solid days, just as Lincolnshire farmers had been doing in Corby every October since King Edward I was a boy. And there were village characters: Charlie the poacher with the three-wheeled car he called the pink pig; Jeff Lamming, who looked like a Disney dwarf with his white beard and his pipe, who ran the service station and talked all day; Farmer Musson, whose cows still wandered out down the village street, although the parish council used to rap his knuckles for it.

It was quiet, it was friendly, it was safe. There was nothing special about it.

When she was 11, Bev failed her Eleven Plus exam and she was upset about that. Her big sister Donna had passed it and she went off every day to the high school in Grantham and everyone had thought that Bev would do the same, because she was bright and seemed to be doing so well at school. When she got the news, Bev went off to see her friends from the primary school and when she found that most of them had failed too, she seemed to make up her mind that perhaps it was all for the best and that there was nothing wrong with going to Charles Read, the ugly new secondary modern school on the edge of the village.

It was while she was at Charles Read, when she was about 12 or 13, that some of her friends began to think that she was not always very kind. Susan Short noticed it. Susan didn't have a lot of good friends. She was a bit shy and gawky with glasses and sometimes she got bullied, but Bev had taken her under her wing and protected her and been like a little mother to her. Everything would be fine and Susan would be minding her own business, and then suddenly it would all go wrong and Bev would start telling

people not to talk to her or start saying bad things about her.
Then just as suddenly she'd come back and be friends again.

Rachel Skerritt was tougher than Susan and stood for no nonsense, but she noticed it too—how Bev always had to be right
about everything and, even if she wasn't right, she would just fib
and say she was. Or if a group of them did work together, she
would quietly tell the teacher that she'd done it on her own. She
kept sucking up to the teachers, especially Mrs Clements and Miss
Pearson, who taught science, trying to score points.

She wasn't always like that. There were times when she would
be fine and friendly. Then suddenly she'd pull you down in front
of people or turn against you. Rachel thought maybe Bev was
upset because a lot of her friends from primary school were going
off and finding new mates at the secondary school.

Rachel noticed how, if Bev was ever about to be in trouble, she
had this way of turning it on to someone else. If the teacher was
out of the room, for example, Bev would get out of her chair and
start dancing about and then Rachel and some of the others would
get up and join in and, when the teacher came back and got angry
with them, they'd turn round and discover that Bev was already
sitting down, and she wouldn't tell the teacher that she was the
one who'd started it. She'd just let the others get into trouble and
sit there with this little smile on her face. Rachel never knew
whether Bev was just lucky or whether she planned it that way.

Rachel began to get fed up with her. Rachel had all kinds of
problems at home. Her parents were getting divorced and her
mum was going to get married and she had to change her name
to Rachel Smith and people were teasing her about it. But Bev
was all right. Her parents didn't go fighting in the street like some
families. They didn't drink too much. They just went down the
Fighting Cocks for an hour or so some nights. And the Allitts
might not have been rich, but Richard and Lillian both worked,
so they were better off than a lot of people on the estate. Bev
always seemed to get whatever she wanted. In fact, Rachel thought
she was really spoiled. She just had to ask for something, like new
jeans or some toy, and she seemed to get it. Sometimes it annoyed
Rachel, because she would tell Bev that she was saving up her
baby-sitting money to buy something, like a little leather jacket
she had seen in Grantham, and then before she'd had a chance to

buy it, Bev would turn up wearing one. And it would turn out that she had got her mum to buy it for her. It was a bit upsetting.

That didn't mean Bev was the favourite in her family. That was the fourth child, Darren, being the only boy. He had his own bedroom, while the three girls, Donna, Bev and Alison, had to squeeze into one room together. Darren had the best of everything, but Rachel thought all the Allitts were spoiled. When she went round there sometimes for a meal, she couldn't believe the amount they used to eat, huge platefuls of stuff. No wonder Bev was getting podgy.

Rachel and the other girls started leaving Bev to play with her brother and sisters. Bev didn't seem to mind too much. She used to spend most of her time with Darren, who was six years younger than her, so she could mother him and take him for walks. The other girls were still friends with Bev. She wasn't that bad. In fact, she could be quite generous if she thought you were on her side, she'd give you sweets or invite you to come with her family on day trips to Wicksteed Park or the reservoir or even on holidays.

Richard Allitt liked to take his family away for a holiday every summer. He couldn't afford a foreign holiday, and he didn't much want one—he'd never been abroad in his life and never planned to either. When the children were young, he used to take them to Heacham, opposite Skegness on the other side of the Wash, where they found a boarding-house to stay in and they spent a week sitting on the beach playing with the pebbles and going for windy walks. They always stayed in the same place.

Then, one Sunday, they were down in Peterborough, visiting Richard's brother Roger and his family, and Roger said they were just off the next day to the Isle of Wight, to stay in a caravan near Whitecliffe Bay. Richard said he wouldn't mind going there and so Roger phoned the woman who ran the caravan site and arranged for both families to go: four adults and eight children. They had a good time and so they went back again next year and then again, every summer for the next ten years or more. Every year, just the same, they'd pack up the car and leave Corby at midnight and drive all the way down to Southampton with Roger and his family in front in their car and arrive much too early for the ferry and then stay for a week in the same caravan site on Whitecliffe Bay,

playing cricket on the same, familiar beach until the fathers got
tired and had to fall asleep in the sun.

There was just one summer when they tried something different
and drove down to Bude in Cornwall instead—Bev thought it was
great and she wanted to go back—but Richard preferred the Isle
of Wight.

Richard liked to take things steadily. Not that he hadn't had
his rocky moments, when his luck turned bad. Everyone in the
village knew that Richard Allitt had an eye for the girls. Most of
the time, no one minded too much—a ram is built for tupping,
they say—but just once he went too far with a woman who lived
on the same estate, who came from a rough family, and her
husband found out and he came round to the Allitts' house and
got hold of Richard and gave him a good thumping. Lillian and
the children were terribly upset, but Lillian forgave him. Bev
would have been very young when that happened, only nine or
ten, and Richard doubted whether she even remembered it. She
was a bit older, more like 14, when Fiat closed the tractor works
and he lost his job, but she didn't seem too worried by that either,
and he was soon working again, driving the wine van for Jeremy
Marshall Roberts.

Bev was always very stable, a good little girl. Richard and Lillian
never heard any complaints about her at all. She was never in
trouble at school and she was very helpful round the house,
looking after Darren, laying the table, helping with meals. Richard
was a little disappointed that Bev and the others were never sporty
like him, but he didn't worry them about it. Bev was a bit too
heavy for sport. Her only real problem was her health. She started
getting ill when she was 13 or 14, and then there seemed to be no
stopping it. Every week she had something different wrong with
her: stomach ache, headache, neck ache, backache, cuts, bruises.
None of them was very serious, and Lillian always bandaged her
up and sent her off to school with a pat on the head, but she did
seem to have a lot of bad luck.

Rachel and some of the other girls were not so sure about these
illnesses. Half the time, Rachel reckoned, Bev wasn't really that
ill at all. She would come in with her finger all bandaged and tell
people she'd cut herself cooking supper for the family and,
although they were quite impressed that Bev was cooking for

everyone, they'd never see a cut or even any mark when the bandage came off a few days later.

Bev always had some story about her illnesses, how she'd fallen off a horse or been knocked off her bike by a passing car or she'd burned her leg or gashed her arm. Rachel and the others didn't believe half of them. They thought she was just showing off, trying to get the teachers to feel sorry for her.

Even the headmaster, John Gleeson, a reserved and careful man, noticed how often she seemed to be ill and how, perhaps, she seemed to make the most of her illness to place herself at the centre of playground attention. Still, he liked her. She seemed quite a bright girl, anxious to please, and he had no worries about making her a school prefect.

Rachel wasn't that bothered. Bev used to tell people that she was Rachel's best friend, but Rachel didn't see it that way. You could never get really close to Bev. If she came into school with a long face, Rachel would say 'What's upsetting you then?'

And Bev would just shrug and say 'Nothing'.

Often Rachel could tell that there was something upsetting her, but she let Bev have it her own way. It was up to her if she wanted to keep secrets. She'd tell you soon enough about her illnesses, all about her latest bandage, but she wouldn't tell you anything personal.

Rachel didn't like going round to Bev's house. There was something about Richard that she didn't like. He would cuddle her when she didn't want to be cuddled and give her big hugs, and if she wore a skirt he'd go on about her legs. She knew he meant no harm by it—he was only joking—but it made her feel uncomfortable. Anyway, Rachel was best friends with another girl by now. It was only a coincidence, but this girl's mum was the one who was caught out when she was carrying on with Bev's dad. Rachel knew Bev didn't like her being with this girl and, sometimes, Bev would try and break them up. Rachel might be away from school for a few days and she'd come back and find everything had changed because Bev had been saying bad things to people about her, or giving little bribes to Rachel's friend, saying she could come and play computer games at her house or play with all her soft toys that she had collected. Or Bev would make a big thing about being friends with someone else, like Susan

Short or Helen Love, who lived in the village and were in the same year as her at school.

Rachel and Bev did become close again for a while. Rachel had some illness. She didn't know what it was, but she kept being sick and, even though she was starving hungry, she couldn't eat anything. Then, one Saturday, she was sick really badly and started bringing up blood and they rushed her to Grantham Hospital and gave her a blood transfusion. They couldn't work out what was wrong with her. In the end, the doctors decided it must have been a reaction to the aspirin which she had been taking and they said there was nothing to worry about. Bev was really kind when Rachel was ill and kept coming round to see her and all the time she was off school recovering Bev came and helped her to catch up with her work. Then, once Rachel was better, they drifted apart again.

When they were about 14, they all started hanging around with boys, and Bev didn't like it. She said she fancied a boy in her year called Martin but she never did anything about it. She used to come to village discos in the old Church room, but she wouldn't dance or talk to the boys. She just sat with Susan or Helen, or whoever her favourite was that week, sipping fizzy drinks and chewing crisps and pretending she wasn't interested. By that time, everyone called her Big Bev and she didn't like it, but it didn't stop her eating so much. She always had sweets in her pocket. Some of her friends had cigarettes in their pockets, and Bev did try smoking once, but she couldn't get the hang of it. Rachel thought she was just afraid of getting into trouble for smoking. She was like that with drinking, too. She would come round to your house and egg you on to take a drink from your parents' drink cupboard, but then she wouldn't drink anything herself. She would say she couldn't because she had a stomach problem. And then, of course, she would make sure your parents found out and everyone except her got into trouble.

Bev had her best times with children, particularly small babies, and ever since they left primary school, she had been saying she wanted to be a nursery nurse or a midwife and she had taken a child-care course at school with Mrs Greatwood. Babies were more or less her hobby and she used to go baby-sitting whenever she could, or she'd knock on doors in the village and offer to take the baby for a walk. She went baby-sitting for a woman who was a nurse at Grantham Hospital, Kate Lock. Bev said Kate Lock told her she would make a good nurse.

Rachel went baby-sitting too. She was very sad when one baby that she looked after died—it was the nephew of the woman who had had the little scene with Richard, the one whose husband beat him up. The little boy was only six months old and he just died. The doctors said it looked like a reaction to aspirin, the same as Rachel had when she was ill. The parents were terribly upset.

Sometimes, Rachel used to take Bev with her when she went baby-sitting, but it didn't always work out. One time, she took Bev with her when she went round to sit for Sue and Phil Binner, and Rachel got really worried because Bev started poking around in their private things, being really nosy, and then she went and woke up the little boy, Luke, and got him out of bed and she was afraid he would start yelling and they wouldn't know what to do. But it was all right in the end because Luke went back to sleep and when the Binners came back and asked if either of the children had woken up, Bev just lied to them. The next thing Rachel knew, Bev was round there every day, baby-sitting instead of her.

Bev was 16, in her last term at school in the summer of 1985, when she had her first boyfriend. He was called Kevin and he came from another village about ten miles away. He was 17 and he had just got his first motorbike and he and two mates drove over to Corby Glen one day and stopped in the Fighting Cocks for a drink. Bev was in there with her sister, Alison, and Helen Love, drinking Coke, and they all got talking, and one of Kevin's mates, Nick, took a shine to Helen. They wanted to go out together, but Helen was a bit nervous so she made Bev come along too, with Kevin.

At first, Kevin felt a bit sorry for her. She told him she had had this bust-up with her family and so she had walked out and gone to live with her granny. She told him, too, about how ill she was. But after they had been out together several times, Kevin began to wonder. He found himself talking to Alison one day and, for some reason, he mentioned about Bev not living with her parents any more, and Alison just shook her head and said 'It's not like that'. He didn't let on to Bev that he knew there was something wrong with her story, but he asked her what this bust-up had been about and she said it was her dad. She said he was a right bastard and she had to get away from him. Then another time, she said it was her mum she couldn't stand, and her dad was always really good to her. Kevin just nodded. Then, her illnesses began to confuse him.

He and Nick got into the habit of going across to Corby several times a week to see Bev and Helen. Nick and Helen were really keen on each other, but Kevin and Bev used to just sit and talk and let the other two get on with it. Every time he met her, Bev seemed to have something different wrong with her: bad lungs, bad stomach, bad appendix, bad kidneys. He couldn't keep up with her and, after a while, he started to think that it just was not physically possible for anyone to have that many illnesses. She'd be dead by now. He told Nick he was going to have to start buying a medical journal so he could hold up his end of the conversation. Mind you, she never really did have an ordinary conversation. They might all be sitting round a table, telling jokes, competing with each other to see who could say the silliest thing and Bev would just be watching and then there'd be a pause and suddenly Bev would say 'Oh, my leg! I really hurt it yesterday, I was running to catch a train' and everybody would say 'Oh, yeah' and then they'd carry on talking. But the next time there was a pause she'd pop up again and say 'You're lucky you caught me, I just got back from Cornwall, on the train. I'm thinking of going to live there,' but they'd know she'd been in Corby all week, and sometimes Kevin and Nick would just make round eyes at each other as if to say 'Who does she think she's kidding?'

It didn't worry Kevin. He wasn't so keen on her. He had tried kissing her once or twice, but she hadn't been that bothered about it, so he just hung around with her to keep Nick and Helen company. Her stories made the evening more interesting. He and Nick used to call her 'The Fable' and before they met up with the girls, they used to say 'I wonder what she's got for us tonight'. And she always had something. She would have sprained her wrist, or just come back from her friend's house where they've got this really great indoor swimming pool, or she'd have got blood poisoning, or she'd been invited to this big, posh party next week, or else she'd just get up and start dancing about—anything, just so long as she got a quick dose of everyone's attention. Kevin just nodded and carried on.

There was one time when Kevin reckoned that Helen was trying to warn him about Bev and her stories. Bev had told him she was going to be away for the weekend, off on some special trip, and anyway, Nick was working so they wouldn't be getting together. But at the last minute, Helen phoned Nick and persuaded him to bunk off work and come over to Corby and she insisted that he bring Kevin, even though Bev was off on her trip. When he and Nick arrived, they found Bev sitting there in the pub.

By now, Kevin wasn't surprised by anything Bev did or said. He said to Nick: 'She said two things that were true tonight — "it" and "the". All the rest was bollocks.'

They had some laughs, though. Nick had a car and he drove them all into Nottingham and they had too much to drink and they got stopped by the police for driving without their lights on, but the police let them go. One night, after they'd taken the girls back to Helen's granny's house for the night, the boys slept in the car and they all met up for breakfast again the next day.

In spite of all her lies, Kevin felt he got to know her quite well. One afternoon, they were sitting together on the war memorial in the market square in the middle of Corby, and her dad drove by in his van.

'Oh, there's dad,' said Bev.

Kevin read the name of Hay Wine, Jeremy Marshall Roberts' company, on the side of the van. 'Oh, he works for that lot, does he?'

'No, he owns it,' she said. 'The normal driver's on holiday.'

Kevin nodded. They sat for a moment in silence.

'He's a bastard, my dad.'

Kevin had heard this before. 'Well, why's he a bastard? What's he done?'

'He gets drunk. He used to come home and he'd be pissed on all these wine samples he gets.'

'Yeah?'

'He hits mum. That's why I left.'

Kevin sighed, and Bev went on. 'I grew to hate him and so I can't live in the same house as him. I couldn't sit back and let him

hit my mum. That's the kind of person I am. That's why I walked
out.'

She sat in silence again. Kevin looked across at her. She had
tears in her eyes. He put his arm round her, in fact he felt sorry
for her, even though he was sure that every word she'd said was
bollocks.

After three or four months, Helen went off to join the Royal
Navy, and she and Nick stopped seing each other. By that time,
Kevin was getting fed up with Bev and her private world—he
wondered just how thick she thought he was—and without Nick
and Helen to bring them together, their short friendship crumbled.

Bev had nothing special to do. She was 16. She had finished school.
She had given up the idea of being a midwife: too much blood,
she said, and she was too squeamish. She wanted to be a general
nurse and work with sick children, but she was two years too
young to start the training so she signed up for a pre-nursing
course at Grantham College and went up to Grantham and back
every day on the bus.

Susan Short went with her, to do a catering course, and some
of the time they were best friends. But then Bev would suddenly
spoil it all. Like in a maths class once, when they had all done a
test, and Susan had worked quite hard and the teacher was just
telling everyone how well Susan had done, and Bev spoke up.

'Oh, is that the one I did for you, Susan?'

And everyone laughed, and Bev smiled to herself, and Susan
felt really fed up with her, but she didn't say anything.

These were dull days. In the evenings, Bev sat around in the
Fighting Cocks, sometimes with a crutch by her side when she
said she had broken her toe, sometimes with her right arm in a
sling, sometimes with her left arm in a sling. She became a regular
part of the pub, particularly after Rachel left. Rachel had been
working there for a long time. She was quite happy, though she
got fed up with the landlady's father teasing her all the time about
the ghost that was supposed to live there. Rachel had been looking
after the landlady's little boy ever since he was a baby but when
she went off on a holiday with her sister she came back to find
that Bev had taken over from her. Rachel tackled her about it,
told her that she had no business playing with the little boy's

emotions like that, but Bev just shrugged and Rachel couldn't be bothered to fight about it so she just gave up. Bev stayed on in the Fighting Cocks, looking after the baby and working behind the bar. She even started seeing the ghost. But mostly she was bored, killing time and waiting for things to happen. Sometimes, they did.

There was the time she broke her wrist in Grantham and she told everyone in the pub how some girls ganged up on one of her mates at the bus stop outside college and Bev went to help her and they all ended up in this public toilet and there had been one hell of a fight and it was lucky Bev was there and it was lucky she was pretty strong or her mate would have been really hurt, but she fought them off, and that was how her wrist got broken. They didn't know what to say to that in the Fighting Cocks. Bev's dad had told them she'd broken her wrist falling down the stairs in Woolworths.

There was the night that Mary Lee died. Mary Lee was very religious and always busy with the Church; she also liked a glass of rum from time to time, and, in the Fighting Cocks, they used to say 'tonight the spirit is moving Mary Lee' and laugh. But everybody liked her. She ran the newspaper shop on the market square and she became an unofficial advice bureau where people went with their problems, from trying to find the bus times to more personal things. Bev worked for her. She delivered newspapers for her and sometimes she looked after the shop as well, on Saturday mornings when Mrs Lee went shopping and on Sundays when she went to Church. Everybody was sad when Mary Lee died so suddenly.

It seemed she died of asthma, which had always troubled her, though they never did a post-mortem. She went across to the Fighting Cocks for a little glass of something, and she seemed fine. Bev was in there that night—she had been working in the pub, cooking and waitressing—and Mrs Lee stayed for a while and then she went home and collapsed and died. Her daughter, Fiona, found her. Everyone was very shocked. Bev and her sister Alison had to run the shop on their own for a little while, and Mary Lee's family were so pleased that they put a little announcement in the paper to thank them. Then they sold the newspaper business to Pauline, who ran the little general store on the other side of the market square, and Bev went to work there instead. Bev had always liked Pauline.

That was the next thing that got them talking in the Fighting Cocks. When they were working in the shop together, Bev and Pauline became good friends. They used to play the fool together, calling each other silly names and giggling in the shop and they often hung around with each other. Then Bev decided to move in to Pauline's house. Pauline was married and living with her husband Merv and their little boy, Danny, and Pauline said Bev was there to help her round the house, but that didn't stop the jury at the bar in the Fighting Cocks concluding that they must be a couple of little lezzies. There was a lot of talk about it. Bev said she didn't much care what they thought. And when she moved out of Pauline's a few months later, back to her parents, she didn't mind hinting to people that it might even be true. She stirred them all up about that and there was not much that Pauline and Merv could do to stop her.

Then, a year later, as if to get them all talking again, Bev not only found a boyfriend but got engaged to be married. She had finished her nursing course at the college and she had nothing special to do. She was just hanging around in Corby Glen nursing her sore kidneys, signing on, and passing time in the Fighting Cocks, which was where she met Steve Biggs, one evening in September 1987.

She was in the bar with Susan Short, drinking halves of lager and playing pool, and they noticed this tall, nice-looking lad with brown hair and one leg in plaster. Steve, who was still recovering from a bad car crash in August, was sitting with his grandfather, who kept nudging him and telling him the two girls were looking at him and he should go up and ask them for a game, and Steve felt shy but in the end he got up and he did ask them, and they said 'All right'.

Bev was very giggly and joking all the time they were playing and Steve lost the game. He didn't mind. The next two nights, he went back again and played more pool with the girls. He had only ever had one girlfriend, and that was not for long, so he wasn't too sure whether he was going to start going out with either of them and he wasn't in any great hurry, but that evening, as the three of them walked away from the pub, Bev took matters in hand.

She stopped by the village phone box and turned to Steve and said abruptly, 'Well? Which one of us do you want to go out with?'

Steve grinned at his feet. No one had ever said anything like that to him before. He could see Bev and Sue both looking at him under the street light, and he didn't want to upset either of them, and he was really not too sure what he should say, so he stammered a bit and finally he said he would go out with Bev. Sue looked very crestfallen and turned and ran off down the street in tears.

'Leave her to it,' said Bev. 'She'll be all right.'

Steve was very sorry about Sue but he was pretty sure he had made the right decision. Bev was fun, a bit of a joker, and he was sure they would have a good time together.

All that autumn, it seemed that he was right. He and Bev spent a lot of time together, drinking half-lagers in the Fighting Cocks and then, when his leg was out of plaster, driving round in a crappy old Escort that he had just got. The doors were rusted and the windows wouldn't open, but it got them around. One night, when they'd had a few drinks in the pub, they went tearing down a country lane and splashing through a ford, which was all swollen with rain, and the car started floating and the water was coming in through the doors and they were laughing and shouting in the middle of it. Steve was glad to be back in the country. He had grown up just down the road, in Bourne, but then his parents had moved to Great Yarmouth and opened a guest-house and he had hated it. He was a soft, innocent lad, and Yarmouth seemed like a very big, dirty place to him. Now, he was back among the fields, living with his grandparents in Corby Glen, working as a road repairman and he had this nice girlfriend and he had only known her a fortnight when they had sex. They didn't do it again for weeks, but Steve guessed that was probably just normal. He was happy.

Bev took him baby-sitting with her and they talked about all kinds of things: the fights she had had with her family, the blood infections she had had since childhood, the ghosts which had tried to touch her in the Fighting Cocks and in her dad's wine shop.

Steve felt very fond of her, and when she told him how Kevin had got her out in a field and pulled out a knife and tried to rape her, he felt so angry for her that he wanted to go out and find Kevin and teach him a lesson. She told him how she had managed to run away from Kevin and how he had followed her round Corby for a while and it had got so bad that she had had to get John, the landlord of the Fighting Cocks, to walk her home in case he tried to attack her again. But it was over now, she said, and there was no point in going after him because she couldn't prove a thing. Steve calmed down. He didn't really want to fight Kevin. He was not the fighting type. He was just happy to be with Bev, though he wished she would let him walk her to her door once, or even come in and meet her family.

Just before Christmas, Bev took matters in hand again. They had patched things up with Sue and they were walking along to her house when Bev stopped him and asked him if he fancied getting married.

'I don't know,' said Steve, who was naturally honest. He shrugged and smiled. 'It's up to you. I don't mind.'

'Well, do you?'

'Yeah. All right. Yeah, I do.'

So they were engaged. Steve took the old Escort into Grantham and went to the Argos catalogue store and bought her an engagement ring. It cost him £40, but he thought it was worth it. He was so happy, he took her to Great Yarmouth to meet his family, and his mum threw a little party. It was odd then, because Steve's brother, who was always good at sussing people out, took one look at Bev and then took Steve aside and said 'Get rid of her'. And Steve could tell that his mum didn't really take to her either. Steve didn't know what they were on about.

He saw Bev every night now. Now that they were engaged, Steve was all for going ahead and naming the day and settling down together, but Bev told him there was no hurry. They would get married later. They couldn't afford it now. They would have to wait. In the meantime, they could start collecting some things they would need. She told him to buy some pottery and some cups and saucers, which she kept in a cupboard at her parents' house.

Richard and Lillian said that if Bev was happy to be engaged, then they were happy for her. She told them that she wasn't too bothered about getting married and it was just Steve who insisted on getting engaged and he had kept going on about it, so eventually she had given in to him—anything for a quiet life. Everyone in the Fighting Cocks congratulated her and some of them even bought her half a lager to celebrate. And Steve felt he had finally arrived in her life when she let him come round to her house for Sunday lunch, and Richard joshed him about being a road repair-man, how he must spend all his time picking bloody holes in the road so he had some work to do filling them in again.

They still didn't have sex very often and, even if they did, it usually ended after a couple of minutes with Bev telling him to get off because he was hurting her. She didn't like kissing or cuddling either. But Steve wasn't worried. He guessed most girls were like that. The only thing that got to him a bit was that she wouldn't hold his hand in public. She said she was embarrassed in case someone saw them, but even when they were engaged she wouldn't do it, even if it was pitch dark and there was no one around. Steve guessed she just wasn't a very affectionate person. She was three months younger than him, but he always thought she seemed more grown up. Sometimes, he felt she treated him like a bit of a baby.

The first time she really upset him was when she crashed the old Escort. He wasn't so worried about the damage to the car, though the front was all bashed in and he'd only just put a new engine in, but it was the lies she told about it. She hadn't learned to drive, but she had kept going on at him to let her try and so one night, when they were on a quiet country lane, he gave her the chance. She was all right for a few minutes, then she took a corner too fast and rammed straight into a tree. Steve immediately put his arm round her and told her it was OK, but Bev was really cool about it all. She wasn't at all upset but she insisted that they had to tell her dad that Steve had been driving and that they had been just outside Corby Glen, even though the truth was that they were miles away, near Stamford. Steve couldn't see the point and he didn't want to lie to Richard, but in the end he agreed.

Then she started saying he was too fat. Steve didn't think he was, but she went on about it. She said that he had to go up to the secondary school on Tuesday evenings for the keep-fit class.

He said he didn't want to, but she insisted. So he went, every Tuesday evening. She wouldn't go herself—she always had a bad arm or a bad leg—and Steve didn't like to say that she needed it more than him because she was pretty big, so he did as he was told, but even when he did the classes she still wasn't happy. She started making him do press-ups and sit-ups.

She'd take him and Sue round to her house when her parents were out and she would sit down on the sofa with Sue beside her and she'd look at Steve and say 'Go on, do 50 press-ups.'

'But I don't want to.'

'Do 'em, Steve.'

And so he would. And sometimes, she'd be happy with that. And sometimes, she'd make him do 100 sit-ups as well, while she sat like Buddha next to Sue with a little smile on her face. Steve didn't like it, but Bev was the first real girlfriend he had had and he just supposed that a lot of girlfriends must be like that.

All he wanted to do was to get on and get married, and so he did his best to please her. But she still wouldn't set a date for the wedding, even though he had agreed to buy an Eternal Beau dinner set for her collection, and when he pushed the point, she really shouted at him and told him to stop bloody pestering her and she'd get married when she was good and ready and not before. They were having sex once a month at most by now and she made it obvious that she didn't like it. Then she did a weird thing—she started walking round holding hands with Sue.

Now, Bev had told Steve that people thought she and Pauline had been having a scene, but she had told him it wasn't true. All that happened, she said, was that Pauline had got drunk one night and tried to get into bed with her and that was why she had left her house. Steve didn't know whether to believe that—and he did suspect that sometimes Bev's stories were a bit exaggerated—but now here she was parading around the village refusing to hold his hand and holding Sue's instead, getting all the gossips going in the Fighting Cocks. Steve could see that Sue didn't like it a bit—sometimes she pulled her hand away and told Bev to get off her—and so he had a quiet word with her and asked her if she thought Bev might be, you know, a lesbian. Sue just shrugged. She didn't know. So Steve plucked up his courage and chose his moment and asked Bev as politely as he could whether she fancied Sue.

For a moment, he thought she was going to blow up at him and pull his ears off, but instead, she was really cool and just said no, as if it was a daft question. She said she was only joking around.

In March of 1988, she made up her mind to train as an SEN in Grantham. She went for an interview, filled in a form, and before Steve knew it, she was announcing that her training would start in September. From that moment, Steve's life started going downhill fast.

She still wouldn't fix a date for the wedding. He kept telling her he loved her, and she just shrugged and never claimed to be the least bit keen on him. She was always grumbling about her pains and dashing off to Casualty in Grantham for X-rays and emergency pain-killers. She learned to drive and started telling him he was a useless driver and once when he was driving she started going on at him and he just pretended she wasn't there and he could tell she was starting to get really angry, and suddenly she turned round and punched him in the jaw. He was doing 60 miles an hour at the time and the car lurched off the road and skidded to a halt on the verge where they had a blazing row.

He persuaded her to come on holiday with him, to a chalet in Yarmouth, where they could be romantic together, but she insisted on bringing Sue and her boyfriend. Then it turned out to be Sue on her own and, when they got to the chalet, Bev announced that she and Sue would share one room, while Steve slept alone in the other. Steve felt really fed up. Then Bev hurt herself in the bathroom. She got her thumb stuck in the tap and it was all red and raw and they had to take her to hospital, and Steve was sure she'd done it on purpose. How could you get your thumb stuck up a tap by mistake?

Once she started training at the hospital, on 12 September 1988, she got worse than ever. Steve told her she could borrow his car and drive in to Grantham each day, but she insisted on leaving Corby Glen and going to live in the nurses' home at the hospital. He said he was going to miss her and he wanted to talk on the phone each day, but she refused to give him the phone number of her block in the nurses' home. He gave her a pile of 50 ten-pence pieces so that she could call him. He would give her a time when he knew he would be in and then he would sit by the phone in his grandmother's house, waiting and waiting and feeling more and more crestfallen as the hours passed and the phone failed to ring. Then suddenly she'd ring another time when he wasn't expecting it and just laugh at him. Steve's grandmother told him she was just messing him around and he'd be better off without her. But Steve wanted her.

For her 20th birthday, at the beginning of October, he spent £15 on a toy dog with floppy ears for her collection, and she just grunted 'Thanks' and never even gave him a kiss. That hurt him, and he let it show. She started to stay up in Grantham on her days off, or if she did come back to Corby, she'd bring work with her.

Steve began to feel very depressed and he wondered if she was going to call off their engagement, but she still told him she was going to marry him and even talked about how many children they would have together. So he stuck with it and tried to make her happy.

They bought a car together, a newer Escort. Steve put in £900 and she put in £375. Then she decided to go on holiday to Spain with another trainee nurse called Nikki Gardener and she announced that he was not allowed to drive the car while she was away and in order to be sure that he did not cheat, she made a point of recording the mileage in front of him and then drew round the wheels with chalk to mark the exact spot on the road where it was parked. Steve tried to fight back. After she'd been away for a few days with Nikki, he took the car and drove over to see a mate. It was a round-trip of seven miles. Then he put the car back on the chalk marks. When she got back, she went mad about it and said he had driven hundreds of miles in her car without permission. He tried to reason with her, but he got nowhere. She said he was seeing someone else and he didn't fool her and she broke off the engagement. Steve was upset, but then she got back with him the same day.

He argued with her again one night in the pub when Bev started talking about the hospital. She was doing two months on a geriatric ward and she started slagging off the patients, saying the old men were always trying to grab at her and touch her up. Steve just snorted. He had learned by now that her stories weren't always true. Then she started saying that some of the patients were so old and feeble that the doctors put them out of their misery.

'What do you mean?'

'They inject them, put them to sleep. They use morphine.'

Steve told her that if he was old and ill, he wouldn't want some doctor creeping round and finishing him off with an injection.

'Well, you wouldn't know about it. And nor would your family. We don't tell 'em about it.'

'You can't do that. You can't just go killing people.'

'You can.'

'Well, if you can and it's all OK, how come you don't tell their families about it?'

''Cos they wouldn't understand, 'cos they're too stupid. They'd only get upset.'

A couple of times, Steve went up to the social club at Grantham Hospital and was amazed to see a Bev he had never met before. She was the life and soul of every nurses' party, always first up to dance, knocking back pints of lager, cracking jokes and clowning about. She and Nikki Gardener kept doing routines from French and Saunders and everyone sat round laughing at her, and Bev kept dancing off with a thin girl called Tracy Jobson, leaving Steve to look after himself. They all thought Bev was great, and they made it pretty obvious that they thought Steve was getting in her way. He began to think she must be seeing other men. He asked her if she was, and she thumped him—belted him in the chest with her fist and knocked the wind out of him. The next time he started complaining that she wouldn't set a date for their wedding, she thumped him again and kneed him in the groin so hard that he fell to the floor with tears of pain in his eyes. He was several inches taller than her, but she was very strong and when she hit him, she wasn't playing around. When she went off on holiday again and put chalk marks round the car again, Steve decided to try and give her a shock.

When Bev came back, he went to see her at her parents' house in Corby Glen and he walked into the hall and he told her that he wanted to finish with her. He had thought she might get upset. He had hoped she would say she was sorry for treating him so badly and then they could be happy again, but she just looked at him as if he was a bit stupid.

'Come in the front room,' she told him. 'We'll talk about it.'

Steve didn't want to talk. He'd had enough and he turned towards the open front door but, as he did so, she pushed past him, slammed the front door, grabbed his hair with both hands and yanked him down on to his knees on the hall carpet.

'You're not going anywhere!' she hissed at him through clenched teeth.

'Get off! Let me go!'

Bev let go with one hand and used it to start thumping him on the back, while one of her chubby knees bashed him in the face. Steve was howling. Bev was swearing. Alison appeared on the stairs.

'Let him go! Let him go, Bev.'

Bev let go and hustled Steve into the sitting room where he sat, subdued, and listened while Bev told him that the engagement was still on.

As a trainee nurse, Bev was doing well. By the autumn of 1989, she had finished the first year of her course and, apart from learning in the classroom, she had had spells working in the hospital with old people, on medical and surgical wards and then on the children's ward, Ward Four, where she spent two months in the summer which she said she really liked. She had put her back out in the first week of training practising a fireman's lift, and then she had had to take off a total of 21 days for various other sicknesses, but she was enjoying herself. There had been a bit of trouble in the old nurses' residence where she was staying. Someone kept hitting the Crash Call button, sending everyone into a panic, but Bev just smiled and shook her head and let all the fuss wash over her. She was quiet at work and got very little attention, but once she was out with her mates, she liked to go wild.

She and Nikki Gardener and Tracy Jobson and the others moved around everywhere in a big gang. They would all meet up in the social club, next to the nurses' home, and drink and have a laugh. Then they might all suddenly decide to get up and go off together and they'd descend on some pub in town, like the Black Dog, and more or less take the place over. It was all a laugh. Sometimes Bev brought nurses home to Corby Glen, for meals at her parents' house, or to go out on day trips.

Nikki was on the training course with her, but Tracy was already qualified and working in the Intensive Care Unit. She was small and wiry with short brown hair and she always seemed to have a cigarette in her mouth. She was going out with a tall heavily-built lad called Andy. One weekend he drove them up to Blackpool—Bev, Tracy and Nikki—and he booked into a hotel room with all three of them standing beside him at reception, and then they all choked with laughter in their room at the thought of how it must have looked, though all they did was drink and fall about and watch television. It was Andy's idea to go to Tenerife in October.

He had been there before and he told Tracy they could get a self-catering apartment, and if four of them went it wouldn't even cost too much, about £300 each for everything for two weeks. So Tracy asked Bev to come, and bring Steve.

From the moment that Richard Allitt dropped the four of them at East Midlands Airport, it was a disaster. Steve wanted to hold hands with Bev; Bev didn't want to. Steve wanted to share a room with Bev, but Bev didn't want to. She wanted to share a room with Tracy, Andy didn't like that, but Tracy said she didn't mind, so Bev got her way. Steve threw Bev in the pool. He thought it would make her laugh, but she sulked, so Steve threw her in again, so she ignored him, so he started drinking too much. Wherever they went, Steve and Bev bickered. They went for a walk on the beach, which was strewn with black volcanic boulders. Bev slipped on one, gashed her leg, got sand in the wound and blamed Steve. She said it wouldn't have happened if he had been holding her hand. Steve said she'd got a nerve, because he was always trying to hold her bloody hand. They went to a clinic and a nurse took Bev into a little room to see to her wound. Outside, Steve and Tracy and Andy sat in silence. Steve was fed up with Bev. Tracy and Andy were fed up with Steve. Then Tracy started to think about something else: inside that little room, the nurse would be cleaning out Bev's wound and washing it with iodine, and although the door was open she couldn't hear a thing. It must be hurting her, but Bev was not making a single sound.

Steve kept hanging around Bev, looking for affection. Bev kept swatting him away. She started accusing him of seeing other girls behind her back in Corby Glen. Steve knew it wasn't true but he

couldn't prove it and he began to worry that Bev must be seeing
other blokes in Grantham. So he accused her, but she just told
him it was none of his business if she was. Now he was convinced.
One night, the bickering got so bad that Bev flew at Steve and
scratched the left side of his face until it bled. He stumbled out
of the apartment and sat alone in the darkness by the side of the
swimming pool with tears on his face and, after a while, Tracy
came out to see him.

'I can't see why she has to be like that,' he said, rubbing away
his tears. 'Why does she have to be so nasty? I love her, you
know, I really love her.'

Tracy said she would go and talk to her and, a few minutes
later, Bev walked out to sit by Steve. Steve looked round at her.
She was in tears. He had never seen her crying before.

'Bev?'

She was sobbing. 'Why didn't you ever tell me that you loved
me?'

'But I did. I'm always telling you I love you.'

'No, you never.'

'But I'm always saying it.'

'Well, I never heard you.'

They drank and fought their way through the rest of the holiday
and, although when they flew home, officially they were still
engaged, Steve knew it was over really. Bev was spending more
and more time with her nursing friends, Steve was afraid to go
round to her house in Grantham in case Richard had a go at him—
Bev told Steve that she had blamed her bruises from her fall on
Steve kicking her—and Steve was left to drink alone in the Fighting
Cocks, waiting for something to happen. In the nurses' home, it
did.

To begin with, it was only little things. The phone would ring,
someone would ask to speak to Nikki, then when she got there,
no one was there. Someone sent Nikki flowers, without a card or
a message. Then one night, when they were all out, someone
started a fire in the little kitchen which they shared. Somone had
stuffed newspaper under the grill and turned it on, the paper had
caught light and, if the nurses hadn't come back then, it could
have got very bad. No one could understand how it had happened.
It was obviously no accident. But it was nastier than that: when

they put the fire out, they found the remains of human faeces on the newspaper. Something very weird was happening.

Bev said it must be this guy who had been going out with Nikki. No one could understand it. Whoever it was, they kept at it. One day, they smeared faeces on Nikki's door. The nurses got so upset that they asked the hospital to call in the police, who made a few enquiries and agreed that there was foul play here, but they seemed to think it was one of the nurses. Bev said they were bloody daft, it must be Nikki's ex-boyfriend. The incidents went on. It was as if some malicious joker was meddling with their lives: superglue in a lock; more superglue in someone's car door; some faeces on paper in the fridge; more faeces on a door; Tracy had her credit card stolen.

The hospital had just hired a new manager for adult wards, Peter Flood, who was trained as a psychiatric nurse. He looked at the Untoward Incident Reports that had been filed from the nurses' home and he worried, in particular, about the mind of the person who used faeces in this way.

'Someone over there is bloody cracked,' he said.

Flood made sure it stopped. He looked through the files, saw that three or four nurses were always involved—Nikki, Bev and one or two others—and he let them know that if this nonsense didn't stop, he would throw them all out. He couldn't tell who was guilty. One of the nurses did try to point the finger at Bev, but Peter Flood had no evidence and after his warning, the malicious joker was never seen again in the nurses' home.

That spring, Nikki decided that when her training ended, she would leave Grantham and go and work in Leicester. Bev didn't seem worried to lose her friend. She spent more time with Tracy now. She began to say that maybe all that trouble with the fire in the nurses' home was down to Andy, because maybe he didn't like Tracy and Bev being such good friends. She and Tracy decided to move out of the nurses' home—the hospital wanted the rooms for new students—and they decided to find a house to rent together.

Bev phoned Steve and told him they weren't engaged any more. By now, he was not too worried at finally losing Bev and soon he was seeing another girl in the village, Carla. But he was worried about their latest car. It was a £4,000 Escort. Steve had paid for most of it and was paying off £1,000 on HP. Now Bev said she was keeping the car. Steve argued. She said he could buy her half of it. He protested that he already owned most of it. She said she had got the car in Grantham and he was not going to get it back until he paid her for it. For a couple of days he fumed, then he went to the bank, borrowed £3,500, paid off the HP, gave Bev nearly £2,000, and got the car back. He decided it was worth it, for a quiet life.

Bev was not doing quite so well as a trainee nurse. She was taking more and more time off sick and by the end of November 1990, when her two years of training came to an end, she had taken off a total of 126 days sick. In her last year, she had made more than fifty visits to doctors, most of them on the Casualty ward. She had injured her head, her left leg, her right hand (twice) and her right foot (twice with broken glass, once by dropping a weight on it). She had suffered with her appendix, her kidneys, her bladder and her abdomen. She had had such trouble with water retention that she now had a catheter for her bladder, she was taking Temgesic to relieve pain, and Asilone and Gaviscon for her indigestion, and Maxolon to stop nausea. She had missed chunks of time on the surgical ward and in gynaecology and, although she passed her final 90-minute exam with an average mark, she had missed numerous tuition days. Her illnesses seemed to be gathering pace, so that in the last few months of the course, she was absent more often than she was at work. Her course tutor thought it was unfortunate, but no cause for concern. Some of the doctors and nurses were not so sure.

Some of the nurses from Casualty were amazed to see Bev Allitt wandering around the hospital in the uniform of a student nurse. For them, in the last three or four years, she had become a familiar, even notorious face with her endless complaints and her recurrent emergencies. There was no doubt in the minds of some of those who had treated her regularly that many, if not all, of her illnesses were works of her imagination.

Back in the summer of 1986, a year after she had stopped going out with her first boyfriend, Kevin, she had insisted that she was pregnant. She was not but she would not believe it, and her GP had had to refer her to a specialist to persuade her that she was wrong. She had come back a few months later, complaining that her belly hurt. She was told once again that she was not pregnant. She suggested she must have ulcers, so the doctors admitted her to hospital and gave her a gastroscopy which showed no sign of any problem at all. She replied with a fit of vomiting, as if to prove that she really was ill. But the nurses noticed that, although she kept showing them bowls of vomit, they never actually saw her throw up. They all agreed that she must be making herself sick.

By the time she started training as a nurse, she had aroused the suspicions of half a dozen different Grantham doctors. A surgeon investigated her gall bladder and decided that her complaints of eating problems were psychosomatic. The physiotherapists who dealt with her stiff hands were puzzled by her patchy symptoms and suspicious of her repeated failure to respond to treatment. After a while, the doctors in Casualty banned her from having any more X-rays on her hands. She replied over the next three months by reporting a series of four different injuries to her left hand and finally a bruise to her thumb which was so severe that the doctors relented and agreed to give her another X-ray. The doctors accused her of deliberately bruising her hands, but she denied it and they found her quite convincing. The next summer, she was given a clean bill of health to start her training as a nurse.

All through her training, doctors at Grantham Hospital recorded their doubts about her: the two-day headaches which had no apparent cause; the blood which she reported in her urine which never showed up in tests; the endless injuries to her hands which seemed to have been self-inflicted; the water on her kidney which she diagnosed and which failed to show up in tests. She claimed she had severe bladder problems but when Grantham Hospital referred her to a specialist in Nottingham in the summer of 1990, he dismissed her symptoms as 'hysterical' and told her to use a bladder catheter. He hoped it would discourage her; she thrived on it. Several of the nurses thought Bev needed psychiatric help and, every time she came in with a new illness, they thought they really ought to try and get her referred for psychiatric treatment, but they never got round to it. During her final year as a trainee, she persuaded a surgeon to remove her appendix. She insisted that it was painful and must be inflamed, but when he removed it, he pronounced it 'grossly normal'. Within a week, her surgical wound was infected and bleeding and the doctors concluded that she had been pulling her stitches and tampering with it. That was in the autumn of 1990, just as she was passing her exams, just as her course tutor was recommending her for work as a qualified nurse without any idea of the truth about her condition.

Some senior staff who dealt with her when she was training on their wards also found her very odd, and when they filled in their reports on her for the training school they recorded their doubts about her. One sister who had supervised her in her final year of training said that she thought she needed counselling for psychiatric problems. But no one did anything about it. Simply because of the number of days she had taken off sick, she was sent to the hospital's occupational health department. She saw them at least three times. But each time, they passed her as fit for work. No one noticed that her behaviour was a classic model of Munchausen Syndrome—that she was apparently obsessed with hospitals—let alone that she might be suffering from Munchausen Syndrome By Proxy, becoming so addicted to hospital procedures that she would find work as a nurse in order to systematically attack her patients. No one understood her problems. No one treated her.

On 5 December 1990, Bev went for her first job interview. It was at Grantham Hospital, where she had decided she wanted to work. She was seen by two of the hospital's clinical service managers, Simon Harrison and Sally Slee. They were interviewing on behalf of all the adult wards in the hospital and they had enough vacancies for SENs to take on all nine trainees who were now finishing their course. Unofficially, their policy was to give work to any of their trainees who wanted it. But they turned Bev down.

They offered jobs to all of the other trainees who were interested. They still had vacancies to fill. They not only turned Bev down, they refused even to offer her work as a bank nurse, filling in occasional gaps in the rotas. They recorded that she was one of the worst candidates they had seen in all their years of interviewing student nurses. They were worried about her sickness record, although they did not know its details, but they rejected her too because she was scruffy and untidy with dirty shoes, a dishevelled cardigan and a hole in her tights, and because she seemed lost when she answered their questions and to have almost no idea of the work she would be expected to do. On 6 December, they sent her a letter with their decision.

Bev Allitt was now in trouble. The ambition which she had held since she was a child was disintegrating. There was no work for her on any adult ward in the hospital. There was only one possibility that remained open to her and, as luck would have it, it was the one that had always been her favourite. She must try to find work on the children's ward, on Ward Four.

Bev's problem in finding work had to take second place to a more immediate problem. She had taken so much time off sick during her training, that, even though she had passed her written exam, she could not officially be registered as an SEN. She need not work the full 126 days that she had missed, but the course tutor ruled that she needed to put in a further ten weeks on the wards. Bev agreed and asked if she could work the time on Ward Four. Sister Barker and her manager, Moira Onions, agreed.

For ten weeks, beginning in December 1990, Bev Allitt worked steadily on Ward Four and enjoyed her new life with Tracy Jobson. They shared a neat, new semi-detached house in First Avenue, a nouveau suburban street on the eastern edge of Grantham with quiet, respectable neighbours who put phoney leaded lights in their windows. They had a great time living together. They had a little grey kitten, and a television, and a video and everything was a laugh. And if half the social club reckoned they were sleeping together, that was their problem. Tracy said it was none of their business, but Bev did nothing to stop the talk. She deliberately dressed in a butch way now, with heavy boots and her trousers sawn off at the calves and she hung around with a pair of nurses who were openly gay, called Jo and Ellen, but she and Tracy kept separate bedrooms, and when Tracy's family started asking her questions about it Tracy told them they were wrong.

Tracy never hid the fact that she cared for Bev. Bev made her laugh, the way she was always clowning around. And she respected her for coping with her problems, right from when she was a kid and she was late starting at school because of her parents breaking up and her being sent off to a foster home. Bev told her about that bastard Steve and how'd he just phoned up and told her he'd got AIDS and that she'd better go and get herself tested.

And about how she had been raped by Kevin, right in front of her girlfriend Helen's eyes, and how Helen had been too scared to give evidence so Kevin had got away with it. Tracy really felt for her when she described how she had had to go off and get an abortion, without her family finding out about it, and she'd gone to this little hospital down in Stamford all on her own. It did occur to Tracy that you probably couldn't get an abortion in Stamford, and she did wonder whether that bit of the story was true. And it struck her that if Bev had tried to tell her that she'd got the abortion in Grantham, she might have been caught out, because there would be records in the hospital. Tracy didn't mind. If Bev wanted to tell stories, that was up to her. She liked her, stories and all.

Bev never told Tracy that she hated men or that she'd given up on them for ever. She said she was living with Tracy because she wanted her as a person and it didn't matter to her what sex she was. It was up to her who she lived with. She did used to tell Tracy that Pauline had been phoning her from Corby Glen trying to persuade her to go back and live with her, but Tracy never actually heard any of these calls. And one night when they were in the social club together, Bev reckoned that she was called out to the car park because Pauline was out there, trying to make her go back with her. Tracy couldn't see why Bev wanted to tell her things like that. It was just Bev's way.

Tracy used to say that Bev was the unluckiest person in the world. If anything could go wrong, it would go wrong on Bev. She had one illness after another. She had to have her appendix out and then she developed an abscess on the wound. Tracy helped her to dress it and it reminded her of how Bev was in Tenerife when the nurse put iodine in her wound: she never made a sound. She seemed to pride herself on feeling no pain. One day when Tracy had a cold and she was complaining that she felt awful, Bev sneered at her.

'You don't know the meaning of pain,' she said.

From time to time, Bev went home, particularly if she had been working a night shift. She would drive straight from the hospital to Corby Glen and let her mother put her to bed and bring her some breakfast and let her sleep all day and then wake her up with a cup of tea. Tracy thought she was really spoiled. She didn't like going there much herself. Bev's dad gave her the creeps. He was always hugging her or trying to sit on her lap, or saying things like 'Oh, I'll come and keep you warm in bed tonight'. He had this way of seeing a sexual meaning in everything, like Tracy might be talking to Bev about something and she'd say 'All right, I'll give it to you tonight' and he would go 'I'll give it to you tonight and all' and start grinning. Bev just used to laugh it off. Bev was always saying that he was carrying on with a woman in the village. Tracy didn't know whether to believe that or not.

Bev's ten weeks of extra training on Ward Four were coming to an end. The ward had been quiet. Bev had done her job. In fact, she had done her job so well that she was known on the ward as 'a sister's dream', always keen, always ready to lend a hand or work an extra shift. Sister Barker certainly seemed to be happy with her. But there was no permanent vacancy there for Bev.

Moira Onions was trying to improve the nursing skills on the ward and she was advertising for a Registered Sick Children's Nurse, a staff nurse with specialist training. Bev knew she hadn't found one. In fact, there was a national shortage of children's nurses, and not one single person had replied to the two advertisements that Moira Onions had placed. Bev suggested to some of the nurses on Ward Four that she might get the vacancy instead, but then she heard of a new training course which was about to start at Pilgrim Hospital in Boston. It was intended to train nurses in children's medicine and it lasted three years. She applied. On 13 February, she went to Boston to be interviewed. The course tutor, Mrs Cottrell-Gibbons and the paediatric nursing manager, Miss Sharples, put her through her paces. And she failed.

She knew nothing about the course, she was vague about her own plans and she seemed disappointed to discover that it would pay no better than her present role as student nurse in Grantham. They told her there and then that she had failed and they suggested that she might like to try again in September when they next started a new course. In the meantime, she should go away and get more experience with sick children, they said.

Bev told Tracy she couldn't care less. She didn't want to work in Boston. But the next day, 14 February, when she went to work on Ward Four, she let everyone know how upset she was. Her extended period of training was about to end, she would finally be registered as an SEN, but she would have no job, nobody wanted her.

Moira Onions was on the ward that afternoon, talking to Sister Barker, and they heard what had happened. They were both worried about the shortage of staff on the ward and so they agreed to interview Bev themselves the next day and see if they could cure their own problem as well as Bev's.

The next day began in some confusion. The key to the Ward Four fridge had disappeared the previous afternoon and no one seemed to be able to explain what had happened to it. Bev Allitt had been given the key-ring to get something from the fridge and she had come back a few minutes later complaining that the key was missing. It was just as well nothing dangerous was kept in there, only eye drops and insulin.

That afternoon, Moira Onions sat in her office, next to the maternity ward, with Sister Barker at her side and they interviewed Bev Allitt. Neither of them was too keen to have her. Both of them had been hoping to hire two fully-trained RSCNs, and one inexperienced SEN like Bev was really no substitute. Sister Barker knew she had a terrible sickness record. Mrs Onions did not feel that Bev really had the right character for the job at all. She knew that she had been rejected by all the adult wards, but it was more than that. She had no access to her medical record, no way of knowing very much at all about her history but somehow she felt that Bev lacked warmth. She had interviewed scores of nurses and she could always tell when someone was right. They couldn't help giving you clues. If they really cared about children, it just bubbled out of them. And there was no bubbling with Bev.

But she had done well in the last ten weeks on the ward and she had been very willing to please. And the nursing tutor had recommended her. And they were short of staff. And the truth was that it was Bev or nothing. And so with some reluctance, they agreed to recommend her for a job. At least, it would be a pair of hands.

Moira Onions had to go to the Hospital Management Group and get special permission to hire a newly qualified SEN instead of the Registered Sick Children's Nurse they had wanted. The management considered the case. No one had gathered together any of the fragments of doubt which lay scattered throughout her past—the doctors and the physiotherapists and the nurses who all thought independently that she was inventing her illnesses, the ward sister and the nurses who thought she needed psychiatric help, the friends who had seen her explode with spite, the fire and faeces in the nurses' home. No one on the board was even aware that this same newly qualified SEN had just been rejected out of hand by every adult ward in the hospital and by their colleagues down the road in Pilgrim Hospital in Boston. As it was, the hospital's management were reluctant to hire her because they didn't want to accept a cut in the skills on Ward Four, but in the end they decided that this was an exceptional case. After all, they reasoned, they had no properly qualified nurse applying for the job, and surely this beginner should be encouraged in her career. It must not be a permanent job, they ruled, only a temporary six-month contract, but during that time, Bev Allitt would be hired to work as an SEN on Ward Four.

It was Friday 15 February 1991.

Bev soon settled into her new role. She was always willing to work and anxious to please, and she became a favourite with some of the more senior nurses who took her under their wing when they heard what she had been through with her boyfriend. He sounded like a real trouble-maker.

She told Kate Lock all about it one evening when they went up to the canteen together for a break, how she had been engaged to him but he was so possessive and jealous that she got fed up with him, and then he had started knocking her about, and once, when they were on holiday in Tenerife, he'd tried to push her off the top of a cliff and so she'd decided she'd had enough and she left him. But he wouldn't let her go. Now he'd been harassing her, phoning her on the ward, following her to work, pestering her every chance he got. It was making her ill.

Kate said it sounded terrible, but Bev said she didn't know the half of it. This Steve had got her arrested. When they had been engaged to each other, they had bought a car together, an Escort, and then, when they broke up, she paid him for his share of it and kept it. But Steve was so bitter and twisted that one night he called the police and told them that she had stolen his car and they had stopped her on the road and put her in a cell and refused to believe that it was her car and refused even to check her story that she was a nurse on her way to work. It was hours before they'd let her go, the bloody bastards. So she'd told him he could keep his bloody car and she'd got one of her own now, and she'd had to sign on with the BNA to do extra work to pay for it.

And even that wasn't the end of Steve's nastiness. He had got hold of Bev's parents and told them that he'd got AIDS and he told them that he wanted them to know about it because he'd caught it from Bev.

Kate did her best to comfort Bev. She felt rather touched that the young nurse had confided in her, and she told her just to get on and do her best and not to worry, and she was sure that everything would turn out all right for her in the end.

Kate and the other nurses were soon afraid that things were turning out to be traumatic. Bev started work as an SEN on the ward on Monday 18 February. On Thursday, 21 February, she was looking after Liam Taylor when he suffered his first respiratory arrest. The next day she specialed him and saw him recover and the senior nurses noticed with approval how she volunteered to come back that evening and work a night shift when Liam's father told her that he would feel happier if she was looking after his son. Then she had to deal with the baby's second arrest and the Crash Team and the terrible death.

The truth was that she did not cope terribly well. Catherine Morris, the Chinese nurse, who was on duty with her, said that she seemed to panic and start dropping things and a charge nurse, David Wiles, who was helping out on the ward that night, had to tell her to calm down. But none of them blamed her. They were worried again ten days later when Tim Hardwick died, while Bev was on duty, and she called in sick that evening. Bev was off work for the rest of that week and then a day after she got back to the ward, Kayley Desmond had two arrests on her night shift. The nurses wondered if it was all getting too much for Bev but, as time went by, and more and more of these arrests happened, she seemed to get much calmer about dealing with them and soon she was talking quite casually about it all to the younger nurses. One night in the canteen, she talked Wendy Sorrell through all the gory details of Liam's final arrest until Wendy was quite sorry she had even mentioned the subject.

She seemed to get so experienced at dealing with arrests that some of the other nurses joked with her about it. Kate Lock, who prided herself on bringing calm wherever she went, turned up for one shift and saw Bev and told her with her motherly smile: 'Oh dear, here's trouble. Wherever you go, things happen. I'm not sure if I want to work with you.' And Catherine Morris told her with a grin several times that she wasn't going to work with her because there were always too many arrests when she was around. Bev knew they were only kidding. She said it was all good experience. She told Lynn Vowles she hoped she could get a job at Queen's Med, in the children's intensive care unit.

Bev was having a bit of trouble with the hospital. She was formally registered as a State Enrolled Nurse now. As soon as she had finished her extended training, she had been given her personal identification number by her professional body, the UK Central Council for Nursing. She was now officially nurse number 8811817E, and she was entitled to work anywhere in the country and she had gone off to the BNA to sign on for extra work with a nice reference from her course tutor and one of the nurses on the ward. But Moira Onions had said she was worried about her sickness record and that she could not be confirmed in her job on Ward Four until she had been to Occupational Health for a medical test. She had gone along and they had taken a quick look and despite her endless sequence of illnesses they had said once more that she seemed fine. But for some reason, the paperwork had got stuck in the pipeline and she was still being paid as though she were only a student. She didn't like that and she complained about it to some of the other nurses.

At their new home in First Avenue, Tracy heard about all these mysterious arrests from Bev, who would come home and tell her about the latest crisis. Bev told her they seemed to think it was a virus or something on the ward and she told Tracy she thought it was weird when she saw Dr Porter drawing a lot of blood from Paul Crampton's groin and sending it off for special tests. What did they hope to find? Tracy told her to take it easy and she joked with her that she was bound to have to deal with a lot of arrests, because she was the unluckiest person in the world. One morning, she waved her off to work and shouted after her 'And try to have a normal day'. But Bev didn't. Tracy was on the Crash Team that hurtled into the ward and found some child struggling for life, and Tracy saw Bev standing there, really calm, almost above it all as everyone rushed around.

Tracy was glad that she wasn't too upset. She had been a nurse longer than Bev and she thought it was unfair the way hospitals recruited people as nurses and never warned them what it was really like, how they were going to see horrible things happening, people really suffering, and their families so upset. Soon after Tracy started, she had had to go to a post-mortem and she hadn't slept for weeks afterwards. Bev did say to Tracy that she always seemed to be around when these things happened and Tracy noticed that she was drinking a lot now, but she had always done that. Mostly, she seemed very happy, and, oddly enough, she had stopped being ill all the time. In fact, since Bev had been given her contract on Ward Four, she hadn't been to a doctor once.

Tracy was upset when their little grey kitten died. She found it one evening when she got back from work, in the front garden, with its head all bashed in. Tracy guessed it must have been run over by a car, though it was odd because First Avenue was a little cul-de-sac, not the kind of place where anyone could drive very fast even if they wanted to. Tracy cried about it for three days. But Bev was all right about it. She said Tracy thought more about that kitten than she did about her.

Bev seemed to be a very strong person. It was as if she could cope with any kind of pain, from all her illnesses or from her personal problems or even from these children dying. She could deal with it. Tracy would be all sympathetic and worried about her, and Bev would just crack some silly joke or twitch her shoulders and say it was nothing.

The nurses on the ward found she was the same. The day that Chris Peasgood suffered his two arrests began with Mary Reet confiding anxiously that she was sure something was going to happen to him. Joan Cottam said she was being super careful. Everyone was checking and rechecking their movements. But Bev just sailed through.

When Clare Winser was upset with her about going off in the ambulance with Chris Peasgood instead of her, Bev made a point of telling her how many arrests she had coped with, as if that made her even stronger, as if that meant there was something special about her.

8

Shortly after seven o'clock in the morning on Tuesday 21 May 1991, Bev Allitt was roused from her bed in First Avenue by a knock on the door. She stumbled downstairs, pulled open the front door and squinted out on to the pavement, where she found six police officers. One of them, a woman, told her that they were arresting her on suspicion of stealing a key from the hospital.

'A key?'

The policewoman went on. 'I am further arresting you for the attempted murder of Paul Crampton.'

Bev stared at them. 'What about work?'

'You can call them from the station and tell them what's happening.'

She shrugged. 'Can I contact my union?'

'Yes.'

Then two of the officers drove her to Grantham police station while the other four stayed and began to search the empty house, two of them up in the bedrooms, two downstairs. It was the upstairs pair who began to make discoveries.

The first thing they found was a syringe. It was lying around in Tracy's bedroom, and, with great care, they picked it up and dropped it into a plastic evidence bag. They found a lot of pills, Temgesic mostly, a yellow pillowcase that obviously belonged to the hospital, some scribbled notes and, finally, in the bottom of the wardrobe, underneath some clothes and wrapped in an old carrier bag, they found a blue school exercise book with 'Ward Allocation Book' printed across the front cover.

Downstairs, as they searched, the front door opened and Tracy Jobson walked in.

Tracy had so many worries that morning that she could hardly tell what worried her the most. She had woken up to the sound of her alarm at 6.15, made herself a cup of coffee and been hit by a wave of nausea which had sent her diving for the loo. She was not usually sick. It had made her feel terrible, but all the same, she had dragged herself out of the house, to the bus stop and off to work. But it had been no good. On the ward, the other nurses had seen she was too ill to be there and one of them had given her a lift home. She couldn't understand what was the matter with her. Just before she opened the front door, she thought there was something odd going on—there were too many cars in the street outside—but it was still a complete shock when she found a policewoman standing right there, inside her home.

The shocks got worse: they had arrested Bev, they were questioning her, they were searching the house, they wanted to question Tracy, too. Tracy told them they were joking. Then her hands started shaking.

She spent the whole day at Grantham police station trying to sort things out. She was completely confused. She defended Bev: she insisted that she would never do anything criminal and although it was true that Bev always did seem to be around when a child arrested, she knew the sort of woman that Bev was and she was sure she would never harm a child. Then she had to defend herself. The syringe was hers, but she only used it to fill her pen. Suddenly it seemed such an unlikely idea, but she had to make them believe it. And she had to admit that on the Intensive Care Unit where she worked, there was a lot of insulin and it was not kept under lock and key, but she swore she had never slipped any of it to Bev. They kept pressing her. She told them honestly that she was Bev's partner, but that didn't mean they were a couple of witches who went round trying to kill children. Tracy was worrying that they would never believe her, but when they started threatening to charge her with stealing a yellow pillowcase from the hospital, she began to feel better. If that was the worst they could throw at her, she must be getting through to them. Later that afternoon they took her home, where she was called by her mother in Peterborough who was beside herself with anxiety because a Central TV crew had got the wrong end of the story and turned up on her doorstep demanding to know why she had been questioned by the police. Tracy spent the night full of fear for herself, worry about Bev, and sheer bloody anger at everyone.

When Bev finally walked through the door 24 hours later, the next evening, it was the anger that had the upper hand.

'What the bloody hell is going on?' Tracy shouted.

Bev stood in the door, her key still in her hand and stared blankly at the question, but Tracy's blood was up and she strode up to her, pointing one finger from her chest.

'You have got a lot of explaining to do. You had better tell me what's going on here.'

Bev shrugged. 'It's all a load of crap,' she said in a voice that reeked of boredom. 'They dunno what they're talking about.'

'What do you mean? You know they bloody had me in as well?'

Bev didn't know. 'It's all crap,' she muttered. 'They're trying to say I did it. I had nothing to do with it.'

Bev walked past her. She was obviously ready to change the subject. She was so off-hand about it all that Tracy didn't know whether to hit her or hug her.

'Are you sure, Bev? They've searched the house, turned the whole bloody place upside down.'

'I had nothing to do with it. It's all crap.'

Tracy turned away from her. Of course, she knew it was all crap. Of course, she knew that. What was she doing shouting at her friend when she'd just been through hell with the bloody police and spent a night all alone in a cell? She was sorry. She was just upset because they'd taken her in too, and she'd never been accused of being a murderer before, and it had been bloody horrible and she never wanted to go through that again and she'd been feeling ill anyway, and she didn't know what was wrong with her, it must have been something she'd eaten, but she felt bad. It was all too bloody weird.

Tracy calmed down. Bev said the police hadn't got any evidence and she'd told them a hundred times that they'd got it wrong and she wasn't even there when some of these kids were ill. They seemed to think she'd been with Paul Crampton when he'd had his last hypo, but she hadn't been; she'd told them she'd been taking a little kid called Martin down to the operating theatre. It was all crap. And they'd got all excited about that allocation book. She'd told them that she had permission to take it—from Betty Asher and from one of the staff nurses, Mandy Poole—and she'd only taken it so that she could write up her diary and answer their questions, and they could hardly blame her for that. Tracy guessed it would all blow over eventually.

As Bev and Tracy made their peace, Stuart Clifton was pacing up and down in Grantham police station, feeling grim. He had thought long and hard before deciding to arrest Bev Allitt. When her name had appeared so clearly in the chart in the incident room she had become his prime suspect. And the chart was not the only finger pointing at her. She had also been on his shortlist of people who were near Paul Crampton in the half-hour when he was attacked. She had already been questioned twice about that and it turned out that she had been on duty for all three of his hypos, on the Saturday, the Sunday and the Thursday—and she had been off work for the three days in between when nothing happened. She had been handling the ward keys when the key to the fridge full of insulin went missing. And it turned out that she had been moonlighting in an old people's home in Waltham on the Wolds where insulin was kept unlocked in large quantities. But Clifton had needed more evidence and he had been faced with a tactical choice. He could play safe and go out and carry on digging in the hope of finding something that would prove the case, but that would take time and risk more attacks on the ward; or he could try a short cut. And, after a lot of pacing up and down in the incident room, he had decided to be optimistic and go for the quick kill. He would take the old-fashioned policeman's approach and simply go and ask her.

If it had worked, it would have saved everybody a lot of time and worry. But they had moved too fast. They had confronted her without enough evidence to force a confession. They'd failed to get her to admit anything, failed to get any kind of evidence to nail a charge to her, failed even to get enough to justify suspending her from work, and they'd alerted her to their suspicions. Now, with Bev Allitt released on police bail, he listened again to the interview tapes and surveyed the damage. They had never got close to a confession. She had sat in that interview room as if she had been handling interrogations all her life—so cool that the younger detectives could hardly believe this was the same girl they had talked to earlier in the inquiry—and she had her lawyer who was being paid by the Royal College of Nursing, and she had her rights, which seemed to multiply every time the House of Commons met.

'I am being accused of doing something I have not done and I would not dream of doing,' she had told them. 'I am telling the truth. God's honour. It's the truth.' She had suggested that she might be carrying some kind of bug that was causing the trouble. She had denied everything so completely that they had even started to believe her themselves and one of the interrogators had had to leave the room to clear her denials out of his head. So they had released her on police bail, and now she was free again, to carry on exactly as she wanted. Clifton picked up the phone and called Martin Gibson.

It was not an easy conversation. In two lines of dialogue, Stuart Clifton shattered Gibson's confident hope that the police would clear his hospital and leave it to the doctors to decide what was wrong on Ward Four. He left Gibson in no doubt that there was a major crime here.

Gibson had been doing his best to hold his hospital together. The Regional General Manager, Brian Edwards, had visited the hospital in person. It was a rare event, and Gibson and his assistant, Peter Flood, had assumed he wanted to talk about the police inquiry. It turned out that he was worried about the budget. He ordered them bluntly to clear up their £200,000 deficit—or heads would roll. Everyone was tense. Peter Flood had been horrified to discover that the fridge key from Ward Four had been stolen without anyone filing an Untoward Incident Report with his office and, even worse, that the missing key was able to open the fridge on every single ward in the hospital. For months, there had been a gaping hole in hospital security, and no one had noticed. He had ordered the Works Department to change all the locks on all the fridges. The managers had done their best to calm the rumours which had been sweeping the hospital. Someone said there must be a bogus doctor, working without any qualifications. Peter Flood had double-checked his records and found that all was well. Someone else suggested that it must be an Iraqi doctor taking revenge for the Gulf War. Flood knew there were a few Iraqi staff—he had listed them in case they were seen as a security risk during the war—but he had checked and reassured himself that they could not possibly have had anything to do with Ward Four.

Now Stuart Clifton confirmed the worst rumour of all. It was one of Ward Four's own staff.

Gibson bounced back from the revelation with surprising calm and asked politely whether Clifton would write him a letter asking for Bev Allitt to be sacked or suspended. Clifton instantly smelled a rat with a legal brief that would end up in front of an industrial tribunal with everybody blaming the police for her wrongful dismissal. Equally politely, he declined. But he wanted her off the ward. He knew now that he was going to have to take the long route to prove his case, and in the meantime the children on Ward Four had nothing more than a camera over the double doors to protect them. And so they compromised, and, instead of being suspended or fired, Bev Allitt began a long holiday. And Stuart Clifton began a long haul.

The next day, he sat down in Grantham police station and worked out a new strategy. It was not easy. If he was right, this young nurse had attacked a dozen different children, many of them more than once. But where was the direct evidence? These kids were perfect victims. Most of them were tiny babies. A poisoner could have stared right into their faces, told them exactly what was about to happen, jabbed them as crudely as could be and then stayed to grin at the result, yet none of them could ever have told, simply because none of them could talk. Only two of them had been old enough to tell: Brad Gibson, who had been asleep, and Tim Hardwick, who had cerebral palsy and had never uttered a coherent sentence in his life. Clifton had little hope of finding any other eyewitness. A nurse's uniform was an almost perfect disguise: everybody trusted nurses. And who would have thought it was odd if they had seen a nurse with a syringe? The woman who poisoned her husband at home was often betrayed by her purse: she had to go out and buy the rat poison or the arsenic and so she left a fatal clue. But a poisoner in a hospital had the whole killer's cutlery laid out for a feast: pills and powders, tablets, toxins, anaesthetics, analgesics, sedatives, narcotics, opiates. A poisoner's paradise.

Clifton decided to think positive. If he had picked the right suspect, then she must have been lying in her interviews, so he would check and cross-check her story. Equally, if it was not simply an outrageous coincidence that she had been present at all these arrests, he now had a dozen different lines of inquiry to pursue. They would have to repeat the operation they had run on Paul Crampton for every one of these kids: set up a time frame for an attack, and then TIE anyone who was present—trace, interview and eliminate them—and see where that left her.

He assigned a pair of detectives to each child; each pair included one officer who had already worked on Paul Crampton and who had, therefore, learned enough of medical procedures and language to avoid looking foolish with nurses and doctors. He set up others to try and track the movement of insulin through the ward and, finally, he called in his brightest inspector, Neil Jones, and gave him the grim job of tracking down the remaining blood, tissues, organs and X-rays of all the suspect children. The blood was particularly important. Clifton now knew that insulin was 'dumped' by the body within 24 hours of an injection. If they were ever going to prove anything, they needed to find blood that had been taken from the victims soon after their arrests and then left in a freezer, where traces of insulin would survive.

The next day, as his officers fanned out across the case, Clifton went to the pub. He drove down to the middle of Grantham, to the Angel and Royal, an old coaching inn full of coats of arms and medieval stonework and there he sat down in the bar for a quiet talk about insulin and blood sugar with the world's greatest expert on the subject, Professor Vincent Marks from the University of Surrey. Clifton had come across the professor by chance. He had been talking to someone at the hospital who said they had been reading about the 'Sleeping Beauty case' in New York where Claus von Bulow had been accused of murdering his millionairess wife with an injection of insulin. They said this professor from Surrey had been flown out there to give evidence. Clifton had called him, and the professor had agreed to meet; his wife, who was a sculptor, was exhibiting her work in Scarborough, and he would make a diversion through Grantham, if that would help. At a quiet table in the Angel and Royal, Clifton now completed his education in body chemistry and persuaded the professor to help him, by testing children's blood for him, including Paul Crampton's sample which had been retrieved from the hospital in Boston.

The new, enlarged inquiry was hard work. The officers who

were trying to track insulin through the hospital stumbled into a swamp. First they went to the hospital pharmacy and seized the computer records of all the insulin that had been supplied to Ward Four. Then they set off to match these against the record of the use of insulin on the ward, where they rapidly discovered that they were wasting their time. Mary Reet and Betty Asher both vaguely remembered dropping insulin vials on the floor and breaking them and no one was sure whether they had been replaced. Lynn Vowles said she thought she remembered seeing a couple of insulin vials in the lotion cupboard in the Treatment Room and she had no idea how they had got there and no one seemed to know whether they had been thrown away or returned to the fridge. No one had any record of how much insulin had been discarded as waste after injections; and a charge nurse on night shifts said that at the end of February he had gone to the fridge and found that some of the insulin was too old to use and so he had borrowed some from another ward. The official monitoring procedure was full of holes. Tracking insulin through Ward Four was like trying to catch a handful of mist.

Neil Jones was wading through a similar swamp in his efforts to find blood and other samples from the children. He had started in the path lab in Grantham, where he had soon found that blood samples were split several different ways and scattered through different laboratories around the country with no reliable record of where they were. He tried the mortuary and found that there too, bits of body and tissue sample were stored in different freezers in different hospitals. And no one seemed to have any central record of the X-rays of these children. Jones was soon reduced to getting down on his hands and knees in front of freezers full of strange packets and bottles and sifting through them in search of evidence. He began to succeed.

In the Grantham mortuary, he found a photograph of Liam's heart, and a large sample from Tim Hardwick's brain. In the Grantham path lab, he found blood from Becky Phillips and Claire Peck, though there was still no sign of the Technicon print-out of the potassium test on Claire's blood—it had just gone. From Martin Gibson, he collected a batch of X-rays, then a few days later, he got some more from Moira Onions and then a further batch from Gibson; they apologized, no one seemed to know what had happened to Becky Phillips's X-rays, they had just gone. Nor did they know what had happened to the print-out from the ECG monitor of Brad Gibson's heart attack, it had just gone too. Neil Jones went to Lincoln, where after rummaging in the bottom of freezers in the County Hospital, he unearthed 77 different tissue samples for children on the list. Every time he found something, he logged it and sent it on for analysis: blood to Professor Marks in Surrey; tissue and organ specimens to the paediatric pathologist at Queen's Med; X-rays to the radiologist at Queen's Med. As a double-check, they sent all the children's medical notes to Professor John Emery in Sheffield, the leading expert on cot deaths.

Once again, Stuart Clifton sat at the centre of the web and watched the results come in.

Professor Marks called him a few days after their meeting in the Angel and Royal. Clifton could hear excitement in his voice.

'I've got the result of your test.'

'And?'

'It's well over the 500 that they measured in Cardiff. Your Paul Crampton had 43,167 milliunits of insulin per litre of blood. It's astronomically high.'

The professor went on to explain that as far as he knew there had only ever been one case of a higher insulin dose, with a doctor who had committed suicide by injecting himself with it. 'It really is astronomically high.' And the C-peptide was low. There was no doubt possible.

Clifton thanked him. The professor agreed to call back as soon as he received any other positive results on the blood of other children on Clifton's list.

The TIE work on Paul Crampton had now narrowed down the time frame. Paul could have been attacked only between 12.45 and 12.55. Only two people went near him in that time, a student nurse and Bev Allitt. And Clifton now believed he could prove that Bev had lied in her interview. It was true, as she had said, that she had taken a boy called Martin to the operating theatre that day, but that had been at noon, and she was back on the ward with plenty of time to spare before Paul was attacked. And both Mandy Poole and Betty Asher denied ever having given her permission to take the allocation book home with her. Clifton had seized her diaries and found that she had not filled them in with any of the details from the allocation book, as she had claimed during her interview. And while they were unravelling that little mystery, another one had cropped up. Some officers had gone to see Sister Barker and she had admitted that she knew the allocation book was missing and she had failed to tell them, and then she told them that a few weeks ago, she'd noticed that someone had cut out the pages from her old diary as well. She didn't know who had done it, but the detectives saw that it had an insider's touch. No outsider would even know this old diary existed, let alone have a chance to gut it of evidence.

It was too early for anything much to emerge from the TIE work on the other children, although it looked as though they all had one common feature: the children were always on I/V drips, which meant that they could be injected through the plastic cannula without their feeling a thing. But the new wave of questioning had had one unexpected side effect. It had spread rumours so far that they had reached the national press who were now moving in on the story. Detectives heard that one of the support staff at the hospital was selling names and addresses of Ward Four parents to the tabloids. Not all of these families were involved, and reporters were beginning to play tricks—calling funeral directors and posing as the friends of bereaved families, sending flowers to nurses they wanted to talk to, so that they could identify them when they walked out of the hospital with a handful of freesias.

Then Clifton had a call from Queen's Med, from Dr David Fagan, the paediatric pathologist who had been examining the remains discovered by Neil Jones. He had been studying the case of Liam Taylor, and he agreed with the Grantham pathologist who said he had died of myocardial infarction, but he had gone one step further and found a reason. Liam's heart had stopped either because he was asphyxiated or because someone poisoned him, probably with barbiturates or insulin. Liam certainly had not died of natural causes. This was now officially a murder inquiry.

Clifton was still absorbing the implications of Dr Fagan's call, when Professor Marks called again from Surrey. The lab had come up with another interesting result. They had looked at Becky Phillips's blood, which had been sent to them by Neil Jones, and it contained 9,660 milliunits of insulin for every litre of blood, another huge reading. Becky Phillips, too, had been murdered.

Becky had not even been on Dr Porter's original list of suspicious cases, because she had died at home after being discharged
from the ward. She was one of the five cases that had been handed
over by the coroner. Professor Marks said it looked as though she
had been given slow-acting insulin which had taken 12 hours to
hit her. Stuart Clifton begged a couple more officers and asked
them to go and see Sue and Peter Phillips.

The Phillips already knew a bit about the police inquiry. The
team that was looking at Paul Crampton had been round to interview them, because they had been on the ward at the same time
as Paul. The truth was that they had begun to get a little fed up
with the questions. They had problems of their own to deal with
and there had been a silly mix-up about a vigilante group.

Sue had been in Boots and she had started talking to Hazel
Elstone, whom she knew from childbirth classes. Sue had been on
the ward when Patrick had had his arrest and was taken off to
Queen's Med with Hazel and Bob and the other twin, Anthony,
behind him. Hazel Elstone said she didn't have much faith in
Grantham Hospital and never had had. She thought it must be
their fault that Patrick had got so bad. Sue said she didn't know,
but it did seem very strange, all these children being so ill. Hazel
said they should form a group of parents to find out what the
hospital had done wrong and get them to sort it out. Sue said that
sounded like a good idea, and Hazel suggested that Peter should
be the leader, because he was so good at talking, better than her
Bob, who was rather quiet.

Sue had told Peter and Peter had told Sister Barker, who understood he meant some kind of vigilante group and—without any
of the hesitation that had blighted the ward in April—she had
gone straight to the police to complain. By the time the police
had got to the bottom of it, Sue and Peter Phillips felt they were
being accused of something and were being quite rude to them.
For good measure, Peter told them defiantly that Bev Allitt was
Katie's godmother, that she had been visiting their home and that
she was very welcome to do so, as were all the nurses from Ward
Four. Bev had become a close friend.

Bev was coming round almost every day now, taking Sue out
shopping, taking Katie out for trips and playing mother to her.
She had got to know them well and they felt she trusted them.

She had even told them about her girlfriend, Tracy, how they had gone on holiday to Spain with their boyfriends and got fed up with them and sent them home so that they could become lovers and enjoy their holiday without them. Bev always seemed to be ill. She had bandages on her arm or on her legs, and one day when she turned up she said she had just burned her eye. But she had been very willing to help. She had taken Katie to meet her parents down in Corby Glen and, one afternoon, she had taken the three-year-old Jamie all the way to Peterborough to have a hamburger and visit Tracy's mum, who lived there. There was one afternoon when she said she was just taking Katie to the park and she had stayed out for four-and-a-half hours and by the time she got back, Sue was going crazy, but Bev had calmed her down.

She had only recently told them that the police seemed to be blaming her for Paul Crampton's problems and that she'd had to have counselling to help her deal with the stress. Sue and Peter told her that that was bloody daft and they would try and help her. Peter knew a couple of private detectives who worked in the town doing odd jobs for local lawyers, and he invited them round one evening and they talked to Bev and told her they would see what they could do to help her. Sue and Peter said they would pay their fees. They didn't see why Bev should put up with being messed about by these cops.

That Saturday, 15 June, Bev came round for lunch. Afterwards, Katie was crying and Sue was busy doing the washing up, so Bev said she would take her out for a quick walk in the buggy. Sue said not to bother, because it was raining. But Bev insisted. Ten minutes later, the front door flew open and Bev was shouting.

'For God's sake, call the doctor. She's going to have a convulsion.'

Sue ran to Katie, who seemed to be fine, and Sue couldn't imagine what Bev was fussing about, but all the same she reached for the phone and called the GP who said she would be right there. Bev watched as Sue picked Katie up from the buggy. Now Sue began to see what Bev was talking about. Katie's face was bright red and bubbling with sweat. Within minutes, the GP's car arrived outside. Katie was now sweating and moaning, Sue was trying to console her, and Bev suddenly said she had to go.

'But can't you just wait?' said Sue. 'Can't you explain that she's going to have a fit?'

'I haven't got time. I've got to pick Tracy up from work.'

And with that, she was gone, leaving the GP and Sue to work out what was wrong. Katie was admitted straight to Ward Four, where they said they weren't too sure what was wrong with her but they were sure there was nothing to worry about.

Two days later, on Monday morning, 17 June, the story broke in the national press, and Sue and Peter were just trying to make sense of a report in the *Sun*, which claimed that several children from Ward Four had been killed, when the police knocked on their door and asked them to come to the station. Sue and Peter had had enough of this and told them plainly that they were fed up with being asked questions, they'd told them everything they knew about bloody Paul Crampton, they'd lost a child themselves and Katie had been very ill, she'd nearly died in April and she'd been very ill again at the weekend and they weren't going to say any more. The officers at the door explained that this was not about Paul Crampton. This was about their own children.

When two detectives told them about the insulin in Becky's blood, Sue and Peter Phillips were full of grief and anger. When they went on to explain that they thought that Katie's godmother was responsible, Peter told them straight: 'It can't be. I don't believe you.'

It was several hours before they got home to discover from one of Peter's teenage daughters, Emma, that Bev had got so fed up with the press hanging round her door in First Avenue, that she had come round and asked if she could stay with them for a while.

Detectives went and found her and told her to stay away from the Phillips.

'I'll keep away from them, if they'll keep away from me,' she said.

Then they went back to the Phillips to talk about Katie. She was still on Ward Four, not yet fully recovered from Saturday's fit, feeding badly, choking and vomiting. The Phillips told DCI Alan Smith what had happened when Bev took her for a walk, and without waiting to hear any more, he seized all the medicine in the house for tests, ordered the nurses to keep Katie's nappies for more tests, and then he posted a police guard outside the door of her cubicle on Ward Four.

Stuart Clifton prayed for another breakthrough.

Bev had been bored stiff. At first, when she'd been sent on leave after the police pulled her in, she had been quite happy. She and Tracy had been planning to go off to the Isle of Wight for a few days with Bev's family. Now Tracy didn't want to go, not with the police everywhere and the press hovering but Bev would have none of it.

'I'm bloody well going,' she said. 'Don't see why I shouldn't.'

So they went. They spent a long weekend at Whitecliffe Bay messing about on the beach and sitting around in tatty cafés. Tracy hated it. She couldn't stop thinking about what had happened, worrying about what the police were going to do next, smoking herself sick. But Bev had a great time. She was dancing and larking about with her sister Alison. Bev had hired a video camera and she got her dad to film her and Alison clowning around, dancing to a Madonna record. Tracy didn't know how she did it. She was glad when they got back to Grantham, but things were no better there.

Bev was going spare sitting around the house all day listening to the radio and picking her nails. She was convinced that the police were tapping her phone. Sometimes, she would drive off to Corby Glen for the day but there was nothing to do there. She went visiting the Phillips, even though Tracy warned her not to because the police wouldn't like it. Bev said it was none of their business.

She went into the hospital and met Mandy Poole outside Ward Four.

'How're you then?' asked Mandy.

'Well, I got arrested,' said Bev in her usual matter-of-fact way. 'And they held me in the cells for two nights.'

Mandy looked shocked, and Bev went on with her exciting story.

'You know they keep on at me about insulin? Well, why would I want to use insulin? If I wanted to do anything like that, I'd use Temgesic. I've got loads of them lying around the house.'

'Oh,' said Mandy. 'Are you coming on the ward?'

Bev said she couldn't. She'd decided she didn't want to come to work any more with all this going on, so she was going to see the management to tell them. She plodded off down the corridor.

A few days later, she distracted herself from her boredom by ringing her old tutor at the hospital, Richard Pitt, and asking him how the police were getting on with their inquiry. He said that as far as he knew, they were still asking questions.

'They were round here the other day,' she told him. 'Wanted to know about this anonymous call I know about, about that Jeanette who got done for stealing things from patients.'

'Yes,' said Pitt. 'What was that?'

'Yeah, the police wanted to know if I knew anything about her. I said I'd worked with her on Ward Seven, back on training, geriatric. But I didn't tell them the other thing.'

'Yes?' said Pitt cautiously, wondering what was coming next.

'That day it all happened with the Phillips's baby, on Ward Four, I was there and I saw this woman down there in uniform that I hadn't seen before, that shouldn't have been there. And I reckon it was her, Jeanette. Well, I can't tell the police. They'll think I'm trying to put the blame on someone else. Do you see?'

'Yes, perhaps.'

'Well, can you tell 'em?'

Pitt wished her goodbye and called the police, who agreed with him that Bev was, indeed, trying to put the blame on someone else. That week, the hospital took two calls from an anonymous woman who insisted that Nurse Allitt was innocent.

Bev still paced the floor in First Avenue. Then the press closed in. An old fellow from the *Daily Mail* kept knocking on the door. There was a television crew hiding down the road, trying to follow her. Now the police said she couldn't stay with the Phillips and she didn't know where to go. It was Tracy's mum who finally came to the rescue.

Eileen Jobson never liked to think bad of people. She was naturally a mother to anyone she liked, round-faced, well-cushioned, with bright little eyes, always full of warmth and consolation. She was the sort of person that other people always leaned on and the truth was that she didn't mind. She never liked to see anyone in trouble. Not even animals—she was always collecting stray cats

and dogs and looking after them. She had made a career out of
caring and from time to time she had worked as an auxiliary nurse.
Recently, she had been through a bad patch, when her marriage
had broken up, but she was settled again now, in a small, terraced
house on a new council estate ringed by dual carriageways outside
Peterborough, and there she lived, calmly caring for her 14-year-
old son, Jonathan, and seeing as much as she could of her daughter,
Tracy, who visited often from Grantham, 30 miles to the north.

She had met Bev quite a few times and thought she was a nice
girl, though rather quiet, and then when all this fuss blew up and
Tracy told her that Bev had been arrested and they were trying
to say she had been attacking all these children, she could see the
state the girl was getting herself into with the police and the press
and so she said 'Look, come and stay here. I'll look after you
until it's blown over.'

Bev had hung back at first, but Tracy said it was a good idea,
and when she was turned away from the Phillips, on 17 June, she
changed her mind and drove down to Peterborough with Tracy.
That first night, they all talked about the police inquiry and Bev
explained that she'd been sacked and it wasn't fair to sack her if
she'd done nothing wrong. Eileen tried to reassure her.

'The police must have made some kind of mistake,' she said.
'You read about these cases . . .'

'I dunno,' said Bev morosely. 'Dunno anything about it.'

'I can't understand why they won't just let you alone. They
must know it wasn't you.'

'They're just, just finding someone to blame, scapegoat.'

'I mean, could you have made a mistake?' Eileen persisted.
'Could you have given these children the wrong drug by mistake,
or something?'

'No, no. More likely be the doctors, do that sort of thing.'

'Well, I don't know,' sighed Eileen, who felt so sorry for this
girl but didn't know quite what she could do to help. 'I'm sure
it'll sort itself out in the end.'

'I'm not bothered.' Bev shrugged and bubbled her lower lip.
'They can't prove anything.'

Something painful brushed through the back of Eileen's mind
so gently that she barely felt it, but then it was gone, and Eileen
stood up and said, 'I'll get some supper.'

That night, Tracy sat Bev down in the sitting room, pushed the *TV Times* off the coffee table and, working from that morning's newspapers and what they had picked up in their interviews, Tracy drew up a list of all the children they thought the police were interested in. Tracy found it hard going.

'You've got to try and remember what you were doing,' she said. 'Come on! Think!'

Bev didn't seem too interested, kept saying she couldn't remember and it was more likely to be one of the doctors who'd done it.

'It couldn't have been me,' she said.

She hadn't been there for half these arrests. She'd been taking a kid to the operating theatre when one of them went off. Some of the children, she said, she had never even heard of. Tracy kept at it. Her first ambition had been to be a policewoman, and now she worked on Bev to recall every detail of the care of the children she had dealt with, the doctors and nurses who had been on duty, the drugs they had been prescribed, the symptoms they had shown, and she scribbled it all down, point by point, and after a while she spotted the pattern.

'They were all on I/Vs!' she said. 'Maybe they're contaminated or something. Do you see? It must be something to do with the I/Vs.'

'Dunno,' said Bev.

Under Eileen's kindly gaze, Bev soon settled into an easy routine in her new home. In the morning, Jonathan would be up and off to school; Eileen, who suffered with pain in her hips, would take her walking stick and hobble round the kitchen getting his breakfast and then tidying the house. Bev would sleep late and then wander down to the shops with Eileen, or watch the tennis on cable TV and play with Jack the terrier. In the evenings, Jonathan and Bev played records and watched more TV, while Eileen enjoyed the warmth of it all and cooked Bev her favourite meals, spaghetti and lasagne and a banana cake, even though no one else liked it. At first, Bev was very quiet and hardly spoke unless Eileen or Jonathan spoke to her first, but after a while she began to relax and Eileen began to feel very fond of her, and Jonathan thought she was a good mate. On her days off, Tracy came down from Grantham to join them. All was calm.

After a couple of weeks, Bev produced some cheap tickets that she had got with petrol coupons for an American theme park in Derbyshire, and that Sunday, 30 June, they piled into Bev's little white Ford Fiesta—Eileen and Jonathan and Bev and Tracy—and, all cramped up shoulder to shoulder, they drove two and a half hours to Derbyshire and spent the day on triple-loop roller-coasters and dodging sheriffs and outlaws in the cowboy town. It was a long drive and it cost a lot—Eileen happened to notice on the way back that all that she had left in her purse was a one-pound coin, and 41 pence in change—but it was worth it, and it all made Eileen feel more and more fond of Bev.

They were still talking about their trip the next evening. They were sitting around in the kitchen, Jonathan was reluctantly doing the washing up to earn himself some pocket money, and Eileen went to her purse to get something to pay him.

'Well, that's funny,' she tutted. 'I know I had a one-pound coin in there. Jonathan, have you been in my purse?'

Jonathan pleaded innocent. Eileen prodded around in her handbag but there was no sign of the coin. There was only the 41 pence in change. That was odd. It was only a pound but it was irritating.

'Are you sure, Jonathan? I know it was there. I saw it yesterday evening.'

Jonathan insisted. Bev said it did seem peculiar.

'Well, I don't know,' said Eileen.

The next day, in the afternoon, Eileen went to the post office to draw her income support. It was not much, but it kept them going and after she had done some shopping, Eileen folded the rest of the money neatly into her purse, two tenners, a fiver and some change. She got home, she did some tidying, she picked up her purse and found that one of the tenners had vanished. Now she felt angry. Jonathan swore he knew nothing about it and Bev did her best to calm Eileen down.

'You must have made a mistake,' she said.

Eileen knew better than that, and felt out of sorts all evening. The next morning, at breakfast, when she looked in her purse, the other tenner was also missing. Now, she was furious. She needed that money. If this was supposed to be a joke, it was not funny. How were they going to eat if they had no money?

'Come on, Jonathan, stop mucking about. Was it you? Did you take it? If it was . . .'

'It wasn't me, mum. What do you think? I wouldn't do that. God! Calling me a thief.'

Eileen hadn't liked even to ask Bev before. She knew the poor girl had enough worries and, after all, she was a guest in the house, but now Eileen asked her, as gently as she could.

'Bev, you don't know anything about it, do you?'

'No. Course not.'

'Well, I can't understand it.'

Eileen liked things to run smoothly in her house, regular meals good and hot, no fights, no nastiness, everything neat and tidy. She felt quite upset, and when her sister Lynn and their mother came to visit the next day, Thursday, she told them all about it. They were sitting round the kitchen table—Eileen and Lynn and her mother with Bev and Jonathan and Tracy—and they were drinking cups of coffee and talking it through, Lynn suggesting all the explanations they had already rejected, when Bev interrupted.

'When we were at the theme park,' she started, 'on Sunday, you know, I saw a ghost.'

Eileen looked at her and chortled. 'You should have said so, we could all have had a look.'

Bev wasn't laughing. 'I didn't want to frighten you. So I didn't say anything. It was a woman. She was in the shop, that souvenir shop, and I saw her.'

'What, are you serious?'

'I've seen 'em before, ghosts. In my dad's shop at home, there's one in there. They're dead scared, though, my mum and dad. Don't tell 'em about this one. They get terrified.'

Eileen had never seen Bev so animated. She seemed really to believe this nonsense. 'What did she look like then, this woman?' she asked, with a grin.

'Sort of tall and thin. There was one in First Avenue and all. Wasn't there, Tracy? Remember? It was in the bathroom. When I was up there, it touched my hair, just touched my hair. Remember?'

Tracy muttered, feeling slightly embarrassed at her friend's outburst. Eileen laughed and swatted away the idea with her hand.

'What a load of rubbish. I don't know, Bev, the things you come out with.'

They changed the subject and Lynn left, Tracy went off to Grantham and Jonathan to bed, and Eileen and Bev were alone together, finishing the washing up, when Bev started again.

'You know that ghost I saw?'

'Oh, yeah.'

'Do you think it might have come home with us?'

Eileen tried to laugh her off again. 'It would have been a bit cramped in the back of that Fiesta! I shouldn't think so.'

But Bev persisted. The ghost was real, it was following her, it had come with them. It must have done. Eileen began to feel frustrated.

'Oh come on, Bev, that's enough. You're just being silly. It's ridiculous, all this.'

'Well, it would explain about your money going missing.'

That weekend, it was true, the house seemed to be possessed by some sort of demon imp who was running around, causing every kind of trouble it could think of. Bev's purse vanished from the wall unit in the kitchen, turned up in the front of the car, vanished again from the kitchen and reappeared in the shelves in the downstairs loo. Eileen's purse also vanished and was missing all Saturday, until Jonathan went to bed and found it under his duvet. In the meantime, his bar of chocolate had disappeared and, in the bathroom, the hot water tap on the sink seemed to have turned itself on, the plug had settled into the plug-hole and, if Eileen had not heard the hot water tank charging and gone to check, the water would have flooded out all over the floor.

By the end of the weekend, Eileen did not know whether to fume with rage or chuckle and laugh. She also did not know what on earth was going on. Jonathan was afraid he did.

'Maybe it is a ghost,' he said. 'Maybe there is something horrible in the house.'

The most ordinary events suddenly became bizarre. Eileen left a bowl of strawberries on the counter top in the kitchen, and it flew up to the top of the cupboard. She left her walking stick in its usual place by the sitting room door, and it leaped over to the two-seater sofa. She put her lighter down in the kitchen while she made some jam, and it tucked itself inside one of Jonathan's slippers, scorching a patch on the sitting room carpet as it went. Bev said it was definitely a poltergeist and Jonathan was beginning to get frightened, but Eileen did not believe in ghosts and demons.

Alone in the house with Jonathan and Bev, she insisted that they should all stay together so that each of them could prove that they were not doing these things. They herded together in the sitting room and made sure that there was nothing wrong in there, they walked together upstairs and checked that everything was fine up there, they went back together to the sitting room where they found that Eileen's walking stick had once again thrown itself across the room, landing this time on the three-seater sofa. Eileen was simply baffled.

One evening, Jonathan found a magazine, *Take a Break*, which had been lying around in the house and it had a story all about ghosts. He read bits of it out to them, about how poltergeists sometimes appear around people who are under stress and steal things and even cause floods and fires.

'Maybe it's me,' said Bev solemnly. 'Maybe it's me that's upsetting it.'

'Well,' said Eileen, who was determined to laugh it off. 'We've nearly had a flood. All we need now is a fire.'

Bev seemed to be relaxing and got into the habit of telling Jonathan jokes. Most of them were about sex, like the one about the Englishman, the Irishman and the Scotsman who were talking about screwing their wives. They made Jonathan squeal with laughter, but he also found them embarrassing.

'You can't say that in front of my mother!' he said. But she seemed to think she could.

The next morning, Eileen decided to go shopping, but when she went to her purse, she found she had lost another £20. Bev was the only other person in the house and so with a heavy heart, Eileen walked through to the sitting room to ask her. She didn't want to think bad of her, but she had to admit she was a funny girl. Just the other day, Eileen had taken her to pick some strawberries on a fruit farm, and when they came back, Bev's arms had been red raw with some kind of allergic rash and Bev had been scratching and scratching till Eileen was afraid she would draw blood, but she wouldn't do anything to make the rash better. She had refused to wash it or put cream on it. She had just scratched and scratched, as if she enjoyed the discomfort.

But even if she was a bit funny, Eileen would never have thought her capable of stealing all this money from her, and when she looked Bev in the eye and showed her the empty purse, Bev almost burst into tears at the question. Eileen didn't know what to think. She didn't want to suspect Bev and she had to admit that Bev had been with her the night before when her walking stick had made its latest trip, so it couldn't be her. Eileen apologized and went off to bake an apple cake.

Cooking always calmed her down and once she had tucked the cake into the oven and set the timer to cook for an hour and a quarter, she decided not to go shopping this morning and, instead, she settled down in the sitting room with a sigh and a cup of coffee and began to feel better. She could smell the cake cooking. It was such a homely, reassuring smell. With any luck, she thought, the money would turn up somewhere, like some of these other things had. She was sorry she'd accused Bev. She'd make it up to her somehow. The cake was smelling very strong now, warm and sweet, but very strong. Eileen flicked through a magazine and finished her coffee and realized that the smell of the cake was now so strong that, unless she was very much mistaken, there was something wrong . . . She dumped the magazine and hobbled as fast as her lame leg would carry her into the kitchen. The smell was overpowering. There was smoke. She looked at the oven: it was right up on maximum. She hadn't put it on maximum. She pulled open the door. Her apple cake was burned to cinders.

'Oh no,' she sighed.

As Eileen cleared up the mess, Bev joined her in the kitchen.

'However could that have happened?' she asked.

'I don't know,' said Eileen. 'But there could have been a fire. If I'd gone to the shops, God knows what would have happened.'

'You see? It's another weird thing,' said Bev. 'It's the poltergeist. You said there'd be a fire. When you going to believe it? That poltergeist has got it in for you.'

Eileen ignored her silliness and carried on hacking charcoal out of the baking tray. Bev seemed quite upset and started to say she could smell burning again.

'It's just the oven,' said Eileen. 'It'll go soon.'

'No. It's fat, fat burning.'

'It can't be, Bev. I'm not doing anything with fat. It's just the cake.'

But Bev insisted. She started feeding scraps of food to Holly the cat on the kitchen floor. 'It is fat. I'm sure it is.'

Eileen really didn't know what this girl was going on about, but then she noticed that the little red thermostat on the side of the chip pan was suddenly glowing, and the switch on the pan was down.

Bev was excited. 'Did you see that? It's just done that by itself, turned itself on.'

Eileen fingered the outside of the pan and was reassured to find that it was cold to the touch.

'It's not on, Bev. I've told you,' she said, as she lifted the lid and was suddenly hit in the face by a thick column of scorching smoke swarming up from the pan. The fat was on fire.

Now Eileen was deeply upset. The smoke had given her such a shock, and that fat was hot, it could have hurt her. This was getting well beyond a joke

That afternoon, when Jonathan came home, Eileen told him what had happened. He was now convinced that there was something supernatural in the house: if the chip pan had still been cold and only just turned itself on, how else could the fat have got so hot in only a couple of seconds? Eileen was trying to find a convincing reply when Bev, who was upstairs, suddenly yelled to them.

'Oh, my God.' Her voice came booming down the stairs. 'Come here! Look at this!'

Eileen and Jonathan scrambled upstairs, into Jonathan's room. The walls were plastered with posters of Madonna and album covers and school notes for his revision and, there in the middle of them, was Bev, standing at the head of Jonathan's bed, staring down at the pillow, which had been stabbed deeply with a knife whose handle still hung in the air like a broken limb. Eileen had to laugh.

'This is getting ridiculous!' she said.

But Jonathan was scared and made no attempt to hide it. It was his pillow that had been stabbed. It was as good as a death threat, and if there was some kind of ghost in the house trying to kill him, then he was not going to sleep here tonight. He had seen enough horror videos to know how that would end up. Eileen tried to reassure him. There was no ghost in this house, she told him, and she took him downstairs and made it as plain as she could that it had to be Bev.

'I'm damn sure it's not me,' she said. 'It's not you, Jonathan. It must be Bev.'

But Jonathan was not having that. He liked Bev. She was always really nice to him, talked to him, watched television with him, she had even bought him a Deacon Blue double album and a Viz T-shirt.

'It's a ghost, mum. What do you want to blame Bev for? Bev wouldn't do that. Leave her alone, it's not fair.'

Eileen did not know what to think. That night, to calm Jonathan down, she agreed that they would all drive over to her mother's house down the road in Bretton and sleep there. They packed up all their overnight things and Jack the dog and Holly the cat and piled into Bev's Fiesta like refugees running from a war zone.

When they arrived, Eileen went upstairs to talk to her mother, who tried to persuade her that it must be Bev who was doing these things. They both agreed that it wasn't Jonathan. His fear was obviously genuine. Eileen knew that it looked like Bev, but she found herself defending her. There were some things she couldn't have done, and anyway, why would she do this to them? Her mother said maybe she thought it was funny. Then Bev came upstairs and told them that she thought the ghost had followed them. She'd seen the front door open all of its own accord and she was not sure what the ghost might have done back at Eileen's. She got Eileen worrying. What if there was a fire or something at home? So they packed up all their stuff again and grabbed the dog and the cat and drove back to Eileen's. Her mother came too.

It felt better to be home. It had been silly really to run off like that. They could sort this out as long as they just stayed calm. Eileen and her mother sat in her room, Bev joined them and together they sat looking through an old jewellery box, reminiscing on engagement rings and wedding rings. Eileen's mother was watching Bev.

'Doesn't anything ever happen in your room, Bev?'

Bev ignored the provocation. 'No, nothing.'

Bev carried on fingering the rings, then she wandered off and barely half a minute had passed before they heard her voice saying 'Oh my God, come and look at this', and when they followed her voice, they found her in her room where the pillow at the head of her bed had been sliced and stabbed with a knife with a 12-inch blade. Eileen's mother stared at the handle.

'But it's one of mine,' she gasped.

Eileen had laughed and fumed at this demon's antics but now, for the first time, she felt afraid. Maybe she was just tired, but she felt her legs starting to buckle and she slumped down on Bev's bed. Whether it was a ghost, or Bev, or someone getting into the house, it was all too much, it was violent, nasty. Jonathan was now refusing to sleep in the house again, and Eileen said he could go and stay with a friend.

Eileen's mother took her off and sat her down in the bedroom with the door closed and they talked about it, and Eileen's mother was very clear.

'It must be Bev. She was on her own in my kitchen and she must have taken that knife. She could easily have done all that to her pillow before she called us.'

'But why?'

'Well, I don't know . . .'

'I mean, we're helping her. She stays here. I don't charge her for her keep, I feed her, I look after her . . .'

'She must have some reason.'

'For God's sake, she's on bail. Why would she do anything so risky? It just doesn't make sense.'

'But who else could it be?'

Eileen decided to go to bed. On the landing, she saw Bev, who pointed into Jonathan's room and said 'What's that there?'

Eileen looked and could see nothing, only Jonathan's door and the pot plant they sometimes used to prop it open, but Bev crossed to the pot plant, crouched down by its side, rooted around in the earth and pulled something out. It was Eileen's wedding ring.

'I thought I could see something,' she said and held it up, triumphant.

Eileen said nothing, but inside, she thought: 'All right, Bev Allitt, I'm going to watch you like a hawk.'

*

While Bev Allitt was settling down in Peterborough, Stuart Clifton was pushing very hard to get her locked up. Clifton now believed that he was hunting a peculiarly dangerous person, someone who, if he was right, had been attacking children roughly once every 48 hours, an intensity of violence which would make her quite simply the most dangerous person in the country. He had heard of no one else who was trying to kill people with that kind of frequency and, if Bev Allitt really were responsible for these attacks, she was peculiarly dangerous because she looked completely normal. At least when you looked at Ian Brady or Myra Hindley, you could see something sinister about them. Peter Sutcliffe looked powerful and almost satanic with his black beard. But Bev Allitt was young and open-faced, apparently completely harmless. She was the girl who stood next to you at the bus stop, just another face in the street, drenched in ordinariness. But if Clifton had ever needed any reminder of the urgency of this inquiry, the sudden panic over Katie Phillips had provided it. They had found no traces of poison in Katie's nappies nor in her medicine bottles, but her sudden fit and Bev's strange behaviour had rung a loud alarm. He had to get more evidence, fast.

Every morning now, he and his entire team sat down in the incident room to pool their knowledge. Each pair of detectives reported on the child they had been studying. New facts started to tumble down on them.

The paediatric pathologist at Queen's Med, David Fagan, reported that he had studied the tissues and samples of all eight dead children, three who had been suggested by Dr Porter and five by the coroner. Liam Taylor and Becky Phillips, they had already established, were murdered. Now he declared that four of the others had died of natural causes but two of them, Tim Hardwick and Claire Peck, had not. He found that the post-mortem reports on both children were wrong. Tim had not died of epilepsy. Claire had not died of asthma. Both of them had been poisoned with some unidentified toxin. Clifton was now looking at four murders.

From Queen's Med, the radiologist, Phillip Small, reported that he had been looking at the X-rays of Kayley Desmond, trying to establish whether her chest infection could have been severe enough to stop her breathing twice in one night. And he had spotted something: high up in her right armpit, in the right axilla, there were dark streaks in her flesh. And unless he was very much mistaken, these indicated foul play. They were, he believed, little bubbles of air. Somebody had either injected Kayley with air in an attempt to stop her heart, or they had injected her with poison in such a hurry that accidentally they had caught air in the syringe. In any event, it was crime. And there was something else.

On the X-rays of Katie Phillips that had been taken after her first arrest, on Friday 5 April, some 12 hours after her twin sister Becky had died, Phillip Small had noticed something strange about the little girl's rib cage. There were tiny wrinkles in the bone, just visible in the sixth and seventh ribs on the right and at the front end of the ninth on the right. An untrained eye might easily have missed them, but the radiologist was in no doubt about them and about their meaning. They were fresh fractures. Someone had broken that little girl's ribs.

In addition to the four confirmed murders, Clifton now also had three confirmed attempted murders—Paul Crampton, Kayley Desmond and Katie Phillips. There were eight other surviving children from Dr Porter's list who were still in the balance.

Some of the new facts caused confusion. Clifton had begun to assume that all the children had been poisoned with insulin, but Professor Marks reported from Surrey that he could find no traces of insulin in the blood samples of any other children apart from Paul Crampton and Becky Phillips. There were some children for whom they had no blood from the time of their arrests, but clearly there were a number who could not have been attacked with insulin.

In the daily conferences, the detectives had already noticed that there were different groups of symptoms. Some children had gone grey and clammy while others had turned dark blue and arched their backs. If the first group was suffering from insulin, it was possible that the second group had been poisoned with another drug. But what would it be?

Looking through the medical notes of the children, the detectives previously had noticed that some of them had unusually high potassium levels in their blood. But when they had raised this with the doctors, they had been squashed. The doctors had informed them that if someone dies—even if they are later revived—potassium leaks naturally from the red cells in their blood and that this was the obvious explanation. The detectives had accepted their word for it. But now they began to wonder. During this inquiry, they had all learned something about the fallibility of doctors. Clifton remembered that Dr Porter had speculated that potassium might have caused the pain which Brad Gibson reported in his arm. And then there was Claire Peck. Between them, the path lab and Dr Porter couldn't agree what results had been reported and which print-outs had been lost by whom, but it was clear that the child had had a lot of potassium in her system, enough to beat the gauge of the path lab machine. It was worth a second look, and Clifton now asked Neil Jones and his twin brother, Paul, to go off and make themselves experts in the chemistry of potassium.

The Jones twins went away and immersed themselves in obscure medical journals. Their first discovery was that they were swimming in waters where few scientists had ventured, but after several days in the depths, they found what they were looking for. They reported back to the daily conference that a group of Swiss doctors had conducted research on the bodies of climbers who had died in the Alps and had measured the rate at which potassium naturally leaked after death. So far as they could tell, this natural rate of leakage did not explain the potassium levels in the children's blood. Clifton was pleased. He ordered blood samples and children's notes to be sent off to two heart specialists, one in Birmingham and one in London. Soon they reported back and, with varying degrees of certainty, they concluded that four children—Liam Taylor, Tim Hardwick, Brad Gibson, and Claire Peck—had probably been injected with potassium chloride. Claire Peck's case was particularly strong since the tests showed that she had more than 16 millimols of potassium per litre of blood, an unnaturally high reading, and this was true not only of blood drawn after her death, which could have been explained as natural leakage from red cells, but also of blood which was drawn when she was still alive. The finding on Brad Gibson meant that Clifton now had four attempted murders as well as four murders, and seven other children still in the balance.

While this steady flow of evidence all tended to prove there had been foul play, there was still very little to show who was responsible. Bev Allitt remained a suspect, not a culprit. Clifton decided to draw up more charts, and he set PC John Griffiths to work again.

Griffiths plotted Bev Allitt's known movements against the suspicious arrests and found that she had been given the drugs key for one reason or another immediately before all but two of the arrests. He tracked her use of insulin and found that she had twice been instructed to inject diabetic children, once on the day that Paul Crampton was admitted to hospital and once on the day that Becky Phillips was injected with her lethal dose. He looked at her night shifts. She had worked only five. On three of them, there had been attacks—Liam Taylor, Kayley Desmond and Brad Gibson. It was all interesting, it was consistent with her guilt, but it did not prove it.

Clifton was worried that the nurses on Ward Four still resented the police inquiry and so he went down to the ward and gathered the nurses together in the Treatment Room and told them what he was trying to do. He explained in great detail the evidence which they had accumulated about Paul Crampton. By the time he had finished talking to them, he believed he had begun to turn the tide.

The nurses, too, now began to believe that there had been foul play and, instead of resentment, they showed their distress. They began to talk more freely. Student nurse Sarah Biggs told them how Bev had assured her early in May that the police would never find the killer because the syringes had already been disposed of. Staff nurse Mandy Poole told them how Bev had stood outside the ward with her at the end of May and explained how personally she would have used Temgesic, not insulin, to attack the children.

Clifton was now ready to think about bringing charges. He decided to summon together all of the medical experts for a conference at which they could pool their information and test the strength of the case. The national press were still sniffing around the story and, as they read each other's fantasies, they became more and more excited. The *Daily Star* produced a fictional story which quoted Stuart Clifton saying that some children had been suffocated with pillows and added that the police feared there was a killer still loose in the hospital. Clifton booked the training wing of Grantham Hospital and at two o'clock in the afternoon on

2 July, he sat down there with his experts to review the evidence, while reporters prowled up and down in the car park outside.

Inside the conference, Stuart Clifton reviewed each case. The detectives reported their evidence, the scientists explained their findings. For the first time, each of them saw the whole picture. Nelson Porter was there and spoke with extraordinary passion of his own conviction that these children had been murdered. Dr Nanayakkara was there and cut a very different figure from his earlier encounters with the police. He no longer argued with his colleague. He, too, conceded that this was murder.

By the time the conference finished, the atmosphere was electric and Clifton was convinced that he was close to being able to charge his suspect. He spoke to the local office of the Crown Prosecution Service, he spoke to the barrister they had chosen to lead the case, John Goldring QC, he asked the hospital to allow them to type out all of the notes of all of the children so that a jury would be able to read them. He was close to the end, he pencilled in 26 July as the day he would charge her—but then an odd thing happened.

His assistant chief constable told him that the Director of Public Prosecutions in London was taking over the case. In 26 years, Clifton had never heard of this before. The DPP was bound to become involved eventually, but not until they had brought a charge, not until they were preparing for court hearings. Clifton would normally go to the DPP, not the other way around. If the DPP came in now, he would have to go back to square one with them. It was bound to cause a delay, possibly a long one. And why were they suddenly so interested? The answer lay in the press. The politicians had heard about the case and had sensed trouble—whatever would happen if someone blamed their management of the health service for this slaughter of children? So the Department of Health had used its influence to call in the DPP, so that they could monitor events, so that it could all be controlled from London. Clifton would have to wait.

In the little terraced house outside Peterborough, Eileen Jobson's life was no longer the same. She'd sit down for a cup of coffee and a TV crew would arrive on the doorstep. She'd pick up her handbag to go out shopping and have to stop and peek out through the curtains to make sure there were no reporters on the corner. One day, the door bell rang and a man from Interflora was brandishing a bunch of flowers. They were for Bev. How nice, she thought. How odd, she thought. It must be the press. So she hobbled round the corner to the flower shop, and gave them back.

She tried to ignore the demon in the house, though it was not always easy, what with the shelving unit detaching itself from the loo wall and making a new home in the cat's basket, her mending scissors taking refuge in the sofa, and her purse emptying itself of cash no matter where she hid it. It was like waking up and finding yourself in the middle of a circus ring full of clowns while everybody else carried on clapping and laughing and eating mouthfuls of popcorn as if there was nothing wrong at all, as if you belonged there. She supposed it must be Bev. She really didn't know.

Bev was no longer shy in the house, but kept up a steady barrage of comedy. There were more smutty jokes for Jonathan. There was a little dancing and clowning around. One night, when they were watching television, Eileen saw a spider—a big one with a body like a prune—lurking in the corner of the room and she shuddered out loud. It was a mistake. Bev instantly reached out and cupped her hands around it and started spooking Eileen with it. Eileen hated spiders and none of her own children would have dared to tease her about it, but Bev did, and reaching across with her hands, she kept pretending to drop it on her.

'Bev, don't,' snapped Eileen. 'It's not funny.'

Jonathan could see she meant it, but Bev carried on, laughing loudly and lurching towards Eileen, who was frantic with fear, until Jonathan finally persuaded Bev to stop.

When she was playing jester, Bev would tease anyone, even Tracy. Tracy liked watching current affairs programmes on television, while Bev seemed to pride herself on her ignorance. Tracy was watching a programme about the tyranny of the former Cambodian leader Pol Pot.

'Pol Pot?' sneered Bev. 'What sort of name is that? Pol Pot? Flower Pot? Bloody daft.'

Jonathan started laughing, and Bev joked on. 'Bloody Chamber Pot, more like it. Keep a Pol Pot under your bed! Pol Pot!'

Tracy told her to shut up. Bev kept on about Pol Potty, Pol Spotty while Jonathan rolled about laughing until finally Tracy blew up at her, told her that she was stupid and ignorant and loads of innocent people had died and all she could do was laugh at his name.

Bev hooted with laughter. 'That's their problem, isn't it? If they've all died. Bury them in a Pol Pot!'

Eileen watched them row. Tracy did think that Bev was stupid. In fact, she was always telling Bev how thick she was, and at first, Eileen had thought she was pretty dense, too. She had been useless when they had tried doing some newspaper competitions together. But now Eileen was not so sure. Sometimes, she caught Bev looking at Tracy with a smug sort of smile on her face, as if to say she could show Tracy a thing or two if only she wanted to. It was just like all this clowning around Bev did. Eileen was beginning to think that acting stupid was just a mask.

One night, Tracy came to visit and she and Bev bought a bottle of vodka. Bev poured them all huge drinks, far bigger than anyone wanted. Eileen took hers to the kitchen and made three weaker ones out of it, but Bev knocked hers back and poured another one, and then another. Tracy started warning her to be careful, but Bev just laughed.

'If you're going to have a drink, this is the way to do it.'

'You're going to be ill,' said Tracy. 'It's stupid, drinking like that. Mum, can't you stop her?'

But Eileen didn't want to stop her. 'There's nothing I can do about it,' she said.

Let her get drunk, she thought, let her get really plastered and maybe then she'll drop her guard and we'll see what she's really like. Bev carried on drinking, Tracy carried on warning her, and, sure enough, Bev started to be sick. They dragged her upstairs and put her to bed, where Tracy cursed her loudly for her stupidity, while Bev lay rolling her head from side to side burbling 'Buddha, Buddha, Buddha'.

Jonathan thought she was hilarious, until he caught her suddenly looking up at him from the pillow with a weird expression on her face, sort of puzzled and maybe disgusted, as if she had just found him on the bottom of her shoe and couldn't work out where he'd come from. Eileen watched her and, in a way, she admired her: legless as she was, she was still not going to give anything away.

'Buddha, Buddha, Buddha,' said Bev, and fell asleep.

The demon poltergeist kept busy. There was more missing money, more moving objects. Eileen found silk flowers and a little china cat laid out on her bedroom pillow. Bev took one look and explained kindly that this was a symbol of death.

Eileen's mother came to stay. She had developed diabetes and she needed to be near people for a few days while she got used to the new pills the doctor had given her to keep her blood sugar down. Eileen, who was now routinely hiding her valuables, stuffed her purse into her mother's handbag. Later, they were making Bev's bed as usual—and there was the purse, under Bev's sheet, with £40 missing. Eileen's mother said that was proof. Stolen property right in her bed! Didn't that show it must be Bev? But Eileen couldn't be sure. Maybe it proved the opposite—that it couldn't be Bev, because if she really had stolen the purse, she would never be so stupid as to leave it where Eileen was bound to find it when she made the bed. Or maybe it was double bluff— Bev had stolen it and left it in her bed, so that Eileen would think that it couldn't be her. Eileen's head whirled. How was she ever going to get to the bottom of this?

In a way, she felt sorry for Bev. Quite apart from all this trouble with the police, she seemed to have had the most terrible life. Bev had told her all about how her parents had split up when she was only two years old and she had been sent off to live with an aunt in Cornwall. That would have been bad enough, but when Bev had gone on to describe how her parents had got back together and asked for her back, only to split up again and pack her off to another aunt, in London, Eileen had thought that it was no wonder she was a little odd and she had felt quite mean for thinking bad things about her. Tracy was always saying that Bev was the unluckiest person in the world: all these accidents she had had, breaking both hands in separate incidents. It was unbelievable, and so sad that it had stopped her playing squash just when she had got into the Lincolnshire county team. Then there had been that dreadful business with the newspaper woman in her village, Mrs Lee, whom Bev had found dead on the floor one night. Bev had obviously hated her—she kept telling Eileen that she was a witch—but it must have been very traumatic to have found her like that and raised the alarm and been so powerless to save her.

Sometimes, Bev just seemed to be one of life's victims. When

Tracy came down, she would tell her the gossip from the hospital, all about the police inquiry and who they were talking to now. And they would all sit round and agree that the police were completely stupid and didn't know what they were talking about, but Bev never went any further than that. She didn't get angry or anxious or do anything to try and fight the police. She just said there must be a load of people who'd really got it in for her and the parents of those kids must really hate her to do this to her. Eileen felt so sorry for her.

'And all the time they're doing this to me,' said Bev, 'there's a bloody murderer wandering around up there.'

To make matters worse, Jonathan was ill. He had not been himself for several weeks. He kept getting dizzy spells and he complained of shooting pains in his legs for several hours each night. The other odd thing was that he was completely addicted to chocolate: endless mugs of hot chocolate and bar after bar of Cadbury's. Tracy kept buying it for him, although Bev said she shouldn't because he was a spoiled brat. They joked about him keeping Cadbury's in business, but then Tracy got serious and said it wasn't natural and they should take him to a doctor. It was true that he did get very aggressive if he couldn't get his chocolate. It was as if he was addicted to sugar for some strange reason. Eileen put it down to his age.

Then Bev said she was ill, too. She couldn't pee and she had pains in her lower back and abdomen. Tracy, who was visiting, told her it was her own fault if she was ill, because she never did what the doctors told her, never took enough fluid, never finished a course of antibiotics. Bev sulked and said it still hurt. As the day wore on, Eileen began to see that she really was in pain and by nine o'clock that evening, it was so bad that they called a doctor who examined her and, despite her protests that she would be all right, sent for an ambulance to take her down the road to Edith Cavell Hospital in Peterborough.

Tracy called Bev's parents in Corby Glen and told them what was happening, but Richard couldn't visit because he was out playing bowls, and Lillian didn't seem to think that she would either. The doctors said that Bev had a bladder infection and they kept her in hospital for ten days, but her parents still didn't visit her. Eileen thought that was very odd. Perhaps Richard was just too busy to visit. Bev had said he worked very hard running this wine business of his and evidently he was always having to go off to France buying wine. It sounded pretty nice to Eileen, to have his own villa in France to stay in, but perhaps that was it, he was just too busy to visit his daughter in hospital. But what about Lillian? Perhaps it was the drink. It was pretty obvious from what Bev said that both her parents were alcoholics. Three or four bottles of wine between them each night! They must be permanently drunk. Bev said she wasn't worried anyway.

'I don't need them,' she said.

In hospital, the doctors were soon puzzling over their new patient's condition. She was certainly suffering from urine retention, though they couldn't discovery why. She also had bouts of very high temperature—up to 105—but the puzzling thing was that her pulse rate never rose. Even odder, her temperature would fall right back to normal within 30 seconds. It did not take the Peterborough doctors long to conclude that Bev was simply heating up the thermometer. By the time she complained that her right breast was swollen, they were sufficiently suspicious of her to look very closely at her symptoms, which was how they came to discover three tiny puncture marks on the upper slope of the breast—the marks of a syringe with which she had evidently injected her breast with water.

While Bev was in hospital, the demon in Eileen Jobson's home was quiet. There was not one incident. Eileen saw her chance. She felt a little guilty about her plan and started to argue with herself: all right, she did feel sorry for Bev; and yes, this was probably a bad thing to do; but all the same, she was going to take advantage of that girl's absence to get some evidence. With Bev out of the house, she started searching her things. First, it was just the pockets of her jacket, then her suitcase and then, still finding nothing, Eileen turned out her whole room, looked in the cupboard, in every drawer, under the carpet. Nothing. These were the belongings of an ordinary girl. No clues. And when she tried to talk to Jonathan about it, he was furious with her and stormed off on his own.

By the time Bev finally returned from hospital, on 24 July, after two weeks away, Eileen was determined to be kind to her and since Jonathan seemed to have got over his mystery illness as well, they celebrated with a barbecue that night on the little lawn behind the house. Bev told them all about her illness and said they were going to have to operate to remove her bladder, and Eileen felt so sorry for her, but Tracy said she was being silly and there were loads of different things they could do before they had to operate like that.

While they were talking, Eileen's walking stick left its place by the sitting room door and landed on the three-seater sofa. The demon was back.

Over the next few days, the poltergeist whipped Eileen's cigarettes from her cardigan and left them in the kitchen and then stole £100 that she had saved up to pay a debt to her sister. Bev and Tracy had just gone back to Grantham when she found the money had gone, and Eileen called Tracy to ask her to check in the car in case it was there. But to Eileen's surprise, Bev and Tracy drove straight back to Peterborough. They said Bev was worried about Eileen, and when Eileen took Tracy aside they ended up arguing. Tracy, like Jonathan, refused to believe that Bev was responsible.

'If you showed me one bit of evidence,' said Tracy, 'I would go straight to the police and tell them. But there is no proof, mum.'

Eileen began to feel that she was losing touch with both children. She felt very isolated. That Saturday, 3 August, she caught Bev lying to her, claiming to have lost £65 from her own purse when Eileen knew she hadn't because she had secretly peeped into the purse earlier to see if her own money might be in there. But she couldn't say anything. She was trapped: unable to confront Bev because she felt sorry for her; unable to talk to her children, because they took Bev's side. It was almost as if Bev had planned it, though Eileen was pretty sure she was not that clever.

On Sunday, Eileen took Bev and Jonathan to Whittlesey Market to do some shopping. Bev was her chirpy old self, and she and Jonathan seemed to be getting on very well, joshing and joking. Bev never did much about the house, but Eileen noticed that she would do little things for Jonathan. Just before they left for market, when Jonathan was eating his toast, she'd made him a drink of blackcurrant juice, and although Jonathan had complained that she'd used a dirty glass, it pleased Eileen to see them teasing each other, to think that Jonathan could make good friends with someone who was seven years older than him.

Jonathan was bored at the market and walked off by himself for a while, but when he came back he made it plain that he had had enough.

'Hang on a bit,' said Eileen. 'I'm not finished yet. Give us a chance.'

Jonathan started saying he felt ill and he wanted to go home, and Eileen was a bit sharp with him.

'Oh, stop it, will you? This is the last time I bring you here.'

'Where's the sun?'

Eileen stared at Jonathan. What was he on about?

'Where's the sun?' he asked again.

And then he started to fall. Eileen saw it happen very slowly: Jonathan falling, his back rigid, his eyes wide open, no sound, and her arms reached him just as he hit the tarmac.

'Jonathan?'

She saw his skin was grey and clammy, his lips were blue, his face was sweating and he was staring ahead with a fixed gaze. The pupils of his eyes were massive and black. She thought he was dead. She needed help. She looked around. There was Bev.

'For God's sake, Bev, help me. Do something.'

But Bev only stood there.

'Bev! Help me!'

Was she in a state of shock? For God's sake, she was supposed to be a trained nurse.

'Bev!'

Bev leaned down out of her trance and looked at Jonathan.

'Is he dead?' she asked, with dull curiosity as if she was wondering about the weather. 'He looks as though he's dead.'

A stallholder came to Eileen's rescue, brought a damp cloth to wipe Jonathan's forehead, said it must be the sun. Eileen shook him, and he started to stir.

'We'd better get you to hospital.'

In the car, on the way to Edith Cavell, Jonathan sat meekly saying that his heart felt cold, but after a while his colour came back and he sucked a fruit pastille that Bev gave him and by the time he got to Casualty, he was feeling quite strong again. The doctors looked at him, tested his blood, said his blood sugar was a little bit low, but basically he had just fainted. Eileen had seen a lot of people fainting over the years and they had always given way at the knees first, never like Jonathan keeling over in a straight line from heel to shoulder. And anyway, why should his blood sugar be low? He'd just had all that blackcurrant juice that Bev had made him at breakfast. But the doctors insisted it was just a faint: make sure he gets some rest, keep an eye on him, nothing to worry about.

On the way home, Bev and Jonathan were joshing and joking as usual.

'Isn't it incredible?' said Jonathan. 'This is exactly what happened to those babies. Imagine if the press got hold of it.'

Bev and Jonathan laughed together. Eileen laughed too, and wondered what would happen next.

9

On the afternoon of 2 July, as Stuart Clifton and his medical experts finished their conference, Judith Gibson arrived home to find that the press had been buzzing around her door again looking for news, and one of the reporters had been asking the neighbours how to get to Ashley Drive. Judith knew a clue when she heard one. She and Steve had spent hours talking to the Cramptons, trying to work out what the police were doing, swapping titbits of information and gossip they had picked up. They had found out the names of half a dozen other families who seemed to be involved but they had no idea who they were. Now, she flicked through the local phone book, looking through all the family names they had gathered until she found one with an address in Ashley Drive. The name was Taylor.

She felt rather nervous as the number rang, like ringing up a blind date, but then a man's voice answered and she explained who she was, and the man said: 'Are you *the* Gibsons?'

'I suppose we are. Are you *the* Taylors?'

'Yeah,' said Chris. 'I think so. You doing anything now?'

That afternoon, the two families met and they started a chain reaction. First, they felt a powerful bond, that they had been through this terrible experience and, even though they were strangers really, they could talk to each other about it and understand what they really meant. Both families had found that other people shied away from the subject or even kept away from them all together, as if their suffering was somehow embarrassing. But when Chris and Joanne talked about losing Liam, and when Judith and Steve talked about the possibility that Brad would always have pains in his legs and problems with his bladder, how he might be on medicine now for the rest of his life, they could say exactly what they felt without fear of offence. Then they arranged to meet the Cramptons and it was the same again. When Kath described the moment that a detective had asked her how it felt to be told that someone had tried to murder your child, she did not have to tell them that she could not explain. They knew.

The three families were very different. The men all worked in the building trade but at quite different levels—David Crampton as a manager, Chris Taylor as a sub-contractor and Steve Gibson as a labourer—they had different incomes, different backgrounds, different prospects, but they had all been through the turmoil on Ward Four and so, despite the differences, they were close. As they met and talked during the following weeks, they began to feel their strength. In isolation from each other, they had felt depressed and confused, but now they began to feel angry, to criticize and to complain.

All that summer, they were waiting for the police to charge Bev Allitt. On holiday in France, David and Kath Crampton had haunted the newspaper shops peeking into the expensive English newspapers to see if there was news. But there was none. They had made friends with enough detectives to know that they felt they were ready to move. The problem was with the DPP. They decided that it was time to give the system a kick. Judith said they could ring up a local TV station and voice their opinion. Chris was all for it. Then Judith said it might be a mistake because if they started to talk to one reporter, it might encourage all the others and then they would never get them off their doorsteps. So, they came up with a better idea. They would hold a press conference and talk to all the reporters at once and in order to make their point more powerful, they would search out all the other families who were involved and invite them to come along, too.

Back home, Judith got busy with the phone book. She made dozens of calls, but all she found was Kayley Desmond's grandmother, who said the family had moved and she was not sure where they were, and a woman who denied being a relative of the Elstones with such vigour that Judith was pretty sure she must be. There had to be an easier way. Finally, she called Grantham police station and found a detective who agreed to give her all the names and addresses, and that day she and Steve tracked down the other families from Ward Four.

Finn and Maggie Desmond were living now in a damp-stained council house in a little hamlet ten miles outside Grantham, where they had moved to get away from some neighbours near their old house in Grantham. Life had got no better for them. They still had the same broken possessions, even the black and white television with the coat-hanger aerial, though Finn pretended now that it was the smoke from the coal fire that could make it work. Finn was still going off into the woods from time to time to get canned up and ask himself 'Why me? Why me?' They had saved up and gone for their first ever holiday in 15 years of marriage, a day trip to Skegness, but Kayley had been ill all day and then someone had pinched all their money so they had come home early. And Kayley was still ill. She was 20 months old now, but she showed no signs of walking or talking. Finn and Maggie could only guess—they weren't doctors—but they supposed it must have something to do with what had happened to her on Ward Four. Sometimes Finn wondered what had happened to Kayley's guardian angel.

Life for Sue and Peter Phillips had been changed entirely by their brush with Ward Four. They had buried Becky in the wind-swept graveyard of St John's Church in Manthorpe on the edge of Grantham, where the hospital chaplain Ian Shelton was the vicar. They were trying to resume life with Katie, full of hope that she would carry no scars, unaware that the doctors had established already that she had suffered permanent brain damage which would afflict her all her life. Their business had crashed, they had given up the brand new Audi, signed on at the labour exchange, and put their house on the market to cover their debts. Peter said it was all because of Katie's illness and the time he had spent by her bedside, guarding her and keeping her safe. Alone among the parents, they had spoken to a reporter and seen their story spread across two pages of the *Sunday Mirror*. There were rumours that they had been paid a lot of money for doing that.

Bob and Hazel Elstone already were beginning to suspect that Patrick had been damaged badly. He and Anthony had been so close. When Patrick stopped breathing on Ward Four, and when he had fits later in Queen's Med, Anthony always went dead quiet. When Patrick had injections, they found marks in the same places on Anthony's skin. But now Anthony was alert and bright, beginning to point and crawl and grab things off the table, but Patrick was being left behind, squeaking with frustration. He had trouble picking things up because his hand kept balling up into a fist, he had no strength in his legs and the doctors said that although eventually he would probably learn to walk, he would always be clumsy. Bob heard that and saw his dream disintegrate. His two sons would never be footballers or runners. Patrick would always be slow.

'Perhaps he could be a boxer?' he asked the doctor.

Creswen Peasgood was not in when Judith and Steve drove round to the grimy, grey estate where she lived outside Newark, so they left a note. An hour or two later, there was a thump on Judith's door, and there stood Creswen, dishevelled and furious, raging that they had dared to come pushing bloody notes through her letter box. Then she calmed down and became a good friend.

The only family who were not contacted were Tim Hardwick's. The detective who had given Judith the addresses advised her not to. He thought they could not cope. He was wrong. Helen Hardwick might have been damaged by her stroke and epilepsy, but her personality was still healthy. She had always loved Tim. When she had been forced to give him up to council care, she had coped with her sadness by filling albums with pictures of him and writing poems about missing him and simply by loving him. She thought he was wonderful. Strangers might have looked at him and seen a broken cripple, but she saw his intelligence and his sensitivity, and she loved him for it. When he died, she survived the same way. The funeral had been a terrible ordeal. Some of the social workers who had looked after him had broken down at the graveside, and Helen had been almost blind with grief. But she never lost sight of her feelings about Tim. Every week, her husband Robert helped her into her wheelchair and pushed her down the windswept pavements, past the bus stops and the chip shops, all the way through Beeston, to visit Tim's grave. It took them two hours to make the round trip, but she would not miss it. And as the weeks passed, she spent hours looking at his photographs, reading over her poems and telling everyone about how wonderful he was and somehow, she found, that even though he had gone completely now and she could not see him even at weekends, she still felt the same way about him, she still loved him just as much as ever. Her eyes sparkled when she talked about him. That feeling filled her up and pushed the pain away.

The rest of the parents started to meet regularly, in a room at the King's Hotel in Grantham. They spent most of their time trying to understand what had happened. Some of them were still not sure whether their children truly had been attacked. Bob and Hazel Elstone had nagged one detective to tell them what he knew but the most he would say was 'Put it this way. Patrick won't get that illness again.' The Elstones, like Belinda King, had discovered with a shock that the hospital had concealed from them occasions when their children had suffered respiratory attacks, incidents they would never have discovered if the police had not been called in.

They wondered sadly together why their children had been chosen. Chris and Joanne Taylor, in particular, couldn't understand what they had done, or what Liam had done, to become the first to be attacked. Had they somehow triggered all this? Kath Crampton remembered how Bev had come into Paul's cubicle early in his stay on Ward Four and Bev had been sniffing and wiping her nose and Kath had said 'Oh, you sound bad. Whatever you do, don't kiss him.' All she had meant was that Bev must have laryngitis, which she had always known as 'the kissing disease' because it can be passed that way. But had Bev thought she was getting at her? Had that singled out Paul as a target? Sue Peck recalled how she had been bathing Claire and seen Bev walking by the room, refusing to stop and smile, and how she had told Claire in a loud voice that it didn't matter if Bev didn't like them. They looked for a pattern, some common factor to explain why their children were chosen, but they were of different ages and sexes, some were very ill and some were on the ward only to reassure the parents. There was no pattern. It was simply random.

As they started to meet and swap their secrets, many of the women discovered that their marriages were showing the same signs of strain. The old emotional habits on which their lives had been built had been dug up and scattered all over the place. One partner would want to cry and grieve openly, the other would say it was over now and time to put it behind them. Grief turned to anger, and since there was no one else to turn it on, they turned it on each other. Often, it was the men who were most disabled.

Sue Phillips walked out on Peter one day because he couldn't pull himself together. She went to see Hazel Elstone, who told her it was just the same with Bob. He was depressed every day, and she had told him he had better buck his ideas up, or she was going.

When the hospital told the press that all the parents had been given counselling, they were incensed. None of them had been given any counselling at all. The hospital revised its statement. Even if they hadn't been given counselling, they had been offered it, they said. But not even that much was true. No one from the hospital had ever given them anything, not even an apology.

Strengthened by each other's anger, they resolved to take this hospital to court. David Crampton made some enquiries and came up with the name of a woman lawyer in Manchester, Ann Alexander, who specialized in cases of medical negligence. That evening, by chance, the parents saw her on television, talking about some other scandal. The next day, David called her and told her that he and the other parents wanted to sue, to win themselves some compensation, to force the hospital to admit the whole truth, to make sure that no other parents would ever have to suffer this painful chaos. Ann Alexander said she would help them.

Most of the parents saw nothing of the hospital. Only the Phillips stayed in touch, because one of their children always seemed to be ill and because they had become very sentimental about the staff. They called them their second family. Even when they discovered the truth about Becky's death and Katie's arrests, they still looked upon the nurses and doctors on Ward Four as protectors, who had saved Katie's life. They could see the strain the nurses felt.

On the day that they discovered that Becky had been murdered, they went into the hospital and met the night sister Jean Savill in the corridor. Peter told her to prepare herself for a shock and then he hit her with the news. For a few moments, she stared at them and then she turned and ran sobbing down the corridor, crying that she could not believe that any of her staff could have done such a thing. They saw her again, a couple of months later, in the canteen, and she apologized for running off like that. She seemed all right, upset about everything, but all right. The next thing they heard, Jean Savill was dead.

She had gone home one Friday afternoon to Leasingham, where

she lived with her husband Barry and their two sons, and she had
written a short note to Barry and left it in the kitchen and then
she had eaten dozens of paracetamol and laid down and died. All
the gossips in Grantham started to whisper that she must have
had something to do with the death of the children. But she hadn't.
In her note to Barry, she asked him to be sure that people did not
think that. The truth was that beneath her bustling and efficient
manner, she had always been an anxious person and she had been
swept by waves of remorse and frustration at her failure to see
what was happening on the ward. She also told some of the nurses
on Ward Four that she felt harrassed by the hospital, as though
they hated her for standing up to them. When the police started
questioning her, she began to panic, she could not remember
simple things they asked her, she began to think they suspected
her and that they were tapping her phone. She felt hounded, by
the police, by the hospital, by her own lacerating guilt. When they
buried her, the church was full and overflowing with nurses from
Grantham Hospital who knew how she had felt.

The nurses on Ward Four were trying to carry on with their
work, but it was not easy. Every move they made recalled the
routines that had let them down. They locked all the drug cup-
boards in the Treatment Room now. They had extra staff at night
now, just like they'd always asked for. All too late. Some of them
tried to blank it all out of their minds. They disconnected the new
alarm over the Treatment Room door to stop it screeching its
reminder at them every five minutes. They reassured each other
that life must go on. But the pain clung to them: more detectives;
more reporters; more gossip in the town; more speculation in the
press; more moments of terror when they looked back at the clues
that they had missed. Some of them saw Bev Allitt in the town.
She turned up at a nurse's wedding. She bumped into Margaret
Geeson outside Woolworths and chatted on as if nothing had
happened.

Stuart Clifton was worried about the parents—he had heard
rumours that some of the men were talking about trying to find
Bev Allitt to lay hands on her themselves—but there was not
much that he could do to quicken the DPP's pace.

The detectives had not stopped pushing since their big conference on 2 July. They had sorted out all the scientific evidence,

Professor Hull had produced a new review of all the children and now they had finalized a list of 12 victims. Starting from Dr Porter's original list of 14 children, they had rejected three as being incidents with natural causes—a girl called Linda Tomlinson whose asthma had stopped her breathing for a few minutes on 3 January; a boy named Edward Crook whose illness showed no unexpected event; and Michael Davidson, whose heart had stopped on 9 April, apparently because he was afraid of needles. Then they had added one case, Becky Phillips, from the coroner's files.

They now believed there were four murders: Liam Taylor, Tim Hardwick, Becky Phillips and Claire Peck. They believed there were also eight attempted murders: Kayley Desmond, Paul Crampton, Brad Gibson, Henry Chan, Katie Phillips, Chris Peasgood, Christopher King and Patrick Elstone. With some children, they had chemical evidence that they had been injected with insulin. With others, there was evidence of potassium. There was evidence too, of the injection of air, of the crushing of ribs, and possibly of suffocation in the case of Patrick Elstone. With some children, they could say only that they believed that they had been poisoned, but there was no clue as to what poison had been used. A senior doctor privately had told Stuart Clifton that he was not particularly surprised to discover that insulin and potassium had been used. They were deadly, they were out of the body within 24 hours of an attack, and, for this reason, he confided, they were used occasionally by colleagues who wanted to speed the end of terminal patients. Clifton was interested. The senior doctor said he knew no more.

In the cases of Henry Chan and Chris Peasgood, there was an element of doubt: some of the doctors still believed that their seizures could have been caused naturally, by Henry's fractured skull and by Chris's blocked airways.

The detectives believed they could explain the timing of the attacks—why they had suddenly started in mid February. They linked it to Bev Allitt's interview at Pilgrim Hospital on 13 February when she had been turned down flat for a job training as a specialist children's nurse. She had already been refused work in the rest of Grantham Hospital. After the Pilgrim interview, she had been taken on to Ward Four on a short contract which would end in August with no prospect of a permanent job. They believed that this had terrified her and that she had made up her mind that the only way to save her career was to go back to Pilgrim for a second interview in the autumn, armed with a wealth of experience in dealing with very sick babies. She had attacked the children, they believed, in order to improve her job prospects. It was hard to believe, they knew, but then it was hard to believe that anyone for any reason would want to kill babies.

After endless hours of interviews with Ward Four nurses, they had found a recurrent pattern in Bev Allitt's behaviour. First, she would be alone with a child, often in a cubicle, frequently one of the ones like Mr Happy that was not close to the nurses' station. Other people who were close would leave, often, it now seemed, as the result of some ploy by Bev to divert them. Before Liam Taylor's fatal arrest, she had dispatched a nursing auxiliary to fetch U-bags to collect his urine; a night charge nurse had wandered in, and she had sent him off to phone for suction catheters; then the auxiliary had come back and Bev had sent her off a second time to fetch a dry sheet. Then she was alone. Then Liam's heart stopped. She had sent Belinda King off for breakfast in the canteen, told Creswen Peasgood to go and have a smoke, sprayed an ampoule of medicine in Lynn Vowles's eyes when Lynn was hovering around Katie Phillips. Once the child suffered the arrest, it was invariably Bev who raised the alarm. Then she stayed at the centre of the commotion as the doctors and nurses and Crash Team descended, but usually she did so as a spectator, watching with faint curiosity, arms folded, impassive unless someone exploded and insisted that she help. She would stay at the centre of the crisis and, if the child recovered and was transferred to Queen's Med, she would volunteer, usually successfully, to go on escort in the ambulance, not to do anything, just to watch, just to be there, at the centre of the storm.

The pattern was so strong that the detectives looked into another case even though they could find no evidence of attack. It involved a 13-year-old boy called Stephen Birks, who was severely diabetic and who had been brought on to the ward on 27 February, four days after Liam's death. Bev had been alone with him in the four-bed area. He had stopped breathing. She had raised the alarm and Kate Lock and Sister Barker had come running and revived him without needing to call the Crash Team. The arrest was mysterious. Even though Stephen often had hypoglycaemic attacks, he always felt them coming and called for help. This one had hit him without warning and without any of the normal symptoms. And it had stopped him breathing, which had never happened before. Even stranger, a BM stick showed nothing wrong with his blood sugar, as if the arrest had been caused by something new, nothing to do with his hypoglycaemia. On his medical notes, the doctors drew a large question mark by the record of the event. But they had no reason to keep any blood samples and now the police had no way of knowing whether or not Stephen Birks had been a victim of crime.

The police had found more evidence on other cases. In the case of Becky Phillips, who had died at home, apparently poisoned with slow-acting insulin, they had established that she had been fed a bottle of milk before she was released from hospital: the bottle had been prepared and given to Becky by Bev Allitt, who had suggested that Becky was hypoglycaemic a full 24 hours earlier. In the case of Liam Taylor, the police had pursued Bev's claim that before his first arrest on the Thursday when he came to Ward Four, the boy had been sick so violently that she had had to go and change her uniform. Margaret Geeson, who had been in charge of the ward, said she was never told that the child had been sick, that Bev had never told her she was leaving the ward to get changed, and that it would be unthinkable for her to leave without saying anything. It looked as though the story of Liam's vomiting had been a lie told to the parents to explain his sudden illness, a lie that might have been uncovered if only the nurses on Ward Four had had time to stop and swap notes about the baby boy's death.

The detectives had also interviewed a nurse who had been working nights on the geriatric ward, who had wandered down to Ward Four unexpectedly one night to try and sell some raffle tickets. When she left, a nurse was standing in the darkness over a child's bed. The nurse was Bev Allitt. The child was Brad Gibson. A few minutes later, his heart stopped.

The police had sent off work schedules and details of 23 arrests to Leicester University, to a medical statistician there named Carol Jagger. She studied the material and tried to compute the risk of a child suffering an arrest when each nurse was on duty. Of the 46 staff who had worked on the ward during the time of the arrests, four rapidly came to the surface. The identity of each of them had been disguised with a number. Nurse 20 was present for seven arrests; Nurse 15 for nine arrests; Nurse 3 for ten arrests; and Nurse 1 had been present for all 23 arrests. The statistician concluded that the risk of a child suffering an arrest when Nurse 1 was on duty was infinite. If Nurse 1 was not there, the risk was zero. Nurse 1 was Bev.

They had visited the old people's home in Waltham on the Wolds where Bev had been moonlighting and they had trawled through patient notes for the seven shifts she had worked there, but they had found no sign of any crime. They had gone back to the bizarre series of fires and practical jokes in the nurses' home in the autumn of 1989 and they had whittled a list of suspects down to three names. It included Bev, but they found no direct evidence that it was her. They had taken final statements from Dr Nanayakkara and from Dr Porter, who had been so tormented by detail that it had taken him six weeks of regular interviews to finalize his account.

Purely as a matter of convenience for a future jury, the hospital had agreed that the police could take on six medical secretaries, arrange for them to sign the Official Secrets Act and then type out all of the hastily scribbled hospital notes for all of the children they were interested in. The job would take two weeks. But as they worked, they made a strange discovery. There was something wrong with Liam Taylor's notes.

For the day he was admitted, when he had suffered his first arrest, while Chris and Joanne were at home, there were two sets of notes, one written by Clare Winser and one by Bev Allitt. One set had to be false. For the night of his second and fatal arrest, there were no notes at all between 8.30, when Bev started specialing him, and 4.30 in the morning, when the Crash Team started working on him. Senior hospital staff said this was absurd and they were sure that the notes had been there at the time. Finally, they found that the notes for the rest of Liam's final night were in the wrong place, in amongst Bev's notes for the day of his admission. It all looked suspiciously as though someone had tampered with the notes, removing some of those that were inconvenient and adding some more. Possibly this was the same hand that had torn the pages from Sister Barker's old diary and taken the allocation book from the ward.

They tried to arrest Bev again to ask her more questions, in the hope that all their extra evidence might force a confession and allow them to charge her more quickly. They set a date for the end of July, but she was in hospital in Peterborough with her bladder infection. They set a date for mid August, but she was back in hospital again with some problem with her catheter. Then the barrister from the DPP's office was out of circulation for the rest of the month, and so they had to wait some more.

Finally, on Tuesday 3 September, Inspector Neil Jones drove down to Eileen Jobson's house in Peterborough and told Bev he was arresting her for the murder of Becky Phillips. Bev remained as cool as she had been before. In Grantham police station, her lawyer sat with her. Very firmly, Bev refused to say anything about anything. After eight hours, they let her go.

For all their hours of work and their pursuit of every lead, the detectives still had no 'smoking gun', no direct proof that Bev Allitt was guilty. At one point, they had hoped that Brad Gibson might break through for them. He was old enough to talk about what he had seen. They had sent two women officers round to spend the morning with him, playing with his toys and trying to win his confidence. But he had seen nothing. If Bev Allitt had attacked these children, she had done so with extraordinary speed and guile: in the minute or so that Kate Lock was fetching Paul Crampton's milk; sometimes in the aftermath of an earlier arrest while other nurses were still treating the sick child. Yet there was no eyewitness. They had a circumstantial case in which they believed, but they would have to rely on a jury to decide whether or not that amounted to proof.

The DPP had stayed in regular touch since gatecrashing the investigation in July. They made no secret of the fact that they needed information to supply to ministers at the Department of Health, who had no official role at all in criminal justice but who were most concerned to keep track of the political implications of the case. The DPP was now routinely collecting information from Lincolnshire police to feed to the Department of Health for ministerial briefings. Now the police sent a full report to the DPP's lawyers, asking for charges. The prosecution lawyers waited a week and asked for a fuller one, for the entire 3,800 pages of statements together with all of the voluminous bundles of medical expertise. They then explained that it would take them several weeks just to read all this, let alone make a decision. All this time, the parents were losing their patience.

The police could not stop them holding their press conference, but they called them in to Grantham police station and begged them not to say anything about Bev Allitt or about anything else which might give the lawyers a chance to complain that she could not receive a fair trial.

And so, on Thursday 10 October, a muted, nervous group of parents gathered in a bare-boarded public hall in Grantham with their lawyer, Ann Alexander. There were rows of reporters, lights, mikes, men with cameras; the whole thing was alien and rather frightening, but they did it. In calm and measured language, they explained that they wanted justice, and they wanted it now. The nightmare had gone on too long. If the DPP did not prosecute this case, they would do it themselves privately.

Stuart Clifton added his own weight of personal pressure, by passing on to the DPP reports which he and the hospital had heard: Bev Allitt was looking for work again, as a nurse.

When the police came to arrest Bev Allitt at Eileen Jobson's house at the beginning of September, Eileen watched her climb into the car and, of course, she felt sorry for her and she wished the police would stop hassling her but there was a part of Eileen that was happy to see her go, if only for the rest.

When Bev was around, there was no peace. Eileen had noticed a pattern: she would hear Bev whistling somewhere in the house with a flat and tuneless sound; then there would be some new incident. She came to dread the sound of whistling. If Bev was not finding a hangman's noose in the garden or limping around complaining that a paving stone had mysteriously fallen on her foot, she was poking around in Eileen's peace of mind in some other way. One night, she suddenly announced that Tracy only ever went out with black men.

'Oh, yes?'

'Yeah, the blacker the better.'

'Well, that's fine with me,' said Eileen, who was less interested in Tracy's choice of men than she was in Bev's reason for wanting her to believe this little titbit.

Even when Bev was in hospital, there was no peace. She had gone back in for a second stay a week after Jonathan's strange fainting fit at the market. She had started creating a stir one Sunday evening when she went to bed early and then suddenly appeared downstairs again, like a two-year-old asking for a drink of water, to complain that she had scratched her foot on an old leather-stitching needle which was supposed to be out in the garden shed but which had transported itself under her duvet. Then half an hour later, she had come down again to report that her catheter had broken and half of it was lost inside her bladder. Eileen had been terribly concerned and started saying they must get an ambulance, and Bev had just waved her aside and said it didn't matter. Finally, she had agreed that she would drive to the hospital herself if Eileen and Jonathan came with her and Eileen had spent the whole journey worrying that she was in pain. But Bev had been tough.

'I can feel it,' she had kept saying, 'but it doesn't hurt me.'

The doctors had sorted out her catheter and agreed to admit her for a few days for observation. Two days later, it had broken again. Then Bev had complained that she was suffering headaches and numbness and described her symptoms with such precision that the doctors had agreed to scan her brain to look for a tumour. There was none. The doctors finally had concluded that she must be suffering from Munchhausen's syndrome but by this time she had been in hospital for ten days and all the time, she was telling the Jobsons that the poltergeist had followed her there. When Tracy went to visit her, she said she had woken up in the middle of the night and looked across at the woman opposite, who was fast asleep, and seen the luminous electronic figures on one of her monitors go crazy and start whirring round until suddenly they stopped on a new number, 666.

'That's the Devil's number,' she had confided, in case Tracy had missed the point.

She reckoned that this same woman had been watching her while she was asleep and told her that there was a great golden eye hovering over her bed, watching her.

Tracy was tough enough to dismiss these stories as a load of silliness, but they intrigued Eileen who found herself guessing and speculating about what was really going on in this girl's mind. With a guilty conscience, Eileen went looking for clues in her belongings again.

Bev came out of hospital in late August and, the very next day, Tracy lost some money from her purse. Bev said that was funny, because there was some missing from hers, too. In fact, her purse had vanished altogether. Everybody started searching everywhere. Eileen went out and looked in Bev's car, under the seats and in the glove compartment, but there was no sign and she went back to the house. A little later, Jonathan suggested that the purse might be in the car boot, so Eileen went out again and she was just looking in the boot, when through the back of the car, she saw the purse under the driver's seat. She knew it had not been there before. Suddenly, she knew something else as well: as fast as she could, she limped back into the sitting room, found her own purse, and opened it to discover that every single penny that had been there had now disappeared. The next morning, Bev came down from her room and announced that she had seen a strange mist in the night over her bed.

No matter how often Eileen realized that it had to be Bev—because these things only ever happened when she was around—Eileen still did not quite believe it. What reason could Bev have? Eileen had racked her brains for an answer. Was it all a game? Was she looking for attention? Did she think it was funny? It just made no sense. Eileen wondered whether Bev was afraid that she might be charged with the deaths of all these children and maybe she was having some kind of nervous breakdown, or perhaps she was so terrified that the police would get her convicted that she was trying to pretend to be mad so that she wouldn't have to go to prison. There had to be some reason for it, but she couldn't see it.

When the police came to arrest her on 3 September, Eileen wanted to say something to them, but she was scared to. She knew Tracy would go wild if she thought Eileen was betraying her friend to the police. Tracy was still adamant that Bev had nothing to do with anything in the house. And Eileen knew that Bev had enough to cope with. So she said nothing, and as Bev got into the police car she looked at Eileen and said she would be back, and, a couple of days later, she was.

Eileen's cash came and went. Jonathan's chocolate bars simply melted away. Bev drove up to the phone box one night and came back saying the ghost had been stroking her knee and turning off the car lights while she was on the phone. An ornamental kestrel took off from the top of the television and turned up behind the waste-paper basket. Bev whistled and the demon came.

Eileen's sisters were in no doubt that it was all Bev's fault, and they were privately urging Eileen to tell her to go and stay with her parents in Corby. Her sister Audrey even suggested that Bev might be guilty of attacking these children in Grantham. Eileen was sure that was not right but whatever the truth about what was happening now in her house, Eileen didn't want to fight with her children. She'd already lost a husband. She had an elder son, David, who lived hundreds of miles away. She didn't want to lose Jonathan and Tracy, too. She couldn't confront Bev. All she could do was to try and catch her out.

She announced without warning that she had decided to decorate Bev's room, so that she had an excuse to turn the whole room out. She found nothing and she had to paint the whole room for her pains. She wondered whether she had missed something, so she told Bev that she had decided to swap the bedrooms around and, once again, she turned out all of Bev's things and still she got nothing, except backache.

A stone from the garden planted itself on the back of the sofa. There was a horrible mess on the back bedroom floor. Bev said it must have been the cat or Jack the terrier, but when Eileen looked closer she found it was woodstain that had been emptied in a puddle on the carpet, ruining it.

Eileen had an idea. She told Jonathan, Tracy and Bev that she wanted them to come into the sitting room. She shut the door and spoke to them as solemnly as she could.

'This has got to stop,' she said. 'I don't believe in ghosts. I don't believe anyone is getting into this house. It's one of us. Now, I know that it isn't me. It has got to be one of you three.'

'Oh mum,' protested Jonathan, but Eileen was determined.

'No. It has to be one of you. And I am going to ask you to swear to me that you haven't done it, swear on the life of the

person you love most in all the world that you have had nothing
to do with taking my money. No! I'm not kidding.'

Eileen turned first to Jonathan and, reluctantly, he agreed to
swear on Eileen's life that he was not doing these things. She
turned to Bev.

'Right, Bev, it's your turn. Who do you love most in the world?'

'Nobody.'

'What?'

Bev twitched her shoulders.

'Well, you must love somebody. Would it be your mother, or
your father, or who?'

'Dunno.'

'Oh, come on, Bev. You must love someone.'

'Not really,' said Bev, with a blank stare. 'No.'

'What do you mean? You don't love anyone? Not even your
mother?'

'No.'

Eileen went on to persuade her that she must love her mother,
and eventually Bev went through the motions of swearing on her
mother's life that the demon was nothing to do with her, but by
that time, Eileen was hardly interested in the oath. What fascinated
her—what chilled her heart—was the sight of this young girl,
looking up at her with blank sincerity on her face and telling her
openly that there was no one, not one soul in the world, not even
her mother, whom she loved. That night, for the first time, she
felt she had glimpsed a little of the truth about Bev.

Eileen didn't claim to be a psychiatrist and she couldn't pretend
to know the whole history of Bev's childhood, but somehow that
girl had grown up cold, without ever loving anyone, without even
loving her own family, and now it seemed that, if there was one
thing which caused her pain, one thing which she simply could
not stand, it was the sight of a happy family. The demon was here
to break them up, to fill them each with anger and guilt and
suspicion and fear—anything just as long as they were bickering
and blaming each other, just as long as they weren't so happy any
more.

The demon began to get nastier. Eileen lived on the edge of a
precipice, waiting every moment for something new to appear out
of nowhere and knock her sideways. She was frightened of each

day, full of dread. One morning, as she was limping along the street on her way back from the shops, she saw Bev pacing out of the house towards her.

'You'd better come home quickly. Something's wrong with Jack.'

As Eileen hobbled along beside her, Bev explained that the little dog had suddenly started frothing at the mouth as if he was having some kind of fit, and she didn't know, but she thought he must have rabies. Eileen said it had happened once to a cat of hers; it had started foaming at the mouth and it turned out it had licked a poisonous toad.

They found Jack in the garden, with white bubbles all around his muzzle, but as they went towards him, he started coughing up on the grass. Eileen crouched beside him, stroking his back and comforting him and, as she did so, she looked at the little puddle of froth which he had spat out on to the lawn and although it made no sense, she was sure she could see something in there.

'It looks like tablets,' she said. She could see them clearly now, the splintered remains of two small, white tablets.

'Yes,' said Bev. 'It does.'

Eileen took some soil from the flower bed and covered the mess, to prevent the cats getting to it, and to give herself a chance to think. She wanted to believe that this was some kind of accident, that somehow Jack had helped himself to some pills. Perhaps he had found her Distalgesic, which she kept for the pain in her hip. Bev said she would check her Temgesic.

Eileen found her pills, all safely in their box, with no sign of teeth marks around them. Bev came back from her room.

'There's none missing,' she reported. 'I know I should have 63 of them and they're all there.'

'How on earth do you know you've got 63 pills?'

'I just do. I know I had 63.'

Eileen shook her head. She couldn't prove it, but she knew Bev had done it. She was supposed to have come shopping with her, but she had made an excuse about wanting to wash her hair. If Jack had not been sick, she would never have suspected. Maybe no one would believe her if she told them, but she knew that Bev had just tried to kill the dog.

On television one night, they saw Judith Gibson being inter-

viewed outside her house, complaining that there was no end to
the police inquiry.

'I don't know what she's got to go on about,' said Bev. 'Her
kid didn't even die.'

Eileen felt her coldness. She was frightened of Bev now. It was
not a fear of violence. Despite Jack's mouthful of pills, she was
sure that Bev would never hurt any of the family, but still she
was frightened of her anger, of the depths of her feeling. It was
so alien to her. She wanted to help her, but she knew Bev would
never admit to being this way.

The more she watched Bev now, the more she saw. She watched
her playing with Tracy's Siamese cat, Holly. She had always
thought she was a little bit rough but now she saw her tormenting
the poor animal, pushing it and pulling it and generally aggravating
it until it howled and lashed out. That cat had been ill, too. Eileen
hardly dared to think why. Twice, at night, the other cat, Vincent,
was dropped from the bathroom window on to the little ledge
over the front door, where he was stuck for hours until morning.
Eileen felt the cruelty of it. She flinched every time she heard her
whistling. Tracy came home and they were all sitting around in
the kitchen and Eileen caught Bev looking at Tracy with the
strangest expression, her jaw stiff, her eyes sullen and dull, and
Eileen thought 'My God, you really hate Tracy, don't you?'

She saw Bev teasing them all, playing with their fears, hinting
that the missing money must be in the garden shed or under a
carpet and then sitting there and watching while they went off
and searched without success. Sometimes when the demon struck,
Bev would watch their reactions and hunch her hands up to her
chest and say 'Ooooooh, I'm frightened.' But Eileen knew she
wasn't.

Eileen no longer slept at night. Jonathan was little better. Both
of them lived on the edge of anxiety, constantly on alert to deal
with the next bizarre incident. Jonathan had a permanent stomach
ache and a feeling of thrill, like when you watch a horror film.
He felt frightened to walk into a room, in case he ran into something weird and so he learned to hesitate at every doorway to give
himself a chance to catch his breath. He was frightened to come
down stairs in case something supernatural tripped him up, he
was frightened to be alone in the dark so he lay with the light on.

And even though neither of them slept through the night, they were no more tired than usual. They were both too full of adrenalin.

In September, Jonathan went off to stay with his uncle in Essex for three weeks, leaving strict instructions for Eileen to record Prisoner on Cell Block H, for which he had a fanatic's devotion. Each week, Eileen made sure she did the job. On the last week, Bev and Tracy were with her in the sitting room while she waited for the programme to start. Bev got up and went over to the video recorder, rummaged around in a bowl where Eileen kept pens and pencils and scissors, popped out the video tape, fiddled with it and put it back.

'What you doing, Bev?' asked Eileen.

'Just writing on it for him,' she said, as she crossed back to the sofa, 'so he knows what he's got.'

Eileen thanked her and pressed the record button. But when Jonathan returned home that weekend and went to play the tape, he could not get a picture. He prodded different buttons and fiddled with the tape and became quite irritated. It was only when Eileen examined the video cassette that she discovered, to her amazement, that the tape had been sliced, cut right through.

'Oh, mum,' cried Jonathan, who was plainly angry with her. 'How could that happen?'

Eileen did not answer. She knew how it could have happened — if Bev had stood in the same room as her and Tracy, right in front of them, and taken the scissors to it. But it was almost unbelievable, so malicious, so devious.

'Put on one of the other ones,' said Eileen. 'I recorded them all.'

Jonathan grunted and did as she suggested. But there was something wrong with this one, too. It took him a while to work it out, but then he realized. This had not been a blank tape at all. This had been his favourite tape, the one with the recording of Madonna in concert, and his mum had gone and recorded Prisoner on Cell Block H all over it. He was furious. How could she have done it? He always put little green stickers on all his tapes, so he knew which was which. That tape had had a green sticker on it, with Madonna written all over it. How could she have done such a thing? Eileen had the answer—someone had switched the green stickers.

She tried to tell Jonathan, but he would have none of it. Bev was his friend and it was horrible to blame her for something that was not her fault. Jonathan stormed off, furious with his mother. And that, thought Eileen, is exactly what Bev wanted.

Bev said she'd lost £7, but then she found it: a £5 note stuck in between the pillows on her bed with a one-pound coin on each side. Out of the blue, she volunteered to cook supper and rushed round all day, buying spaghetti and the ingredients for a tomato sauce, but when they sat down to eat, Eileen suddenly was not hungry. She didn't know why, but she just couldn't eat. Bev seemed disappointed.

'Maybe have some later,' she said.

But Eileen didn't.

The demon tried to set fire to the bathroom and left the towels and curtains black and scorched. It stole the key to the little wooden chest where Eileen had taken to hiding her purse. Eileen's sisters told her she must call the police. They said someone was going to get hurt. Eileen wouldn't. She couldn't without losing Tracy and Jonathan. She tried once more to persuade Tracy of the truth, if only to protect her. But Tracy would have none of it. And Eileen had no proof.

She sat with Tracy in the sitting room, a storm of feelings raging in her chest: fear of Bev, fear of losing Tracy, anger at Bev, anger at herself for being so weak, shame at wanting to cause trouble for a girl with such terrible worries. Bev was in the kitchen washing up. Eileen was grateful for that. She did precious little to help around the house, unless Tracy was there to show off to. She smiled her thanks when Bev came to join them. And as Bev sat down, at that moment, for the first time, Eileen sensed there was something wrong.

'Ooh, whatever is that smell? It's like bleach or something. Have you been using bleach?'

'No,' said Bev.

'I'd swear I can smell bleach. Where is it coming from?'

Tracy said she could, too, and Bev said, well, she'd seen a bit in the bottle in the kitchen cupboard, so she had put just a dab on the dishcloth. Eileen got up and they all went into the kitchen and found the bottle of bleach, which was nearly empty.

'There should be more than that,' said Eileen. 'It was nearly full.'

'Dunno,' said Bev.

They went back into the hall and traced the smell, slowly, up the stairs, across the landing, into Jonathan's room.

'God,' said Tracy, 'it's in his fish tank.'

But it wasn't. They started to search the room. The smell was very strong. They looked under the bed, under the chairs, behind the curtains, on top of the cupboard. There was nothing and they turned to go, and Eileen with an absent mind lifted the corner of Jonathan's duvet and found the edge of a swamp of bleach. The whole of his bed was awash with the stuff. As she lifted the duvet, the fumes stung her eyes and caught her throat like smoke, and she started crying.

'That's it. I can't take any more. I just can't.'

Eileen slumped on to the floor, sobbing. Tracy thought this was all bloody stupid and she started stripping the sheet and the duvet cover off the stinking bed and then trying to grab the mattress which was dripping with bleach. Bev stood watching her without a word.

'Well, help me then!' barked Tracy.

Together, they dragged the sodden remnants of Jonathan's bed into the bath and poured cold water over them and helped Eileen back downstairs. They sat in the sitting room and, for a moment they did not talk, only sighed and shook their heads. Then Tracy turned on Bev.

'You did that, didn't you?'

'I didn't.'

'You bloody did. It must have been you. You're the only one that could have done it.'

'I didn't. I bloody didn't.'

To her surprise, Tracy could see tears in Bev's eyes, but she kept at her.

'It must have been you. Don't lie to me. Who else could it have been?'

'It wasn't me.'

'I know it wasn't mum and I know it wasn't me. That only leaves you, doesn't it. Doesn't it?'

Eileen watched, half-thrilled, half-frightened as they slammed words into each other's faces until finally Bev blew up, scattered a shower of abuse over Tracy and ran out of the room in tears. It was the first time Eileen had ever seen her show any real emotion.

Tracy stayed downstairs and fumed for several hours. Bev stayed upstairs in her room. Eventually, Tracy went up to see her and found Bev lying on her bed, still insisting that she hadn't done it and that the bleach could have been put there any time by anybody, not her.

When Tracy came back downstairs, Eileen asked her 'Well, what has she got to say for herself?'

'She swears she didn't do it.'

'But, Tracy, she must have done.'

'I know. But what can I do? She swears she didn't.'

Eileen and Tracy talked then, and for the first time since Bev had started driving them apart, they were almost close. Eileen found herself asking a question which, until then, she had not even dared to ask herself. Could Bev have done something to Jonathan?

To Eileen's relief, Tracy did not blow up at the idea. She looked at it rationally, and she agreed that Jonathan might have collapsed like that because his blood sugar was too low, and maybe it was only a little bit low by the time they got to hospital because Bev had given him a fruit pastille to suck on the way there in the car. And the police were talking about insulin. But that didn't mean Bev had attacked Jonathan. They both agreed that she couldn't have attacked those children. And anyway, said Tracy, the only way to give someone insulin was by injection. And she could not possibly have injected Jonathan without him knowing it. Eileen agreed. She couldn't have attacked Jonathan. It must just be a coincidence.

Still, Tracy finally had seen what Eileen had been seeing for three months now. Eileen was relieved. The truth was out. At the very least, Bev would have to stop her silly tricks now. Then maybe they could talk about it and work out what to do for the future. That night Eileen slept, without the sound of whistling.

At lunch-time the next day, Tracy laughed when she saw Eileen hunting around in a kitchen cupboard retrieving her purse from the casserole dish where she had been hiding it.

'Oh, you wouldn't believe some of the places I've had to hide this purse while all that nonsense was going on. It'll be a relief to keep it in my handbag again.'

She opened her purse. Six pounds were missing. Gone, since she had gone to bed last night. Gone, since Bev had been caught out with the bleach. Eileen's heart sank. This would never end. Bev must really hate her to do this to her. Then Eileen's cigarettes vanished.

Tracy did not know what to say, or whose side to take. She decided to get Bev out of the house, and the next morning she persuaded her to drive her back to Grantham. Eileen called her mother. For several weeks, she had been avoiding her family because they had been pressing her so hard to call the police. Now she needed them and her mother and sister, Audrey, turned up within half an hour.

'We're going to call the police' said Audrey, 'before someone gets hurt.'

Eileen was terrified. If they did that, Bev might try and get her own back. She might hurt Tracy. She might even tell the police that Tracy had something to do with the dead children. 'No, I don't think you should.'

'But you know it's her. Your own common sense tells you that. You don't believe in poltergeists.'

Eileen insisted that Tracy might be in danger. They mustn't do anything that would turn Bev against her. Audrey began to see the threat. She, at least, believed that Bev could have killed the children in Grantham, and blaming Tracy for her crimes was the least of what she might do if she lost her temper.

Eileen had an idea. 'Let's call her parents. Let's get them down here and try and sort it out with them.'

Audrey agreed and went to the phone. For nearly an hour, Eileen sat with her mother and sister, rehearsing the events of her bizarre three months, wondering over and over how she could have let it go on so long, trying to decide what they would say to Richard Allitt to persuade him that his daughter had been behaving this way.

But when he arrived, Allitt asked no questions. 'Do you want her out?' he asked, as he stepped into the hall.

Eileen was taken aback. 'It's not a case of wanting her out,' she heard herself say, and then she stammered through her prepared speech: the total of £300 she had lost, the bed full of bleach, the ruined carpet.

Allitt broke in. 'And Beverly is doing these things?'

He started to talk about how he and Lillian were surprised at Bev, at how little emotion she was showing over the police business, how she was just like one of her uncles who never showed his feelings. Suddenly, he seemed to make up his mind. He would go back to Corby and get Lillian and Bev and they would all come down and sort it out. Eileen sat down again with Audrey and her mother to wait, trying to guess what Bev must have done in the past to make her father so ready to assume that she was in trouble again. They talked and drank tea for several hours, and Eileen decided to walk up the road with Audrey to the phone box to call her other sister, Lynn. On the phone, she found herself once more protesting that Lynn should not call the police. Lynn said she had decided they must. Eileen started arguing in defence of this girl whom she knew very well had been causing all her problems.

'I think I'm going round the bend here,' she said.

Then Bev's car pulled up next to the phone box and Tracy jumped out. She was furious. Eileen handed the phone to Audrey. Tracy was yelling, complaining bitterly that Eileen had asked Richard Allitt for £300 and for more money for a new bed and for new carpets, and how dare she! Eileen was trying to protest that she had said no such thing. But Tracy would have none of it. Bev had spoken to her dad. And Bev said that was what had happened. And Bev wouldn't lie.

Eileen was walking back to the house, with Tracy marching along beside her shouting, and Audrey scampering along behind them. As Eileen reached the house, Bev drove up beside her in her car, threw open the door so that it slammed into Eileen's arm and towered up from the driving seat, fucking and blinding into Eileen's face and then grabbing her by the arms and shouting some more.

Audrey pulled her off. 'If you want to discuss this in the street, I am quite happy, but I think it would be better to go inside.'

Inside, Bev shouted on, demanding that Audrey leave the room, commanding that Eileen's mother vanish. Audrey stood up to her. Eileen could see she was terrified. She thought she was frightened of Bev. The truth was that Audrey was frightened of the police. Unknown to Eileen, Lynn had called the police just before Eileen rang her. Unknown to Eileen, they were already outside. Audrey had spotted them as she came out of the phone box and begged them to stay away for ten minutes. Now Audrey was terrified they would turn up in the middle of this row and send Bev into some kind of unstoppable fit, which would end up hurting Tracy. She had to get Bev out of here before they came in. She told Bev to calm down. Bev obeyed. They all consented to work on Bev's level. Bev said it was all the fault of the poltergeist. They nodded. Bev said it had to be investigated. They wondered who should do that. Bev didn't know. They sympathized. Well, what about the police, they asked. No police, said Bev.

'You call the police and I'll get 25 years.' Then, jabbing a thumb towards Tracy, she added: 'And she'll get another five.'

'How can Tracy get five years? She's done nothing.'

'They think she helped me. They think I did all these things at Grantham and they think she helped me.'

'But she didn't!'

'Yeah, but Tracy can't prove that.'

Eileen looked at Bev now and saw a monster. Audrey knew she had to cut this meeting short. She had to think of something, some kind of compromise, some way of getting Bev out of here before the police walked in.

'What about the Citizens' Advice Bureau? Maybe they could help.'

'Eh?' said Bev.

Audrey knew it was a daft idea but she stuck to it and, just like a dream, Bev went for it. They all agreed that Audrey would talk to the CAB and ask their advice about the poltergeist, Bev and Tracy would go back to Grantham, and they would talk tomorrow and all be bound by the CAB's advice.

Now, Eileen was terrified. Her daughter was about to go off with this crazy person, this person who had been acting like a demon in her house for three months, starting floods and fires, stealing, poisoning the cat and the dog, who was threatening to get her five years, who—if Audrey was to be believed—really had attacked those children in Grantham, who might attack Tracy now to try and cover her tracks. But there was no stopping her. Tracy had taken Bev's side. And Audrey was hurrying them both out of the house as if they were contagious.

The door closed. Eileen cried. Audrey spun round on her: 'Prepare yourself for a shock. The police are outside. I made them wait.'

Eileen's mind flared in panic. They'd arrest Bev. Bev would blame Tracy. Tracy would go to jail. Eileen was furious with Audrey and Lynn and everybody. She was sure, through her tears, that she would not tell the police a thing. She had to keep quiet. It was the only way to protect Tracy. The police were at the door.

Neil Jones smiled at Eileen and nodded his head, as if to say he understood. He sat down next to Eileen on the sofa in the sitting room. Eileen hunched forward and cried. He crooked one arm around her shoulder and said there was no need to say a thing.

'I can see you've been through a hell of a time here. You don't have to, but I think you should tell us. We're not going to write anything down. Just tell us what's gone on.'

It worked. Eileen suddenly trusted him, and she started to talk. It was 4.00 in the morning when she finally stopped, and Neil Jones thanked her and said goodbye.

The next day, Bev and Tracy came back, and Audrey persuaded them that she had spoken to the Citizens' Advice Bureau, who had come up with a plan: Eileen and Jonathan were to stay in Peterborough; Tracy was to go back to Grantham, Bev to her parents. Then they could see where the poltergeist was. The truth was that Audrey had not spoken to anyone, but she and Eileen were determined to get Bev out of the house and, much more important, to split her up from Tracy. It nearly worked. Bev believed the story and agreed to most of it, but she insisted that she would stay in Grantham with Tracy. Eileen bit her lip in fear as she watched the two of them drive away again.

Over the next eight days, Eileen spent hours talking to the police, recording a statement that ran the length of a small encyclopaedia. And the police talked to her. They told her about the

children on Ward Four. Eileen refused to believe it. But her sisters
did. They said Tracy was away, alone, with a very dangerous
person. Eileen couldn't bear it. Bev couldn't be guilty. But she
knew she was dangerous. She had seen it for herself. The police
begged her to get Tracy away from Bev. Eileen called her on the
phone, but Tracy wouldn't leave. She would not blame Bev unless
she had proof. Eileen knew Tracy. She knew she would want the
truth and she would keep on at Bev until she got it. And what
would Bev do? Eileen could still hear Bev, swearing and shouting
as she dragged her by the arms. The hatred in her. Eileen now
was afraid for Tracy's life. And there was nothing she could do
to help her.

Eileen's whole life was now consumed by speculation about
Bev, and fear for Tracy. She looked back over Bev's time in the
house, at her sheer cunningness. That night when Eileen had made
them all walk round the house together and yet somehow her
walking stick had flown across the sitting room—she could see
now that Bev was the last to leave the room as they walked out
and all she had to do was flip the stick into the air as she closed
the door. It was so easy. Or the chip pan. It had not suddenly set
fire to the fat in a matter of seconds. It had been heating up for
half an hour or more and the red light which had suddenly come
on was just the warning light. And Bev had been hanging around,
feeding the cat, finding any excuse to stay and watch the fun.
Eileen felt such a fool. Except for that one time—when she had
refused to eat the spaghetti Bev cooked. Maybe there had been
some sixth sense warning her. And as she admitted to her mother
that she thought Bev might have wanted to harm her, she thought
again about Jonathan. That was all very odd.

'I mean, Tracy's right,' said Eileen. 'She couldn't have injected
him.'

'No,' said her mother.

'So it must have been the sun or something. But I don't know.
For all I know, a nurse like Bev would have some other way of
tampering with your blood sugar. I mean, there must be other
drugs apart from insulin that could do that.'

'Well, of course there are. That's what my tablets do.'

Eileen froze. Her mother's tablets. For her diabetes. They
weren't insulin. They were Diamicron. But they had the same

effect on blood sugar. And her mother had been staying in the house when Jonathan fainted. And her tablets had been in the kitchen, on the bread bin, right next to the sink—where Bev made Jonathan a drink of blackcurrant juice that morning—in a glass which Jonathan said had something mucky in it. It had to be! She'd tried to kill Jonathan.

And now Tracy was alone with her.

In their much-loved house in First Avenue, Tracy and Bev were having a difficult time. Bev was bored again, truculent about the press and still full of defiance for everyone in Peterborough. She couldn't find any decent work and she was filling in at the wine store in Corby Glen. And Tracy was beginning to boil.

For months now, ever since the police had arrested her and accused her of helping Bev to kill these children, she had been tugged inside herself between loyalty to Bev—her closest friend, her trusted partner—and a fear that pulled at her with growing strength, as first the police and then her aunt Audrey and then her aunt Lynn insisted that Bev was guilty.

She had never believed that Bev was doing these things down in Peterborough. For one thing, Bev had kept telling her that they ought to call the police to investigate. And why would she say that, if it was her that was doing it? It looked to Tracy as though it must be her mum who was doing it all. Bev said she was drinking ever such a lot in the evenings, so much that Bev was having to pay for all the shopping because Eileen was just drinking her income support. They wondered whether she was going a bit crazy with the mixture of all that alcohol with the pain-killers which she was taking for her bad hip. Tracy had kept telling Bev to get out of Peterborough and go and stay in Corby Glen, but Bev had refused. She was too worried about Eileen; she had to stay and look after her. Tracy couldn't help believing her. But then there was the bleach in Jonathan's bed. Bev wanted her to think that that was her mum, too. But Tracy had been there, and she'd seen it. She knew Bev was lying about it. She knew her mum wasn't really a drunk. Now, she started to pick at Bev's shell.

'Tell me the truth will you? That was you with that bleach. Wasn't it? Go on. Tell me.'

But Bev wouldn't. Tracy kept picking, trying to catch her out with some detail of the demon's behaviour. Sometimes, Bev just shrugged her off. Other times, she yelled at her.

'You prove it. You see? You don't bloody know, do you? You got no proof.'

One night, when Bev was out somewhere, Tracy sat at home and drank wine from the top of a bottle and by the time Bev came back she was drunk enough to go for her. As soon as Bev walked in the door, Tracy was up and striding towards her.

'Right, you better sit down here and listen to me . . . I don't believe you're innocent . . . You did them things at my mum's. You know you did . . . Didn't you? You're a bloody liar.'

Bev glared at her. Tracy went on. 'And you killed them kids.'

There. She'd said it at last. For a moment, Bev just sat and fumed. Tracy dug again. 'Didn't you? You killed them kids!'

Then Bev was up off the sofa, spitting with rage and lashing out with her fists. She caught Tracy in the mouth. Tracy lashed back. Then just as suddenly as they had started, they stopped and staggered away from each other, but now they were at war.

Tracy went to work the next day and told the other nurses that the blue bruise on her lip was ink from a pen she'd been sucking. And when she got back home, she pursued Bev again. This time Bev crumpled and whined and said she couldn't stand it and, if Tracy thought she was guilty, then that was it, she was going to kill herself.

Tracy felt like the lowest of the low. How could she even think of her friend doing these things on Ward Four? She said she was sorry, she made up her mind to look after Bev, but then the suspicion came back to haunt her, stealing her thoughts no matter where she hid them, and she found herself turning out Bev's pockets and wondering out loud whether Bev might have done something wrong that would explain why the police were hunting her. And Bev would crumple and ask her how she could think that she was guilty. Tracy would probe her story. Where was she on this day? Had she really never been near that child? Bev always had an answer. Tracy could not talk to their friends about it. None of them would begin to suggest that Bev might be guilty. Tracy was on her own. Once, when she pushed too hard, Bev ran to her room, grabbed a packet of 50 Temgesic and tried to run

out of the house. Tracy had to stand in the door and tell her she
didn't mean it. Bev raged.

'I'm gonna kill myself. If you think I'm guilty, I'm gonna kill
myself. I'd rather kill myself than go to prison.'

All the time, the tug of war went on in Tracy's mind. Her
mother would call, pleading with her to come home. Tracy would
tell her there was no reason: 'You've got no proof.'

'But, Tracy, you don't know what she's like.'

Tracy now knew that Bev was not normal: one minute she was
all right, and the next minute she was some weird maniac doing
all these things in Peterborough. And if she was capable of doing
those things, she might be capable of attacking the children. She
began to watch Bev very closely, and after a while she came to
realize that she was watching her not because she hoped that she
would find some clue, but simply because she was beginning to
be scared of her. She wondered whether Bev would want to poison
her. Of course not. She wouldn't do that. But she watched her all
the same. Would she use a knife on her, maybe when she was
asleep at night? Maybe she had a syringe full of insulin in the
house. Tracy thought about leaving. But she couldn't: if she left
and Bev did kill herself, Tracy would never know the truth. She
had to have proof. So she kept digging at Bev to tell her. And the
more she dug, the more she feared. When Bev offered to make
her a cup of tea or coffee, she sat like a fly in a web and watched
every tiny move she made. When Bev drove down to Corby Glen
one day, Tracy sat in the passenger seat beside her, and, as they
hurtled down the Great North Road, Tracy was rigid, thinking
to herself 'Any moment now, she's going to kill us both. She's
going to swerve into a lorry and kill us both.'

After a couple of weeks, Tracy could take no more. It was early
November. Bev had gone home for the weekend. Tracy had waved
her goodbye and said 'See you Monday' but, on Sunday, alone in
the house, with some cameraman hanging around on the pavement, Tracy called her mother and said she was coming down.
She caught a train to Peterborough.

When she arrived back home, she was not sure how long she
was going to stay. Eileen made up her mind for her. She had called
her mother and her two sisters and now they sat her down and
Eileen said 'Right, even if we have to lock the doors to keep you

here, you have to face facts. You are going to sit and listen to what we have to say.'

It was a terrible scene. There was a lot of shouting and gesticulating and crying, and Tracy tried to stick up for Bev and kept asking 'Why? Why would she do all these things?' and they said they didn't know 'but, Tracy, she did them,' and eventually Tracy gave in and said that she knew in her heart that they were right. The next day, Tracy called the hospital and they said she could take time off work and then she called Bev and made some excuses and told her she wasn't coming back.

'All right then,' said Bev.

Stuart Clifton had been tidying up loose ends and waiting for the DPP to make a move. The hospital had picked up a strong report that Bev was looking for work in local nursing homes and one of the managers tried to head her off by calling the district health authority with an off-the-record tip to the nursing home regulator about what was going on. The Grantham branch of the BNA nursing agency, who had hired Bev to moonlight in the old people's home, sent an action memo to all its branches, warning that she should not be hired.

Clifton had been talking to psychiatrists, trying to find some motive in this case. They reckoned that Bev Allitt was a classic example of the condition which Dr Porter had heard about at his conference, Munchausen Syndrome By Proxy—named after the exaggerated fantasies of Baron von Munchausen—an insatiable lust for attention which was satisfied first by making up stories and pretending to be ill and, in its advanced stages, by inflicting illness on others.

The psychiatrists said that, in applying to be a nurse, Bev was following a path that was well worn by those who suffered from Munchausen Syndrome. They were effectively addicted to hospitals, to medicine and treatment, and they often applied to become doctors and nurses so that they could spend every day in the embrace of the hospitals they loved. The psychiatrists told the police that many of those who suffered from this simple version of Munchausen Syndrome remained entirely harmless, content to enjoy their orgy of medication. But a few progressed and developed the syndrome 'by proxy'—instead of making themselves ill, they inflicted illness on those around them.

Clifton sent case papers to a paediatrician in Leeds, Roy Meadow, who had been the first to identify and name this advanced version of the syndrome. Meadow explained that in the classic model, a mother who had scored attention by pretending to be sick, then picked one of her children and repeatedly made it ill in order to attract the attention of doctors. These mothers could be astonishingly ingenious. One had fed her child a stone inside a toffee and then mixed her own blood with the child's urine sample to persuade doctors that the child was suffering with a kidney stone. Others rubbed caustic soda into the child's skin to produce a rash, fitted an undersized arm cuff to increase blood pressure readings and used a syringe and nasogastric tube to remove the child's feed from its stomach to justify a complaint that the child was losing weight. One woman who knew she was suspected of tampering with her child hid a tablet in her mouth and secretly passed it on to her child in a kiss.

But there were examples, Meadow explained, which did not involve a parent. These were more rare, but much more lethal, and they involved nurses. Clifton discovered that around the world there had been a series of cases where people with Munchausen Syndrome had become nurses and started to murder their patients. In Toronto in 1981, 36 children were murdered in hospital; in Vienna in 1989, a group of nurses used insulin to kill 49 patients; in West Germany, a nurse who enjoyed the title Angel of Death murdered 17 of her patients. The American authorities had uncovered a rash of cases: in Maryland, Long Island, Michigan, Los Angeles and, most striking, in San Antonio in Texas, where a nurse named Genene Jones had been blamed for the murder of 16 children in her care. Her case, complete with its history of fantasy stories and imaginary illnesses, had been described in detail in an American paperback, *The Death Shift*. The book was mentioned in newspaper stories and soon became a hot property in Grantham bookshops; there was an explosion of rumour that Bev Allitt had been seen reading it in the hospital. Clifton investigated and found there was no truth in it.

The parents were still worrying Clifton. Some of them had staged a public protest and marched into Grantham police station with a huddle of TV crews behind them, demanding action. They were talking about going to London to camp outside the DPP's office to force them to make a decision. Bev Allitt had been seen in Grantham and he feared for her safety. Bob Elstone was saying openly that he would 'swing for her'. Peter Phillips had spotted her twice and Sue had had to talk him out of confronting her. A friend of the Taylors lived within sight of Bev's house in First Avenue and there was talk of people lying in wait for her.

For his part, Clifton felt his work was nearly done. He had cut down his team to one sergeant, who was taking care of the paperwork. He had several new murder cases to work on. There was a teenage lad who had been found dead on a country road and who had been put down as the victim of a hit and run driver, until someone noticed that the blood on his face had run in the wrong direction. In other words he had been beaten up and dumped in the road before anyone drove over him. And there was an axe murderer at work in Lincoln. He was also struggling to finish his Open University degree. But the Allitt case would not be closed.

First, a junior doctor spoke up about the case of Michael Davidson, the six-year-old boy who had suffered a cardiac arrest apparently brought on by his fear of needles. This doctor's name was Karen Bradshaw and, although she normally worked on a surgical ward, she had been with Michael on Ward Four, because he was recovering from surgery. She was the doctor who had been trying to resite his I/V drip when it all happened. And the point was, the thing that worried her, the thing she wanted the police to know, was that she had not set up the injection herself. The person who had filled Michael's syringe and then passed it to her, the person who had been standing quietly watching as she started to run the fluid into Michael's bloodstream, the person who had done nothing as the boy suddenly went rigid and stopped breathing, that person was Bev Allitt. Clifton said they'd better take a look.

Then Mrs Jobson called to tell them two things. Tracy had come home and she was ready to talk to them. And there was something else that worried them, that they thought the police ought to know about—Jonathan's mysterious fainting fit. Clifton recruited four more detectives to the team and set them to work.

At first, Tracy found it hard to talk to the police. It felt like a betrayal. She still missed Bev and, even now, she found it hard to know what to believe. She talked more to Eileen. For hours on end, they juggled the facts, looking for a pattern. Why had Bev done that to them? Maybe she had wanted to be caught and it was all some kind of cry for help. Maybe she had deliberately made herself ill so that she would go to hospital and stop hurting them so much. Maybe she whistled like that because she heard voices and she was trying to cover their sound. Maybe she was trying to prove that she couldn't be hurt, that she could take a rash on her skin, or a broken catheter, or half a bottle of vodka and never feel the pain. Maybe she just hated everybody who was happy, even Jonathan. They looked back at the weeks when he had complained of pains in his legs, when he had been addicted to chocolate and they began to accept that perhaps he was being poisoned slowly over a period of time—and that was why the demon had kept stealing his bars of chocolate, to stop him refuelling his blood sugar. Jonathan now believed that Bev had attacked him and he said he wanted to get on a train to Grantham and kill her for what she'd done. His aunt Audrey said she'd go with him. And as the mysteries of Jonathan's collapse sank in, Tracy began to turn, to feel that she was the one who had been betrayed. Still, she was in a tangle about it and when the police started asking her—discreetly, but nevertheless directly—about the two of them being lovers, she felt like her privacy was being raped. She gritted her teeth and told them that it was true, she really had cared for Bev and there was nothing wrong in that. Then she wished the police would leave her alone. She was still in a tangle about it, when the police turned up one day, not to interview her, but to show her a letter they had been given.

It was the sort of letter that is usually sent by blackmailers in B-movies, written in a clumsy jumble of printed letters hacked out of newspapers and magazines. The message was just as blunt: 'I have ruined your life. I am glad.' But there was some subtlety to it. It had been sent to Bev Allitt, 22 First Avenue, Grantham, but it was postmarked in Peterborough, as if it had come from Tracy, as if Tracy were trying to celebrate her success in blaming Bev for her own crimes.

Tracy shrugged at it. 'Yeah?'

'What do you make of that?'

'I don't know. Someone's playing stupid games. I never seen it before.'

'Do you know anything about it?'

'No!'

'You didn't send this letter to Bev?'

'I swear to God I didn't send that letter. What would I want with sending letters? Why don't you take my fingerprints, whatever you like? Why would I send a stupid bloody letter like that?'

The police backed off. 'It's all right. We think we know where it came from.'

The letter was bound up with tape. The detectives found that it came from the hospital and, on the adhesive, they found familiar fingerprints. It was Bev's revenge. Two days later, Bev's lawyer passed them another one. The detectives kept it in a file.

Tracy thought Bev was being stupid, but she saw what it meant. She and Bev were finished. It really was over. She probably would never see her again. It really looked as though everything they said about Bev was true. It really looked as though her best friend had tried to murder her brother.

The next time the police came to talk to her, she felt less guilty and she talked more freely, just roaming backwards and forwards through the three years she had known Bev, looking for clues, finding almost none, wondering about all the trouble with faeces and fire in the nurses' home, when Tracy's credit card was stolen, and about the day that Bev was arrested and what had made Tracy so sick that day, and about that little grey kitten that had died in First Avenue that seemed at the time to have been run over by a car, and trying not to believe it when the police said that Bev was probably responsible for all of these things, then suddenly remembering with a shock of recognition the fragment of a minute, months ago—a moment that had meant nothing at the time— when they had been quiet on the Intensive Care Unit one morning towards the end of April and Tracy had been sent down the corridor to work on a geriatric ward, and she had been looking after an old lady who had just been rushed in, in some sort of coma, because she had had a hypoglycaemic attack, lost all her blood sugar and no one knew why, and now Tracy remembered— as if it was happening right now—how she had looked at that old lady's notes and seen that she had come from the old people's home in Waltham on the Wolds and she had thought to herself 'Oh, that's funny, that's where Bev worked last night'. Now she remembered. It made her want to scream.

The detectives searched out their new leads. With Tracy's help, they established that the old lady she had dealt with in April was named Dot Lowe. She was seventy-three, she was nearly blind and she was senile and she normally lived at Lancaster House old people's home in Waltham on the Wolds. At the home, where they had previously thought there was no sign of crime, they found no record of her having been given any insulin other than her normal routine injections at breakfast each morning. Then a care assistant told them that at 5.00 in the morning on 27 April, she had been walking past the room which Dot Lowe shared with two other elderly ladies and she had seen Bev Allitt giving her an injection. She had assumed that she was supposed to.

The detectives, who had learned to believe the unbelievable, could hardly accept the ruthlessness of it. If they were right, this had happened five days after Claire Peck died. As Nelson Porter finally raised the alarm and tore round the hospital warning that there was a murderer at work on Ward Four—when, finally, it became dangerous to attack children there—the danger had moved and, while the hospital tried to pretend that there was no reason why they should call the police, ten miles down the road an old lady had been poisoned in her sleep.

Stuart Clifton heard from the prosecution lawyers. They wanted another conference where the police and the doctors could sit down with them and review the evidence on the main block of 12 children to make a final decision. Clifton booked a room in Nottingham, well away from the press, and set aside 20 and 21 November, two days so that they could take each case in turn and discuss it in as much detail as the DPP wanted. They met, they talked, they made decisions and by the afternoon of the first day, they had finished. The DPP agreed: Bev Allitt could be charged.

At 7.00 that evening, 20 November, Stuart Clifton called Bev Allitt's lawyer. His name was John Kendall and he was the crime man in Grantham, who handled more of the local muggers and vandals than any other solicitor. Clifton knew him well and he trusted him.

'Will you bring her in, John?'

Kendall agreed and drove down to Corby Glen to fetch his young client. She was at home with her parents. When Kendall came to the door and told them that it looked as though the police were going to charge her, Richard said he would come to the station with her, but Bev said no, it was OK, she wasn't worried. And Kendall drove her off into the darkness, alone in the passenger seat, calm as usual, while Richard and Lillian stood in the door of the house where she had been born and wondered whatever would happen next.

It was just after 8.00 when Neil Jones went to the interview room, where Bev sat with John Kendall, and charged her not once, but 20 times—with murdering four children, with attempting to murder eight other children, and finally, as a back-up, with causing grievous bodily harm to the same eight children. Bev said nothing. She was led down to the cells, where she tucked herself under a blanket, curled up and was soon soundly asleep. At 9.00 the next morning, when they came to take her to court, she was still sleeping peacefully, and all over Grantham police station, they wondered at her calm.

It was on television, on the main national news, a big story. In the little terraced house outside Peterborough, Eileen Jobson sat with her son and daughter and watched the crowd outside the court-house: the parents of the Ward Four children, some of them in tears as the reporters made them run a gauntlet of questions; the police with stern faces; the spectators yelling 'Bitch' and 'Scum'; the round-faced girl they knew so well sitting in a van in the middle of it all with handcuffs and a dull expression.

Bev was remanded in custody in New Hall women's prison in Wakefield to await her trial. The prosecution said she had to be locked up, for her own protection.

For the parents of the Ward Four children, the charges brought a kind of relief. At least now everyone knew what they were talking about. Bev still had to be tried. She might be convicted, she might be acquitted. But at least now, they felt, the dreadful, unbelievable ordeal was coming to an end.

But it was not ending. It was simply changing. On Ward Four, they had been at the mercy of doctors and nurses, people whom they had trusted and who had let them down. Now, they were in the hands of policemen and lawyers and bureaucrats, and they saw no reason to trust them either. No one told them anything. Most of the parents still had no idea what had happened to their children. Steve and Judith Gibson had been to see Dr Porter several weeks after the police had been called in and he had tried to tell them then that Brad's heart attack might have been caused by a virus. He never even mentioned foul play. They guessed he had been ordered by the police not to tell them the truth. The parents now knew that the children had been killed and damaged, but they didn't know how, or by what drug, or how the drug was given, let alone what the hospital knew about it and why they hadn't done more to stop it. The hospital held on to their medical notes. No one would even let them read the post-mortem reports. The police held on to their files.

The Regional Health Authority announced it was holding an internal inquiry. It said it wanted to restore public confidence. It appointed a team of three worthy citizens, none of whom ever approached any of the parents to see if they had anything to say. The hospital unions refused to talk to the internal inquiry and insisted that the jobs of all Ward Four staff should be guaranteed. The Community Health Council, which was supposed to be the public's watch-dog, never asked the parents if they had any complaints and dealt out bland reassurance on all sides. The Health Secretary, William Waldegrave, wrote to the Regional Health Authority to say he was concerned about the effect on other children's wards. As far as the parents could see, everyone seemed very concerned to restore public confidence in the hospital, but no one seemed to care about them. Martin Gibson even arranged to have a new photograph of himself sent to the *Grantham Journal* in which he was looking more serious and concerned than in the old smiling picture which they had on file. The parents felt abandoned.

Hazel Elstone was cornered in the Isaac Newton Shopping Centre by a woman she barely knew who complained bitterly that it was the fault of Hazel and the other parents that this innocent nurse had been wrongly accused of these crimes. 'You should leave her alone,' the woman shouted. 'She hasn't done nothing. The nurse that killed herself. I bet she done it.'

Hazel thought the woman must be mad but, to her surprise,

she found that other parents were running into similar reactions. Joanne Taylor had nearly come to blows with a taxi driver who had made a similar speech to her without realizing that her child was involved.

At parents' meetings, they talked about how angry and isolated they felt. But they had to admit their impotence. They agreed that there should be a proper public inquiry. The truth mattered, for them and for other parents who were taking their children to other hospitals around the country. But they didn't know what the truth was. David Crampton went to see the local MP, the Foreign Office Minister Douglas Hogg.

David's aim was to flush out all the facts about the hospital's handling of the crisis. He had talked to a detective on the inquiry who had told him that the police could not understand why it had taken the hospital so long to call them in but the hospital had been telling the press that there had been no delay. Following the Grantham grapevine, he also discovered that the police had compiled a report on the various breaches of rules and procedures which they had discovered in their inquiry, from the confusion in the path labs to the bending of rules on the handling of drugs on Ward Four. But all this was confidential, he was told, and unlikely to be made public. After meeting David Crampton, Douglas Hogg agreed to do what he could to secure a public inquiry after the trial.

The only people who paid any real attention to the parents were the press. They began to dominate their lives, often in a most profound way. The parents discovered a strange truth about life in Britain in the 1990s, that any ordinary person who suffers a disaster can expect within days to find a stranger with a notebook on the doorstep. This stranger will insist not only that their grief be public but also that it should be made public for a price. Their grief, in short, was commercialized.

Peter Phillips led the way. He had already spoken to the *Sunday Mirror*, advertising his suffering, inviting millions of strangers to consume his grief. Perhaps it had helped him. Perhaps it was some solace to feel that everyone now knew exactly how much it hurt, to believe that in towns and villages all over Britain there were people who felt sorry for him. But there was something else. Although he had claimed that he would never take money for his story, that it was too private and too painful, he later told the other parents that he had signed an exclusive contract with the paper and been paid handsomely. They said they understood, but they didn't want to sell their own stories.

When Bev Allitt was finally charged and brought to court, Peter Phillips was there along with the other parents, who were amazed to see him darting over to the reporters and inviting them to bid for pictures he had taken of Bev with his children. After the hearing, he invited the press back to his house and, despite his exclusive contract with the *Sunday Mirror*, he told them that they should bid for the family's story. He encouraged the other parents to do the same. They would all make a fortune, he said. Newspapers were going to make a fortune out of it, and so should they. He badgered some of them. Bob Elstone said his story was not for sale, but he had talked to some people for free, because he wanted the world to know what had been done to his Patrick. Peter Phillips told him he was pathetic.

Then Peter discovered that Central Television, to whom he had sold some photographs, had been selling them on to newspapers. He was furious and tried to sue them and went to a parents' meeting, announcing that Central had caved in and sent round a motorbike messenger with a cheque for £40,000. After the meeting, on the strength of this windfall, he was buying brandies for the other parents and offering to pay for an African safari holiday for Chris and Joanne Taylor.

It took the other parents a while before they discovered that this was a fantasy, that Central had not sent him any £40,000, that Peter Phillips was lost in grief and was looking for an artful dodge to escape, hoping somehow that if he acted lucky, maybe he would be lucky. By that time, somebody who resented his boasting had reported him to the DSS for failing to declare his capital. He blamed Creswen Peasgood, though she fervently denied it.

The Phillips sold their story for a second time, to the *Sun*, who agreed to pay them £5,500. The other parents refused to sell anything to anyone, but the reporters would not give up. They called Judith Gibson so often that she was scared to pick up the phone and had to go and see a psychiatric nurse for her nerves. They posed as detectives. They posed as house-hunters. One of them approached David Crampton and told him he was the only parent who had not spoken to him. David felt guilty, called Judith and found the reporter had given her and all the other parents exactly the same line. None of them spoke. But Peter Phillips stormed on, converting his grief into newsprint.

He arranged for Katie to be christened and let the press take photos of the ceremony. He went on to Ward Four with a camera and was outraged when hospital staff concluded that he was taking pictures to sell to the papers. He sacked Ann Alexander as his lawyer and hired his own solicitor who would, he said, win him a fortune in compensation. He asked an estate agent for details of £200,000 houses. Parents' meetings became sour affairs, dominated by talk about money. They talked about setting up a trust fund to collect money for the children. Peter Phillips said that was all right, but he had had two children damaged, so he would have to have twice as much money as everyone else. The economy was in recession. Steve Gibson had been laid off. Bob Elstone was taking home only £38 a week for 40 hours in a taxi. Mick Peasgood was out of work. Other parents began to capitulate to the press.

Sue and David Peck agreed to sign up with the *Sun*, not because they wanted to but because it was their only hope of peace. Once the other press knew that they had signed, they finally stopped banging on their door. Helen Hardwick signed with the *Sun* as well. She had never dealt with reporters before, nor with anyone like them. She thought it sounded like the right thing to do, to celebrate Tim's life. When she discovered that they had paid her less than a fifth of what the other parents were getting, she did not understand. She was too shy to make a fuss, but she did write to the *Sun* to ask why that was. They didn't reply. Finally, Chris and Joanne Taylor signed too, exhausted by reporters on their doorstep, and encouraged by Sue and David Peck in the hope that this would finally buy them some peace for their grieving. The *Sun* was now content. It had purchased the emotions of all four families whose children had died. Then they went after Bev Allitt's story. Her lawyer said that once the trial was over and Bev was acquitted then she and her family would sell their story. He suggested the bidding might start at £150,000.

On 11 February, as the lawyers and the DPP prepared to stage Bev Allitt's committal, one of Clifton's detective sergeants drove north up to Wakefield and went to see Bev Allitt. There he told her that he was charging her with the attempted murder of Michael Davidson on Ward Four on 9 April, with the attempted murder of Dot Lowe in Lancaster House old people's home in Waltham on the Wolds on 27 April, and with the attempted murder of Jonathan Jobson in Peterborough on 4 August. He also charged her with causing grievous bodily harm to all of them. Six more charges. Twenty-six in all. Bev said nothing and went back to her cell to wait for her trial.

10

It is a rainy day in Nottingham. All the plate glass and concrete on the sprawling new courthouse is smeared with drizzle and every time anyone walks up the main steps at the front of the building there is a crackle of light in the gloom as the photographers swarm forward with their flashguns snapping. Inside the heavy revolving door, there are queues of reporters and lawyers and detectives and stray members of the public all lining up to be scanned by the security men. Upstairs, on the first floor, a scrum of people is already pressing against the door of court number one, badgering the usher who is feeding numbered raffle tickets to the grasping hands. 'First come, first served,' he calls. It is Monday 15 February 1993. The trial of the Crown versus Beverly Gail Allitt is about to begin.

Inside, the court is already filling up: little knots of barristers chatting and hitching their robes, the court clerk testing the sound system, detectives in tight suits cradling twelve-inch heaps of paper, court officials flushed and grave as they check every detail. Alone and apart, at the far end of the court room, sits Bev.

She is sitting on an armless grey chair gazing at the waist-high wooden fence in front of her, her face looked into a frown of concentration, her line of sight fixed so unerringly on this one spot on the fence that it seems as though she is frightened to look away in case everything collapses without her stare to hold it all in place. She is sitting absolutely still, tipped slightly forward with her shoulders rounded as if someone has justed jabbed her painfully in the belly. On the other side of the fence that runs around the dock, the solicitors and barristers in their suits and robes now take their seats, the prosecution to her left, the defence to her right, all of them with their backs to her, waiting for the judge to take up his position behind the grainy wooden desk on the raised platform at the far end of the room. All around her on the outer edge of the room, the benches have now been filled by reporters and spectators and, over to her right, in the far corner, the jury, seven men and five women, are lined up in two rows of six.

Bev looks at none of them, but they all look at her. The reporters look and whisper wise-cracks in each other's ears. The television artists look and scribble little notes (surreptitiously, because it's against the rules to draw in court). The members of the public who have queued outside for precious tickets look at her open-mouthed as if her mere appearance would satisfy their curiosity. They have all seen her photograph in the paper, but now when they look, they see an unsightly, unfamiliar figure. She is completely changed. During the fifteen months she has been waiting for her trial, she has lost four or five stone, maybe more. They say she has anorexia nervosa, 'the slimming disease', but perhaps there is more to it than that. She is scrawny like a featherless bird, with bony cheeks and blackened eye sockets and skin so pale it is yellow. She looks as though she is dead.

Now, as the whispering dies, Mr Justice Latham strides in to take his place and John Goldring QC rises to his feet to begin the opening speech for the prosecution. He is a small, sharp-featured man with piercing eyes, rather like a raven in his black gown. He nods once at the jury and begins to speak. 'In Grantham, not very far from Nottingham, there is a hospital. It has been there for many years. It is a typical general hospital . . .' And so the story which for nearly two years has been the subject of so much fearful rumour is finally laid out for the public to consume. The speech is a model of simplicity.

Goldring begins by recalling the confusion on Ward Four as children collapsed without explanation in the spring of 1991. 'Nothing like this had ever happened before. Nothing like this has happened since. What on earth was going on?' In answer to his own question, he produces the case of Paul Crampton and draws out from it the clean, uncomplicated evidence of malice: 'It was clear that there was a criminal at large on Ward Four.' He goes on to describe the old ward diary, the pages of which had been cut out—more evidence of crime, he suggests—and then the ward allocation book which mysteriously disappeared. 'Someone took it. Who? The person who cut the pages from the old diary?'

He moves in on his target, explaining that when the police arrested Bev Allitt, they searched her house. 'And what do you think was found in her wardrobe? The allocation book! What was it doing there? Her explanation was wholly unconvincing.' Now he has named his criminal and he begins to catalogue the suffering of the child victims, taking them one by one, sketching out a 'chilling pattern' of sudden catastrophe and linking it always and only to the accused, who still sits frozen in indifference behind him.

As his opening speech winds through the afternoon, John Goldring's simple story becomes strained with the hint of doubt. 'We can't say in each case exactly what the defendant did to a particular child,' he tells the jury with an apologetic air. 'No one was watching her. Nurses are not expected to assault their patients.' He suggests that she may have injected the children with insulin or potassium or perhaps she suffocated them with her hand or possibly interfered with their oxygen supply. He cannot say for sure.

There are other, deeper doubts which John Goldring does not even mention. There is no eye witness to the crimes of Ward Four, no scientific evidence to implicate Bev Allitt, no fingerprints, no footprints, no evidence of any kind to forge a direct link between the young woman in the dock and the collapsing children. All that John Goldring can offer the jury is a circumstantial case—always the most difficult kind of case to prove—and this one carries with it a special difficulty, because Goldring cannot even take it for granted that the crime in question has ever occurred. There is no corpse riddled with bullet holes or stab wounds to prove that anyone has been murdered or attacked. There is Paul Crampton's blood sample, which has always suggested foul play, but even that has developed an evidential hole: the blood which contained the 'astronomically high' quantity of insulin was originally lost between Grantham and Boston hospitals because it was wrongly labelled, an error which could enable the defence to complain that there is no proof that this blood came from Paul Crampton or anyone else on Ward Four. The prosecution cannot prove it with a DNA test, because the sample has all been used up in insulin assays. And so far as all the other collapses are concerned, the evidence of crime consists only of the conflicting hypotheses of a small army of scientists and doctors.

In pre-trial hearings, Bev Allitt's barrister, James Hunt QC, has already advertised his strategy. He will argue that these so-called victims of crime were simply sick children who became sicker, that the sequence of collapses on Ward Four was merely a particularly unfortunate cluster of natural incidents of the kind which doctors and nurses often encounter. And if there is evidence of one crime—against Paul Crampton—there is no evidence to show that it was committed by Bev Allitt. He does not need to prove that Bev is innocent. All he has to do is to create in the minds of the jury a reasonable doubt.

Right up to the beginning of the trial, the police have been searching for some new advantage. Briefly, they thought they had found it when they came across the strange case of Natalie Barlow, a five-month-old baby with asthma who arrived on Ward Four early in the sequence of collapses. She was wearing a crucifix on a light chain around her neck and one day, she had a choking fit. The nurse who was looking after her discovered the crucifix loose in her cot, but there was no sign of the chain—until the next day, when it turned up in her nappy. Clearly, she had swallowed it and passed it through her system. What caught the eye of the police was that the nurse who was looking after her at the time was Bev Allitt, and Natalie's mother insisted that the crucifix and chain had been fastened with special child-proof catches. The police were so interested in the case that they re-opened the incident room, took statements from everyone involved and concluded that Bev had probably fed the chain down the little girl's throat deliberately and then raised the alarm when she started to choke. But the Director of Public Prosecutions decided that the case was too weak to be added at such a late stage.

Even as the trial opens, the police are still trying to strengthen their attack, sending off the last remaining samples of children's blood for one final chemical sweep. But the fact is that for all the work by Stuart Clifton and the Lincolnshire detectives over the last 22 months, for all the 4,000 pages of witness statements and the hundreds of hours of expert opinion, the trial of Beverly Allitt now looks as though it may finally be decided not by all the complicated subtleties of evidence but by the simple instincts of the jury. Each side will lay out its facts and its arguments and then appeal for common sense. The prosecution will unfold a sequence of disasters, all unexpected, all unexplained, all with only one common link, and they will urge the jurors to accept that this one link must be the key to the truth. For them, the truth is in the pattern. The defence will simply defy the jury to believe the unbelievable: there was no motive for these crimes, they will say, no profit, no hint of six, no reason at all; no one kills babies, they will say—least of all this 24-year-old girl whose lifelong ambition has been to care for them.

On this first afternoon of the trial, John Goldring tries to reduce this one central doubt. 'Why should a nurse do these things? The short answer is that we do not know. However, as a matter of law, we do not have to prove what the motive was.' He looks sternly at the jury. 'If you are satisfied that she did it, you must convict, even if you are baffled as to why she should have done it.'

The truth is slightly more subtle. The prosecution are confident that they do know why Bev Allitt attacked the children—because she was suffering from the lethal personality disorder Munchausen Syndrome By Proxy. They have commissioned two experts to study her medical history and both are agreed that she is a classic example of the disorder, but Mr Justice Latham has ruled that these psychiatric reports are inadmissible. They would serve only to suggest to the jury that Bev Allitt was crazy and if they thought that, the judge argued, the jury might then convict her regardless of the strength of the evidence and that would be unfair. There is to be no mention of Munchausen Syndrome. The result is that the prosecution are left with a considerable mystery in the centre of their case, and nobody who sits in Nottingham Crown Court for the opening of the long-awaited trial can be sure how it will end. Nurse Allitt may be convicted of nothing.

At the end of the room, with her hands folded neatly in her lap, Bev sits with a mask of disdain as the man in the black gown weaves chains of words around her.

By the time that Bev Allitt finally appeared in the dock at Nottingham Crown Court in February 1993, the events on Ward Four had long since ceased to be merely a matter of crime. By then, they were covered with the fingerprints of politicians.

As soon as it became clear that the police were uncovering evidence of murder, the tide of anxiety that had risen in the children's ward welled up to consume all the managers of Grantham Hospital. Martin Gibson and his deputy, Peter Flood, talked about it incessantly with the other senior managers. They had done nothing wrong, they agreed, but still they were fearful. Would Ward Four have to close? Would parents start to boycott it? Could it get so bad that the whole hospital would have to close? And who would be blamed? Would heads roll? And if so, whose? 'I'll tell you what,' said Flood at the end of one bout of managerial soul-searching. 'We're going to need our Teflon suits.'

The anxiety rose higher. In the headquarters of the Trent Regional Health Authority in Sheffield, it reached Brian Edwards, the general manager, and Sir Michael Carlisle, his chairman. They could see the whole future of Grantham Hospital could be at risk. Sir Michael wrote to the Grantham MP Douglas Hogg to tell him plainly: 'Our most pressing concern is that public confidence in the paediatric services and indeed the whole hospital, be re-affirmed as quickly as possible.' But they could see that the risk was even greater than that, and so they talked to the Department of Health and spread the anxiety right to the top of the political tree where the Secretary of State for Health, William Waldegrave, imagined the danger spreading across the whole country and he, too, wrote to the Grantham MP Douglas Hogg to warn him: 'It is extremely important that the public do not lose confidence in children's hospitals.'

From the first days, the health authority tried to calm public fears with reassuring statements: the hospitals was safe; they were simply looking at 'the possibility of discrepancies in the use of some prescribed drugs'; the police were involved simply as a precaution; security had been reviewed and there was no cause for alarm. Later, as the national press closed in and the Ward Four parents found their voice and started asking questions, the statements became more defensive. On 10 October 1991 the parents called a press conference and demanded a public inquiry. The Regional Health Authority prepared a detailed response which touched for the first time on the most controversial question of all: had the hospital been too slow to call in the police? In a fax which was sent to Martin Gibson on the afternoon of 11

October, the legal department of the Regional Health Authority laid down an official version of events for public consumption. 'We have been cooperating closely with the police since calling them in at the end of April,' they said. 'This was done as soon as it was identified that there was the possibility of a prescribed drug on the Children's Ward being misused.' It was a reassuring line. since the truth was that a full two and half weeks had passed between Dr Porter receiving the result of Paul Crampton's blood test and Martin Gibson's eventual call to the police, it also happened to be a lie. Four more children had been attacked during that time, and since one of them had died and one of them had been permanently damaged, it appeared also to be a lie which had been constructed deliberately to conceal the hospital's errors.

The reaction of the authorities became tougher and more ruthless as the evidence of crime hardened, and with it the threat of scandal. If there had been delays, if some or all of these deaths turned out to have been avoidable, then some hospital staff must have been guilty of mistakes. But that was not the real problem. Staff could be dealt with at the cost of only the slightest political damage: all institutions are vulnerable to human error. But supposing it went further than that. Supposing some of these delays and mistakes reflected faults in the management of the hospital. That was the political nightmare. There was nothing special about Grantham Hospital. All of the procedures and practices and rules and regulations that applied to it, ran through the whole of the National Health Service. What was more, all of the controversial health reforms which had been introduced by the Government, all of the changes in funding, the whole idea that a hospital should be treated as a business in an 'internal market'—all of these highly contentious, politically volatile new policies touched every part of the National Health Service. And the National Health Service was the biggest public institution in the country, the service that consistently rose to the top of public opinion polls as the touchstone of public trust, one of the key issues for the general election that was due to be held in the spring of 1992. If it was mismanagement of the health service which had allowed a murderer to run loose on Ward Four, then the havoc wreaked by Nurse Beverly Allitt could yet reach out and poison the heart of Government.

The threat concerned all of the politicians and the officials who were involved, from the little hospital on the edge of Grantham right up to the office of the Secretary of State, but there was no obvious defence and there was no easy agreement among them. As the scandal crashed into them, they scattered like termites all running in different directions offering different solutions to fix the damage. The policy that finally emerged was by no means supported by all of them.

Within weeks of the parents' press conference, the Regional Health Authority declared their opposition to any kind of public inquiry. Instead, they announced in November 1991 that they would organise their own internal inquiry whose aim, they said quite openly, was to restore public confidence. But if any of the political fixers thought that this was the tranquiliser which would cure everyone's anxiety, they quickly discovered that they were wrong.

The inquiry team had three members: the former manager of Leicestershire Health Authority, Ken Baddiley, who was the chairman; the former matron of Sheffield Children's Hospital, Nerys Owen, and a consultant paediatrician from Wakefield, Roddie Macfaul. On 9 January 1992, they sat down in the seminar room at Grantham Hospital for their first full meeting and immediately received a barrage of bad news about Ward Four.

Moira Onions, the nursing manager, came and told them that there were not enough doctors on the ward, that there were too many locums who didn't know the ward, that the junior doctors did not have enough experience to care for children, and that medical care on the ward had become less competent as the hospital drifted apart from Queen's Med. Then Dr Porter and Dr Nanayakkara separately told them the same story with even more passion.

Dr Nanayakkara informed them that for nearly two years he had been warning the Regional Health Authority that the shortage of doctors on the ward was so bad that he could not guarantee a safe service. His junior doctors were often inexperienced, he said, and when he worked with out-patients in Newark, he simply had no junior doctors at all. He had tried to make the ward run more smoothly by organising monthly divisional meetings of everyone involved in the care of children, but they had disintegrated because staff were too busy to spare the time for meetings. Dr Porter echoed his words. There was no safety net on Ward Four, he said. If one of the consultants was there, all would be well. But if they were away—at meetings, on holiday, off sick, called to Casualty—the junior doctors could not be relied on. There had been a time when all their junior doctors had been sent routinely to Queen's Med for a two-week crash course in paediatrics, but the personnel department had stopped that because they could not afford to pay for locums while they were away. The result was that most of the junior doctors literally did not know their job, and furthermore, Dr Porter told the inquiry, the ward was short of vital equipment.

The barrage of bad news continued as the inquiry team was informed that the supply of nurses was just as bad as the supply of doctors. Sister Barker, her deputy Margaret Geeson, and three of the night sisters took it in turns to lead the inquiry team into all the dark corners of life on the children's ward: the shifts where there were no staff nurses at all, only SENs to run the ward; the endless reliance on temporary bank nurses; the equipment they had to beg and borrow from other wards; the play leader who had left and never been replaced; the teacher who had left and never been replaced; the entire management structure which lacked any training in child care. The message from the witnesses was unmistakable, but it was spelled out even more clearly in the letters that had been written in the spring of 1991 while the sequence of mysterious collapses was taking place. There was Sister Savill's cry for help, written on 4 April 1991, alerting the entire hospital management to the fact that there had been a run of seven cardiac arrests on the ward, begging for more staff and ending with the sombre hope that someone would answer her appeal 'before a tragedy occurs'. The posthumous voice of Jean Savill was eerie, but even more powerful were the letters that had been written in Moira Onions to her boss, the mouse-like Hannah Newton, who was based at Pilgrim Hospital in Boston.

In one letter, written on 22 March, after three children had collapsed, Mrs Onions had said it was urgent that she be allowed to hire more nurses for the ward: there was no cover when nurses went sick; staff were having to cancel holidays and work on their days off; and now they were in danger of losing the help of student nurses because the nursing college had discovered that the senior staff had no time to teach them. Miss Newton had received the

letter but she had failed to solve the problem. As more children
fell ill and the nursing staff had been stretched to breaking point,
Mrs Onions's anger had poured out in a second letter, written
two days after the death of Claire Peck, on 24 April. This time,
she had gone even further: they were so short of staff and they
were relying so heavily on nurses who had no paediatric training
that Ward Four was now—in the view of the ward's own nursing
manager—'an unsafe environment'. But still there had been no
solution to the problem. Miss Newton had replied three weeks
later with a tart little note, criticising Mrs Onions's management
style and complaining that she had listed problems without offering solutions.

This was all political dynamite. On the evidence of the most
senior staff, the children's ward of Grantham Hospital was a
danger to its patients before Bev Allitt even stepped through the
door, simply because of the way it was being managed and funded.
And who was to blame for this? Who set the budget and laid
down the rules for the hospital personnel department and stone-
walled the letters of protest from the doctors and the managers?
It was the Regional Health Authority, the very same body that
had been so keen to use this internal inquiry to restore public
confidence in its service. Then the bad news got even worse, when
the name of Sister Teresa Schuch appeared in the inquiry.

On 10 January 1992, the inquiry team had been handed a copy
of an internal audit on the hospital's Special Care Baby Unit which
had been prepared two months earlier by the Mid Trent College
of Nursing and by Sister Schuch, who had been in charge of the
unit since Mary 1991. On the face of it, it was a dull bureaucratic
survey, designed simply to ensure that student nurses and mid-
wives would be well treated there. But when the inquiry team
read it, they discovered a bombshell. Bluntly, the audit stated:
'Medical staff are not up to date and provide sub-standard care
for the babies, which is dangerous.'

More danger to children in Grantham Hospital. And more
dynamite, because the medical staff who ran the Special Care Baby
Unit were the same ones who ran Ward Four: Dr Porter and Dr
Nanayakkara and their regime of over-stretched, under-
experienced junior doctors. If the audit was right—if these doctors

really were 'dangerous'—then it was not only the Regional Health Authority whose future was in jeopardy.

The inquiry team were told that Sister Schuch was now preparing a full report on the alleged dangers of the doctors she worked with on the Special Care Baby Unit. Two weeks later, the report fizzed into their in-trays. If it was correct, it was devastating.

According to Sister Schuch, doctors made errors with drugs and exposed babies to numerous unnecessary risks, by operating with dirty hands, leaving babies undressed and freezing, ignoring anti-infection procedures, injecting into red and swollen sites and using inaccurate drug doses. She described at length the case of a baby who had been born with signs of a bowel obstruction. She reported that she had pleaded with doctors to transfer the child to Queen's Med but they had delayed for a full 24 hours, during which time they had given the baby an entirely unnecessary enema and failed to replace the fluid lost in the process. Another baby had been born with its cord wrapped twice around its neck and, she claimed, it had been exposed to a grave risk of infection by a junior doctor who had cut its umbilical cord and inserted a catheter into its stomach, all without washing his hands. She accused the doctors of ignoring the confidentiality of patients and claimed they had once discussed a mother's abortion in front of two other families.

She was particularly scathing about Dr Nanayakkara. She claimed she had seen him handle a baby's testes in a freshly soiled nappy and then, without pausing to wash his hands, run his fingers inside the baby's mouth to check the condition of its palate. She said he had over-ridden a care plan for a mother who was supposed to stay in the unit to learn how to administer Theophylline to her baby; the mother had gone home without understanding the drug and had accidentally given her child a massive overdose. She claimed that when the Royal College of Physicians was due to visit the unit to assess the need for an extra doctor, Dr Nanayakkara had ordered his juniors to admit more babies and not to discharge any that were ready to leave, even though this was likely to cause unnecessary distress to the parents.

All this seemed damaging, but Sister Schuch saved her hardest blows for the end of her report, when she gave her account of the relationship between the two consultants. She said it was dreadful. They did not communicate or work well together. They did not even like to be in the same room together. They did agree to meet for ward audits, but she said: 'The meeting is constantly filled with the consultants snapping at each other. They rarely talk to each other and prefer to talk through a third party'. Dr Nanayak-kara, she claimed, was particularly difficult. He had mood swings, he was arrogant, he was a male chauvinist who made excuses for male junior doctors but was hard on females, and if anyone criti-cised him, he became impossible to work with.

By the time that the inquiry met for its third day of evidence, a fortnight later on 12 February, there was a state of suppressed panic among the hospital authorities. Three of the most senior officials in the Regional Health Authority had descended on Gran-tham Hospital for an emergency meeting with Sister Schuch and the two consultants. It had been a stormy session with the two consultants complaining furiously that they had been called to the meeting without any warning of what it was about and that Sister Schuch had fired off her report without raising her worries with them. They had bitterly denied her allegations and at one point said they would refuse to work with her any more. Afterwards, Dr Porter had written a letter to the management, full of indignation, warning that Sister Schuch had a personality problem and that this was causing safety worries on the Special Care Baby Unit. Within a week, Sister Schuch had replied—with a new report, listing more complaints and describing, amongst other cases, a baby with breathing trouble who was laid in a cot with his head in a oxygen box to help him. She claimed that the doctors had first insisted, in the teeth of nurses' protests, that the baby should be dressed, with the result that it started sweating, then they opened the flaps of the oxygen box to cool it down with the result that it lost oxygen and started to have fits, and finally they removed the oxygen box all together and accidentally dropped it on the new-born infant's head.

The big question now for the Regional Health Authority and its internal inquiry was whether Sister Schuch was right. It was by no means clear that she was. While the hospital managers tried to broker a peace agreement between the sister and the two consultants, the inquiry team started asking their witnesses what they thought. It soon became clear that the truth was more compli-cated than it appeared in the Schuch report.

There was no shortage of witnesses who agreed that there was friction between the two consultants, though they picked their words with discretion. Several nurses said the two consultants were 'very different'. A senior doctor said there seemed to be 'a communication problem'. The Community Health Council suggested that the two men had had a problem and that they 'should try harder to get on together.' Sister Barker, who had been working with the two men for the last six years, went furthest. Dr Nanayakkara had frightened people in the past, she said, and he did seem to have trouble dealing with women, and the two men did sometimes change each other's prescriptions, apparently just for the sake of it—Dr Porter was particularly prone to this, she said—and she agreed that she had heard the two men arguing.

But none of the witnesses thought their relationship was as bad as Sister Schuch made out and no one supported her most damaging allegations, of dangerous practice and of errors in the administration of drugs. There were also some witnesses who directly contradicted her. A professor from Leicester, Hamish Simpson, who was asked to submit a formal report that the two consultants, was full of praise. He cleared them of any bad practice and said their teaching was particularly good. The chairman of the medical staff committee said he had not seen any evidence of a problem between the two men. Dr Porter and Dr Nanayakkara came to defend themselves, admitted that they sometimes had disagreements, but insisted that the nurses did not suffer as a result and that they got on better than many other consultants around the country. They were not asked about the details of Sister Schuch's report; the Region had decided that they should not be confronted with them. The inquiry team sat through it all, solemnly taking notes as the dazzling clarity of the Schuch report faded before their eyes.

It became clear that the friction between the consultants was only one skirmish in a whole battle field of clashes around Ward Four. The doctors didn't get on with the managers. Sister Barker didn't get on with Moira Onions. Nurses had to tell junior doctors how to do their jobs; and some of the junior doctors refused to listen. Social workers felt excluded by the doctors. Physiotherapists felt isolated by the nurses. The consultants were at odds with the anaesthetists because the consultants wanted to set up an intensive care cot for very ill children but the anaesthetists refused to cooperate on the grounds that most of them were not trained to deal with children. The ward was at odds with the personnel department over the need for more staff. And the whole hospital was out of step with its sister hospital in Boston, because there was not enough money to make the two places complementary. Even the hospital chaplain joined in, submitting a paper in which he complained that the hospital resisted change and suffered from an incestuous climate.

The inquiry witnessed one of the skirmishes at first hand when Martin Gibson came to give evidence and began to describe the financial cage in which he had been confied. He had been unable to set up clinical management teams so that consultants could work alongside managers, because the Regional Health Authority denied him the cash to pay for them and would not even allow him to borrow from next year's budget to fund them. Then two of the Region's most senior officials came to the inquiry and complained that Martin Gibson was a weak manager and, in particular, that he had failed to introduce the clinical management teams recommended by the Department of Health. The hospital, they complained, was old-fashioned and backward.

The inquiry witnessed one of the results of all these bad relationships when they attempted to discover whether Ward Four was operating with any formal guidelines for the care of children. They found that the Department of Health in London had failed to issue any national guidance at all because they were preoccupied with issuing white papers to reform the system. The Region, however, had issued a document entitled 'Welfare of Children in Hospital', but the inquiry then discovered that the document had never been discussed by district health officials and that neither Martin Gibson nor his Quality Assurance Officer had ever laid eyes on it. Grantham Hospital's management had, however, drawn up their own Paediatric Standards Document. Unfortunately, this had never been shown to any of the staff on Ward Four.

The inquiry that was supposed to restore public confidence had uncovered a rat's nest: the hospital was riven with management problems, many of them known to the Region, who had done nothing about them. All that stood between the Regional Health Authority and a full-blooded scandal was the ignorance of the public at large. Sister Schuch was a puzzle for the political fixers. If she was right, then the two consultants were behaving so irresponsibly that they were ripe for blame for almost anything that went wrong on the ward, so much so that they might even distract attention from the history of mismanagement. The trouble was that it was now clear that she was not right. And if the public ever heard that she was saying these things about the consultants, it could damage the management who should have done something to sort out the problem. So far as public confidence in the hospital was concerned, the worst thing that could happen would be if the Schuch report ever became public.

In court number one at Nottingham, no one mentions a political fix. The witnesses come and go while Bev sits shrivelled in the dock, refusing to reward any of them with the merest glance of recognition.

Nobody calls her Bev any more. The judge turns towards the jury with a sheaf of old nursing notes and points out the defendant's handwriting. The lawyers brandish charts logging Miss Allitt's movements. The nurses from Ward Four come and stand twitching with anxiety in the witness box and they remember babies 'going off' without an explanation, collapsing like dolls, turning dusky grey and blue, dying, and they all agree that always 'Nurse Allitt was there'. The parents of the children come and take their turn to recall the days when ordinary life was suddenly infected with terror. Chris Taylor's eyes bristle with tears when he describes Liam's last few waking minutes. Sue Phillips is icy calm and she dissects the detail of her daughter Becky's death and of her other daughter Katie's everlasting injuries. Looking straight at the jury, she speaks firmly and clearly and then, when she is finished, she staggers outside and heaves with sorrow on Peter's shoulder. David and Kath Crampton, Judith Gibson, Creswen Peasgood, Belinda King, Hazel Elstone, Sue Peck all tell their stories and they all agree that always 'Beverly Allitt was there'.

When they have finished their evidence and taken their places on the benches at the side of the court, the parents of the Ward Four children clutch their partners for safety and, flushed with nerves, they stare at the lawyers for a minute or two before they can bear to turn their eyes to the dock at the end of the courtroom.

In a story full of mysteries, Bev is the biggest mystery of all. Why has she changed so much? It is not just that she has lost weight, though that has been dramatic. More than that, her whole personality has withered. There is no more Big Bev, no sign any more of anyone assertive or confident, no clue that she ever danced drunkenly across the floor of the nurses' social club or spun out dirty jokes or doled out grief to her fiancee. It is as if all the outward sign of normality—the body that was robust and healthy, the eyes that looked when they were looked at, the mouth that spoke or even smiled—all this shell of everyday familiarity has cracked and fallen away, exposing this creature that had been living secretly inside.

The press have been saying that Bev has anorexia, but that is mostly a pleasing fib they have been fed. The truth is tucked away behind her blank stare, behind the scarred walls of New Hall women's prison in Wakefield, where Bev Allitt was taken when she was finally charged with murder 15 months ago, in November 1991.

It took a while for her to find herself behind bars. When she first arrived in the prison, she was quiet, overawed by her surroundings just like any other new inmate. They kept her in the hospital wing in case she tried to kill herself, saying it was a routine precaution which they took with anyone who faced such serious charges, although it was clear that they were concerned, too, that some of the other prisoners might convict her and punish her themselves. After a few weeks Bev began to find a role. She became louder, bossier, more bumptious. She found that most of the others on the hospital wing were weak, inadequate characters and soon she was the boss of the walk, referee of all disputes, keeper of the television controls, maker and breaker of friends, centre of attention. When her parents came to visit her at weekends, she was a jovial, back-slapping host, dispensing orders to the prisoner officers, calling up more cups of tea, lobbing jibes across the visitors' room at other inmates. She seemed impervious to her surroundings, quite undaunted by her fate. When she went to court for a remand hearing, she caught Judith Gibson's eye and flashed her a grin that made Judith churn with anger.

She wrote to Tracy asking her to visit, promising that she would swear in front of a priest that she had had nothing to do with attacking any of the children. When she received no reply she sent a prison probation officer as a messenger, but Tracy would not come. Bev heard that the police were planning to charge her with trying to murder Tracy's brother, but she still pleaded with her to visit and wrote sadly to another nurse to complain that Tracy had deserted her. 'So much for friends!' she said.

From time to time, she went to the prison doctor: she had sprained her wrist, she had banged her arm, she had bruised her finger. Once or twice, she took too many sleeping pills. The hospital officers calmly absorbed her complaints and sent her back to the wing. Then, early in the new year, Bev seemed to grow bored with her bumptious, bossy role. Suddenly and decisively, she stopped eating. She said she couldn't swallow anything, she felt too ill, the thought of food just made her feel sick, she wondered if perhaps she had anorexia. The prison officers in New Hall were not impressed. They'd seen it all before. They said she was just trying to con them. They said she was just looking for attention again—or, more likely, a transfer to hospital. And they were pretty sure she was sneaking Mars bars from other prisoners during association. They refused to play her game and simply continued to offer her food. Bev simply refused to eat it.

By June, Bev had lost four stone. She became so thin that the police were afraid that she might be declared unfit to face trial, but a Home Office psychiatrist visited her and said she was healthy enough for the law's purposes. Then the game changed. Suddenly in late summer, Bev began to vomit, regularly and violently. The prison doctors could not understand it. If she was not eating, how could she have anything in her stomach to throw up? And what was making her vomit like this? They were sure she was not really ill but eventually, reluctantly, they gave in and transferred her to the local hospital, Pinderfields. They did so in a cloak of security—false name, false story, a guard outside her door—not so much to stop her escaping as to protect her in case someone found out who she was and tried to kill her. The doctors at Pinderfields watched her closely. The prison officers did, too. And after a few days they believed they had solved the mystery of her sudden vomiting, although the answer really only made the mystery deeper. They discovered that she was swallowing her own faeces. The discovery proved that the prison had been right all along— Bev was not really ill at all. But, in a sense, it proved the opposite— that she was suffering from some illness that was so profound that it beggared the imagination.

She was transferred to the secure hospital at Rampton, where she was hydrated and sedated and, from time to time when she devised some new affliction for herself, she was transferred to the general hospital at Bassetlaw to be revived. But she survived the months of waiting to be presented at Nottingham Crown Court, where she sits now, scowling into space. And silently, relent- lessly—and whether she means to or not—she is committing judicial suicide. If her best defence is to persuade the jury that she is a normal young woman who could not conceivably have committed these crimes, then her own appearance now as a wretched freak is the most powerful evidence against her.

As the trial moves on, Bev's barrister, James Hunt, starts to skirmish with witnesses. He is tall and heavily built with half- moon glasses and a booming voice. He pounces on the junior doctor Harshad Tailor, forcing him to admit that when he was trying to resuscitate Liam Taylor he accidentally pushed the tube down the baby's foodpipe instead of the windpipe and blew oxygen into the stomach. Hunt chases the error, looking now for an admission that this could have been the cause of the baby's sudden death, but Dr Tailor quietly insists that Liam's heart had already stopped. Hunt tries a different line to explain the death of Tim Hardwick, suggesting that he must have suffered an unseen epileptic fit just before his death. He corners a nursing auxiliary, Lesley Davies, and paws her from side to side trying to persuade her to agree that she wiped foam from the boy's mouth. She resists him. He pursues her.

'Your recollection is not very clear,' he suggests.

'Oh, I thought it was pretty good,' she says, with a nervous grimace that makes the jury laugh and loses Hunt his point.

The defence keep punching, testing every weak spot in the prosecution case. For hours at a time, the trial disappears into the mire of everyday detail, picking over old nursing notes and temperature charts in an endless effort to establish Nurse Allitt's exact whereabouts at exact moments in the history of terror. It becomes boring. The tabloid reporters grumble that John Goldring has deprived them of their best headline by failing to call Bev 'the angel of death'. They begin to slip away. The spectators follow. Soon Bev is sitting in an almost empty room, bereft of drama.

Behind the scenes, there are wild lurches of fortune. The final effort by police to find new evidence has paid off: one of the blood samples which was sent away in the first week of the trial has come back positive. The blood belonged to Claire Peck and it contains traces of the anaesthetic lignocaine, which is available on Ward Four. The first analysis suggests that this small trace is all that remains of a deadly overdose which was given to Claire and which paralysed her heart before most of it was flushed out of her system by her dying liver. This remaining trace is like some weak and distant wireless message desperately signalling the truth from the dying child. Its discovery causes euphoria in the prosecution camp. It is proof of foul play. Claire Peck's case has now become as clear and certain as Paul Crampton's and the trial is stopped while the defence absorb the implications. On the day of the discovery, Stuart Clifton is outside the court and passes one of the defence lawyers, who waves him a cheery hello.

'What are you so cheerful about?' asks Clifton.

The lawyer stops and leans towards him. 'When you've been shot in the head and kneed in the balls, the best you can do is to go down smiling.'

But within days, it all falls apart. The scientists cannot agree about the meaning of the lignocaine. While some say that it is the last remains of a deadly overdose, others say that it is simply a normal, therapeutic dose which was not filtered by the liver because the liver had shut down with the rest of Claire's body, that it could not have done the child damage and it was probably given quite legitimately during the resuscitation. It proves nothing, they say. Worse than that, it causes confusion. The prosecution have previously said that Claire died of potassium poisoning. But if it was really the lignocaine which killed her, then why is her potassium so high? Are the prosecution now going to change their minds and say that this potassium is the natural result of red blood cells leaking after death? Or will they stick to the original theory and say that the lignocaine caused no harm? Or will they say that she was given lethal doses of two different drugs at the same time?

Whatever they say, they know that James Hunt can now use the
lignocaine to spray their case with confusion and create more
reasonable doubt in the minds of the jury.

Then, just as the court settles down again, an unexpected bundle
of documents bobs to the surface. The jury and the spectators
know nothing of this, but it causes consternation in the corridors
of the courthouse. Somehow, someone has got hold of the
Regional Health Authority's secrets—including Sister Schuch's
report.

Some of the political fixers had worked hard to make sure that no
one outside the hospital knew anything that had been uncovered
by the internal inquiry. It had not been easy.

The first time it nearly broke out was during the election campaign in the spring of 1992. The National Health Service was at
the top of the agenda and the Labour Party was at the top of the
polls. The Department of Health asked the hospital to produce a
briefing paper, designed to offer a discreet explanation for this
delicate situation in Grantham to the Labour candidate who
looked likely to be the next Secretary of State for Health. The
hospital agreed. A few weeks later, the Labour Party was thrown
onto the defensive in the War of Jennifer's Ear, when they were
accused of twisting the facts about a girl's experience in hospital
in order to score political points. Apparently terrified that the
Labour Party might seize on Ward Four to mount a counter
offensive, the Department of Health asked for a second briefing
paper, this one designed to blow the Labour Party out of the
water. But the Labour Party did not seize on the story and failed
to provide the next Health Secretary, so the health service officials
kept their secrets.

Still they had to deal with the report of the internal inquiry
which was drafted and redrafted during the early summer. On 2
July, the inquiry team took their third draft to the office of
Brian Edwards, the general manager of Trent Regional Health
Authority, and showed him the mass of bad news. The political
headache now was acute. The Region had publicly announced that
they would publish the results. They had taken advice from the
Lincolnshire police and from their own lawyers and they had been

assured that as long as they did not gather evidence about Bev Allitt or about the children she was alleged to have attacked, they would be able to publish their report without interfering with the forthcoming trial. Now the report was ready and it was time to fulfil their promise and tell the public what they had found. A month passed. It was August. Some of the Ward Four parents were growing restless, asking what had happened to the internal inquiry. David Crampton was becoming more forceful in his demands for the truth. He had been to see Douglas Hogg, the Grantham MP, and had won his support for a full public inquiry and now he was asking to see the hospital management. Another month passed. Then on 17 September, the Region finally played their card: they announced that the report would not be published after all.

They said they were sorry. They had intended to publish. But now, they said, their lawyers had changed their minds and decided that it might interfere with the forthcoming trial. And they could not ignore their lawyers' advice. 'This is a matter of great regret,' they said. The Ward Four parents found that hard to believe.

But the Region were now on the offensive. With the internal report suppressed, they launched a campaign to clear up the mess that had been revealed by Bev Allitt. They started shifting key figures out of their posts. Several had already gone: Sister Barker had been moved to a 'community liaison role'; Hannah Newton had been relieved of her position at Grantham and replaced by Peter Flood; Martin Gibson had left to take up a new job at Leicester Royal Infirmary. None of the moves was officially linked to Bev Allitt and no evidence was ever produced to suggest that they deserved to lose their jobs. Martin Gibson said he was going of his own free will. But those who were left behind believed that their colleagues had been unfairly pushed and there were angry mutters that they were being sacrificed to protect their political masters. Then the new manager arrived, and they began to fear that the sacrifices were only just beginning.

The man who took over Martin Gibson's office was an abrasive Scot named Allister Stewart. He was bald and stout, built like a second-row forward, with a manner to match. He went down to Ward Four and told the staff that he was not going to repeat the mistakes of the past. The nurses, who had always liked Martin

Gibson, were suspicious. Suddenly things started to change and the financial drought that had seemed eternal was over. A deluge of money poured through the hospital.

The health politicians wanted management consultants, so they were hired—one for the outpatients, another for 'organisational development', and one for district services; one was flown over from Spain with flight and accommodation paid and a £900-a-week fee, another was charging £450 a day. They wanted to improve the image of the hospital, so they hired a smart London PR firm called Westminster Strategy, starting a bill that ran into tens of thousands of pounds.

The old medical physics room, where they kept the big gamma camera, was suddenly taken over and splashed with money—redecorated, refurnished, sealed off with new locks, bars on the window and fancy electronic security. It became a no-go area, so secret that nurses said they saw officials checking their dinner trolley in the corridor outside to make sure it was not bugged. Inside, the new manager and his lawyers and PR advisers formed themselves into a group they called GAT, the Grantham Advisory Team. Every piece of paper that referred in any way to Beverly Allitt or the troubles on Ward Four was removed from staff, sometimes without their knowledge, and stashed away inside the GAT suite. The entire affair was now becoming a secret. When journalists approached the hospital for information, they were turned away by Westminster Strategy. When a reporter from Central TV protested at his treatment, they searched the manager's office when he left to ensure that he had not left a listening device behind him. Behind this veil of secrecy, the Region now pushed through their biggest change: they took the management of Ward Four away from Grantham Hospital. The ward would stay physically within the hospital's four walls but in the future it would be run by Queen's Med in Nottingham. And all jobs of all the doctors and all the nurses would be in jeopardy. They would all be made redundant by Grantham and would then be re-hired by Queen's Med only if they passed an 'assessment interview'.

The hospital unions were crazy with rage. They demanded to read the internal inquiry report to see whether there was any justification for the Region's action. But the report was secret. The unions asked if their solicitor could read if after giving a legally binding undertaking not to reveal its contents. No, the report could not be seen by anyone. Then more managers were moved. Moira Onions was told she must go; she fought but lost. Peter Flood disliked the new regime and resigned in disgust. By November, the head of personnel was the only member of the old hospital management who still survived. In December, he went, too.

This all seemed to be a cynical strategy. To some staff and the parents of the Ward Four children this was a desperate effort to conceal the truth and to pre-empt a public inquiry by clearing out everyone and anyone who was tainted by Bev Allitt's time at Grantham, regardless of their guilt. It seemed that the Region's main wish was to be able to turn to the world once the trial was over and tell them that the problem was solved. All that mattered, it seemed, was the politics.

The Regional Health Authority and their PR consultants denied this fervently. The secrecy, they said, was forced upon them by their lawyers because of the forthcoming trial. The job changes were simply part of a redesign of the hospital management. They agreed that they did not want a public inquiry, but they said that that was simply because it was unnecessary. The trial and their own internal inquiry would do the job. As friction between the hospital and the parents continued, the parents were disappointed to discover that Douglas Hogg who had lined up with them to demand a public inquiry, now stepped away and said he was no longer so sure. Perhaps a public inquiry would cause too much distress to witnesses, he said. Perhaps it was not necessary after all.

At the end of December, after a sequence of meetings involving the most senior health officials in the area, the GAT team produced a confidential report for the Department of Health. A month later, on the eve of Bev Allitt's trial, they produced another. Together, they presented the new Secretary of State, Virginia Bottomley, with an official account of events on Ward Four. They pressed hard to avoid a public inquiry.

They proposed that they should conduct a second internal inquiry, to start disciplinary proceedings against some staff under the Health and Safety laws. Once blame was established, they would hold a series of meetings with the families of the Ward

Four children, but these would take place behind closed doors with both sides agreeing not to disclose anything to the world outside. In the meantime, they would deal with the parents and with their lawyer, Ann Alexander, whom they described as 'an ardent publicist', by persuading the Treasury to provide £500,000 for a trust fund to start paying compensation to the damaged children.

The reports carried no suggestion that the Regional Health Authority had any responsibility for what had happened. They gave no detail about the shortage of nurses and doctors and equipment and carried no analysis of the results of these shortages for the children who were attacked. The reports also made no reference to the phone calls which had been exchanged between Martin Gibson and the Region as the police were being called in to the hospital. They said nothing of the Region's direct involvement in advising the hospital manager not to close the ward at a point when a consultant, armed with a blood test and supported by the Professor of Paediatrics at Queen's Med, was insisting that there might be a murderer loose among the children. Instead, the blame was shunted downwards.

One of the reports, dated 31 January, mentioned the letter which Jean Savill had written, begging for staff and equipment to deal with the collapsing children. There was no suggestion in the report that it was the Regional Health Authority who had created the problem and who had habitually refused to allow the hospital to solve it. Instead, the report criticised Martin Gibson for failing to produce 'an adequate, co-ordinated response'.

The same report also referred to Sister Schuch's allegations about the doctors on Ward Four and, although it noted that the two consultants had had no chance to reply to the detail of the allegations, it failed to record the evidence which supported them. Instead, it examined the long delays in reacting to the collapses among the children, said nothing about the failures of the hospital management and concluded simply that there had been 'from the beginning to the end of April a series of inappropriate and inadequate statements and actions from Dr Porter which add up to an apparent failure to act as resolutely as he could have done, compounded by Dr Nanayakkara's failure to accept that there was a problem beyond the inadequacy of equipment and staffing during the period and by the failure of the two consultants to work together.'

Some officials disagreed, but if others had their way, they would control the flow of information about what had happened on Ward Four. They would blame the two consultants and, if necessary, the former manager Martin Gibson, but they would make very sure that the Regional Health Authority and its political masters came nowhere close to blame. All they had to do was to keep it quiet.

At first, it is only a few of the Region's secrets which bob up to the surface of court number one in Nottingham: the letter from Sister Savill pleading for help; other letters from nurses and sisters complaining that the ward is unsafe because of staff shortages, and, most sensitive of all, the report of Sister Teresa Schuch on the doctors in the Special Care Baby Unit. The judge wants to know why none of these documents have surfaced earlier. He is clearly irritated. The Regional Health Authority say they gave everything to the police; the police say they passed on everything they had to the DPP; the DPP say they gave everything to the defence; but the defence deny it. They say they have heard about some of these documents and they have been asking for them but only now have they finally been able to see Sister Schuch's pitiless attack on Dr Porter and Dr Nanayakkara and the history of disquiet on Ward Four. The judge demands the truth. The defence are seeing rainbows. At last, they seem to have found what they have always been looking for—an alternative explanation for these children collapsing. Bev Allitt finally has more than mere doubt to work with as a defence. Once more the trial is stopped for both sides to get to grips with the new documents.

The consternation in the courthouse is matched by the fuss that now breaks out in the corridors of the Department of Health. Senior officials there have been infected with the Region's desire for secrecy and have started to advise the Secretary of State, Virginia Bottomley, that a public inquiry will be too expensive and that the deaths on Ward Four do not raise any issue of sufficient public interest. Now, the balance of political risk has suddenly shifted. If these documents break into the public domain through the courtroom, it may be most unwise to pursue a policy

of concealment. And there is worse to come for the health politicians: the defence decide to embark on a paper chase, demanding
to see what other useful documents are still hidden away in the
health authority's vaults. They want access to the GAT suite in
the hospital. The hospital resist, the defence insist. Within 24
hours, they are inside the hospital's secret sanctum, leafing through
the papers stored there. They find little. They suspect there is
more. Where is the evidence collected by the internal inquiry?
Where are Martin Gibson's personal logs? Where is all the corre-
spondence about staffing levels on Ward Four? Now they demand
access to the Regional Health Authority's headquarters in Sheffield. There is a round of table banging with lawyers trading
threats and allegations. It reaches the brink of a row in open
court before the Region finally surrender and hand over two large
cardboard boxes full of paper. The defence start to plough through
it and are nearly ready to return to court, when there is an urgent
call from Rampton. Bev is ill.

It seems she has collapsed in her room. She is clearly weak and
in need of more treatment than Rampton can give her and so,
once again, she is strapped into a stretcher and bundled into an
ambulance and taken down the road to Bassetlaw General Hospital. There, doctors sedate her and feed a thin tube up her right
nostril and down to her stomach so that they can pump fluids
into her starved body. With her own peculiar magic Bev has
succeeded once again in becoming the centre of attention and
sympathy.

By the time the trial resumes—with Bev now absent in her
hospital bed—the defence have found a store of treasure: details
of a cluster of deaths among newborn babies that took place when
Nurse Allitt was no longer in the hospital; an earlier incident
when a nurse accidentally injected a child with the wrong drug;
more and more about the shortage of staff and equipment on the
ward. Now the defence are spoiling for a fight. They call Dr
Nanayakkara and Dr Porter to the witness box and James Hunt
starts to drag them through this swamp of allegation. And it all
goes wrong.

The two consultants have already given evidence half a dozen
times, describing the collapses of various different children, and
they are now calm and confident in the witness box. They deny

almost everything that Sister Schuch has said about them. If they admit anything, it is only to justify their behaviour and to explain that Sister Schuch does not understand the medicine involved. Hunt throws one dart after another in their direction; the doctors simply swat them away. The jury sit back and cease to take notes. At the end of Dr Nanayakkara's evidence, John Goldring stands up and asks the consultant if there is any connection between the mysterious collapses on Ward Four and the contents of Sister Schuch's report about the Special Care Baby Unit. Dr Nanayakkara pauses, leans down to the microphone, pauses again and says: 'None whatsoever.'

The defence had planned to call Sister Schuch to give evidence herself, but now they have discovered that her report was written for her by her boyfriend, a schizophrenic; that it includes comments which she cannot support, and that in her previous job at a hospital in Kent she filed a similar complaint about the doctor she was working with there. It is the beginning of the end for the defence. Sister Schuch's allegations are clouded with doubt and damned as irrelevant. And the health authorities are in trouble: there has been a haemorrhage of confidential information and the cornerstone of their story—that the two consultants should take the blame—has just started to crumble in open court. There is a bizarre skirmish during a break in proceedings when Judith Gibson goes to one of the detectives to complain that a stout man with a bald head sitting next to her in the public gallery has been muttering furiously under his breath, grunting 'Liar!' while the consultants are giving evidence. The detective has a word with the man. It is Allister Stewart, the new manager of the hospital, who apologises to Judith and leaves the court.

The defence never really recover their momentum. James Hunt throws all his weight at the team that tried to resuscitate Claire Peck, trying to make them admit that they gave the dying girl lignocaine, or that they might have given it and forgotten, or that someone else might have given it without their noticing, or, at the very least, that it would have been appropriate to give it. None of them concedes an inch. At the end of a tough day, most of the potential confusion about the lignocaine has dissolved. On the evidence in court, there is no possibility that Claire was given the drug legitimately. The scientists can still argue about how much she was given, but all the evidence now suggests that the injection was unauthorised and improper.

Hunt has a little more success with Alice Stewart, the care assistant who says she saw Bev inject Dot Lowe in the small hours of the morning at a time whe nobody should have been injecting the elderly lady with anything. Alice Stewart is the nearest thing in the whole case to an eye witness.

'Nurse Allitt was stood at the side of Dot with her back to the door injecting into Dot's arm,' she tells the jury. 'She looked shocked at seeing me. She took the injection out of Dot's arm and put the syringe in her pocket.' Forty minutes later, she says, she and Bev went back to check on Dot. She just looked as though she was going to die . . . Nurse Allitt just stood there and would not help. She did not say anything.'

Hunt's line of attack is that Alice Stewart failed to mention this for months and invented the story only after she had seen Bev Allitt on television. Mrs Stewart says that she said nothing simply because she assumed Bev was supposed to be injecting the old lady.

Hunt is forthright. 'I suggest you never saw Beverly Allitt injecting Dorothy Lowe at all.'

Mrs Stewart bridles. 'I suggest I did.'

'When the police came to you and started making investigations, this is something you have invented and developed as it has gone along.'

'Sorry, no.'

Hunt attacks her credibility with brilliant force and finally leaves her dazed and obviously shaken. As the trial moves into its final stages, the small army of experts who have been trying to decode the fragments of evidence in the case are called in. Both sides are agreed that this is the real battle ground. If James Hunt can cast lasting doubt on their conclusions, he can pull up the prosecution by the roots and deny that any crime ever took place on Ward Four. It is all about the fallibility of scientists.

Dr Terry Marshall flies in from Australia and concedes frankly that having conducted three post-mortems on children from Ward Four—Liam Taylor, Tim Hardwick and Becky Phillips—and having concluded that all three died of various natural causes, he now realises he was wrong on all three occasions. He says he did try to alert the coroner to the doubts about Liam's heart attack, but he failed. Pathology, he tells the court, is an inexact science. Hunt can do little to restore the pathologist's respect for his own work.

Dr David Fagan, the paediatric pathologist from Queen's Med who has reviewed the cases for the police, comes into the witness box and carefully reconstructs as much of the truth as he can. The four deaths were unnatural, he says, and he is clear that Becky Phillips was probably killed by an insulin overdose. The others, however, are not so clear. Liam Taylor may have been suffocated or he may have been injected with some poison. He is 'very deeply suspicious' that Tim Hardwick was poisoned but he cannot say what the poison was. He is sure Claire Peck did not die of asthma—he says that Dr Klaus Chen's post-mortem findings were 'inadequate'—but he cannot be sure of the real cause.

James Hunt rises to cross-examine Dr Fagan. It is a decisive moment in the trial. Hunt must create doubt here, and he begins by quoting Dr Terry Marshall.

'I am sure you would agree with others that paediatric pathology is an inexact science.'

'I would agree.'

Hunt pushes him a little further. 'You are indulging in professional, intelligent guesswork?'

'I am giving my professional opinion.'

It is the ambiguity which lies at the heart of the case. The two men now push and pull across this dividing line. Hunt persuades the doctor to agree that he has never seen anything like Liam Taylor's heart before. The logic is clear: if Fagan has never seen it before, he lacks any previous experience with which to interpret it. So he must be merely guessing. Now Hunt offers him several alternative explanations. It was the tube going down the baby's foodpipe? No, says the doctor, that would have made little difference.

Hunt tries again. 'The ultimate cause of death was probably hypoxic brain damage, was it not?'

'That, I think,' says the doctor sternly, 'is the ultimate cause of death in everyone.'

'If you ignore the heart and take into account the lung

pathology—this is a speculative question—what would you have called it if Liam Taylor had just died at home?'

'I would have been unhappy. I would have asked the coroner to investigate more thoroughly.'

'It would probably have been classed as Sudden Infant Death Syndrome, would it not?'

'Not by me, no.'

The tussle goes on for hours, moving from case to case, but the pattern is now established. Hunt can show that the whole truth is not known, but he cannot deliver an alternative which takes the blame away from Bev Allitt. It may be fragmented and partial, but the evidence of crime is undeniably there. There was a murderer on Ward Four.

The credibility gap which separates Bev Allitt from conviction is now beginning to close. When David Fagan is replaced in the witness box by Professor Roy Meadow, an eminent paediatrician, the unbelievable finally begins to sound commonplace.

Professor Meadow is the man who first observed and defined Munchausen Syndrome By Proxy. He is not allowed to mention the syndrome in court, but he can describe its effects. 'On a great many occasions,' he begins, 'I have encountered situations in which adults have harmed and killed children in ways which even I had not considered to be possible . . . I have been involved with about 100 children who have been given drugs and poisons either to make them ill or sometimes poisons causing them brain damage and death . . . I have been involved with 50 to 60 children who have been suffocated . . . When it first begins the child usually struggles to breathe. If the child is lying on its back, you have to put your knee on to them to hold them, but it's not difficult with a small child . . . I am aware of cases where it has been done by an adult to a child sitting on their knee.'

John Goldring asks if suffocation leaves any tell-tale signs.

'It doesn't necessarily leave any marks at all. In the great majority of cases in which I and other paediatricians have been involved, no marks have been found.'

The effect of Roy Meadow's evidence is eerie, like a doctor telling an apparently healthy patient that for years there have been unseen tumours growing inside him. The apparently reliable assumption that adults care for children and protect them turns out to be full of doubt and—at least in Roy Meadow's world—little better than a comforting delusion. If Bev Allitt was hoping that the jury would accept that that no one kills children, Professor Meadow has just damaged her badly. Only one small chink now remains in the credibility gap, and John Goldring moves to close it. 'Is it, in your experience, looking at the ward situation, something that is difficult to do on a ward or not?'

'No,' says the professor with the sad air of a man who has seen it all. 'It is not difficult to do on a children's ward.'

The trial is nearly over. After eleven weeks of prosecution witnesses, the defence can fill only three days with their few experts. It is not that Bev's lawyers have not tried. They have reached out all over the world in search of help. It is simply that Bev has too much to explain.

An insulin expert, Professor Edwin Gale, called by the defence, says Dot Lowe was routinely being given too much insulin and was, therefore, 'an accident waiting to happen', but he cannot explain why Bev Allitt should have been seen giving her an unauthorised injection in the middle of the night. The professor goes on to suggest that Becky Phillips's sudden death is so unlike any other death from insulin that he has heard of that he finds it hard to believe that it was insulin which killed her, but he cannot explain the huge quantity of insulin which was found in the dead baby's blood. A defence scientist produces a glass of blackcurrant juice and demonstrates to the jury that if you crumble a tablet of Diamicron into it—as the police say Bev did in her attack on Jonathan Jobson—the chalky scum sits on the surface of the drink as well as floating to the bottom. This contradicts the description give by Jonathan, who reported scum only at the bottom of his glass. Then the scientist admits that if you simply scrape the scum off the top of the drink with a spoon, the blackcurrant juice is left looking exactly as Jonathan described it.

On Tuesday 11 May, after a week of final speeches, the jury retires.

Within an hour of the jury's retirement, a desperate tension has travelled through the crown court building, infecting all of those who are waiting, provoking a torment of speculation about the

jury's deliberation, cancelling all other thought and all other conversation, reducing several hundred individuals to one common
mass of anxiety. It must have started with the parents, who now
work together as a matter of instinct (when Sue Peck volunteered
to give evidence about Claire's death, half a dozen couples turned
up for the day simply to sit near her in case she needed them).
For them, a guilty verdict on their child would be full of meaning
they can barely decipher: a turning point in their ordeal; maybe
a release from some of the pain; revenge; a debt paid to the child
who suffered; something to do with the truth being accepted in
the eyes of the world; justice, in a word.

A few of the parents have been unable to make it. Helen Hardwick is now more ill than ever, with cancer of the lymph glands
in addition to her epilepsy and her withered left side, but she still
sparkles with excitement at the memory of Tim and, although she
is housebound, Tim's sister Elaine has come to join the waiting
families. The unstable life of Finn and Maggie Desmond has finally
collapsed after a day of hopeless confusion in Skegness, when Finn
took Kayley and her older sister Zara for a day by the sea and
ended up being arrested in a drunken state. Now the girls have
been taken into care, Maggie has found another man, and Finn is
alone in the run-down council house with the ruins of his life.
But the other parents wait for the jury. David Crampton has
been questioning doctors in the corridors of the courthouse and
discovering to his amazement that the doctors at Queen's Med
really had no suspicion about Paul's strange hypoglycaemic attacks
and discharged him with no inkling of the truth, simply because
he was better. The Gibsons and the Peasgoods race each other
with crossword puzzles and break off to smoke and talk about
the jury. Sue and David Peck have become close friends with the
Taylors and they sit together now. The Pecks have had a new
baby, a girl called Jennifer. Joanne Taylor has been unlucky: a
year ago, she was pregnant but in an evening of nightmarish
cruelty, she not only lost the baby but was taken back to Grantham Hospital to do so. Few of the parents want anything to do
with the hospital now. One night shortly before the committal
last year, Creswen Peasgood suffered an asthma attack which was
so bad that an ambulance was called to take her to hospital. She
was lying prone on a stretcher in the back of the ambulance

breathing into an oxygen mask when she suddenly realised where they were taking her. She sat up, tore off the mask and told them she'd rather bloody die than go to that place. The ambulance was diverted to Mansfield.

The tension in the courthouse reaches out to embrace three nurses from Ward Four who have come to wait for the verdict on their former friend and colleague. Many of the nurses have been sunk in depression, having trouble sleeping, losing weight, tormented by the special pain of discovering that it was one of their own kind who was the cause of all the misery, consumed by needless guilt and by the terrifying idea that they could conceivably have stopped her. After several bruising arguments with the unions, the hospital did agree to provide counselling for them, but it was soon stopped. The nurses have been suffering, too, from Peter Phillips, who was involved in a series of quarrels on the ward and threatened to punch one of the night managers in the mouth. The nurses then received a letter addressed to Sister Barker and the staff of Ward Four. It was signed by Sue Phillips and it seethed with bitterness. 'Thank you for ruining my life and my family's,' she wrote. 'We have been given a life sentence because of the incompetence of staff on Ward Four, so you can all have one as well. Every year on April 5th a sharp reminder will appear in the local paper "Becky Grace Phillips, murdered on Ward Four because of the incompetence of staff". You are all responsible for my beautiful Becky's murder—I hope you can live with that for the rest of your lives.' Margaret Geeson has inflicted particularly severe punishment on herself, replaying repeatedly the long week in April when she was acting sister on the ward and when she knew from Dr Porter and Moira Onions that someone might be tampering with the children, when she saw more children collapsing and dying, and when she was forbidden by strict instructions to say or do anything to warn them. Two years later, she simply cries at the thought of it. Now, Margaret sits with Lynn Vowles and one of the night nurses, Doreen Fardell, all three of them determined that they will subdue their nerves and sit through this final ordeal alongside the parents.

When Margaret first came to court, to give evidence in the first week of the trial, Joanne Taylor saw her standing pale and nervous outside the courtroom and spontaneously walked over and kissed her on the cheek. It was the beginning of peace between the nurses and the parents; even the Phillips stop now to tell them that they know it was not really their fault at all.

There has also been an end to all the squabbling on Ward Four. All the nurses were made redundant as part of the plan to allow Queen's Med to take over the management of the ward, and during the trial they have been running the ward, travelling to Nottingham to give evidence and then waiting to go for interviews to discover whether they still have their jobs. In the event, all of them have been taken back except for Sister Barker who has lost even her 'community liaison' role and who is a broken figure when she appears in court, waxily pale and stunned.

Dr Porter and Dr Nanayakkara are finally united in defence of their careers and have often sat together drinking cups of coffee in the courthouse canteen. They continued to squabble long after the police were called in. They had a bitter little wrangle about Patrick Elstone, which began when Dr Porter wrote a line in Patrick's medical notes recording that the family had been shocked to discover from Dr Nanayakkara that Patrick had suffered not one, but two arrests on the day he was attacked in April 1991. When Dr Nanayakkara read this note, he banged off a sharp letter to Dr Porter, denying that he had disclosed any sensitive information to the Elstones and complaining that Dr Porter had recorded this 'allegation' without consulting him. He then insisted on discussing it formally with Dr Porter and wrote a long note in his own defence in Patrick's file. They are still very different characters: giving evidence, Dr Nanayakkara strode into court with his neat, new suit and his military bearing; Dr Porter stumbled along, late for his first day because he was still in his pyjamas when the witness bus arrived at his home to collect him. But now, the two men are closer. A few months before the trial started, the hospital tried to persuade them to take a year's sabbatical. They refused, sensing that this might be the beginning of an attempt to lock them out. Then the hospital insisted that they would both be so busy in court that they would have to take special leave and they agreed and now they have been told that there is no place for them under the new regime of Ward Four. They are out of work. And the parents and the Ward Four nurses share their sense of injustice at the decision: they may agree that

Light 345

the doctors made mistakes but they cannot see the fairness of blaming them and only them.

They have discovered enough by now to know that Bev Allitt found weak points all over the hospital and the entire machine turned out to be running on moving parts which were all worn out. Under the normal stress of routine hospital life, the machinery was more or less able to do its job but, confronted with a crisis, it simply collapsed under the strain. The weaknesses that had been built into the system by lack of funding and by sheer inertia suddenly became lethal.

The nurses knew there was no secret about any of this. Error was a part of everyday life: doctors working on that thin line between science and guesswork; delays in handling path lab samples; the accidental loss of X-rays, test results, children's notes; the production of thick tomes of procedural advice which were never read. It was the same in most hospitals. There was no secret, either, about the fact that the delicate network of personal contacts on which the children relied for their welfare was hanging in shreds.

All these weaknesses, it was now clear, were embedded into the system and then aggravated by shortages of staff and of equipment. Ward Four was trapped by habit and lack of supervision, by low morale and lack of funds, staked out and helpless, the perfect victim. The problems which the health service inflicted on the hospital conspired together to set the scene for Nurse Allitt's crimes and then enables her to get away with them. In her behaviour as a student nurse, she had littered the hospital with warning signs—the faeces and fire in the nurses' home, the thefts from Ward Four, her history of imaginary illness—and even without knowing of these, other wards and other hospitals turned her away simply because she was not up to standard. She was hired on Ward Four, the parents and the nurses now knew, because they were desperate for staff. Once there, she was often left alone with children. No one had the time to supervise her. When she started attacking the children, nurses and doctors missed clues largely because they were too busy to see them. It was clear now that there had been mistakes—human errors—but that was not the whole truth. Even if the jury deliver justice in the courthouse, it is not at all clear to those who wait that the authorities will do the same in the hospital.

Tuesday afternoon passes and the jury are sent to a hotel for the night without delivering any verdicts. Everyone is back on Wednesday morning, all tired and some of them hungover after a restless night. Steve and Judith Gibson went walking at one in the morning to try and calm themselves down. And the tension, it appears, has now spread from the courthouse all the way to London, to the office of the Secretary of State for Health, Virginia Bottomley.

At the end of the week before, the Regional Health Authority scored an almost overwhelming victory in their campaign to prevent a full public inquiry. They failed to restrict the post-mortem to the internal disciplinary inquiry which they had secretly proposed but they did succeed in persuading the Secretary of State that there should be only a limited investigation. She agreed that it should be conducted in private by a chairman selected by them, with a panel appointed by them and terms of reference to be agreed by them, and with no powers to compel witnesses to give evidence or force the disclosure of documents. As word of all this leaked, the Ward Four parents and the hospital unions were furious: to them, it was no better than allowing Bev Allitt to pick her own judge and decide on the charges she should face. On Monday and Tuesday, the health union, COHSE, and the families' lawyer, Ann Alexander, bombarded Douglas Hogg and the Department of Health with faxes and late Tuesday night, Virginia Bottomley bowed to the pressure and agreed to meet the following morning — Wednesday — to reconsider her decision.

Wednesday morning passes with still no word from the jury, and the two sides in the political struggle — the PR men from Westminster Strategy, Ann Alexander and the union officials — prowl round the courthouse door, all pushing portable phones to their ears to beat the roar of the traffic, waiting for news from London. Both sides are worried. In the hospital, one of the managers has been desperately running around the wards trying to find nurses who shot video pictures of the Christmas parties, where managers traditionally serve the food wearing fancy dress of the nurses' choice. The video of the 1989 party shows Martin Gibson and Peter Flood dressed as Arabs in a harem, but the 1990 party, which took place only six weeks before Bev Allitt began attacking the children, is much worse. At the time, it was all a good-humoured joke, particularly when the party was over and Martin Gibson discovered that he didn't have his coat and had to tip-toe all the way down the main corridor through the centre of the hospital sporting a little white fairy's dress and wellington boots. The hospital, terrified that the press might get hold of the pictures, have offered £150 for copies of the video. The nurses, who have little affection for the new management, have turned down the offer and protected their old manager simply by keeping the picture to themselves. News finally leaks out of Whitehall and into the portable phones. The Region have had to agree to a new chairman for the inquiry—the former Ombudsman, Sir Cecil Clothier QC—but the Region has kept its grip on the rest. Clothier will have no powers and he will work in private with terms of reference to be agreed by the Region. The parents still smell injustice. Later that afternoon, the judge sends the jury away for their second night in the hotel, still without verdicts.

By Thursday morning, the tension is turning to worry. In the unofficial betting, most of the detectives had put their money on a verdict by Wednesday afternoon. Now, they begin to wonder out loud whether all their work is going to waste. It looks as though the jury are having problems. Maybe it is just that they can't be sure that Bev wanted to kill those children who survived, so they are going to reject the attempted murder charges. That worries no one as long as they convict on the alternative charges of causing grievous bodily harm. But perhaps the defence succeeded in creating enough doubt about the whole case. Perhaps the jury are just hopelessly split and unable to agree on anything. It has been more than 48 hours now.

Everyone involved in the long saga of Ward Four sits and waits, except for the central figure. Bev is still in hospital, being fed by a nasal tube and with a telephone by her bed on which she will hear the jury's verdicts from her lawyers. In a way, her absence makes no difference. Even if she were still sitting in the dock of court number one, frowning into the middle distance, she would be little more than a symbol standing in for all the mysteries she represents. She is so full of contradictions: desperate for sympathy but remorselessly cruel to anyone who gives it to her; denying pain and vulnerability but constantly pretending to be stricken and sick; defiant and indifferent but addicted to approval; a nurse but a killer. She sees herself as a victim—of family, of friends, of her whole existence—and somehow it relieves her to make victims of those around her. Perhaps her love of illness is, in fact, a cry for help from the healthy remnant of her personality, an attempt to translate all her inner madness into something which can be seen and treated and cured. The psychiatrists are all happy to say that she has Munchausen Syndrome, but that begs more questions than it answers. The truth is that no one understands her. It is part of the terrible irony of her life that that is probably exactly how she has always felt inside.

Even if she is not here any more, all those who wait feel just as strongly about her. Almost all of them hate her—because they can't understand her, because they couldn't stop her, because she humiliated them and hurt them beyond measure. Creswen Peasgood dreams of strapping her to a bed in a bare, white room and injecting her over and over again. There is talk of hanging, of what they will do to her if she is freed. No one feels sorry for her. Even if she is sick, even if she was once a happy little girl whose mind caved in under the weight of overwhelming sickness, even if she has been dragged through life by her personality disorder like a cart behind a runaway horse, they can only hate her. The law supports them. If she is convicted of murder, the judge will have no option but to send her to prison for life. Her lawyers may plead that if she is guilty, it is because she is sick, but the law will punish her.

Suddenly, the courthouse tannoy shouts 'All parties to court number one' and everyone's breathing is a little faster as they come from all the corners of the building and take their seats around the courtroom. Every seat is filled, except the one in the dock, and as the judge settles on his high-backed wooden chair, the whole room falls silent. There is only the occasional rustle of paper as 150 frightened people listen to the thumping of their hearts. Minutes pass. Finally, the door at the back of the court opens and the jury file in, looking exhausted. They slump into their seats, staring into their laps while all the eyes in the room search their faces for a clue and the judge, whose face is stiff with tension, smiles as best he can and asks the jury foreman to stand.

'Have you reached any verdicts upon which you are all agreed?'
'Yes, sir, we have.'

A ripple around the room. A peak of expectation. But then the judge turns the screw one more time by telling the jury that they must go back to their room without announcing their decision so that the foreman can organise what he has to say. Fifteen more minutes pass. By the time the jury file back in again, the entire room is locked into an agony of anticipation. No one speaks. Nothing that anyone can say can begin to match the words which the foreman is about to deliver. Sue Peck and Joanne Taylor have begun to weep gently. Stuart Clifton has his hands clasped on the top of the bench in front of him like a man in prayer. The foreman of the jury stands. The clerk of the court stands and begins to read the long list of charges.

On the charge of murdering Liam Taylor? 'No verdict.'

Joanne Taylor hangs her head.

On the charge of murdering Tim Hardwick? 'No verdict.'

It is becoming hard to breathe in court number one.

On the charge of attempting to murder Kayley Desmond? 'Not guilty.'

This room is now poised on a knife edge. On the alternative charge of causing grievous bodily harm to Kayley Desmond? Everything hangs on the next word. 'Guilty'.

Now the whole room gasps as one. She's guilty—the word the parents have waited two years to hear. The jury believe she did it. And she did: Bev Allitt did it. The parents faces are set in stone as the clerk of the court reads on. No verdict on Paul Crampton, nor on Brad Gibson—then guilty again of causing grievous bodily harm to Henry Chan.

And now another murder charge—the death of Becky Phillips. The clerk reads the charge, the foreman looks once at his notebook and says 'Guilty'. This time, it is a strangled cheer which leaps up from the public gallery and the usher shouts for silence and Sue and Peter Phillips sit impassive as all the parents who have turned round to squeeze their hands turn back to watch again as the clerk of the court reads on. No verdict on Katie Phillips, nor on Michael Davidson, nor on Chris Peasgood—then guilty again of causing grievous bodily harm to Christopher King. No verdict on Patrick Elstone. And on the charge of murdering Claire Peck? 'Guilty'.

For a moment or maybe two, it is quiet. Sue Peck turns slowly to David, sitting at her side.

'Is that it? Is that Claire?'

David nods, his face as pale as paper, and slowly Sue begins to bow, her head sinks down and she begins to cough up huge sobs of tears. As she hides her head on David's chest, the other parents stand and huddle round her. Chris and Joanne are both crying now. Judith Gibson, too. And it is not only the parents. In the public gallery and on the reporters' benches, men and women are wiping their eyes, the nurses from Ward Four are slumped on to each other's shoulders. After months of misery, after all the doubts and worries, the sheer tension is now relieved. The truth is told. In the well of the court, Stuart Clifton is standing quietly with the palm of his hand cupped over his face, crying too.

That evening, the defence lawyers travel to Rampton to see Bev in her hospital bed where she lies, still skeletal and when they tell her what has happened, she does something which none of them has seen her do before. She sheds a tear. Then she makes a decision. She tells the nurses to remove the tube that runs into her nostril and down into her stomach. It is her only source of nourishment. Without it and with her body weight already cut by half, the Rampton doctors warn her, she will not last a week. Bev says she doesn't care. She says she's had enough.

It takes the jury another four days to finish their work but finally at 3.45 on the afternoon of Monday 17 May, they declare their final verdicts. Bev is guilty of all four murders; of attempting to murder three of the survivors—Paul Crampton, Brad Gibson and Katie Phillips—and of inflicting grievous bodily harm on the six other surviving children. The jury reject the two victims from outside the hospital, Dot Lowe and Jonathan Jobson. The police can see that there was reasonable doubt about them and understand why the jury find Bev not guilty, but at home in Peterborough, Jonathan goes up to his room and sits alone and thoughtful, while Eileen cries again and wishes she had been allowed to go to court to tell the jury of all that happened in her home.

The defence persuade the judge to delay sentence for ten days to allow them to gather evidence of Bev's Munchausen Syndrome. It may persuade the judge not to recommend that she serve at least 30 years and it may encourage the Home Secretary to agree that she should serve her sentence in a secure hospital, but it cannot change the simple demands of the law for any person convicted of murder. Nurse Beverly Allitt will be sentenced to life. Only those closest to her know that she had opened an escape route by withdrawing her consent to treatment; some of them think she will soon eat again, that it is just another gesture from a girl who feels best when she feels ill.

Now, the parents leave the crown court to be greeted by a pavement full of press and by an official announcement that the Secretary of State for Health is going to allow the Regional Health Authority to establish an inquiry into the affair. It will be led by Sir Cecil Clothier, who will sit in private and who will set out with no powers to compel witnesses or to uncover documents.

The parents drive away from Nottingham. David Crampton is full of fight, intent on forcing a proper public inquiry that will uncover the truth which he knows is being hidden. Sue and Peter Phillips are off to Florida, on a holiday which is being funded by a television programme to which they are giving an interview. Belinda King has been off work for the three months of the trial but now she is supposed to go back to work at Grantham Hospital; she cannot quite see how she can bear to do it. Judith and Steve Gibson go home to Brad, who still limps a little.

Chris and Joanne Taylor drive up the hill through the new estate on the edge of Grantham, back to the neat, new, semi-detached house, where the picture of Liam hangs on the sitting room wall. They will never forget him but they know that there is no going back. Joanne takes her time to get out of the car. She is pregnant again.